Research Methods for Environmental Studies

The methodological needs of environmental studies are unique in the breadth of research questions that can be posed, calling for a textbook that covers a broad swath of approaches to conducting research with potentially many different kinds of evidence.

Written specifically for social science-based research into the environment, this book covers the best-practice research methods most commonly used to study the environment and its connections to societal and economic activities and objectives. Over the course of the chapters, Kanazawa introduces quantitative and qualitative approaches, mixed methods, and the special requirements of interdisciplinary research, emphasizing that methodological practice should be tailored to the specific needs of the project. The book also provides detailed coverage on key topics including the identification of a research project; spatial analysis; ethnography approaches; interview technique; and ethical issues in environmental research.

Drawing on a variety of extended examples to encourage problem-based learning and fully addressing the challenges associated with interdisciplinary investigation, this book will be an essential resource for students embarking on courses exploring research methods in environmental studies.

Mark Kanazawa is a Professor of Economics at Carleton College, USA. He has also held visiting positions at Stanford, UC-Berkeley, and the University of Illinois, and he has been awarded the Jacobs Fellowship at the Huntington Library and the Simon Fellowship at the Property and Environment Research Center. Kanazawa has published research in the areas of American economic history, law and economics, new institutional economics, water policy, economics of sports, and the economics of natural resources. He teaches courses in environmental and natural resource economics, western economic history, economics of sports, econometrics, and research methods in environmental studies.

'This book provides a holistic approach to research methods in environmental studies by looking into the epistemological underpinnings of contemporary issues in environmental studies. The contents are comprehensive; and the examples and case studies apt. Students in environmental studies will find the book a useful toolkit to reflect on how best to design research projects.'

Girma Zawdie, University of Strathclyde, UK

Research Methods for Environmental Studies

A Social Science Approach

Mark Kanazawa

LONDON AND NEW YORK

First published 2018
by Routledge
2 Park Square, Milton Park, Abingdon, Oxon OX14 4RN

and by Routledge
711 Third Avenue, New York, NY 10017

Routledge is an imprint of the Taylor & Francis Group, an informa business

British Library Cataloguing-in-Publication Data
A catalogue record for this book is available from the British Library

Library of Congress Cataloging-in-Publication Data
A catalog record for this book has been requested.

ISBN: 978-1-138-68016-6 (hbk)
ISBN: 978-1-138-68017-3 (pbk)
ISBN: 978-1-315-56367-1 (ebk)

Typeset in Goudy
by Deanta Global Publishing Services, Chennai, India

Printed and bound by CPI Group (UK) Ltd, Croydon, CR0 4YY

Contents

Figures

Tables

Boxes

1 Introduction to research methods in environmental studies

Introduction: The recent growth of environmental studies

In August 2009, a story appeared in the news magazine *Newsweek* that reported an explosion of interest in studying the environment on college campuses all over the United States. According to the story, so-called green majors had suddenly become a "hot commodity," and colleges and universities were scrambling to establish new programs in order to meet a sudden upsurge in demand for environmentally related curriculum. It reported, for example, that in 2007 alone, universities launched at least twenty-seven new programs, degrees, or certificates relating to study of the environment, up from a mere three in 2005 (Kliff 2009).

This picture of sudden, avid interest in studying the environment among college students is reinforced by more systematic data collected by the National Council for Science and the Environment. In a survey conducted in 2008, it was found that 652 colleges and universities in the United States offered 840 different interdisciplinary programs that focused on study of the environment. These included programs in environmental science, environmental studies, natural resource management, environmental policy and planning, environmental management and risk analysis, and a number of others. Roughly *two-thirds* of these programs had been established since 1990 (Vincent 2009).

And the growth of environmental programs has by no means slowed since then. By 2012, when a follow-up survey was conducted, the number of colleges and universities offering environmental programs had increased to 838. This represented an increase of 29% in a scant four years. Meanwhile, the number of degree programs at these college and universities had increased by 57% (Vincent et al. 2012)!

Clearly, we are currently experiencing an enormous boom in academic study of the environment, which is showing no signs of letting up.

Why is there so much interest in studying the environment?

Why has study of the environment become such a hot topic lately? Surely, much of the reason has to do with the state of the environment. If you have progressed far enough in your study of the environment to be now taking a course in research methods, you are aware of the many pressing environmental issues facing local communities, cities, states, countries, and the international community. These issues include: ongoing climate change, air and water pollution, increasingly scarce fresh water resources, production of hazardous wastes, depleted natural resources, destruction of rain forests, habitat destruction, growing lists of endangered species—the list goes on and on.

At the same time that the list of serious environmental challenges is growing, it seems as if the complexity of these challenges is growing as well. Some issues, like climate change, are dauntingly complex. Addressing climate change requires that we consider not only climate science and technologies for mitigation and adaptation. Also critical to consider are a variety of economic, political, cultural, and social factors that influence human behavior and, therefore, our willingness to take individual actions to mitigate or adapt to climate change. Also increasingly important lately are popular attitudes toward science, which impact our ability to muster political consensus on what steps to take, how serious the problem is, and even to agree on whether there is a problem at all.

But even "smaller" environmental problems, such as contamination of local groundwater supplies or disposal of toxic wastes, can still present numerous complex challenges. Indeed, many of the issues we observe with climate change also appear with many environmental issues that are more local in nature. For example, in the case of local groundwater contamination, we are often presented with issues of science and technology, such as the geology of the local aquifer and the availability of different technologies to clean up groundwater supplies. Solutions are also affected by the whole gamut of human factors, which may influence zoning decisions, decisions on where to site facilities, local support for bringing in potentially polluting businesses because of jobs created, and so forth.

The seriousness and complexity of environmental issues present important challenges to attempts to address environmental problems. I would argue that they have also given rise to a great deal of interest among both college students and faculty in studying the environment in a systematic way. The urgency of environmental problems seems to demand a concerted response. We need to understand these problems better to be in a position to suggest possible solutions.

Undergraduate research in environmental studies

Understanding environmental problems requires knowledge that has been produced by a number of academic disciplines in the natural sciences, social sciences, and the humanities. This knowledge relates to how the natural world works, the mutual relationship between the natural world and human activities, and how humans understand their relationship to the natural world. In previous courses, you have undoubtedly encountered many important concepts, ideas, and theories that constitute what we refer to as knowledge. But you may not yet have a clear idea of how knowledge in general comes to be generated: how concepts are formulated, ideas are conceived, and new theories are discovered and verified.

Here is where research comes into the picture. The creation of useful knowledge requires a set of systematic procedures to take existing knowledge and carefully combine it with new ideas and new evidence, in order to gain new insights into real world phenomena. All of the knowledge you have encountered in previous courses has been gained through an arduous, painstaking process involving countless hours of hard work by previous researchers.

Consider, for example, anthropogenic climate change, the idea that climate change is occurring due to human activities, especially the burning of fossil fuels. Though many people, including most scientists, practically take this idea for granted today, this wasn't always the case. The idea that the earth's atmosphere could serve as an insulating blanket that traps solar radiation (the so-called *greenhouse effect*) was first conceived by the great French mathematician and scientist Joseph Fourier in the 1820s, nearly two centuries ago (Rodhe et al. 1997). This idea did not, of course, come to Fourier out of thin air (so to speak), but rather was the result of detailed, precise calculations of solar radiation and a painstaking process of ruling out alternative possibilities.

However, nobody thought that human activities could cause the earth's temperatures to rise until the 1890s, when the Swedish scientist Svante Arrhenius decided to try to quantify how much carbon dioxide (CO2) and water vapor it would take to warm the planet. His idea was to capitalize on detailed readings taken by the American astronomer Samuel Langley on radiation from the full moon. By combining these data with data on global temperatures, he performed a series of calculations to estimate how much of the radiation was absorbed by ambient CO2 and water vapor in the atmosphere (Crawford 1997, p. 9).

Literally tens of thousands of calculations later, Arrhenius had his answer: if CO2 levels doubled, the earth's temperature would increase by 4–6 degrees Celsius (Crawford 1997, pp. 9–10; Sample 2005). He then concluded that the practice of widespread burning of coal, which was known to generate CO2, could result in significant warming of the planet.

Arrhenius's conclusions were not immediately embraced by other scientists, some of whom pointed out what they said were countervailing factors, such as absorption of CO2 by the oceans. However, gradually over time, as more data were collected and more scientific studies were done, there emerged the scientific consensus that we know today. This consensus is that Arrhenius was basically correct, even if his calculations on the precise relationship between CO2 buildup and global temperatures have had to be adjusted and refined.

Bottom line: It took a series of scientists, doing painstaking research and building on previous scientific findings, to give us the knowledge of global warming that we have today.

The notion that research involves building on the work of others has been famously attributed to renowned British scientist and mathematician Sir Isaac Newton (see Box 1.1). Like many young men of his time, Newton was educated in the teachings of the famous Greek philosopher Aristotle (who we will encounter again in Chapter 2), as well as the French philosopher Rene Descartes and the astronomers Galileo and Johannes Kepler. It was only by building on their ideas that Newton was able to make his major breakthroughs in physics and mathematics.

Box 1.1 The cumulative nature of research

"If I have seen further, it is by standing on the shoulders of giants."

Sir Isaac Newton

If you are like many undergraduates, you may feel like you are being given a tall order. Doing original research to come up with knowledge that no one has thought of before? How is that even possible for me to do? Part of the answer is that everyone has to start somewhere. Even Isaac Newton knew nothing about math and science before he enrolled in school at the age of twelve and started receiving instruction in Latin, Greek, and mathematics.

And you should view your starting point as just that: a starting point. Developing research expertise is a gradual, cumulative process that takes time and investment in learning a range of different skills. These include:

- Understanding the information content of evidence and what it means;
- Methods for collecting and managing data and other forms of evidence;
- Practical methods of analysis;
- Systematic ways to familiarize yourself with the research of others;
- Facility with various computer software programs;
- Understanding and practicing ethical behavior;
- Effective communication of research results, both oral and written.

Developing these skills takes time, training, and experience. Furthermore, over time you will have the opportunity to develop increasingly sophisticated skills, which will allow you to tackle more challenging research questions and perform more sophisticated analysis. All of this can make the development of research skills a life-long learning process. There is always more to learn. But if you stick to it, the rewards, both personal and professional, can be great.

The many and varied types of research questions

As it turns out, in studying the environment, there are many possible research paths to pursue. This is in part because there are many different types of questions you could ask about the environment. In this textbook, we will focus on research methods used by social scientists, as opposed to the methods of natural scientists such as Fourier, Arrhenius, and others who studied climate change. This means that there will be a great deal of emphasis on the human and social dimensions of environmental problems and the research methods that are appropriate for addressing the questions that arise.

Consider, for example, the research questions listed in Box 1.2. Each question deals with some aspect of human interaction with the environment, but the nature of the questions being asked are subtly different. The first two questions are about the effects of environmental changes on human activities. The third question is about taking a classic environmental text and wondering how influential it was, in fact, in changing public attitudes. The fourth question is about social interactions among groups who are potential partners in efforts to promote environmental protection. The fifth question is about the effectiveness of an environmental policy.

Box 1.2 Social science research questions

What were the economic impacts of depleted summer streamflows on whitewater rafting in New Mexico in the early 1990s?

What was the impact of climate change on national park visitations in the Canadian Rocky Mountains in the late 1990s and early 2000s?

How influential was Rachel Carson's book *Silent Spring* in contributing to changing public attitudes toward use of DDT?

What factors affect the success of activist coalition-building among grassroots environmental organizations?

Do households in southern Africa that are located in areas with integrated conservation and development programs receive more tourism-related benefits than households that are not?

The varied nature of these questions itself suggests that the methods used to answer them may have to vary as well. One might think, for example, that answering the first two questions might require methods that permit you to measure the impacts, perhaps using numerical data, simulations, or statistical procedures.

The third question *could* be about measurement (of the influence of Carson's book), but it could also be about identifying other factors that might be responsible for changes in public attitudes.

The fourth question does not seem to be about measurement at all, but rather about identifying factors that contribute to the success or failure of different environmental organizations to work together. However, you can imagine that methods might vary greatly because these factors could be many things, including: size and member composition of the organizations, organizational procedures for getting things done, member attitudes toward other groups, and so forth. For the third and fourth questions, it may be unclear to you exactly what evidence might be collected or how it might be systematically analyzed to answer the question.

Finally, the fifth question could be tackled in a number of ways, because the word "benefits" could be defined in a number of different ways. If you are accustomed to defining benefits monetarily, then this seems like a question that you could try to put a number to. This might involve testing a hypothesis to answer this "yes" or "no" question, based on differences in benefits across the different regions. But benefits could also take other forms, including environmental, social, or psychological. In this latter case, it might be less clear what method one might use to go about answering this question.

There are two points being made here. The first is to point out the wide range of research questions that could be asked about the environment, using the social science approach. The second is that there might be a variety of different methods available to researchers who wish to take a social science approach to studying the environment. Much of the discussion to come in the rest of this book will focus on developing this variety of approaches more fully.

Disciplinary vs. interdisciplinary research

One thing that makes it interesting to study the environment is the fact that many environmental issues seem to have so many different dimensions. For any given issue, there often arise, for example, questions of science, economics, politics, culture, law, and ethics. If you think about all of these different aspects of an issue, you may wonder how to bring them all together to make sense of an environmental problem. This raises the question of how to use the knowledge, ideas, and techniques of different academic disciplines.

The traditional model: Disciplinary research

It has been a longstanding tradition in colleges and universities in the United States to structure courses and programs according to academic discipline (Brewer 1999, pp. 331–3). This is why, for example, most colleges have departments of economics, sociology, psychology, chemistry, physics, history, philosophy, and so forth. Each department has a distinctive curriculum: a set of courses that is pretty standard across different institutions that reflects a disciplinary consensus regarding what students should be taught. This includes subject matter, of course, but it also includes a particular set of research methods that are used most commonly by researchers in the discipline.

For example, at my institution—a small college in Minnesota—all economic majors are required to take courses in intermediate microeconomics, intermediate macroeconomics, and econometrics. The fact that all economics majors are required to take these courses reflects general agreement among our economics faculty that knowledge in all these areas is required for a solid, rigorous, and well-rounded education in economics. And the research training received by economics majors reflects the ideas, concepts, and tools that are specific to the discipline of economics, which relies heavily on numerical data and statistical methods.

At larger universities, you commonly have the same disciplinary options. Consider the University of Minnesota—which has roughly twenty times as many undergraduates as my college—where you can major in basically all of the same disciplines. However, in addition to the basic set of majors offered at my college, there are many more options, as you might expect.

For example, in addition to economics, the University of Minnesota allows you to major in the related field of applied economics, where you can focus specifically on economic issues related to natural resources, agriculture, and the environment. Similarly, instead of majoring in psychology, you can major in child psychology, which focuses specifically on early childhood development. Or you can major in biology with a minor in entomology. All of these examples reflect disciplinary and subdisciplinary focuses and, again, specialized methods for conducting research.

An important recent trend: Interdisciplinary research

Over the last forty years or so, however, we have witnessed an important trend in higher education: the greater integration of the approaches of different disciplines. At my college, though the traditional departments dominate the curriculum, we now have majors and programs where coursework is taken from different disciplines. These include: American Studies, Neuroscience, Political Economy, Women's and Gender Studies, and Environmental Studies. In each of these programs, faculty have decided that proper study of the subject requires coursework in multiple disciplines.

And to the point of this book: this means that research questions and methods are also drawn from multiple disciplines. This development reflects the growing area of *interdisciplinary* research. Box 1.3 provides a standard definition of interdisciplinary research (Committee on Facilitating Interdisciplinary Research 2004, p. 2).

Box 1.3 Interdisciplinary research

"Interdisciplinary research is a mode of research by teams or individuals that integrates information, data, techniques, tools, perspectives, concepts, and/or theories from two or more disciplines or bodies of specialized knowledge to advance fundamental understanding or to solve problems whose solutions are beyond the scope of a single discipline or area of research practice."

As Box 1.3 makes clear, the basic idea behind interdisciplinary research is that there are certain inherent limitations to relying solely on the ideas and methods of individual disciplines when one is trying to solve certain types of problems.

So interdisciplinary research may involve, for example, bringing together researchers from the natural sciences with researchers from various social science and humanities disciplines, such as economics, political science, sociology, anthropology, psychology, history, and philosophy. By putting their heads together to solve a problem, researchers may be able to gain insights into solutions that researchers from individual disciplines cannot.

To be clear, interdisciplinary research need not necessarily involve teams of practitioners from different fields, as it is being portrayed here. Individual researchers are capable of, and increasingly are, doing interdisciplinary research. However, it is not yet common for individual researchers to have extensive training in multiple disciplines. It is hard enough to master one field, let alone several! However, we are increasingly seeing programs at colleges and universities that attempt to instill interdisciplinary education in their students.

The different disciplinarities

To be clear, if you read about interdisciplinary research, you will find people using a number of different terms that seem like the same thing. For example, in addition to interdisciplinary, you will also commonly hear the terms *multidisciplinary* and *transdisciplinary*. These terms are all related in that they all refer to bringing together the content and methods of different academic disciplines. Where they differ is in the degree of integration that occurs among the researchers from the different disciplines.

For example, Box 1.4 lists definitions of the different disciplinarities as provided by one scholar, Patricia Leavy (Leavy 2012, p. 210). According to Leavy, as you move from multidisciplinarity to interdisciplinarity to transdisciplinarity, the degree of integration among the disciplines increases.

Box 1.4 The different disciplinarities

	Level of collaboration between disciplines
Multidisciplinarity	Collaboration between two or more disciplines without integration.
Interdisciplinarity	Collaboration between two or more disciplines with varying levels of integration of concepts, theories, methods, and findings.
Transdisciplinarity	Collaboration between two or more disciplines with high levels of integration causing the development of new conceptual, theoretical, and methodological frameworks.

Multidisciplinary research means research that uses the ideas, methods, and findings of different disciplines, but where there is no real attempt to integrate material from the disciplines. So a multidisciplinary research team might consist of natural scientists and social scientists, but researchers from each discipline work essentially in isolation from their counterparts in other disciplines. They all contribute to the final research report, but each one does her own "thing." Multidisciplinary research is illustrated in Figure 1.1, where all of the disciplines A through F are being pursued on separate tracks, largely in isolation from each other.

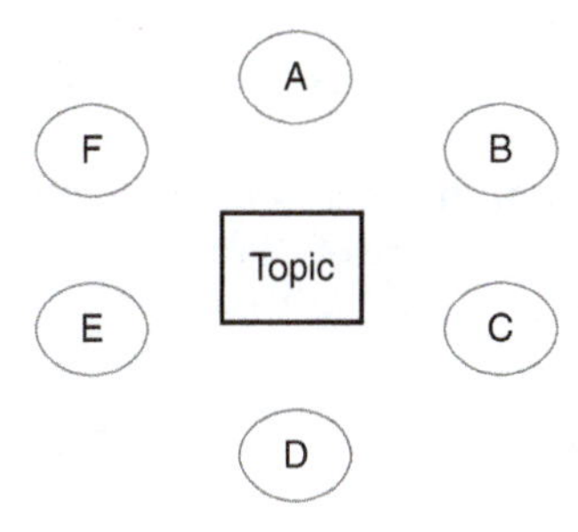

Figure 1.1 Multidisciplinary research.

Source: Author.

Interdisciplinary research also involves researchers from multiple disciplines working together. However, in contrast to multidisciplinary research, an attempt is made to integrate the content, methods, and findings of the different disciplines. This is illustrated in Figure 1.2, where the different disciplines are achieving a certain degree of integration with each other.

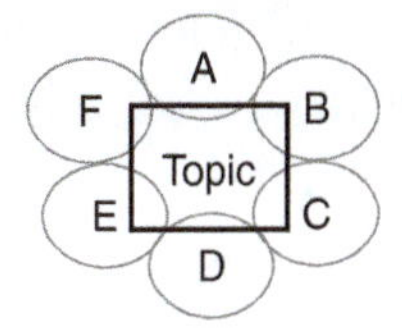

Figure 1.2 Interdisciplinary research.

Source: Author.

Finally, transdisciplinary research involves "high levels" of integration among the disciplines. It thus raises the stakes for researchers in terms of cross-fertilization of ideas and methods. This is illustrated in Figure 1.3. Furthermore, transdisciplinary research involves not merely taking and using existing theories and methods, but

Figure 1.3 Transdisciplinary research.

Source: Author.

rather developing new theories and methods. Thus, it attempts not merely to integrate the disciplines, but rather to transcend them.

To be honest, it is often hard to draw a clear distinction among the three disciplinarities, because much of the distinction depends upon "how much" integration is occurring. Can it ever really be said that *no* integration is occurring, which seems to be the distinction between multidisciplinary and interdisciplinary? How much integration is necessary before we would consider research to be truly transdisciplinary rather than "merely" interdisciplinary?

These are challenging questions to answer. In this book, we will generally not draw a distinction among the three, but rather will refer to any research that combines multiple disciplines as "interdisciplinary." This is, technically speaking, not strictly correct, but will be used here given the practical challenges of distinguishing among the disciplinarities. However, you should be aware of the distinction, as it is commonly made among researchers working in multiple disciplines.

Interdisciplinary research in environmental studies

It turns out that interdisciplinary research is extremely important in the social science approach to environmental studies. This largely has to do with the nature of many environmental research questions that social scientists consider. A lot of these questions bring together multiple disciplines.

Referring back to Box 1.2, consider the research questions posed there. The first question on the impacts of reduced streamflows on whitewater rafting involves issues of natural science and economics. The second question involves behavioral responses to climate change. The third question is about the impact of various social factors on the dissemination of scientific findings. And so forth. Each question focuses on the intersection between two or more traditional disciplines.

To get a better sense for the value of interdisciplinary research in studying the environment, let us consider a couple of more extended examples.

Saving the Cape Hatteras historic lighthouse

The researcher David Policansky describes an interdisciplinary research effort that was undertaken in the late-1980s by the National Research Council (NRC) (Policansky 1999). At the time, coastal erosion was endangering an old historic lighthouse located at Cape Hatteras in North Carolina. The NRC was invited to advise the National Park Service to explore options and make recommendations on how to protect the lighthouse from the encroaching sea.

Saving the lighthouse was quite a complex problem with many dimensions, including issues of science, engineering, environmental impacts, economics, law, and policy. Technical options included either moving it to a safer location or fortifying and reinforcing the existing foundations. However, saving the lighthouse was not merely a technical issue of engineering, as there was a question of how much the different options would cost, in an era of reduced federal budgets.

Furthermore, the lighthouse was considered to be of historical significance, as it dated back to nearly the Civil War era. This meant that there was value to trying to preserve both it and the configuration of surrounding buildings in their original state (United States National Park Service).

Finally, legal issues arose because reinforcement options ran afoul of state laws that prohibited the building of certain types of structures on the North Carolina coastline (United States National Park Service).

In order to address the variety of issues that arose, the committee that worked on options and recommendations included a geographer, a constitutional lawyer, two construction engineers, a civil engineer, a historian, an economist, a coastal geologist, two ecologists, and an expert on masonry (Policansky 1999, p. 387). In the end, the lighthouse was relocated. But the point here is that it required an interdisciplinary effort in order to come up with reasonable options for how to proceed.

Climate change impacts on the North Shore of Lake Superior

The second example is based on an interdisciplinary research project that I was recently involved in. This project involved researchers from a number of different disciplines, including climate scientists, sociologists, tourism experts, and an economist (me). We were interested in projecting the impacts of climate change on communities on the North Shore of Lake Superior in northern Minnesota, the local economies of which relied heavily on tourism dollars. This was a big question with many moving parts, because it raised issues of climate science, subjective attitudes toward local environments, behavioral responses to climate change, and economic impacts on the local communities. Since we will be referring to this study at various junctures in the chapters to come, let us give it a name: the *North Shore Climate Change* study.

To give you a sense as to why we formed this interdisciplinary team to carry out the project, consider two of the project's components. One of these was to estimate the impact of climate change on historical visitations to state parks in northern Minnesota. This analysis was done in order to try to quantify the likely impact of future changes in climate. For this part of the project, I worked with a couple of climate scientists from the University of Minnesota.

I collected the social science data, including visitors numbers, economic variables, and so forth. The scientists collected climate data and worked with climate models that provided projections of future climate conditions. This division of labor made sense because the natural scientists knew nothing about the quantitative methods of economists, and I knew nothing about climate science. By working together, the end result was one that neither I nor the natural scientists could have accomplished working in isolation from each other.

Another part of the project involved better understanding the likely behavioral responses of tourists to climate change. This analysis combined notions from economics and sociology to determine the importance of "place-based attachment" for visitors' willingness to pay for climate change mitigation. Place-based attachment, which means psychic connections made to places on the basis of previous experiences, is a factor that economists do not typically consider when they attempt to measure the determinants of willingness-to-pay. In our results, it turned out to be a systematically important factor. If I had worked by myself using only concepts from previous economic studies, it is unlikely that I would have uncovered this result.

The challenges of doing interdisciplinary research

I hope that these examples effectively convey the potential value of taking an interdisciplinary approach to studying the environment. However, this discussion would be incomplete if it did not mention certain challenges to doing interdisciplinary research.

Perhaps the major challenge is that there are a number of structural issues that can get in the way of achieving true integration of different disciplinary perspectives. First, researchers in different disciplines have different types of expertise and specialized vocabulary for describing the things that they do. This means that researchers from different disciplines often have to take some time to learn how to effectively communicate with each other (Brewer 1999, p. 335; Policansky 1999, pp. 388–9).

Based on personal experience, I would strongly recommend not underestimating this issue. It is quite easy for researchers from different disciplines to spend a significant amount of time talking past each other, simply because they have different understandings of particular words, phrases, or concepts. Furthermore, they often have an imperfect understanding of the content of each other's disciplines, which can also lead to miscommunication because each "side" may lack the proper context to really understand what people on the other side are saying.

Second, the very fact that people are coming from different disciplines means that an interdisciplinary research team can be populated by researchers with a wide range of views. This range of views is commonly wider than that of a team composed of researchers from the same discipline, who are more likely to share similar perspectives on things like appropriate approaches to take and methods to use. The wider range of views on an interdisciplinary team may make it harder to achieve consensus on things like how to solve a problem, and even defining exactly what the problem is.

Third, there is an understandable tendency for researchers in individual disciplines to believe that the approach and methods of their discipline are the correct ones, sometimes at the expense of the approach and methods of other disciplines. Involvement in an interdisciplinary team requires each researcher to be open-minded about, and to see value in, the approaches and methods of other disciplines. Sometimes it can take time for researchers on an interdisciplinary research team to fully gain each other's trust, respect, and confidence in their expertise.[1]

Bottom line: Interdisciplinary research holds great promise for fruitfully studying a wide variety of environmental issues. At the same time, it presents a number of challenges to environmental researchers that stem from different assumptions, outlooks, vocabularies, and knowledge bases.

Conclusions

As we shall see, conducting research on the environment can be tremendously rewarding, allowing us to gain important insights into many vexing environmental problems. As the same time, there are many things to consider and numerous challenges to overcome every step of the way. However, thanks to all of the researchers who have gone before you, there are many things we know regarding what to do and what not to do. Here is where this textbook may help you. This is because this textbook is designed to do three main things.

First, it is designed to introduce you to a wide variety of approaches to doing environmental research. Knowing different approaches is important because there are many types of environmental research projects that you can do, depending upon the research question you wish to answer. As a practical matter, students using this textbook will likely have a wide range of interests in the environment, both in terms of the topics they wish to tackle and the type of research project they wish to do. This textbook is designed to accommodate a wide variety of projects on a wide range of topics.

As we shall begin to see in Chapter 3, there are two basic approaches you can take in conducting research in general. You can take a *quantitative approach* or you can take a *qualitative approach*. Though there is certainly overlap in the two approaches, they are sufficiently distinct to merit separate discussion. This fact provides a natural organizing framework for the book, which contains two main sections.

The quantitative approach is discussed in Chapters 4 through 8, and the qualitative approach is discussed in Chapters 9 through 14. Chapter 15 is then devoted to a discussion of how one can bring the two approaches together in the *mixed methods* approach. Each of those discussions will provide practical guidance regarding how to design and carry out various types of research projects.

Second, this textbook provides many illustrative examples of actual research projects undertaken recently by environmental researchers on a number of environmental issues. These examples are intended to do three things: (1) to illustrate a variety of principles of good research method; (2) to illustrate a number of practical nuts-and-bolts issues that arise when you undertake environmental research; and (3) to provide you with ideas regarding interesting, feasible research projects on the environment.

Finally, this textbook is designed to provide you with a number of tools that will be useful in helping you carry out environmental research. These include: practical matters of data collection, tools for statistical analysis, working with different kinds of evidence, practical issues relating to administering surveys and conducting interviews, ethical issues in research, and the nuts-and-bolts of developing a research proposal. In some matters, the textbook discussion will need to be supplemented with additional material, simply because space constraints do not permit as complete a discussion as may be warranted on certain points. Whenever possible, guidance will be provided on additional resources to consult.

Note

1 For more on the challenges of interdisciplinarity, see Brewer (1999), p. 335; Jacobs and Frickel (2009).

References

Brewer, Garry D. "The Challenges of Interdisciplinarity," *Policy Sciences* 32(December 1999): 327–37.

Committee on Facilitating Interdisciplinary Research, Committee on Science, Engineering, and Public Policy. *Facilitating Interdisciplinary Research*. National Academies, Washington: National Academy Press, 2004.

Crawford, Elisabeth. "Arrhenius' 1896 Model of the Greenhouse Effect in Context," *Ambio* 26(February 1997): 6–11.

Jacobs, Jerry A., and Scott Frickel. "Interdisciplinarity: A Critical Assessment," *Annual Review of Sociology* 35(2009): 43–65.

Kliff, Sarah. "Green Degrees in Bloom," *Newsweek*, August 8, 2009.

Leavy, Patricia. "Transdisciplinarity and Training the Next Generation of Researchers: Problem-centered Approaches to Research and Problem-based Learning," *International Review of Qualitative Research* 5(Summer 2012): 205–23.

Policansky, David. "Interdisciplinary Problem Solving: The National Research Council," *Policy Sciences* 32(December 1999): 385–91.

Rodhe, Henning, Robert Charlson, and Elisabeth Crawford. "Svante Arrhenius and the Greenhouse Effect," *Ambio* 26(February 1997): 2–5.

Sample, Ian. "The Father of Climate Change," *The Guardian*, June 6, 2005.

United States National Park Service. "Moving the Cape Hatteras Lighthouse," April 14, 2015, https://www.nps.gov/caha/learn/historyculture/movingthelighthouse.htm

Vincent, Shirley. "Growth in Environmental Studies and Science Programs," *Association for Environmental Studies and Sciences* 2(2009): n.p.

Vincent, Shirley, Stevenson Bunn, and Sarah Stevens. "Interdisciplinary Environmental and Sustainability Education: Results from the 2012 Census of U.S. Four Year Colleges and Universities," *National Council for Science and the Environment* (September 2012).

2 A brief history of knowledge and argumentation

Introduction

Why do we do research? There are actually a lot of different answers to this question. Some answers are highly abstract (to divine the truth) and others are highly concrete and practical (to get an A in my science class). But I would like to focus on one, which I think is central to the enterprise or at least, it should be. We do research because we want to know more. The more knowledge we have, the better we can understand how the world works and our relationship to the world. And the better positioned we will be to offer informed solutions to vexing environmental problems, such as deforestation, climate change, water pollution, toxic waste disposal, and extinction of endangered species.

But thinking about knowledge and what we know raises additional questions. We all have an intuitive idea of what it means to know something. Roughly speaking, to know something is to believe it to be true. However, the world is not black and white. We can all think of countless things that we believe to be true but about which we are not sure. Some things we are more sure about than others. What counts as knowledge? How do we come to believe certain things? And are there things that it is impossible to know?

What is knowledge?

In environmental studies, we are often concerned with a particular type of knowledge, what is called *scientific knowledge*. Scientific knowledge is systematic, evidence-based knowledge about the physical and natural world that is based on established physical principles. We can think of plenty of examples of scientific knowledge. The sun-centered nature of the solar system. The elliptical orbits of the planets. The recent warming of the earth's atmosphere due to the build-up of greenhouse gases. The germ theory of disease. The role played by the heart in the circulation of blood. All of these examples are things we believe about the physical world, objective facts that characterize the nature of things, how things work.

The contingency of scientific knowledge

Why do we believe these things? The short answer is because they have been through a rigorous process of scientific discovery and confirmation. At one time, none of these things were believed to be true. It took inspiration and careful thought by scientists to come up with an insight, and then countless hours of additional work to confirm that this initial insight could be believed.

Our base of scientific knowledge is also determined by things that we believe not to be true. We do not believe that the sun revolves around the earth. We do not believe that fires occur because all flammable materials contain a combustible element called *phlogiston*. We do not believe that it is possible to transform base metals such as iron and lead into gold. We do not believe that the disease cholera is spread by *miasma*, or foul-smelling air.

Many people used to believe all of these things. But few people do anymore, because the same scientific process that has led us to believe certain things has also led us to not believe other things. As some things have been confirmed, others have been rejected. As more people have come to believe that the earth revolves around the sun, fewer believe that the sun revolves around the earth.

One thing that all this should tell you is that we need to draw a distinction between what we believe and what is actually true, in a scientific sense. Scientific knowledge is in a constant state of flux: as new discoveries are made, some knowledge is confirmed, and other knowledge is rejected.

Even now, there is no way that our present scientific knowledge base can be considered the final word on any matter, despite the best efforts of really smart scientists and all of our extremely sensitive measuring instruments, supercomputers, and massive amounts of data. In other words, all of what we know should be considered as *contingent knowledge*, subject to change as new information comes to light.

Some have interpreted this argument as implying that we can never know the truth, which calls into question the value of science. Years ago, famous scientist and science writer Isaac Asimov was confronted with this very argument in a letter written to him by a student. The letter was written in response to one of Asimov's essays, in which Asimov had extolled science and all the scientific progress that had been made in the last century. The letter writer had argued that Asimov's faith in science was misplaced because all of what we know is still wrong.

Asimov responded politely that the letter writer was laboring under a misconception of what science was all about. It is important to recognize, Asimov argued, that in science there is no right or wrong. Rather, there are various degrees of wrong. Scientific progress is not about getting things right: rather, it is about getting things less wrong. This argument was contained in Asimov's famous essay "The relativity of wrong" (Box 2.1).

Box 2.1 The relativity of wrong

"My answer to him was, 'John, when people thought the earth was flat, they were wrong. When people thought the earth was spherical, they were wrong. But if you think that thinking the earth is spherical is just as wrong as thinking the earth is flat, then your view is wronger than both of them put together.'

The basic trouble, you see, is that people think that "right" and "wrong" are absolute; that everything that isn't perfectly and completely right is totally and equally wrong …

What actually happens is that once scientists get hold of a good concept they gradually refine and extend it with greater and greater subtlety as their instruments of measurement improve. Theories are not so much wrong as incomplete."

Isaac Asimov

Knowledge in the social sciences

In the social sciences, it is equally true that all knowledge should be considered contingent, but for slightly different reasons. The obvious difference between the natural sciences on the one hand and the social sciences on the other is that in the latter, there are the added social, political, economic, and cultural dimensions. The nature of knowledge is still about what we believe to be true. However, there are two important complicating factors.

First, compared to the natural sciences, the social element makes it more challenging to pursue the same research strategies to develop our knowledge base. It is more difficult to create laboratory conditions and controlled experiments that allow for clean tests of theories. This is especially true in certain of the social sciences like sociology and anthropology, which often emphasize research on individuals in their social and cultural settings. And this is also often true of environmental studies. But even in economics—the social science that tries to emulate the methodology of the physical and natural sciences most closely—it is not always easy to collect appropriate data or to create convincing tests that effectively add to what we already know.

Second, by virtue of its subject matter, much social science research defines knowledge differently than do the natural sciences. Research in the natural sciences relies heavily on physical data that have been carefully collected, measured, and categorized. The scientific ideal is to let these data speak for themselves, and for scientists to conduct experiments and tests in an even-handed manner. The resulting knowledge base is then intended to be objective, based purely on physical facts and phenomena not open to individual interpretation.

By contrast, social science research is commonly aimed at characterizing social behavior, attitudes, and beliefs. Knowledge is based not just on physical facts and phenomena, but also often on people's perceptions and beliefs about these things. Thus, in much of the social sciences, knowledge has both objective and subjective components. Indeed, certain types of social science research, especially in sociology and anthropology, emphasize the subjective component as much as, if not more than, the objective component.

We should probably dwell on this point for a moment, because it is extremely important that the argument not be misunderstood. When people say there is a subjective component to knowledge, they are not saying that whatever one subjectively believes is true. At the same time, in much social science research it is often assumed that how people subjectively perceive things can have real, substantive effects on their behavior and attitudes toward the world. Later on in this chapter, for example, we will encounter the notion of social construction, which ascribes an important role to social factors in affecting people's perceptions of the world around them. And we shall see many examples of beliefs, attitudes, and perceptions mattering in a number of environmental issues.

In order to better understand the various methods used by researchers to acquire knowledge, let us begin by briefly examining the human quest for knowledge over the years. Here, we will be mostly hitting the highlights, as this discussion is merely meant to give you a sense of the main arguments that have been advanced regarding: how humankind has thought about knowledge, the various means to acquire knowledge, and the more fundamental question of what it means to know something. In this discussion, I will be focusing mostly on the western tradition, where many of our ideas about *epistemology*—the study of knowledge—come from.

The origins of knowledge in the ancient world

The quest for knowledge has been going on for millennia, for as long as people have wondered about why things happen. The notion of scientific inquiry originated in ancient Greece, in the centuries before the birth of Christ. Prior to this time, people told stories, or so-called *myths*, to try to explain natural phenomena. These myths often involved titans, gods and goddesses, and other supernatural beings. Lightning occurred because the Greek god Zeus, or the Norse god Thor, hurled thunderbolts. Fire was not a chemical reaction, but rather a gift from the titan Prometheus, who stole it from the gods. These myths and many others were believed to be the reasons for the existence of lightning, fire, and many other things experienced in the real world. Myths were how people made sense out of the world.

The ancient Greeks

The ancient Greeks changed all that by starting to think about how to explain natural phenomena without relying on supernatural forces. The Greek philosopher and mathematician *Thales of Miletus* (620–546 BC) was apparently one of the first to attribute natural phenomena to causes within nature rather than the gods. This included a physical theory of the origin of earthquakes (O'Grady, "Thales of Miletus").

A number of other Greek scientists, philosophers, and mathematicians would make major contributions to advance our understanding of the world. These include: *Anaximander*, who advanced a theory of evolution centuries before Darwin (Russell 1942, p. 27); *Leucippus* and *Democritus*, who theorized that matter was made of atoms (Russell 1942, pp. 64–5); and *Eratosthenes*, who provided the first known accurate measurement of the size of the earth (the Greeks knew it was round!). The celebrated Greek physician *Galen* did extensive study of human anatomy and physiology (Thorndike 1922; Nutton 2002).

How did the ancient Greeks go about their attempts to acquire knowledge? Here is where an important issue of research method arises. There were actually two schools of thought on this very issue. One was that knowledge was acquired by *reason*. The other was that knowledge was acquired by *experience*.

The idea that knowledge is acquired by reason has been traced to certain so-called *pre-Socratic* philosophers; that is, philosophers who lived prior to the time of the famous Greek philosopher *Socrates*. However, currently this idea is usually associated with Socrates' pupil, the Greek philosopher *Plato*. According to Plato, in our search for knowledge we cannot trust the evidence of our senses, because appearances can be deceiving. In *The Allegory of the Cave*, Plato likens our everyday existence to living in a dimly lit cave, where all we can see are vague shadows of real things, never the things themselves (Figure 2.1). This is the best we can expect to know from our imperfect senses (Plato 1948, pp. 546–9).

A contemporary example of this Platonic argument can be found in the movie *The Matrix*. In this movie, all of humankind is living in a world where nothing that they experience is real and, therefore, all of what they think they know about the world is nothing like the true reality.

According to Plato, the only way to truly know the world is to reason things out. To do this, we begin with statements that are unquestionably true; namely, ones that do not depend for their truth on any experiences we might have. For example, a statement that is unquestionably true is: "Two plus two equals four." There is no experience that we could ever have that would contradict two plus two being equal to four. Statements like these have come to be called *innate ideas*.

How did people get these innate ideas? Well, Plato had the view that these ideas reside in one's soul, which is eternal. Being born is part of a process of reincarnation, where we start to experience the world anew. The process of gaining knowledge is basically a process of remembering these rules; for example, when we learn how to add numbers in elementary school (Plato 1948, pp. 215–18; "Innate idea", New World Encyclopedia). So, according to Plato, even though experience matters (a great deal!), it is reason that ultimately determines what we make of it.

Figure 2.1 The allegory of the cave.

Source: Wikimedia commons.

The school of thought based on these ideas of Plato is now commonly called *classical rationalism*. To this day, the general notion of using reason and deduction to produce knowledge is one of the two main pillars of research methodology.

The other school of thought emerging from ancient Greece was *classical empiricism*, which took a very different stance on the origins of knowledge. These Greeks argued against the idea that reason was the ultimate source of knowledge. Rather, they emphasized the importance of what we experience through our five senses. This position is commonly associated with the famous philosopher *Aristotle*.

Why did Aristotle believe that experience was what was most important? Aristotle just did not buy Plato's notion that innate ideas were ultimately responsible for knowledge. Rather, he believed that knowledge can only begin to accumulate when we start having experiences with the world ("Innate Idea", New World Encyclopedia). You can think about it this way: at birth, we are a *blank slate*, with nothing written on it. It is only through experiencing the world that things get written on the slate.

This is not to say that Aristotle did not believe in reason. Far from it. But he thought that knowledge was impossible without experience. Once you start to accumulate experiences, this triggers the use of reason to make sense of the world. Only then can we observe patterns and understand how the world works. But experience had to come first.

It is interesting that Aristotle was a student of Plato. In fact, he studied for twenty years at an academy founded by Plato. With such diametrically opposed beliefs about paths to knowledge, one can only imagine the debates and arguments they must have had. In Figure 2.2, we see an artist's depiction of Plato and Aristotle engaged in one of their philosophical discussions. Here, the famous Renaissance artist Raphael has chosen to symbolize their different views on the way to obtain knowledge. Plato, on the left, is pointing towards the heavens, which symbolizes his view that knowledge comes from universal abstract principles. Aristotle, on the right, is gesturing towards the earth, which symbolizes his view that knowledge is grounded in experience and observation.

The knowledge of the Greeks was absorbed into the Roman Empire when Rome conquered Greece in the second century BC, but scientific inquiry was not pursued with the same vigor under Roman rule. And when the Roman Empire fell to invaders in the fifth century AD, this effectively put an end to most scientific inquiry in Europe for a long time.

The medieval period

The ensuing *medieval period*, sometimes called the *Middle Ages*, was a period in which there were relatively few new developments in Europe in the way people

Figure 2.2 Plato and Aristotle.

Source: Wikimedia commons.

thought about knowledge and how to obtain it. We will return to this issue shortly. But before we do, it needs to be mentioned that major scientific advances were occurring in other parts of the world, especially in China and parts of the Muslim world.

Scientific discovery in the non-western world

Over a long time period stretching back into Roman times, the Chinese made many important discoveries and inventions, including gunpowder, the compass, printing, and the process for making paper (Needham 1954–98). In the eleventh century, a Chinese scientist was perhaps the first to propose a theory of how lands are formed, a precursor to the current academic discipline of geomorphology (Sivin 1982, pp. 47–51). And during the later Middle Ages, the Chinese made major advances in mathematics and astronomy. However, for a number of complicated reasons, Chinese science began to stagnate after the fifteenth century or so (Lin 1995).

Similarly, the Middle Ages were a time of major scientific advance in the Islamic world, which encompassed mostly the Middle East and northern Africa. Major discoveries were made, for example, in astronomy, mathematics, and medicine (Grant 2008, p. 507). Indeed, the word "algebra" comes from an Arabic word, reflecting its origins in the Islamic world.

There are a couple of reasons why science flourished in the Islamic world during this period. First, when Islamic armies went out and conquered new lands, the Islamic world learned about the ideas of many of the ancient Greek scientists and philosophers. Over time, it became the practice of certain Islamic scientists to rely on experimentation rather than arguments based on philosophy. This included the great Islamic scientist Al-Haytham, who made important early discoveries in the field of optics (Dallal 2010, p. 39).

Second, science was viewed as a way to support practicing the Islamic faith. This view was, for example, expounded by the Islamic philosopher Averroes (see Box 2.2). Indeed, some scientific discoveries were made precisely to support Islamic religious practice. Astronomers put their heads together to produce extremely accurate and detailed maps, for example, so that anyone anywhere in the Islamic world would know the precise direction to Mecca. This was, of course, so they would know exactly which direction to face in order to pray (King 1997).

Box 2.2 Averroes on science

"Anyone who studies anatomy will increase his faith in the omnipotence and oneness of God the Almighty."

Science in the medieval western world

Meanwhile, knowledge production stagnated through most of the Middle Ages in Europe, in part because the ideas of Plato, Aristotle, and other Greek philosophers were largely absent for most of this period. This was because the capacity to speak Greek—and, therefore, to translate the ancient Greek texts—largely disappeared in Europe. To make matters worse, few translations of the Greek philosophers had been made into the language that did survive: Latin (Spade, 2016, *Stanford Encyclopedia of Philosophy*).

Nevertheless, in Europe the tradition of learning was preserved through the growth of Christianity. Monasteries were established, where monks and priests taught themselves to read and write. And these monks and priests also opened up schools, to teach others. And not surprisingly, the nature of knowledge inquiry changed to one that focused intensively on religious inquiry. This entailed answering questions such as: How do we know God exists?

The method for answering questions also changed, to one that relied heavily upon religious authority. Knowledge was not to be obtained through reason or experience, but rather through study of scripture. Over time, however, knowledge of the ancient Greeks filtered slowly back into Europe. This was probably at least partly due to the spread of Greek ideas from the Islamic world (Lindberg 1978; Brown, n.d., *Internet Encyclopedia of Philosophy*).

We then witnessed the rise of the *scholastic* movement, which applied some of the methods of the ancient Greeks to the study of scripture. Important among these was the application of reason and logic in order to make sense of the world. However, the objective was not the generation of new knowledge, but rather the mastery of what was already known. This mostly meant questions like: What do the scriptures really mean? What is the real basis for faith? (McGinn 2014, pp. 12–16).

The heavy reliance on reason meant that experience and evidence were downplayed by scholastics in the search for knowledge. The single-minded focus on scripture and ancient Greek texts led many scholastics simply to ignore experience altogether. A famous example of this is the *Story of the Horse's Teeth*, which is often attributed to the Renaissance philosopher Francis Bacon.[1]

In this story, a bunch of friars were sitting around one day arguing over the number of teeth in the mouth of a horse (Box 2.3). The answer, they believed, must be contained somewhere in the ancient texts. But no matter how much they searched those texts, they just could not find the answer. Then at one point a young friar says: "Hey, there's a stable out back. Why don't we go take a look?" As the story goes, the rest of the friars were aghast at the insolence of this young friar in proposing the consideration of anything but the ancient texts, and they promptly threw him out of the order. Though possibly apocryphal, this story conveys well the single-minded reliance of the scholastics on established authority, sometimes to the exclusion of everything else.

Box 2.3 The scholastics and the *Story of the Horse's Teeth*

In the year of our Lord 1432, there arose a grievous quarrel among the brethren over the number of teeth in the mouth of a horse. For 13 days the disputation raged without ceasing. All the ancient books and chronicles were fetched out, and wonderful and ponderous erudition, such as was never before heard of in this region, was made manifest. At the beginning of the 14th day, a youthful friar of goodly bearing asked his learned superiors for permission to add a word, and ... beseeched them to unbend in a manner coarse and unheard-of, and to look in the open mouth of a horse and find answer to their questionings. At this, their dignity being grievously hurt, they waxed exceedingly wroth; and, joining in a mighty uproar, they flew upon him and smote him hip and thigh, and cast him out forthwith. For, said they, surely Satan hath tempted this bold neophyte to declare unholy and unheard-of ways of finding the truth contrary to all the teachings of the fathers. After many days more of grievous strife the dove of peace sat on the assembly, and they as one man, declaring the problem to be an everlasting mystery because of a grievous dearth of historical and theological evidence thereof, so ordered the same writ down.

Having just read about how Islamic scientists did it, you may be wondering how the European scholastics fit reason and faith together. It is common to assume that either you believe or you do not believe, and reason or logic have nothing to do with it. In a world where Christian scripture matters so much, how would reason ever even get a foothold? And wouldn't the ancient Greek philosophers be considered to be pagans not worth even thinking about?

Scholastic philosophers did struggle with these questions, but a breakthrough reconciling faith and reason occurred in the writings of the scholastic philosopher St. Thomas Aquinas. Aquinas, born in 1225, is widely considered to be the most important philosopher of the medieval period. Aquinas addressed the faith-reason dilemma by arguing that there were two types of laws governing the universe: natural law and eternal law. Natural law governs the workings of the world, while eternal law is ultimate truth (God's law). Natural law may be discovered through reason, while eternal law is only knowable through faith.[2] By drawing this distinction, Aquinas opened the door for reason- and evidence-based inquiries into the world separate from questions about God's existence (Rothbard 2002, p. 4–6]).

The views of Aquinas would turn out to be enormously influential in promoting the free pursuit of knowledge. After Aquinas, faith in the written word of the scriptures began to decline as an obstacle to scientific inquiry. The grip of the Church on inquiry into new knowledge was loosened. People became increasingly free to think for themselves about the world and to discuss their views with others. And they felt increasingly free to consider other sources of authority besides the Church. This led many to turn back to the ancient Greeks for ideas and ways of thinking about the world. All of this gave birth to the next important stage in humankind's quest for knowledge: the *Renaissance*.

The Renaissance: Beginnings of modern knowledge

The period known as the Renaissance in Europe dates from around 1400 AD to 1700 AD. This was a period in which scientific and humanistic inquiry flourished, which led to revolutionary changes in science, literature, art, architecture, and music. During this period, many important scientific discoveries occurred. This included Robert Boyle's theory of gases and William Harvey's theory of the circulation of blood, as well as the invention of the telescope, microscope, compass, and thermometer. It was also during this period that Copernicus theorized that the earth revolved around the sun, which the ancient Greeks had known but which had been lost during the Middle Ages with the dominance of the Church.

The new scientific breakthroughs were enabled by a fundamental change in the way science was done. Instead of being largely a matter of faith, inquiry into knowledge became more an exercise in applying reason and logic. And once people began to look beyond the word of authorities, they started to rely much more heavily on actual observation of how the world seemed to work. In this, they were heavily influenced by the views of Francis Bacon.

Bacon vs. Aristotle

To understand Bacon's views, let us return briefly to Aristotle, whose ideas Bacon sharply criticized. According to Aristotle, there were four possible explanations for phenomena in the natural world. These were known as the *Four Causes*. To understand these causes, let us consider a concrete example.

Consider an acorn, which you know grows to be an oak tree. The question is: What are the various ways we can understand what an acorn really is? According to Aristotle, we can understand an acorn to have four causes: a *material* cause, an *efficient* cause, a *formal* cause, and a *final* cause (Aristotle 2008, pp. 38–42).

The *material* cause of an acorn is the physical stuff it is made up of, like water, protein, minerals, and tannin, which makes it taste bitter to us, even though squirrels like them.

The *efficient* cause of an acorn is what causes it to be what it is: the oak tree that produced it, and the process of photosynthesis that feeds on sunlight, rain, and warmer temperatures in the spring.

The *formal* cause of an acorn is what it is when it has reached its full potential: the large oak tree that it grows up to be.

And the *final* cause of an acorn is its purpose, the reason for its existence; namely, to produce more oak trees and, therefore, more acorns. Aristotle would have believed that all of these were important, complementary ways to think about what acorns were.

Bacon thought that a lot of this was a bunch of mumbo-jumbo. He didn't quarrel with the first two causes: he thought it was important to know what things are made of and how they are made. But he did not think it was important to think about what things potentially could be: he was just interested in understanding things as they really are. And to do this, he certainly did not think we needed to ascribe any purpose to their existence (Rychlak 1993, pp. 390–1; Klein, 2012, *Stanford Encyclopedia of Philosophy*). It might be fun or reassuring to think all things had a purpose, but he did not think that this was a proper province of scientific inquiry.

Bacon called for careful observation of events in nature, to collect data and to think carefully about what the data are telling us. In the process, we need to be skeptical of what we see and hear and try not to infer more than is warranted by the facts. Of particular usefulness are data that seem to go against what we think we know, which forces us to rethink. If necessary, we may need to go out and collect more data. In this way, we gradually build up a base of knowledge in a careful and systematic way, and are as sure as we can be that our beliefs are warranted.

All of this adds up to an approach that is heavily empirical, which is why Bacon is sometimes called the *father of empiricism*. The Renaissance scientist William Harvey saw himself very much as taking this approach (see Box 2.4).

> *Box 2.4* William Harvey
>
> "I ... learn ... anatomy not from books but from dissections, not from the tenets of Philosophers but from the fabric of nature."

We should remember that Aristotle himself did believe that experience and evidence were the ultimate sources of knowledge, as we saw earlier. However, there were two important differences between Aristotle and Bacon. The first was that hard-headed Bacon did not see the need to bring in issues, such as purpose, that were essentially unknowable from the facts. Bacon was saying: Let's just stick to what we can really say about the important questions of what things are and how they work. And let us not uselessly speculate on questions like what is their purpose in life.

A key distinction: Inductive vs. deductive reasoning

The second important difference was that Aristotle was a firm believer in the use of *deductive* reasoning to understand things about the world, whereas Bacon was a firm believer in the use of *inductive* reasoning (Cajori 1925, pp. 85–6; Godfrey-Smith 2003, p. 236). This is a crucial distinction to understand, so let us spend a little time making sure we know what the terms mean and how they are different.

In using deductive reasoning, Aristotle would start with a premise, such as "All men are mortal," a statement that seemed to be unquestionably true. From this uncontroversial statement, he could reason his way to the conclusion that Plato was mortal by simply noting that Plato was a man. This illustrates deductive reasoning, in which you start with a general premise and reason out its logical consequences to be able to draw conclusions about some specific situation.

Notice that when you use deductive reasoning, you can be very confident about the conclusions you draw, as long as you start with a valid premise. Given that *all men are mortal* and that *Plato is a man*, it is hard to see coming to any conclusion other than: *Plato is mortal.* Thus, you can use deductive reasoning to generate conclusions that you can be very certain about.

However, notice also that how much certainty is warranted depends crucially on whether or not your premise is valid. If instead your premise was "All men are tall," your logical conclusion would have to be that Plato is tall, which may or may not be true. This illustrates the crucial importance of having valid premises if you are going to use deductive reasoning. In this example, if you measure Plato and discover that he is indeed short, you may want to go back and re-examine your premise.

In championing the use of inductive reasoning, on the other hand, Bacon believed that you should start not with general principles, but rather with specific instances. This means that one begins by collecting empirical evidence and then seeking patterns in the data. From these patterns, one then discerns general principles.

To illustrate induction, let us consider a classic example from the history of science. Suppose you see a swan and it happens to be white. You may think nothing of it except to admire its gracefulness and beauty. However, suppose you keep walking around seeing swans and every one happens to be white. A general principle may start to form in your mind: *All swans are white.* This is an example of induction. You are taking specific encounters with swans as evidence and using them to state a general principle about the world.

Notice that when you use induction, you can never be certain about your conclusion. Just because every swan you have ever seen has been white, this is no guarantee that *all* swans everywhere are white. Maybe you don't get out much. Maybe you have bad eyesight. Maybe you just haven't been looking in the right places. All we can really say is that given our experience to date, this is our tentative conclusion. We may be pretty confident, perhaps because we have done extensive fieldwork all over the world. But using induction, we can never know for sure.

Bottom line: Whereas deduction involves moving from the general to the specific, induction involves moving in the opposite direction: from the specific to the general. And deduction permits certainty about our conclusions, but only if we are starting with valid premises. With induction, none of our conclusions can be stated with certainty.

Empiricism

Bacon's views would turn out to be extremely influential and are considered to be the beginnings of the application of the *scientific method*, which is based heavily on the collection of evidence and using it to draw conclusions about the world. As we have seen, they sparked a scientific revolution, a period of extraordinary achievement of new discoveries in science, technology, and mathematics. And Bacon's ideas were pursued and developed by a number of important philosophers who became known as the *empiricist* school. One of the key figures here was the seventeenth-century British philosopher *John Locke*.

Locke is known for many important ideas in philosophy and political economy, but here we will focus specifically on his ideas relating to knowledge and how it is acquired. As an empiricist, Locke is known for resurrecting Aristotle's old notion of the mind as a blank slate (Pinker 2002, pp. 5–6; Godfrey-Smith 2003, pp. 19–20). Like Aristotle, Locke did not much care for Plato's notion that people are born with innate ideas. He believed that it made a lot more sense to think that all knowledge came from experience, which imprints itself on the mind so that what we know is simply the sum total of all of our experiences, like all of the writing on an originally blank slate.

The question of whether we should think of the mind as a blank slate has provoked widespread and heated debate among academics in a wide variety of fields (see Pinker 2002; Fromm 2003). Here, let us focus on two problems that relate specifically to knowledge and how it is acquired. First, there really do seem to be ideas that many people have that do not seem to originate in experience.

A simple example of this is "2 + 2 = 4." Everyone accepts this statement regardless of their experiences with the world. And to accept it, we do not have to ascribe to Plato's notion of remembering innate ideas from past lives. As a component of our knowledge base, it's just true. The empiricists never provided a satisfactory answer to this objection to pure empiricism.

A second issue related to an apparent contradiction that one encountered if one subscribed to empiricism. The problem was, some people argued, that we never experience the world itself. We only experience sensations derived from our five senses. So if: (a) all knowledge comes from experience, and (b) we never really experience the world, then: (c) how can we ever know anything about the world (Godfrey-Smith 2003, p. 19)? The people who argued this were known as *skeptics*. The skeptics argued that it was impossible to discern any sort of objective reality: all we can know is our personal experience of the world, which is completely subjective.

Twentieth-century thought

Logical positivism

The views of the skeptics created real problems for the empiricist approach, and it created real problems for scientific inquiry in general. How in the world can we acquire knowledge about nature if all of our knowledge comes from our senses and we can't trust our senses? The people who offered a way out of this conundrum were a group that was known as the *Vienna Circle*, which was formed after World War I. This group of philosophers created a new approach that became known as *logical positivism*.

First, they tackled the problem plaguing the empiricists that innate ideas such as "2 + 2 = 4" really do seem to exist in the world. They did this by creating two different categories of statements, or propositions, about the world.

The first category was called *analytic propositions*. These are statements about the world that are true regardless of experience, like "2 + 2 = 4." These are true not because they are handed down from on high or resided in our souls, as Plato argued. Rather, they are conventions: statements that we as a society simply agree are true. We can all agree because every one of the components of an analytic proposition has a particular meaning that we all agree upon. For example, in this statement, we all agree about the concepts that "2" and "4" embody, and we all agree about what it means to add things to each other.

The second category was called *synthetic propositions*, which may or may not be true, depending upon experience and evidence. These are statements like: "All men are over six feet tall." The logical positivists argued that only synthetic propositions are a legitimate subject of scientific inquiry. Statements like "All men are over six feet tall" can be investigated and we can decide that they are either true or false (Godfrey-Smith 2003, pp. 25–6).

The second way in which the logical positivists offered a way out of the empiricist conundrum was essentially to redefine what is meant by "meaning." The question of what a statement means, argued the logical positivists, really comes down to only one thing: Is it possible to verify whether or not a statement is true? The logical positivists argued that only if verification is possible in principle does a statement have any meaning. This meant, of course, examining evidence and seeing what it told us about the statement.

We can see how this argument applies to synthetic propositions like "All men are over six feet tall." Here is where scientific inquiry would come into play, with data collection and analysis. And because it is possible to summon evidence to determine that this statement is either true or false, logical positivists would say that this statement is meaningful.

So what sorts of statements would this principle rule out? They would be synthetic propositions such as: "Trees have standing," "Animals have rights," or something that Albert Einstein reputedly once said: "The theory of relativity is beautiful." They may or may not be true, but one cannot imagine any evidence that would allow us to verify one way or the other. The ability to verify was key. To logical positivists, any statements that are incapable of being verified are meaningless (Godfrey-Smith 2003, pp. 26–7).

Recall the objection of the skeptics to the empiricists about the hopelessness of ever knowing anything, if all we can rely on is evidence. Notice how this argument addressed this objection. If statements are meaningless if they cannot be verified, then it is meaningless to speak about the difference between the objective world and our subjective perceptions of it. This is because no evidence exists that would allow us to distinguish between the two. This clever argument permitted the logical positivists to sidestep the objection that evidence and experience were inherently unreliable.

> **Bottom line:** According to the logical positivists, the only statements that have any meaning are ones that we can use as evidence to verify that they are true.

Post-positivism

So logical positivism provided a way out of the serious problems faced by the empiricists. However, some serious problems with logical positivism soon became apparent. One was a concern that some philosophers had with reliance on verification. They argued that using verification as the standard for testing the truth of a proposition created some serious problems of interpretation. The philosopher who more than anyone else is identified with this position is the Austrian-British philosopher *Karl Popper*.

Popper saw the following problem with verification: it is just too easy to take any piece of evidence and interpret it as verifying a statement. The classic example of this, provided by Popper himself, was the view of economic change proposed by the nineteenth-century socialist economist Karl Marx.

Popper was not a big fan of Marxism. Marx would say things like: "Economic change occurs because of class struggle." So when a revolution came, Marx could say: "See? The proletariat are throwing off their chains. This proves my statement is true." Then somebody would say, "Not so fast. Here's another case where there is no revolution." Marx, or one of his followers, would respond: "Well, that is because the dominant class is repressing the proletariat, making economic change impossible. That also proves my statement is true." So no matter what happened, class struggle was driving everything. Marxists could not lose! Everything that happened could be interpreted as supporting Marx's proposition, which then must be true (Popper 2002).

Popper argued that rather than using verification, researchers should rely on *falsification*. Under this view, scientific progress occurred not by continually trying to verify that propositions were true. Rather, the purpose of scientific research was to progressively rule out propositions that were false. This was to be done by posing hypotheses capable of being falsified, and then collecting data to test these hypotheses. Through a gradual process over time, we would inch closer to the truth, never knowing for sure if we got there. You may notice that this is Asimov's notion of the relativity of wrong, which we saw earlier (Godfrey-Smith 2003, pp. 58–61).

> **Bottom line:** Rather than relying on *verification* as the criterion for assessing the knowledge value of statements, Popper argued that we should rely on *falsification*. This insight would pave the way for widespread application of the modern scientific method.

The notion of falsification has a couple of important implications for how research should be done. First, hypotheses must be sufficiently simple in order to yield clean tests. The problem is that the world is a complex place, with much going on all at once. It is important to cut away a lot of that complexity, which is our only hope if we wish to pose hypotheses that can actually be tested.

The trick is to be able to cut away only what is not essential to represent what is going on. This is why social science disciplines like economics often use simple models of the world. This method of reducing things to their essentials is why the scientific method is sometimes referred to as *reductionist.*

Second, it is important that researchers be objective in performing hypothesis tests and interpreting the results. Among other things, this means that researchers need to minimize bringing value judgments to their work. They should set up their tests fairly, without knowingly introducing bias, and they should let the results speak for themselves. Without doing all of this, it is not clear that a process that relies on falsification will yield reliable results, in allowing us to appropriately rule out objectively incorrect conjectures.

This picture of science I have just been painting conjures up images of scientists in white lab coats puttering around a laboratory filled with beakers and test tubes. This picture really is a gross stereotype of science in action. The way science is actually done in the real world is much more complex and frankly, much more interesting, than this. And this brings us to a second objection of the post-positivists to logical positivism. Namely, that it left out a very important component of science: the human and social element.

Science, and research in general, does not occur in a vacuum. There are social reasons why certain research questions get asked and others do not. There are social reasons why certain research programs obtain financial support and others do not. And there are social reasons why certain research findings gain traction among other researchers and the general public and others do not. Without considering social factors, the picture we are painting of: (1) how research is done and (2) how it benefits society remains grossly incomplete.

In this chapter, we have already seen evidence of the importance of social factors in influencing what research gets done and how it is received. During the Middle Ages, the dominance of the Church heavily influenced which questions were asked by the scholastics and which answers they could even consider. For the scholastics, it would have been impossible to consider any ways of thinking about knowledge that did not centrally involve God. And you are probably aware that during the early Renaissance, religious authorities staunchly opposed the theory that the earth revolved around the sun.

But it hasn't just been the Church. In the nineteenth century, the Hungarian physician *Ignaz Semmelweis* noticed that in hospitals in Vienna, many women were dying in childbirth. Noticing that deaths were higher in certain hospitals where doctors were handling cadaverous material, Semmelweis proposed that doctors wash their hands prior to delivering babies. And he backed up this proposal with careful studies that showed that hand washing could dramatically reduce mortality rates (Hempel 1966; Miller 1982; Gillies 2005).

However, Semmelweis' ideas were not accepted by the medical community and many doctors simply refused to consider washing their hands. Tragically, Semmelweis was later committed to an asylum, where he died after being beaten by the guards. He was later vindicated when Louis Pasteur came up with and confirmed the idea that diseases could be transmitted by tiny microorganisms, or germs. It was only gradually over time that the *germ theory* gained public acceptance.

The scholastics, the sun-centered theories of Kepler and Copernicus, and the tragic story of Ignaz Semmelweis all illustrate that there is a second important element of the research process that the logical positivists did not really consider. In addition to what I will call "nuts-and-bolts" research—collecting data, conducting experiments, and testing hypotheses—there is also the larger social context in which questions are asked and answers are shared with the rest of the world.

The post-positivists proposed that we widen the focus of our notion of research. They argued that there are actually two important complementary contexts in which to think about research. The first is the narrow day-to-day setting of researchers doing nuts-and-bolts research. The second is the broad social and scientific context where questions get asked, funding decisions are made, and research findings are broadcast to the rest of the world. The first is called the *context of justification*, and the second is called the *context of discovery* (Godfrey-Smith 2003, p. 29).

It is important to emphasize that the context of discovery includes both the state of scientific understanding at a particular point in time, and the larger social context in which research is being done. When Copernicus proposed his sun-centered models of the solar system, he was challenging an existing scientific understanding about the fundamental nature of the solar system. But he was also doing it during a time when Church doctrine was dominant, which made it difficult for his ideas to gain headway. The distinction between the state of scientific ideas and the social context in which science is done is important to keep in mind if we wish to understand the contributions of another extremely important post-positivist philosopher: *Thomas Kuhn*.

Kuhn was actually a physicist who became interested in the history of scientific ideas, and his writings have had a tremendous impact on the philosophy of science. His ideas are expressed in one of the most influential books of the twentieth century: *The Structure of Scientific Revolutions* (Kuhn 1996).

In this book, Kuhn draws an important distinction between nuts-and-bolts science, or what he calls *normal science*, and science that leads to *paradigm shifts*: fundamental changes in the way we think about things (Kuhn 1996). Most of the time, normal science is not very glamorous: it is about solving problems, and tweaking and refining theories. So unless you get a charge out of doing these sorts of things, it is usually not very exciting.

Sometimes, however, in the process of doing normal science we encounter things that are hard to explain, given the current understanding. At first, we may write them off as curiosities, or caused by bad data or faulty instruments. But they keep coming. And then other people start getting the same findings. It becomes a more persistent mystery, no longer easy to simply dismiss. And eventually they force us to fundamentally change our views about what is going on. And the end result is a new way of thinking about things: a new paradigm.

For example, in the nineteenth century physicists believed that light was transmitted through space in a mysterious, invisible substance called *ether*. Given what they knew at the time, it was the only way they could understand how light could move from one place to another. But if light was indeed transmitted by ether, this meant that we would have to observe it traveling at various speeds, depending upon conditions.

Then two physicists, Albert Michelson and Edward Morley, devised an extremely sensitive way to measure the speed of light and discovered that light always travels at the same speed. If this was really true, it cast major doubts on the theory that light was transmitted through ether. However, no matter what they did, they and others kept coming up with the same finding, which caused a crisis in the field of physics. Suddenly, physicists had no idea how light moved from one place to another (Shankland 1964; Livingston 1987).

Fortunately, along came Albert Einstein, whose theory of relativity did not rely upon ether or any other such substance to explain how light traveled through space. And since it predicted that the speed of light was constant, it provided a new way of understanding light propagation. This was a paradigm shift in our understanding of this scientific issue.

However, Kuhn went further than positing scientific progress as a series of paradigm shifts. Kuhn argued that in the process of doing science, scientists always bring a set of theoretical premises and scientific methods to the practice of science that are particular to the social and professional context in which they work (Box 2.5). These collective assumptions provide a backdrop to their work and constitute part of the prevailing scientific paradigm.

Box 2.5 Thomas Kuhn on the practice of science

"Far from being magisterial in its objectivity, science was conditioned by history, society, and the prejudices of scientists."

But social factors don't simply enter in at the macro-level when we are considering major shifts in scientific paradigms. They can also exist on a day-to-day level. Many people have agreed with Kuhn and argued that there is inevitably a social element involved in doing normal science. As the philosopher Paul Boghossian has put it:

> No one should deny … that knowledge is often produced collaboratively, by members of a social group, and that contingent facts about that group may explain why it shows an interest in certain questions over others.
>
> (2006, p. 20)

So scientists, being human beings, bring their own personal values, interests, and prejudices to the task of doing science. The questions are: Can we continue to have faith in the legitimacy of scientific method? Can we trust the results of scientific experiments?

These questions are a bit controversial, but many philosophers would argue that the answer to both questions is yes, if scientists are careful. What they mean by this, roughly speaking, is that even if scientists cannot avoid bringing their social baggage to the exercise of posing research questions, they can be careful once they don their white suits and enter the laboratory. Copernicus may have been a social creature of his time, but that didn't stop him from using evidence to correctly interpret the elliptical orbits he postulated. If scientists all do this, then science should move forward and we will ultimately get to where we should be going.

In making this argument, philosophers of science are distinguishing between the context of discovery and the context of justification. The argument is that even if the first stage is infested with social factors, proper science can be done if scientists are careful in trying to be scientifically objective in the second stage. One reason this is a controversial argument is that some find it hard to believe that social factors, if they enter into the first stage, will not enter the second stage as well.

Social construction

For all their disagreements, the positivists and post-positivists did agree on one thing: that there is such a thing as objective truth. We may never know what it is, but it does exist. And searching for it is a legitimate goal of the human quest for knowledge. Kuhn and many post-positivists may have believed that scientific practice itself was infected with the prejudices of scientists, but they never doubted the ultimate goal of learning the objective secrets of nature.

There is another approach, however, that downplays the idea of the search for objective truth. This is the approach called *social construction*. Social constructionists believe that knowledge is heavily influenced by social factors, such as how you were raised by your parents, interactions with your siblings, and the attitudes of the social groups you belong to. All of these factors influence how you perceive, interpret, and create meaning out of the things you experience[3] (see, for example, Hacking 1999; Boghossian 2006). If you think about what this means, there are two immediate implications.

First, social constructionists heavily emphasize social influences on human behavior. The idea here is essentially that humans are primarily and inevitably social creatures. What we think, say, and do are heavily influenced by social and cultural factors. This includes social and cultural norms, societal and community expectations, and our interactions with others: our parents when we were growing up, our friends at school, our bosses and co-workers, and so forth. This is in stark contrast with the post-positivist approach, which largely treats human behavior as individualistic and internally driven.

Second, this approach typically gives rise to studies that attempt to portray human behavior in all its real-world complexity. This is in stark contrast to the reductionist approach of post-positivism, which takes much of this complexity and ignores it for the sake of a tractable analysis and plausible hypothesis tests. Social constructionists would argue that the reductionist approach risks losing much useful information that may provide valuable insights into people's behavior. So social constructionists pick up on things that most post-positivists would not: feelings, personal opinions, attitudes, body language, tone of voice, intonation, figures of speech, conversational dynamics, and so forth.

It might help to be concrete about the difference between the post-positivist approach and the social construction approach. One way to view the evidence summoned by scientists for hypothesis testing under the post-positivist approach is that it exists outside, or independent, of any social context. Global temperatures are what they are, regardless of whether you live in the United States, Indonesia, or rural Norway, or regardless of whether you live in middle-class America or an indigenous village in Papua New Guinea. We all believe dinosaurs existed tens of millions of years ago, because we have a fossil record and dinosaur bones that constitute overwhelming evidence. These forms of evidence are an objective reality: facts that can be precisely measured and quantified.

As opposed to the factual evidence used in scientific studies, the evidence used in many studies using the social construction approach is of a different nature. The attitudes of rural Norwegians towards climate change are not facts, they are beliefs. They do emanate from and belong to the individual, to be sure. We all hold our own personal beliefs. But what determines these beliefs? We can all understand the scientific process that results in fossilization of dinosaur bones. What process determines what we believe about climate change?

There are many social factors that influence our beliefs about things: how we were brought up by our parents, interactions with our peers, norms in the community in which we were raised, and so forth. Many argue that these social factors may play an influential role in determining our beliefs about dinosaurs and climate change, completely aside from any "objective" evidence that any scientist could provide. If so, then we would say that our beliefs regarding dinosaurs and climate change are at least partly socially constructed.

For example, religious beliefs about the duration of geological time may lead some to question scientific claims that dinosaurs lived over sixty-five million years ago. Similarly, politically based suspicions that scientists are conspiring to paint the consequences of climate change as being excessively dire might lead some to question projections of climate change weather impacts, or even question whether climate change is occurring at all. For many social constructionists, these social factors can vastly outweigh objective science in shaping people's attitudes and beliefs.

Bottom line: Social constructionists tend to ascribe importance to social factors in affecting behaviors, attitudes, and perceptions of the world. This tends to lead to non-reductive methods of analysis that emphasize the complexity of human behavior. These analytical methods may then rely on a wide range of different types of evidence.

Conclusions

The purpose of this brief history of knowledge has been to convey how the quest for knowledge has changed over the years, to help you think about what knowledge is and how humans have tried to acquire it. As you can see, there have been many approaches, but they all basically come down to the use of reason and/or experience. In the chapters to come, we will be exploring a variety of research methods that use and combine the two in various ways.

As you might expect, at times the multiplicity of approaches will seem to be incompatible. For example, there would seem to be no middle ground between the positivist emphasis on objective facts and the constructionist heavy reliance on personal experiences, attitudes, and perceptions. However, the field of environmental studies is incredibly varied and rich, leaving room for various approaches depending upon exactly what topic you want to research. The trick will be to find a match between your particular research interests and the appropriate methodology to employ.

Exercises/discussion questions

(1) The relative roles of reason and experience in determining what we know may be captured in the following thought experiment, from Robert Pirsig's *Zen and the Art of Motorcycle Maintenance*. Imagine that someone was born without any of the five senses: sight, hearing, smell, taste, or touch. But imagine that this person was somehow, through artificial means, kept alive until she became an adult. What, if anything, would she know?

(2) Consider the *Story of the Horse's Teeth* attributed to Bacon. Can you think of any times in your own personal experience when you suspect that you may have relied too heavily on received authority, at the expense of evidence?

(3) Which of the following are examples of *induction*, and which are examples of *deduction*? Explain.

- What is the next number in the sequence? 1, 2, 4, 8, 16, 32, ___
- All even numbers are divisible by 2, and 38 is divisible by 2; therefore, 38 is an even number.
- Summer days are hot, so that means the 4th of July this year will be hot.
- In each of the last five years, the average temperature of the earth has increased. Therefore, global warming is occurring.
- Global warming occurs when ambient levels of carbon dioxide increase. Carbon dioxide levels are increasing. Therefore, global warming is occurring.

(4) Suppose you wanted to answer the research question: *Are all swans white?* Describe a research strategy based on inductive reasoning. Describe a research strategy based on deductive reasoning.

(5) Consider the statement "2 + 2 = 4." In your opinion, is this a statement which is simply true, regardless of experience?

(6) Which of the following statements are *falsifiable*?

- All swans are white.
- Some swans are white.
- The sun will rise tomorrow morning.
- Global warming is occurring.
- Global warming may or may not be occurring.
- Environmental quality gets worse as income levels rise, and then gets better (see Figure 4.1, *The environmental Kuznets curve*).

(7) In this chapter, we have seen a couple of examples of so-called *paradigm shifts* in the history of science: the move from an earth-centered to a sun-centered picture of the universe, and our understanding of how light is transmitted through space. Would you consider recent developments in climate change science to constitute a paradigm shift? Can you think of other scientific developments that you would characterize as paradigm shifts?

(8) In performing science, we have seen the distinction between the *context of discovery* and the *context of justification*. Many post-positivists influenced by Thomas Kuhn would argue that social factors enter heavily into the context of discovery, influencing the questions that are asked, the answers that can be considered, and the ability to obtain funding for research programs. However, they might also argue that social factors can be largely kept out of the context of justification, where nuts-and-bolts science is conducted. Do you agree?

Notes

1 Though commonly attributed to Francis Bacon, the true origins of this story are not really known.

2 To be complete, you should be aware of two other types of law that Aquinas was concerned with: *divine law* and *human law*. But these other types of law are not important to discuss here.

3 You should be aware that there are two related terms: social *construction* and social *constructivism*. The distinction sometimes made is that the former refers to factors relating to social interchange, while the latter tends to refer to your internal cognitive processes (see, for example, Guterman 2006). For the purposes of this discussion, I will not draw a sharp distinction between the two.

References

Aristotle. *Physics* (Oxford World Classics, 1st ed.). Oxford: Oxford University Press, 2008.

Boghossian, Paul. *Fear of Knowledge*. Oxford: Clarendon, 2006.

Brown, Christopher M. "Thomas Aquinas," *Internet Encyclopedia of Philosophy*, n.d., http://www.iep.utm.edu/aquinas/

Cajori, Florian. "The Baconian Method of Scientific Research," *Scientific Monthly* 20(January 1925): 85–91.

Dallal, Ahmad. *Islam, Science, and the Challenge of History*. New Haven: Yale University Press, 2010.

Gillies, Donald. "Hempelian and Kuhnian Approaches in the Philosophy of Medicine: The Semmelweis Case." *Studies in History and Philosophy of Biological and Biomedical Sciences* 36(2005):159–81.

Godfrey-Smith, Peter. *Theory and Reality*. Chicago: University of Chicago Press, 2003.

Grant, Edward. "The Fate of Ancient Greek Natural Philosophy in the Middle Ages: Islam and Western Christianity," *Review of Metaphysics* 61(March 2008): 503–26.

Hacking, Ian. *The Social Construction of What?* Cambridge: Harvard University Press, 1999.

Hempel, Carl. *Philosophy of Natural Science*. Englewood Cliffs: Prentice-Hall, 1966.

King, David. "Two Iranian World Maps for Finding the Direction and Distance to Mecca," *Imago Mundi* 49(1997): 62–82.

Klein, Jürgen. "Francis Bacon," *Stanford Encyclopedia of Philosophy*, December 7, 2012, https://plato.stanford.edu/entries/francis-bacon/#SysSci

Kuhn, Thomas. *The Structure of Scientific Revolutions* (3rd ed.). Chicago: University of Chicago Press, 1996.

Lin, Justin Yifu. "The Needham Puzzle: Why the Industrial Revolution Did Not Originate in China," *Economic Development and Cultural Change* 43(January 1995): 269–92.

Lindberg, David C. *Science in the Middle Ages*. Chicago: University of Chicago Press, 1978.

Livingston, Dorothy Michelson. "Michelson-Morley: The Great Failure," *The Scientist* (July 1987).

MacDonald, Scott, and Norman Kretzmann. "Medieval Philosophy," in *Routledge Encyclopedia of Philosophy* (Taylor & Francis, 1998), doi:10.4324/9780415249126-B078-1

McGinn, Bernard. *Thomas Aquinas's* Summa theologiae*: A Biography*. Princeton: Princeton University Press, 2014.

Miller, Patti J. "Semmelweis," *Infection Control* 3(Sept./Oct. 1982): 405–09.

Needham, Joseph. *Science and Civilization in China*. 7 volumes. Cambridge: Cambridge University Press, 1954–98.

New World Encyclopedia, *Innate Idea*, April 16, 2014, http://www.newworldencyclopedia.org/entry/Innate_idea

New World Encyclopedia, *Tabula rasa*, November 11, 2015, http://www.newworldencyclopedia.org/entry/Tabula_rasa

Nutton, Vivian. "Logic, Learning and Experimental Medicine," *Science, New Series* 295(February 1, 2002): 800–01.

O'Grady, Patricia. "Thales of Miletus," *Internet Encyclopedia of Philosophy*, n.d., http://www.iep.utm.edu/thales/

Pinker, Steven. *The Blank Slate*. London: Penguin, 2002.

Pirsig, Robert. *Zen and the Art of Motorcycle Maintenance*. New York: Bantam, 1975.

Plato. "Phaedo," in Scott Buchanan (ed.), *The Portable Plato*. New York: Viking, 1948: 191–278.

Plato. "The Republic," in Scott Buchanan (ed.), *The Portable Plato*. New York: Viking, 1948: 281–696.

Popper, Karl. *Conjectures and Refutations* (2nd ed.). London: Routledge, 2002.

Rothbard, Murray. *The Ethics of Liberty*. New York: New York University Press, 2002.

Russell, Bertrand. *A History of Western Philosophy*. New York: Simon and Schuster, 1942.

Rychlak, Joseph F. "Intention in Mechanisms and the Baconian Criticism: In the Modern Cognitivist Reviving Aristotelian Excesses?" *Journal of Mind and Behavior* 14(Autumn 1993): 389–98.

Shankland, R. S. "Michelson–Morley Experiment," *American Journal of Physics* 31(1964): 16–35.

Sivin, Nathan. "Why the Scientific Revolution Did Not Take Place in China – or Didn't It?" *Chinese Science* 5(June 1982): 45–66.

Spade, Paul Vincent. "Medieval Philosophy," *Stanford Encyclopedia of Philosophy*, March 15, 2016, https://plato.stanford.edu/entries/medieval-philosophy/

Thorndike, Lynn. "Galen: The Man and His Times," *The Scientific Monthly* 14(January 1922): 83–93.

3 General research design principles

Introduction

There were a couple of important takeaway messages from the last chapter. One is that there are two fundamental components to the production of knowledge: reason and experience. We have seen reason and experience combined in different ways, depending upon whether you take a rationalist or empiricist point of view, like Plato vs. Aristotle. We saw that both were largely submerged for a while during the Middle Ages when church doctrine led to heavy reliance on religious texts. And we saw there have been serious controversies over the years regarding how experience is to be used and interpreted. But by now, you should be hard pressed to imagine a quest for new knowledge without the use of both reason and experience.

Second, you should now have a broad conception of what we mean by evidence. If you are like many students entering a research methods course for the first time, you may come in thinking of evidence as numbers and statistics. And those types of evidence will certainly be an important part of the picture moving forward. However, if evidence can also consist of beliefs, attitudes, and perceptions—which play an important role in the social construction approach—then we can now treat potentially many other things as evidence. The question is: How exactly is this done?

This chapter will start to answer this question by outlining some general research principles. In doing so, it will focus on the specific needs of your research project. These needs include: choosing a topic, asking a researchable question, and thinking about how one uses evidence to try to answer this question.

What is a research question?

When you are just starting out on a research project, you will need a research question. By this, I simply mean a question where you propose to do research in order to answer it. But more specifically, I mean research where you will be collecting evidence to answer the question.

This may still seem pretty broad. But thinking back on Chapter 2, notice how many possible questions we have just eliminated from consideration. We have eliminated, for example, questions like "Is 2 + 2 = 4?", "Do triangles have three sides?", and "Is the theory of relativity beautiful?" Again, this is because these are all questions for which there is no evidence we can imagine collecting that would allow us to answer them.

The first trick to posing a research question, then, is to make sure it is one where it makes sense to even consider collecting evidence. "Is global warming occurring?" would fit the bill, because we can easily imagine collecting data on global temperatures and seeing if they are rising over time.

This is not to say that doing this would necessarily provide a definitive answer to the question. If you have ever seen actual data on average global temperatures, you know that temperatures go up and down from year to year. It is hard to tell for sure if extreme weather events (like floods, droughts, and tornados), another sign of global warming, are becoming more frequent over time. At the end of the day, you may still not be sure what the answer is. But as long as the evidence can shed light on the answer *in principle*, you may consider it a valid research question.

Now, let's think about this argument a little bit more. Suppose your question was: "Is it *possible* that global warming is occurring?" Is this a valid research question? Most researchers would say not. If we observe a rise in temperatures, we might be tempted to conclude that the answer is yes. But if we observe that temperatures are falling, it is not at all obvious that the answer is no. This question does not seem amenable to analysis of the evidence because all kinds of evidence are consistent with it being true. The word "possible" makes this question too vague to be a legitimate target of inquiry.

In posing a research question, it helps to be both specific and concrete. Such research questions are not always easy to come up with. So to give you a better idea of what would be a reasonable research question, Box 3.1 provides a few examples. These are all questions from actual studies that we will encounter later on in the book.

Box 3.1 Research question examples

- What climatic factors systematically impact state park visitations in northern Minnesota?
- How do interest group pressures influence the listing of endangered species under the Endangered Species Act?
- What explains the success or failure of local referendums for environmental protection?
- What factors determine the success of local organizations in developing and managing irrigation water supplies?
- What psychological factors might inhibit individual support for policies to combat climate change?
- What accounts for the failure of local grassroots organizations to successfully collaborate on local environmental issues?

In addition to being both concrete and specific, all of these questions have an important thing in common. They all try to provide insight into an environmental issue by examining some cause-and-effect relationship. The effect of climate factors on state park visitations. The effect of interest group pressures on listings of endangered species. The unspecified factors that determine the success of local environmental referendums, or the success of local organizations in developing and managing water supplies. And so forth. This is a very common form taken by many research questions about the environment.

All of these questions work as research questions because they are all amenable to an empirical analysis. In every single case, it is possible to collect evidence and draw some meaningful conclusions that provide an answer. Does a particular factor matter? How much? If there are multiple possible factors, which ones matter and which ones do not? Answering these kinds of questions often provides important insights into particular environmental issues.

A key distinction: Quantitative vs. qualitative research

As I mentioned earlier, there are two broad categories of research that you could conduct: *quantitative* research and *qualitative* research. These are different types of research projects that you might do, depending upon your interests and your research question. Box 3.2 provides some representative definitions of quantitative and qualitative research.

Box 3.2 Some definitions of quantitative and qualitative research

(1) Quantitative research:

- "primarily involves the collection and analysis of numerical data" (Seale 2012, p. 587);
- "is a means for testing objective theories by examining the relationship among variables" (Creswell 2009, p. 4);
- "entails constructing hypotheses and subsequently testing them from empirical research" (Spicer 2012, p. 482).

(2) Qualitative research:

- "research primarily dealing with non-numerical data, such as images, fieldnote observations, texts, video and audio" (Seale 2012, p. 587);
- "is a means for exploring and understanding the meaning individuals or groups ascribe to a social or human problem" (Creswell 2009, p. 4);
- "involves an inductive process in which theory is derived from … empirical data" (Spicer 2012, p. 482).

Quantitative research

Quantitative research grows out of the positivist and post-positivist traditions discussed in Chapter 2. Studies in this vein generally assume that there is an objective truth out there, and there is a mostly objective way of getting at it. This is typically done through some variant of the scientific method (Heyink and Tymstra 1993, p. 291). Most quantitative research tends to ignore or play down the importance of social factors in determining what research questions get asked and how social factors may affect the answers.

Quantitative researchers often start with a theory that generates testable hypotheses, proceed to collect mostly numerical data, and then subject the data to tests, usually statistical in nature. The hypothesis tests then shed light on the theory or some application of the theory. Notice that the process is generally *deductive*: starting from a general understanding and moving to a specific situation.

Qualitative research

Much qualitative research, on the other hand, grows out of the social construction tradition. Many qualitative studies do not assume there is an objective truth waiting to be discovered. Rather, these studies focus on how social problems, including environmental ones, are perceived and experienced by people (Heyink and Tymstra 1993, p. 292).

Though qualitative studies use evidence, there is often little in the way of numerical data and formal hypothesis testing. Rather, qualitative studies often rely on non-numerical data, such as texts, journals, images, audio and video recordings, and observation of behavior in its natural setting. This evidence may be used to generate a theoretical understanding of what is going on.

Notice that the qualitative method is largely *inductive*: starting with empirical evidence and the specific details of a situation and then inferring general principles. This is why qualitative research is sometimes thought of as a process of *generating* theory. This is in contrast to quantitative research, which is commonly thought of as concerned with *testing* theory, through testing of hypotheses generated by theories.

Since all of this tends to be new for many students, let us expand on this discussion using a particular environmental example.

An example: Social construction of wilderness

Many of us are accustomed to thinking of wilderness in a specific sense: as an undeveloped place (largely) devoid of a human presence, filled with forests, lakes and streams, birds, and animals (see Figure 3.1). This description emphasizes the physical features of wilderness, the physical things that we associate with the idea of wilderness.

Figure 3.1 Wilderness as undeveloped place.

Source: Wikimedia commons.

But the notion of wilderness often goes beyond this mere notion of a physical space, as there is often an associated notion of being a place where one can go to escape civilization. The environmental historian William Cronon has nicely encapsulated this notion of wilderness:

> a pristine sanctuary where the last remnant of an untouched, endangered, but still transcendent nature can for at least a little while longer be encountered without the contaminating taint of civilization.
>
> (Cronon 1995)

Cronon, however, has a very different take on the concept of wilderness. Rather than being a physical space characterized by the absence of civilization, he argues that the concept of wilderness is a social construction. By this, he means that wilderness has always been what society has made it out to be.

At one time, for example, people associated wilderness with wild, barren, desolate places: places to be feared rather than embraced. This belief about wilderness gradually changed over time.

By the eighteenth century, the image of wilderness had begun a radical transformation. Rather than something to be feared and shunned, some people had started to regard it as a place filled with wild beauty that needed to be preserved and protected for all time.

By the late nineteenth century, amidst growing concern over some of the ills of civilization and economic development, wilderness had come to evoke nostalgic images of a simpler, trouble-free time. At the same time, it also began to be viewed as a place of recreation, a place to "get away from it all," especially among the well-to-do. Summarizing this history, Cronon says:

> [T]here is nothing natural about the concept of wilderness. It is entirely a creation of the culture that holds it dear, a product of the very history it seeks to deny.
>
> (Cronon 1995)

Today, Cronon says, our conception of wilderness has come to mean, for many people, an escape from the bitter reality of our humdrum lives (Figure 3.2). This has led to both an idealization of wilderness and an implicit condemnation of civilization. According to Cronon, setting ourselves outside of nature, viewing nature as something "over there" in the wilderness, gives us permission to justify and rationalize our own "business-as-usual" behavior:

> We work our nine-to-five jobs in its [civilization's] institutions, we eat its food, we drive its cars (not least to reach the wilderness), we benefit from the intricate and all too invisible networks with which it shelters us, all the while pretending that these things are not an essential part of who we are. By imagining that our true home is in the wilderness, we forgive ourselves the homes we actually inhabit.
>
> (Cronon 1995)

Cronon's take on wilderness is a good example of the approach of many qualitative researchers. Rather than focusing on the objective physical characteristics

Figure 3.2 Wilderness as escape.

Source: Wikimedia commons.

of wilderness, he focuses on what wilderness has meant to people over the years. Starting as a scary place to be avoided, it later became a place of beauty to be preserved, and then gradually over time it has come to symbolize a refuge from the ills of modern civilization.

In making this argument, Cronon brings no evidence in the positivist sense of the term. But his perspective may be very important in helping us interpret what is going on. And it may well help us understand how to proceed moving forward, in terms of our ability to effectively address environmental issues in an appropriate way.

So, for example, Cronon comes to the perhaps surprising conclusion that "wilderness poses a serious threat to responsible environmentalism," and calls for a radical re-thinking of how we view wilderness. Rather than thinking of it as a pristine area "out there" somewhere, he argues that we should recognize nature wherever it exists, even as the apple tree in our own backyard. Doing so will connect us better to nature and provide a healthier balance between our concern for wilderness and other pressing environmental issues.

What is evidence and how is it used?

One of your first decisions in designing a research project will be to decide whether you will take a quantitative or qualitative approach. This will depend upon your research question, of course. Consider the following three questions from Box 3.1:

- *What climatic factors systematically impact state park visitations in northern Minnesota?*
- *How do interest group pressures influence the listing of endangered species under the Endangered Species Act?*
- *What psychological factors might inhibit individual support for policies to combat climate change?*

From what we have said so far, you might well suspect that you will want to use the quantitative approach to tackle the first question and the qualitative approach to tackle the third one. The second one you may be unsure about. And you would be right in all three cases! But the question is exactly why?

The answer has to do with the nature of evidence and how to use it appropriately. You may already suspect that there are many kinds of evidence you can use to support an argument: an embarrassment of riches, if you will. However, the type of evidence you will want to use for your specific project will vary greatly depending upon your specific objectives.

There are three broad categories of objectives in environmental research: (1) quantifying relationships and testing hypotheses; (2) characterizing environmental processes and mechanisms; and (3) divining the meaning of environmental issues and concepts, like wilderness. Let us consider these in turn.

Quantifying relationships and testing hypotheses

A great many research questions about the environment involve quantifying relationships and testing hypotheses about various environmental issues. First, it is often important to know how large an impact is. Consider, for example, the first question, which was one of the questions asked in the *North Shore Climate Change* study: *What climatic factors systematically impact state park visitations in northern Minnesota?* It might be important for park managers to know how much rising temperatures affect state park visitations. With temperatures likely to continue to rise under ongoing climate change, such information would help inform decisions on park hours, hiring of employees, expansions of facilities, and the like.

Second, it is often useful to test hypotheses regarding environmental relationships. For example, you may know that ongoing climate change is likely to have two separate impacts on temperatures: gradual average increases over time and increased frequency of intense heat events. You might suspect, however, that moderate increases in temperatures will have a different impact on park visitations than intense heat events. It might be important to test to see if this is true.

Both of these questions are amenable to a statistical analysis of numerical data on the number of visits to the state parks, along with data on various indicators of climate conditions. This is a good example of a project that would be amenable to the quantitative approach. One would be working with objectively measured numerical data on visitors and climate variables, in order to come up with our best guess as to the true relationship among the variables.

Characterizing environmental processes and mechanisms

Another general research objective might be to understand the process that generates an environmental outcome. The second question: *How do interest group pressures influence the listing of endangered species under the Endangered Species Act?* is a good example of this. You are interested in explaining how the Fish and Wildlife Service (FWS) lists endangered species in the United States: why some get listed and others do not and, perhaps, the timing of these listings. You suspect that political factors might matter.

Answering this question might entail: (1) examining how the process works, (2) identifying the points where political pressures on the agencies might be brought to bear, (3) identifying the actors who participate in the process, and (4) documenting the factors that seem to make some groups more influential than others.

The evidence you might use could include: the text of the original enabling 1973 Endangered Species Act legislation that specifies listing procedures; the subsequent political history of reauthorizations and adjustments to the law; the history of actual listings of endangered species; and the record of public comments in the *Federal Register* on FWS proposals to add species to the list (Ando 2003, pp. 147–8).

What we have just described is a very different animal from the quantitative approach described for the first question. Most obviously, it is not at all clear whether you would be using any numerical data, quantifying any relationships, or explicitly testing any hypotheses. This fact alone would make the collection and analysis of evidence very different exercises. These quantitative procedures are not necessarily ruled out: it might well be possible to collect data and test some hypotheses as part of the project. But these would not be an integral, or even necessary, part of a qualitative study.

A perhaps more subtle difference is that the quantitative approach to the first question is focused on *outcomes*, whereas this question is focused on the *process* that leads to those outcomes. The distinction between outcomes and process is sometimes an important way in which quantitative and qualitative studies differ.

Typically, when we do a quantitative study, we analyze data in order to quantify a relationship among variables and, this is important: *We let theory tell us what we think is going on to cause changes in some variable to lead to changes in others*. But as a rule, we do not throw ourselves into the details and examine how the process unfolds on the ground in the real world.

On the other hand, when we do a qualitative study, we sometimes have little theory to guide us in interpreting real-world patterns in evidence. Recall that qualitative research is commonly inductive, starting from evidence and generating theories toward an understanding of what is going on. This means that we are often looking for rich descriptions of behavior, the social context in which it occurs, and how processes unfold over time.

To understand this point, it might help to examine Figure 3.3, which contrasts this project with the previous one. The project that tries to characterize the impact of climate change on park visitations focuses on merely quantifying the relationship, without examining the process or mechanism whereby park visits are affected. In effect, what happens in between is a black box which we cannot see inside. In contrast, the study that examines political influences on ESA listings is very much interested at looking inside the black box to see how political factors affect the listing of species. What happens in between is of keen interest to the researcher.

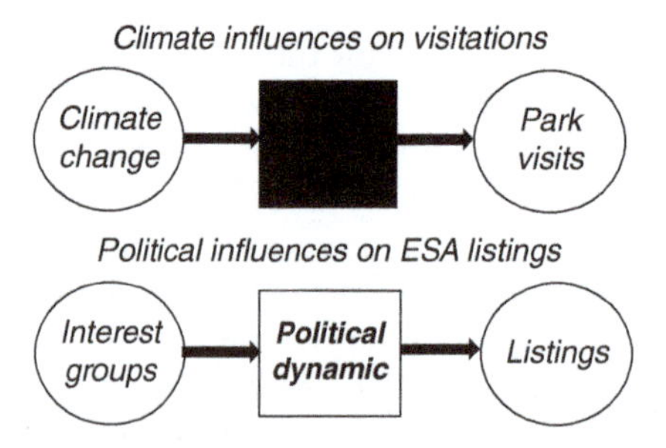

Figure 3.3 The focus on processes in (some) qualitative studies.

Divining meaning

A final research objective might be to try to understand the meaning that people ascribe to environmental events. We saw earlier, for example, Cronon's argument that wilderness should be viewed as a social construction rather than a physical place. In that case, we saw how this different perspective could have some important implications in terms of balancing concern for wilderness vs. other environmental goods.

Also exemplifying this objective is the third question listed above: *What psychological factors might inhibit individual support for policies to combat climate change?* This is a question which is asked in a study we shall encounter in Chapter 11. In this study, the author is trying to understand why residents of a rural Norwegian community only weakly support strong measures to combat climate change, despite a tradition of progressive attitudes toward the environment in general and a general belief in the efficacy of government intervention (Norgaard 2012).

In carrying out this study, the author delves into attitudes toward climate change in this rural community by traveling to the site and conducting interviews of various local residents. The evidence that she gathers from these interviews allows her to paint a complex psychological picture of these residents. This picture sheds light on the question of why relatively well-to-do, well-intentioned, and well-informed people may nevertheless take little action to combat what they know to be a serious problem.

Identifying interesting, feasible research projects

Now that we are aware of the different types of research projects that can be undertaken, let us turn to the practical question of how to go about identifying one that is right for you. It turns out that there are a number of factors to consider, having to do with: originality, feasibility, and interest you have in the topic.

Originality: Avoiding reinventing the wheel

Here, it is important to keep in mind the ultimate purpose of doing research: to contribute to our understanding of an issue. In order to ensure that your research is indeed a contribution, it is important to know what other researchers have done: the specific questions they have asked, the answers they have come up with, and the research methods they used. All of this points to the importance of doing a thorough reading of previous studies related to your topic—what is commonly called a *literature review* (see Box 3.3).

Useful electronic resources

A few words about doing an effective literature review. First, it is important to be thorough when you are looking for previous studies, because you don't want to miss anything important. The problem is that there are many, many studies out there on every conceivable topic. How do you ensure you are covering your bases, gathering all of the relevant studies?

There are several useful resources that you should be aware of, which you can access on the internet and perhaps even through your university library. One important resource is the digital library *JSTOR*, which your university may subscribe to. In JSTOR, you can search for scholarly journal articles and books using keywords, and for most articles, you can download PDF files to your computer.

Two words of warning. First, in JSTOR there is something that is sometimes referred to as the "moving wall." This means that for copyright reasons, JSTOR does not allow you to download or even read an article if it has been published more recently than in the last several years.

Second, even for older JSTOR articles you do have access to, it is a bit of an art to conduct JSTOR searches in such a way that you are able to cover every article and book in its database that is relevant to your study. Your faculty member or reference librarian can give you useful tips on how to make your JSTOR searches more efficient and comprehensive.

Another valuable resource is the on-line search engine *Google Scholar*, which contains an enormous number of references to scholarly journal articles, conference papers, dissertations, abstracts, and technical reports. Google Scholar is similar to JSTOR in that you can search for sources using keywords. Compared to JSTOR, it has the disadvantages that: (1) it is not as easy to search efficiently, and (2) many of the articles and other sources you will find cannot be directly downloaded.

On the other hand, Google Scholar contains a much more comprehensive database of sources, so you can be more confident that your search will not be overlooking anything.

In addition, Google Scholar has the *forward citation searching* feature, which JSTOR does not have. This means that when you find a source, it is possible to see the subsequent studies that cited it. By noting these studies, and the subsequent studies that cite *them*, and so forth, you can trace an entire scholarly conversation among researchers about a topic from its origins in the literature up to the present time. *Web of Science*, another database that your library might have, is another citation indexing service that also has this very useful feature.

Critically reading scholarly studies

Once you are satisfied that you have collected a comprehensive set of studies, the next step is, of course, to start reading. Here, your primary focus should be to identify the specific contribution of your research project. You do this by noting two things about the studies you read: *what they say*, and *what they do not say*. The idea here is that you need to know the findings, and the methods used to produce those findings, but you also need to know the limitations of the studies: what remains unknown or not well understood at the end of the day.

Box 3.3 The purpose of your literature review

"Novices may think that the purpose of a literature review is to determine the *answers* about what is known on a topic; in contrast, experienced investigators review previous research to develop sharper and more insightful *questions* about the topic."

(Yin 2009, p. 14, emphasis added)

To understand the findings, you should identify the questions they asked and the answers they arrived at, based on their evidence. Most of the studies in your literature review have tried to answer a question that is related to yours. For example, for the *North Shore Climate Change* study, I did a JSTOR and Google Scholar search for previous studies and came up with the ones listed in Box 3.4.

Box 3.4 Partial literature review example

Albano, C. M., C. L. Angelo, R. L. Strauch, and L. L. Thurman. "Potential Effects of Warming Climate on Visitor Use in Three Alaskan National Parks," *Park Science* 30(2013): 37–44.

Dawson, J., and D. Scott. "Managing for Climate Change in the Alpine Ski Sector," *Tourism Management* 35(2013): 244–54.

Elsasser, Hans, and Rolf Burki. "Climate Change as a Threat to Tourism in the Alps," *Climate Research* 20(2002): 253–7.

Fisichelli, Nicholas, Gregor W. Schuurman, William B. Monahan, and Pamela S. Ziesler. "Protected Area Tourism in a Changing Climate: Will Visitation at U.S. National Parks Warm Up or Overheat?" *PLOS One* (June 17, 2015).

Jones, Brenda, and Daniel Scott. "Implications of Climate Change for Visitation to Ontario's Provincial Parks," *Leisure* 30(2006): 233–61.

Maddison, D. "In Search of Warmer Climates? The Impact of Climate Change on Flows of British Tourists," *Climatic Change* 49(2015): 193–208.

Nyaupane, G. P., and N. Chhetri. "Vulnerability to Climate Change of Nature-based Tourism in the Nepalese Himalayas," *Tourism Geographies* 11(2009): 95–119.

Richardson, R. B., and John B. Loomis. "Adaptive Recreation Planning and Climate Change: A Contingent Visitation Approach," *Ecological Economics* 50(2004): 83–99.

Scott, Daniel, Brenda Jones, and J. Konopek. "Implications of Climate and Environmental Change for Nature-based Tourism in the Canadian Rocky Mountains: A Case Study of Waterton Lakes National Park," *Tourism Management* 28(2007): 570–9.

As you can see from the article titles, these studies were all previous attempts to understand the effect of climate change on tourism activity in some specific context: Alaskan national parks, the European Alps, Ontario provincial parks, the Nepalese Himalayas, and so forth. Reading all of these studies and noting their findings will give you a sense for the state of the frontier of our knowledge on this issue.

Often, when you read studies for your literature review, you will find that studies disagree on the answer to a question. For example, in this climate change example, you might find that some studies are finding a significant impact of climate change and others are not. In cases like this—where the jury is still out—another study of the effect in a different context may be valuable in lending support to one side or the other, making us more convinced that the answer is either yes or no. Either finding could be considered a contribution toward making our understanding "less wrong," as Isaac Asimov would put it.

However, another potential contribution might be to refine our understanding of the factors that make the answer "yes" in some cases and "no" in others. Maybe the effects are different in summer versus winter. Maybe the effects are different depending upon local conditions: for example, coastal locations versus prairie versus higher elevations. By examining the regularities in the findings, you might gain new insights that allow you to make more refined predictions about the impact of climate change.

As it turns out, in most of these studies, climate change was found to be indeed having significant effects on local tourism. Even in this case, however, there may still be a contribution to be made. It did not happen to be the case in the climate change topic, but sometimes the studies are older and their findings are based upon evidence that is out of date. In this case, a study based on recent evidence might reveal different effects, perhaps because conditions have changed.

More generally, it may be that existing studies have overlooked some important factors that may be important ones to consider. For example, the studies listed in Box 3.4 investigate the effects of average changes in climate variables, while not investigating the implications of increased incidence of extreme climate events. Looking forward into the future, this may be a serious omission, because most climate scientists agree that such extreme events are likely to become more frequent under continuing climate change.

Box 3.5 Checklist: Originality

- ✔ Use JSTOR and Google Scholar for your initial reference searches.
- ✔ Use forward citation searches to ensure your literature review is up to date.
- ✔ Read studies both for what they say and what they do not say.
- ✔ Seeming consensus on an issue does not necessarily rule out a project.
- ✔ Research answers are not only "yes" or "no" but also: under what conditions?
- ✔ Pay attention to whether existing studies may be out of date.
- ✔ Be continually asking yourself: What are these studies overlooking?

Feasibility: Can this project be done?

Another issue to consider when choosing a research topic is feasibility: Can your project be brought to successful completion within the time frame you have to do it? Your research project may be a class assignment, for which you have been given a semester or only part of a semester to complete it. Or your project may be an independent study project, under the supervision of a faculty member. Or your project may be a senior thesis, for which you may have more time.

Obviously, the more time you have, the bigger a project you can take on. Regardless, it is important not to bite off more than you can chew. "Is climate change occurring?" is certainly an interesting, many would say extremely important question, but may not be a question that can be answered in the context of an undergraduate research paper. All of the research questions in Box 3.1 work because they are narrowly defined and have a very specific focus. This makes it easier to collect evidence and still have time to do the analysis.

When doing certain types of projects, time can be an especially pressing issue. A general piece of advice is to not underestimate the amount of time it might take to collect your data. At present, there is a great deal of data available online, which can be extremely useful for many quantitatively oriented projects (a few of these sources can be found in the appendix to Chapter 5). However, it is not always in a format that is easy to use, and reformatting and organizing it into usable form can take time. In some cases, you may have to *scrape* the data (see also Chapter 5), which can also take time, as well as expertise in coding.

Sometimes, in the course of doing your literature review, you will read studies that make reference to specific public data sources. Whenever possible, write these sources down, if the data set appears to be relevant to your project. This is often a really good way to get data.

However, beware of relying on the authors themselves to furnish you with their data. It is tempting to do so since it is so easy to send e-mails nowadays. Even if they are willing to share their data with you (and not everyone is), it may take time for even completely well-intentioned researchers to respond. It is important to keep in mind that you are asking a stranger to do you a big favor. Probably the last thing you want to do is to be sitting there for weeks, waiting in vain for a great-sounding data set that never shows up.

There are several other ways in which time can become a pressing factor. We shall encounter these in later chapters, but let me just mention a few now. One is when you are doing a so-called *mixed methods* study, which simply means a study with both quantitative and qualitative components.

When doing a mixed methods study, sometimes the quantitative and qualitative analyses are done sequentially because you are looking for the results of one analysis to inform the framing and design of the other. In this case, you might have not one, but *two* data collection efforts, with the second one occurring only after the first analysis is complete. We will talk about how to deal with this issue in Chapter 15. But for now, you can imagine how you might find yourself pressed for time to complete both analyses.

Second, in Chapter 14, we shall encounter an approach to research known as *action research.* As we shall see, when you do action research, the project does not end when you turn in your research report. Rather, the report becomes the basis for action to be taken to address an issue. The actions taken are then observed, reflected upon, and may then became the basis for further research. This added stage of observation and reflection will require you to budget additional time to make sure it gets done, to inform further research either by you or other researchers.

Finally, some research projects involve working with human participants. This occurs, for example, if you survey or interview people in order to collect evidence for your study. In this case, you will have to obtain clearance from the institutional review board (IRB) at your institution. This will involve presenting an application for approval by the IRB before you can move forward with your evidence collection. Sometimes these processes can take time, so you should make sure you budget time to get through the process. We will talk more about this issue in Chapter 18.

Box 3.6 Checklist: Feasibility

- ✔ Don't bite off more than you can chew.
- ✔ Pose your research question as narrowly and specifically as you can.
- ✔ Be sure to budget enough time to get everything done.
- ✔ Scan studies in your literature review for data sources.
- ✔ Do not rely on the authors of studies to furnish you with their data.
- ✔ If you are doing a sequential mixed methods study, you will need to leave enough time for both data collection and analysis efforts.
- ✔ If you are undertaking action research, you will need to allocate time for the follow-up observation and reflection stages.
- ✔ Leave time for the IRB approval process, if your project involves working with human participants.

Interest: How much do I care about the answer?

As we saw earlier, "Is climate change occurring?" seems like a better research question than: "Is it possible that climate change is occurring?" And the argument there seemed to be that one can only really effectively bring evidence to bear to answer the first question. However, let us set this issue of evidence aside. When we think about these two questions, there may be another good reason to prefer the first question. Honestly, you may just find it to be a more interesting question. I mean, who really cares if it is *possible* that climate change is occurring? But a lot of people would very much like to know if climate change is *in fact* occurring.

This issue—whether a question is one that you find interesting—is, in my opinion, sometimes underrated. You might be asking yourself: Why in the world would I pose a research question that I do not find interesting? One answer might be that it is a class assignment and you were just handed the topic. Another might be that your research project is a class assignment and you have limited time to do what you really want to do. Or perhaps you are having difficulty identifying an interesting topic, so you pick one just to satisfy a requirement of your program. Finally, you may be part of a student research team and your team is having difficulty agreeing on a question, so everyone has to compromise.

The thing is: having a real interest in the answer to a question can be quite sustaining during what can be a long and sometimes arduous research process. Properly done, you will be reading a number of books, articles, reports, blogs, and websites; gathering evidence of various kinds; performing analysis; and writing up the results. This is a lot of effort to have to expend to answer a question that you are not really all that interested in knowing the answer to. If necessary, I would recommend spending a bit of extra time early on in the process to come up with a research question you are really happy with.

However, the point here is not merely: Do I find the question interesting? You might ask yourself: *Why* do I find it interesting? Aside from pure intrinsic interest, there might be good reasons to care about the answer.

One important reason is that the answer might really matter, if not to you then perhaps to others. Later on in the book, for example, we will encounter some examples of research projects that are designed specifically to benefit underprivileged, underserved communities. In one case, toxic releases of lead were causing significant health problems among local residents. A research project that raised awareness of the issue while pinpointing the location of the releases could provide major benefits to local residents.

An extended example: Local impacts of climate change

To illustrate some of these issues, let me describe the *North Shore Climate Change* study in a bit more detail. As I mentioned earlier, this was a team project to improve the capabilities of tourism-based coastal communities in northern Minnesota to adapt to ongoing climate change. The project team consisted of natural scientists, social scientists, and tourism experts. We came together to study the challenges facing communities heavily dependent upon outdoor recreational tourism. These communities are likely to be deeply affected by projected changes in temperatures, precipitation patterns, and extreme weather events.

The project was motivated by a recognition that climate change has probably already started to cause changes in local weather in northern Minnesota, and that these changes are likely to continue into the foreseeable future. Communities on the North Shore of Lake Superior are heavily dependent upon outdoor tourism activities, including hunting, fishing, hiking, and canoeing in the summer and downhill and cross-country skiing, snowmobiling, and ice-fishing in the winter. Over one million tourists visit the North Shore during the summer months alone.

Climate change has already started to cause warmer temperatures, drier conditions, and decreasing snow depths and ice thickness on lakes in northern

Minnesota. If current climate trends continue, there could be major impacts on the quality of the tourism experience, possibly reducing the number of tourists coming to visit. This in turn could have major socioeconomic impacts on the local communities that are so dependent upon tourism dollars.

Given the scale of the project, we posed multiple research questions, including the one we saw earlier: *What climatic factors systematically impact state park visitations in northern Minnesota?* This question was asked because there are a number of popular state parks situated along the entire length of the North Shore, for which there exist detailed historical numerical data on park visitations and detailed climatic data. Answering this question would give us a sense of the quantitative impact of changing climate on the level of tourism activity. It also allowed us to test some hypotheses on the impact of various climate factors.

In addition, we thought it was important to get a sense for the subjective factors that influence tourist interest in visiting the North Shore, including psychological ties, place-based identification, and what the area means to tourists on a personal and emotional level. Hence, we posed additional questions such as: *How important is place-based identification in influencing tourism activity? How important is a sense of attachment in influencing how much people value planning for climate adaptation?*

Quantitative analysis

In order to answer our research questions, we pursued a two-pronged approach that included both quantitative and qualitative components. For the quantitative analysis, we first performed a literature review of previous studies of climate impacts on outdoor recreational tourism activities. This literature review provided guidance in terms of helping us to identify statistical models and methods that had been used to analyze tourism activities in past studies. It also revealed the current state of understanding regarding the impact of climate factors. Finally, it revealed a gap in our understanding of the impact of climate factors; namely, that the impact of extreme weather events such as floods and heat waves is not well understood.

Based on these findings from existing studies, we then performed a statistical analysis of daily state park visitation data for both the summer and winter months for the years 2002–2014. This permitted us to quantify the impacts of different climate variables on park visitations, and we also discovered the importance of extreme weather events in affecting tourism. We then used climate models to project future climate conditions, including the projected incidence of extreme events. This allowed us to derive projections for the likely impact of climate on park visits in the future (Kanazawa et al. 2016).

Qualitative analysis

For the qualitative analysis, we performed a separate literature review that focused heavily on prior studies of the factors that shape attitudes to changing environmental conditions, including climate change. One message of this literature review was that the importance of psychological factors such as emotional attachment and personal identification was not well understood.

In order to carry out our qualitative analysis, we administered surveys to tourists at various locations along the North Shore: parks, roadside rest areas, outfitters, lodges, and so forth. The questions in these surveys asked visitors about a number of different topics.

The topics included: the purpose of their current trip (what recreational activities); their trip expenditures on lodging, food, gasoline, and so forth; their likely visitation responses to changes in climate conditions in the future; their willingness to pay for climate change adaptation planning; and their attitudes toward the North Shore. This last category of questions was about things like emotional attachment, personal identification, depth of feeling, and the uniqueness of the North Shore experience.

Based on their responses, we were able to draw some conclusions about the importance of place-based emotional connections on people's willingness to pay for adaptation planning. This in turn led to a distinction we drew between occasional visitors and "dedicated" visitors (that is, those with particularly strong place-based emotional attachment). This distinction had some useful policy implications regarding adaptation planning and funding for adaptation efforts (McCreary et al. 2016).

Conclusions

This chapter has laid out some basic general principles of research design, which are important to follow to ensure that you are undertaking a project that is original, feasible, and interesting. Key steps along the way are:

- Identifying a specific and well-defined research question;
- Thinking carefully about your research objectives; and
- Grounding your project in a scholarly literature.

In addition, you will have to think carefully about whether your research topic calls for a quantitative or a qualitative approach. Depending upon which one you choose, the next two sections of this book are designed to develop much more of the specific details involved in both kinds of research projects.

Exercises/discussion questions

(1) Are the following legitimate research questions? How might you improve them?

- Is the sky blue?
- What color do people see when they look at the sky?
- What makes the sky look blue to us?

(2) Consider Cronon's argument about social construction of wilderness and, specifically, the general idea that it is a creation of culture. Can you identify *specific* cultural factors that might determine how wilderness is socially constructed? How might these factors influence our ability to set in place policies for wilderness protection? Endangered species protection?

(3) Watch the 60 *Minutes* video clip: "Shaleionnaires," 60 *Minutes*, November 14, 2010, http://www.cbsnews.com/video/watch/?id=7054210n. Brainstorming with two other students, come up with FOUR research questions raised by the shale gas video: two that take a purely disciplinary perspective, and two that take a multidisciplinary perspective. In the manner of the popular TV quiz show *Jeopardy*, please phrase each of them in the form of a question.

(4) Consider the following research questions. Which ones seem to warrant taking the quantitative approach and which ones the qualitative approach? Why?

- What political and economic factors keep some endangered species from being listed as endangered?
- Do endangered species listings mostly reflect biological considerations, or political considerations?
- How are endangered species listings affected by which political party is in charge of Congress?

(5) Take the following quantitative research question and do a literature search in JSTOR for an academic journal article that you think is relevant to answering this question.

What is the most cost effective method for reducing nitrogen loads into the Mississippi River, in order to address hypoxia in the Gulf Coast?

In addition, do each of the following:

- State, in fifty words or less, the underlying theory that is either explicit or implicit in this research question.
- One reasonable interpretation is that there are two: one economic and one scientific. If you think there is more than one theory, describe them both. Which do you think is more central to answering the research question, and why?
- Briefly summarize the findings of the research. What is the answer it gives to the research question?
- Describe how you went about finding the journal article, including naming any databases you consulted.

(6) Take the journal article you found in question (5) and find two other related studies, one that was published *beforehand*, and one that was published *afterwards*. Give an *overall* summary of the evidence (that is, from the three studies combined) in terms of insights into the theory.

References

Ando, Amy W. "Do Interest Groups Compete? An Application to Endangered Species," *Public Choice* 114(January 2003): 137–59.

Creswell, John W. *Research Design: Qualitative, Quantitative, and Mixed Methods Approaches.* Los Angeles: Sage, 2009.

Cronon, William. "The Trouble with Wilderness; or, Getting Back to the Wrong Nature," in William Cronon (ed.), *Uncommon Ground: Rethinking the Human Place in Nature.* New York: Norton, 1995: 69–90.

Heyink, J. W. and T. J. Tymstra. "The Function of Qualitative Research," *Social Indicators Research* 29(July 1993): 291–305.

Kanazawa, Mark, Bruce Wilson, and Kerry Holmberg. "Local Consequences of Climate Change: State Park Visitations on the North Shore of Minnesota," Working paper, November 2016.

McCreary, Allie, Sandra Fatoric, Erin Seekamp, Jordan Smith, Mark Kanazawa, and Mae Davenport. "Risk Perceptions and Meanings of Place: What Influences Visitors' Willingness to Pay for Climate Change Adaptation in Nature-based Tourism Destinations?" Working paper, September 2016.

Norgaard, Kari M. "Climate Denial and the Construction of Innocence: Reproducing Transnational Environmental Privilege in the Face of Climate Change," *Race, Gender & Class* 19(2012): 80–103.

Seale, Clive (ed.). *Researching Society and Culture* (3rd ed.). Los Angeles, Sage: 2012.

Spicer, Neil. "Combining Qualitative and Quantitative Methods," in Clive Seale (ed.), *Researching Society and Culture* (3rd ed.). Los Angeles: Sage, 2012: 479–93.

Yin, R. K. *Case Study Research: Design and Methods* (4th ed.). Los Angeles: Sage, 2009.

4 General principles of quantitative research

Introduction

In the last chapter, we encountered the quantitative approach to research and contrasted it to the qualitative approach. As we saw, the two approaches are quite different, both in research objectives and in the way they use evidence. In the next five chapters, we will develop the quantitative approach in considerably more detail. In this chapter, we begin by developing some basic principles of quantitative research, including: drawing the important distinction between theory and hypotheses, using theory to generate testable hypotheses, the challenges involved in testing hypotheses, and the use of data in hypothesis testing.

One thing to keep in mind during the discussion of the quantitative approach is that this approach is largely in the positivist/post-positivist tradition. For the most part, we will assume that the evidence we are using is not socially constructed. We will also be assuming that the goal of the research is to add to our understanding of how the world works in some objective way. Our ultimate goal, as Asimov would put it, is ultimately to get less and less wrong about how we think about a particular environmental issue.

What is quantitative research?

To begin with, Box 4.1 reproduces part of Box 3.2, which laid out some definitions of quantitative and qualitative research. There are several takeaway messages here. Apparently, quantitative research examines the relationship among variables. In doing so, it poses testable hypotheses. It tests hypotheses by collecting evidence and using it to perform the tests. The evidence is numerical in nature. And, finally, the results of the tests are intended to shed light on a theory.

If we think carefully about what all of this means, there are several important implications. First, the quantitative method is largely *deductive*, not inductive. We start with a theory, which is an internally consistent way to think about how the world works. And we proceed from there to examine evidence to understand what happens in particular instances. We do not generally start with the evidence and use it to generate a theory. Again, this is in sharp contrast to the typical approach of qualitative researchers.

Box 4.1 Some definitions of quantitative research

Quantitative research:

- "primarily involves the collection and analysis of numerical data" (Seale 2012, p. 587);
- "is a means for testing objective theories by examining the relationship among variables" (Creswell 2009, p. 4);
- "entails constructing hypotheses and subsequently testing them from empirical research" (Spicer 2012, p. 482).

Second, the hypotheses are generated from the theory. Recalling the approach of the positivists and post-positivists from Chapter 2, there needs to be some way to tell whether or not a theory should be believed. The positivists argued that there must be some way to *verify* that a theory is true. The post-positivists, famously Karl Popper, argued instead that it must be possible to *falsify* a theory. In either case, however, evidence needs to be brought to bear.

The modern quantitative approach uses the falsification criterion. This means posing falsifiable hypotheses that seem to be implied by a theory, and subjecting them to rigorous testing. If rigorous testing leads us to reject a hypothesis, this would seem to be evidence against the theory that generated it. This in turn might lead us to rethink the theory, either searching for a new theory or modifying the existing theory to be consistent with the new evidence. If testing leads us to not reject a hypothesis, then this is taken as supportive of the theory from which the hypothesis is derived.

Third, the emphasis on numerical evidence means that there is heavy reliance on statistical methods. The statistical method uses data collected in samples to draw inferences on a target population that is the subject of analysis. These inferences include quantifying relationships and testing hypotheses. The validity of these inferences depends upon a number of factors, including our sampling procedure and the creation of statistics that capture certain important properties of our variables. These properties include the magnitude and variability of variables, and co-movement across different variables.

The relationship between theory and hypotheses

The distinction between theory and hypotheses is not always fully appreciated by those studying quantitative methods for the first time. So, since this distinction is crucial to understanding the quantitative approach, let us spend a little time making sure we know the difference.

As we have seen, quantitative research starts with theories that we devise to order and interpret knowledge about the world. For example, there is a theory known as the *greenhouse effect* that is based upon the scientific relationship between greenhouse gas emissions and global temperatures. According to the theory, emissions of greenhouse gases such as carbon dioxide and methane lead to the build-up of these gases in the atmosphere, which captures and contains solar radiation and causes global temperatures to rise.

As an example from economics, there is a theory known as the *environmental Kuznets curve* that characterizes the relationship between environmental quality and the level of a country's economic development (see Grossman and Krueger 1995; Dasgupta et al. 2002). This theory holds that environmental quality declines as countries move from low to moderate levels of economic development. But thereafter, continued economic development is associated with improved environmental quality. This relationship is illustrated in Figure 4.1.

Theories, of course, do not spring from out of nowhere but are created and refined over time by researchers in various disciplines. Two hundred years ago, no one had ever heard of the greenhouse effect or the environmental Kuznets curve. Someone had to think that they might exist and summon reasoning and evidence to support their existence. Even then, they might not have been believed, especially if the new theory was in sharp contrast to the existing understanding.

For example, in Chapter 2 we heard about the medieval scientist Nicolaus Copernicus, who advanced the idea that the earth revolved around the sun rather than vice versa. It took a long time, in the face of determined resistance by religious authorities, for him and his followers to convince people that this was indeed the case. It was only gradually, as evidence was collected that seemed to corroborate the new theory, that we gained greater collective confidence that the new theory was really true.

In the case of the greenhouse effect, the theory was conceived at the end of the nineteenth century, when the Swedish scientist Svante Arrhenius proposed the new idea that the burning of fossil fuels could cause the earth's temperature to rise. However, for a long time this idea was received with skepticism. Again, it was only gradually over time, with the accumulation of corroborating evidence, that this idea has come to be widely accepted in the scientific community.

These examples point to two key components of the process of coming up with theories to explain environmental relationships. Theories need to be generated, and then once generated, they need to be tested and, if necessary, refined.

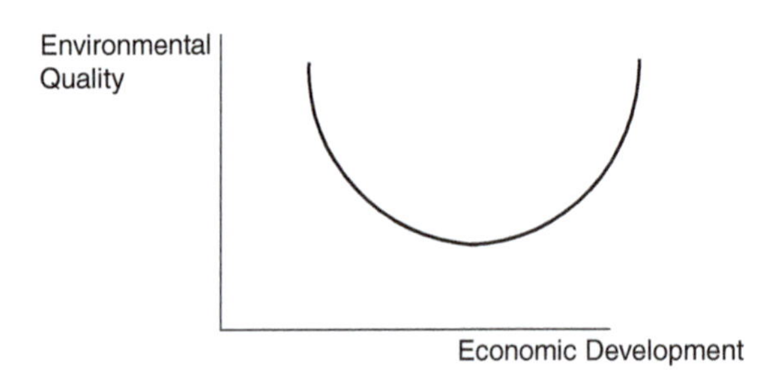

Figure 4.1 The environmental Kuznets curve.

The renowned inventor Thomas Edison once spoke to this distinction when he famously said that "genius is one percent inspiration and ninety-nine percent perspiration." The one percent referred to coming up with a new idea such as a lightbulb, and the ninety-nine percent referred to bringing the idea of a lightbulb to complete commercial fruition.

The distinction between theory generation and theory testing is not entirely clear-cut. It can be argued that no theory springs from nowhere, fully formed: rather, theories build on the work of others (recall Box 1.1, Newton's famous quote about standing on the shoulders of giants). However, it is a useful distinction here, because it speaks to an important distinction often drawn between quantitative and qualitative research. Namely, that quantitative research is largely about *testing* theory, while qualitative research is largely about *generating* theory.

To be more precise, we need to distinguish between theories and hypotheses, which are not exactly the same thing. The band *They Might Be Giants* gives a pretty good layperson's definition of a scientific theory: "A scientific theory isn't just a hunch or guess—it's more like a question that's been put through a lot of tests" ("Science is Real"). What they are saying is that theories are a way of modeling or thinking about the world that has been subject to repeated testing until we believe they have explanatory value.

The greenhouse effect is a theory because it is a way of thinking about global warming that is supported by scientific principles regarding the impact of greenhouse gas build-up on the trapping of solar radiation in the earth's atmosphere. It is supported by various forms of evidence, including data on long-wave radiation both entering and leaving the earth's atmosphere.

Hypotheses, on the other hand, are like "hunches or guesses" regarding what may be true, such as whether global warming is occurring. If enough hypotheses are confirmed regarding global warming that are consistent with the greenhouse effect, then it blossoms into a theory that scientists believe.

A key concern of quantitative research is the testing of hypotheses which are generated by theories, such as the greenhouse effect or the environmental Kuznets curve. Repeated testing of hypotheses provides evidence either for or against a theory. But if the results of enough hypothesis tests support a theory, then it becomes largely accepted as a way of understanding the world.

Using theory to generate hypotheses

Okay, so quantitative research is largely about testing hypotheses, in order to allow us to test theories regarding how the world works. But how exactly do we go about testing hypotheses?

It is important to keep in mind that falsifiable theories have specific implications that may be either consistent with evidence, or inconsistent. These implications form the basis for hypotheses that we test using data. Let us see how theories can generate specific testable hypotheses with a couple of examples.

Example 1: The greenhouse effect

The greenhouse effect implies that global temperatures should be rising in recent years, when we have experienced measurable, substantial increases in ambient greenhouse gases (GHG) in the atmosphere. If this is true, then we can imagine the implication illustrated in Figure 4.2. Here, increases in ambient GHG are associated with higher global temperatures.

To be clear, I have represented this relationship with a straight line, but there is nothing in the theory of the greenhouse effect that implies the relationship is linear. Indeed, there is much in the theory that suggests the relationship may not be linear. However, as a rough approximation to reality, a linearity assumption may not be bad and is often an initial assumption that is made in actual quantitative research.

If you are new to quantitative research, it may seem strange to you that we have reduced an extremely complicated natural phenomenon to this incredibly simplified graphical relationship. You may be asking yourself: Aren't we in danger of oversimplifying and missing a lot of important factors that might tell us whether or not the greenhouse effect is real?

It is important to keep in mind that simplifying complex issues is central to the quantitative approach. As we saw in Chapter 3, one big difference between the quantitative and qualitative approaches is that qualitative research often entails examining all of the messy details of the processes and mechanisms underlying a relationship.

Quantitative research, on the other hand, shoves all of those messy details into a black box, which is part of the simplification process. It is not that those messy details are unimportant in the real world. It is just that they are not relevant to the specific research question we have chosen and, therefore, we choose not to worry about them when we do the quantitative analysis.

For example, the mechanism of the greenhouse effect involves short-wavelength visible sunlight passing through the atmosphere, while the re-radiated infrared radiation gets trapped under the atmosphere. Because greenhouse gases such as carbon dioxide strongly absorb infrared radiation, the result of greenhouse gas build-up is the greenhouse effect. While all of this is obviously important, none of it needs to be taken into account when we set up a hypothesis test about

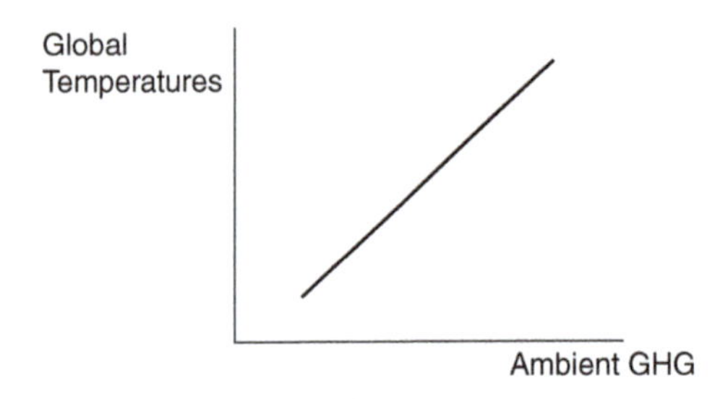

Figure 4.2 Hypothesis based on the greenhouse effect.

the relationship between ambient greenhouse gases in the atmosphere and global temperatures.

In addition to largely ignoring the underlying processes and mechanisms, another aspect of the simplification process is to ignore factors that should not affect the basic cause-and-effect relationship. In terms of the greenhouse effect, we might reasonably argue, for example, that the location of the emissions sources should not affect the basic relationship. So it might be safe to ignore whether or not a particular ton of GHG was produced in the United States, Canada, or India.

All of this simplification is part of the *reductionist* method of quantitative research that we have referred to a few times already. Again, by this we mean reducing matters to their bare essentials, in order to focus on answering a specific, narrowly defined research question.

It should be stressed here that the success of this reductionist approach depends heavily on being careful when we are deciding what we can and cannot assume. For example, in our simple model, we would not want to ignore the location of the emissions sources if it was in fact an important factor in determining the greenhouse effect. It is kind of like the example we encountered in Chapter 2 of trying to figure out Plato's height. In that example, we started with the premise that "All men are tall" and concluded that Plato was tall because Plato was obviously a man. When we start with a faulty premise, we may introduce serious errors into our analysis.

Returning to the relationship between ambient GHG levels and global temperatures depicted in Figure 4.2, you may recognize that this relationship can be expressed as follows:

$$\textit{Global Temperatures} = a + b\ \textit{Ambient}\ \text{GHG}$$

This is, of course, an application of the general algebraic representation of a straight line, where a is the vertical intercept and b is the slope.

This is a very useful equation, because it takes the theory of the greenhouse effect and translates it into a simple, very specific testable hypothesis: *Is* b *positive?* If so, then there is a positive association between global temperatures and ambient GHG levels, which is consistent with the greenhouse effect. If not, then there is either a negative association or no association, which would be taken as inconsistent with the greenhouse effect. The entire theory thus hinges on the value and sign (positive or negative) of one number.

To be clear, this equation is unquestionably an oversimplification of the relationship between ambient GHGs and global temperatures. However, perhaps surprisingly, it is not drastically different from some models used by some academics to conduct tests of the greenhouse effect. For example, a model used by Thayer Watkins of San Jose State University predicts changes in the earth's temperature using levels of carbon dioxide, sunspot activity (a measure of the intensity of solar radiation), and current levels of earth temperatures. His equation imposes some assumptions suggested by physics, but in general form, it is not terribly more complex than this one (see Watkins, http://www.sjsu.edu/faculty/watkins/ GWstat2.htm).

Example 2: The environmental Kuznets curve

As another example, let us consider the theory of an environmental Kuznets curve. Recalling Figure 4.1, this was the notion of a "U-shaped" relationship between environmental quality and economic development. Obviously, the assumption of a linear function will not suffice here. However, notice that a U-shaped relationship can be captured with a quadratic function:

$$\textit{Environmental Quality} = a + b\ \textit{Economic Development} + c\ (\textit{Economic Development})^2$$

Recalling what you know about quadratic functions, this function can capture a number of different relationships between environmental quality and economic development depending upon the values of b and c. Notice that the characteristic U-shape of the environmental Kuznets curve can be captured when $b < 0$ and $c > 0$.

So in this case, the hypothesis might be tested by asking: *Is* b *negative and is* c *positive?* Notice that both parts of the statement have to be true in order to support the existence of a U-shaped relationship between environmental quality and economic development. If either or both are not true, then this would be inconsistent with the theory of the environmental Kuznets curve.

Prelude to hypothesis testing

Once we have generated testable hypotheses, the question becomes: How do we actually go about testing them? Chapters 6 and 7 will provide a good deal of specific details in order to answer precisely this question. In the meantime, however, let me just say a few general words about quantitative methodology.

The general takeaway message so far is that we create simple models that provide clean, simple tests of hypotheses that we generate from theories. Once we have generated our hypotheses, it would seem to be straightforward to determine whether "b is positive" in the greenhouse effect example, or whether "b is negative and c is positive" in the environmental Kuznets curve example. However, when you actually examine real-world evidence, it is often not at all immediately clear what the answer is to questions like these.

For example, consider the evidence on global temperatures shown in Figure 4.3. Over this time span, it is well established that ambient GHG levels have been steadily rising. If the greenhouse effect were real, we might expect global temperatures to be steadily rising as well. However, the evidence in Figure 4.3 shows nothing of the kind: there have been all sorts of short-term fluctuations of various lengths and severity. And even though the overall trend appears to indicate gradually rising global temperatures, we may feel uncomfortable concluding this with complete confidence.

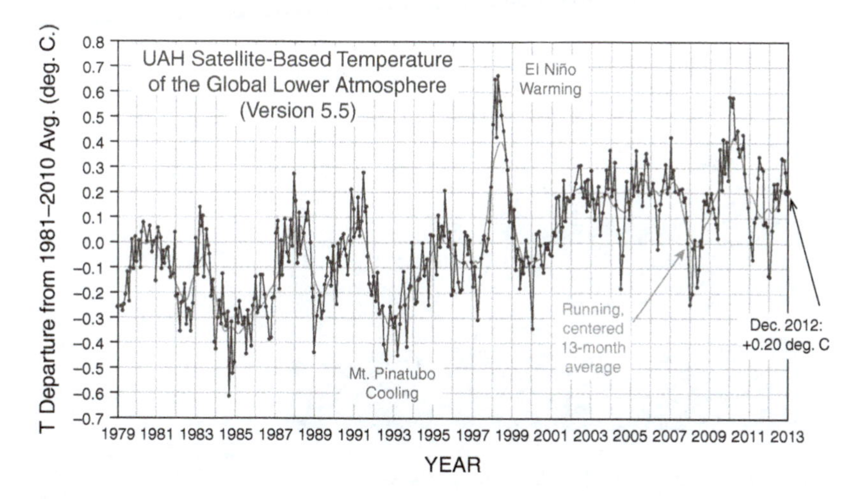

Figure 4.3 Global temperatures, 1970–2016.

Source: NASA.

More generally, it is commonly the case that real-world evidence appears ambiguous when we are using it to test hypotheses. The question is: With evidence like this, how can we determine whether or not the greenhouse effect is real?

A reasonably complete answer will have to wait until Chapter 7, but for now, let me just state the short answer: *We cannot know for sure one way or the other: we can only make probabilistic statements*. That is, based upon the evidence, there are some things we will be able to say with confidence and there will be others that we will not be able to say with confidence. The question is: How *strong* is the evidence? The stronger it is, the more confidence we will have in the results of our hypothesis tests.

Here is where the statistical method comes into the picture. This method involves taking numerical data and using them to construct statistics that allow us to determine whether variables such as ambient GHG and global temperatures are correlated with each other and if so, how strongly.

One key to understanding this approach is to recognize that there may be a great many factors that affect a relationship among variables. In Figure 4.3, for example, notice that there were other things going on during this period that affected global temperatures. One of these was the eruption of Mt. Pinatubo in June of 1991 (Figure 4.4).

The eruption of Mt. Pinatubo in the Philippines was the second-largest volcanic eruption in the world during the twentieth century. During the eruption, over a cubic mile of material was ejected into the atmosphere, which formed an ash cloud some twenty-two miles high and over one hundred miles across. Included in the ejected material was some twenty million tons of sulfur dioxide. The material acted as a shield, which reduced the amount of solar radiation that entered the earth's atmosphere. The result was a temporary drop in global

Figure 4.4 The eruption of Mount Pinatubo, 1991.
Source: US Geological Survey.

temperatures by roughly 0.5 degrees Celsius (USGS 1997). This appears in Figure 4.3 as a drop in temperature from 1991 through 1993, at which point the effect began to dissipate.

The eruption of Mt. Pinatubo is the most prominent example of another factor—besides the secular build-up of ambient GHGs—that has affected global temperatures over the past forty years. More generally, many factors may affect global temperatures. This includes the warm ocean currents that periodically cause the El Niño phenomenon, which Figure 4.3 shows dramatically increased global temperatures in 1998.

When you consider that there may be a lot of different factors acting in complex and sometimes unpredictable ways on global temperatures, the jagged, fluctuating pattern of global temperatures shown in Figure 4.3 becomes more understandable.

It needs to be emphasized that there is nothing about these other factors that necessarily negates the greenhouse effect theory. Just because Mt. Pinatubo erupted and caused a temporary reduction in temperatures does not mean that there is no connection between GHG build-up and global temperatures. These other factors just complicate the picture when we are trying to determine, based on the evidence, how much credence to place in the theory.

But they also do mean that we can never be certain. And sometimes there may be so many other factors that matter that it becomes extremely difficult, if not impossible, to perform convincing tests of hypotheses. As a matter of methodology, when we perform statistical analyses we will attempt to control for other factors such as Mt. Pinatubo and El Niño in order to try to isolate the effect of GHG build-up. But we may not be successful, for two reasons.

First, in a complex world, there may just be too many confounding factors. Second, even if we are able to identify all of these other factors, it may not be possible to collect the necessary data to control for them. This leads into the final set of things to consider when doing a quantitative analysis: the use of data.

Representing variables with data

In all of the discussion in this chapter so far, we have been ignoring the question: How do we capture with data the variables that theory tells us are important? For example, if we want to test for the existence of the greenhouse effect by establishing the relationship between global temperatures and ambient GHGs, we will need data on these two variables. Furthermore, these data will have to be numerical if we want to have any hope of applying the statistical method.

But exactly how do we measure ambient GHGs? Do we use levels of CO2? Levels of methane? Both of these are GHGs. Some weighted measure of the two? Science tells us that methane is a much more potent GHG than CO2. If that is true, what weights do we use? And what about other GHGs such as nitrous oxide and ozone? By simply stating the greenhouse effect theory as the relationship between temperatures and GHGs, we are masking a huge can of worms in terms of implementation. The question is: How do we define the variables that form the basis for a statistical analysis?

Similarly, if we wanted to test for the existence of the environmental Kuznets curve, how do we represent economic development? How do we represent environmental quality? Here, the same problems arise: What specific data can we use that will accurately capture these two theoretical variables?

The answer is, of course, going to vary from project to project, but here are a few things to think about. First, no matter what data you use, you are only going to be approximating the variables that are important in theory. But keep in mind that if you have a choice, some variables will be better than others.

If, for example, you want a variable that captures the level of economic development, you will find that there are a great many candidate variables for which you will be able to find data. Two variables that are commonly used are *gross domestic product* (GDP) and *per capita gross domestic product.*

GDP is the most common way in which economists measure the economic activity of a country. Per capita GDP simply takes the GDP of a country and divides it by the country's population. Both would seem to capture the overall level of economic development, but the latter captures the level of welfare of an average individual in a country. In principle, this would seem to provide a better measure of the determinants of public concern for environmental quality than total country economic activity. Therefore, many studies prefer it to GDP (Grossman and Krueger 1995).

Choosing an appropriate variable to capture a theoretical concept is an issue that comes up repeatedly in both quantitative and qualitative research. The issue is referred to as *construct validity* and it will be discussed at length in both Chapters 6 and 9.

Second, despite the fact that your data variables will only approximate the theoretical concepts, there may be ways to make them more precise and, thus, to better serve your research purposes. One would be to narrow your research question, which could cut down on the variable definitions that make sense for the purposes of your study.

A few years ago, I had a student who was very interested in the idea of an environmental Kuznets curve and wanted to see whether it existed in the data. But since the variable *environmental quality* was too broad, he decided to focus on endangered species, which was the aspect of environmental quality that he was most interested in. Using the number of endangered species as a narrower measure of environmental quality (and controlling for a lot of other factors), he used statistics to show that lo and behold, there did seem to be evidence for an environmental Kuznets curve for endangered species.

Finally, there are ways in which you will be able to capture variables that do not seem amenable to representation using numerical data. You might be asking yourself, for example, if I wanted to investigate the greenhouse effect using data on economic development and GHG levels, how in the world would I control for the effect of the eruption of Mt. Pinatubo in 1991? Fortunately, the answer is that you might very well be able to, using methods that we will describe in Chapters 6 and 7.

Conclusions

The quantitative approach to research is one of the two main ways in which research on the environment is done. It is very much in the positivist and post-positivist spirit discussed in Chapter Two, and it typically involves starting with a theory, generating hypotheses, quantifying relationships among variables, and testing hypotheses using objectively measured data. The next four chapters will develop various aspects of quantitative research in considerably more detail. By the end of that discussion, you should have a good sense of various issues associated with working with and analyzing data.

Exercises/discussion questions

(1) Consider the research question: *Is there an environmental Kuznets curve for deforestation?* Explain why this is a falsifiable statement.

(2) Which of the following are theories?

- The earth revolves around the sun.
- The sun revolves around the earth.
- The moon is made of green cheese.
- There is an environmental Kuznets curve for deforestation.
- The universe originated in a Big Bang nearly fourteen billion years ago.
- The universe was created in seven days.
- Certain features of the universe are best explained by an intelligent cause, not an undirected, random process such as natural selection.

What do you conclude about what constitutes a theory?

(3) Would you consider the following to be theories or hypotheses? Explain.

- The planets move in elliptical orbits around the sun.
- Globalization causes polluting activities to locate in poor countries with weak environmental protection policies.
- Stringent environmental regulation can increase social welfare.

(4) You may have heard of the *Gaia Hypothesis*: that organisms interact with their inorganic surroundings on Earth to form a self-regulating, complex system that helps to maintain and perpetuate the conditions for life on the planet (Wikipedia). Some people consider it sufficiently well-established to merit the name *Gaia Theory*. At what point does a hypothesis become a theory? What would it take for you to be sufficiently convinced to call something a theory?

References

Creswell, John W. *Research Design: Qualitative, Quantitative, and Mixed Methods Approaches*. Los Angeles: Sage, 2009.

Dasgupta, Susmita, Benoit Laplante, Hua Wang, and David Wheeler. "Confronting the Environmental Kuznets Curve," *Journal of Economic Perspectives* 16(Winter 2002): 147–68.

Grossman, Gene M., and Alan B. Krueger. "Economic Growth and the Environment," *Quarterly Journal of Economics* 110(May 1995): 353–77.

Newhall, Chris, James W. Hendley II, and Peter H. Stauffer. "USGS Fact Sheet 113-97: The Cataclysmic 1991 Eruption of Mount Pinatubo, Philippines," *United States Geological Survey*, February 28, 2005, http://pubs.usgs.gov/fs/1997/fs113-97/

Seale, Clive (ed.). *Researching Society and Culture* (3rd ed.). Los Angeles, Sage: 2012.

Shaftel, Holly (ed.). "Global Climate Change: Vital Signs of the Planet," *National Aeronautic and Space Administration*, 2016, https://climate.nasa.gov/vital-signs/global-temperature/

Spicer, Neil. "Combining Qualitative and Quantitative Methods," in Clive Seale (ed.), *Researching Society and Culture* (3rd ed.). Los Angeles: Sage, 2012: 479–93.

Watkins, Thayer. "A Statistical Test of the Global Warming Hypothesis," *San José State University*, n.d., http://www.sjsu.edu/faculty/watkins/GWstat2.htm

5 Quantitative data and sampling

Introduction

When you do environmental research, you will be marshaling evidence to support whatever conclusions you reach. In principle, there are a great many different kinds of evidence available to you. What evidence you choose depends on your research question, of course. However, your choice of evidence also depends crucially on whether you will be taking a quantitative or qualitative approach. Qualitative studies generally tend to use a wide range of types of evidence so that there will be a lot of ways to make your case.

When you decide to do a quantitative study, however, you will be working with a very specific kind of evidence: numerical data. In some ways, you may find this limiting because there will be many issues you will be unable to resolve, questions you will be unable to answer. However, in other ways, reliance on numerical data opens up a number of possibilities for analysis, because you will have a wide variety of quantitative methods at your disposal. For certain types of questions, analysis of numerical data can provide powerful insights into environmental issues and problems.

Data: The basics

The importance of data in environmental research has to do with two key objectives of the quantitative approach: quantifying relationships and testing hypotheses. Many environmental questions center on the relationship among variables. For example, we may be interested in factors that can reduce nitrogen loading in surface waterways in a cost-effective manner. Or we may be interested in the effect on local farming activity of restricting diversions of surface irrigation water in order to protect fish habitat. Or we may be interested in the impact of ongoing climate change on economic activities of various kinds, including agriculture and nature-based tourism. With a little thought, you can come up with many similar examples.

In each of these and many other examples, several important questions arise: Is there an effect? How certain are we that there is an effect? If there is an effect, how large is it? And how certain are we that it is as large as it seems to be?

To illustrate, let us consider the second example: the effect of restrictions on surface water diversions on local farming activity. In many rural localities in the western United States, surface waters in rivers and streams serve at least two functions: they can be left in place in order to provide habitat for wildlife, or they can be pumped from rivers and streams to irrigate farmlands.

If they are left in place to provide habitat, this reduces the amount of water farmers can use to irrigate. However, farmers may respond to reductions in water availability by growing other kinds of crops. Or it may provide them with incentive to conserve water, through more careful water applications or employing irrigation practices, such as drip irrigation, that use less water. So even though it seems like there should be a negative effect in principle, in practice questions arise regarding how large the effect is and, indeed, whether there really is a negative effect at all.

Here is where the primary functions of quantitative data analysis come into the picture. With numerical data, we can test for whether or not there actually is an effect, and if there is, we can make estimates of how large it is. Chapters 6 and 7 discuss some methodologies for quantifying relationships and testing hypotheses. For now, we just note that none of those methodologies would work without numerical data.

Two important concepts: Unit of analysis and unit of observation

To perform quantitative analysis of data, it is important that the data be in a very specific format, which will be reflected in the structure of your database. All databases need to have the same structure in order to perform valid data analysis. In order to understand this point, let us begin by defining two important concepts: *units of analysis* and *units of observation*.

Units of analysis

In quantitative research, the unit of analysis is defined as the object, individual, or entity that is the focus of your study, about which you collect information and draw conclusions. To put it simply, it is merely *who or what is being studied* ("Units of Analysis", 2016). It is very important to be as clear as you can be in defining your unit of analysis, as this will determine both what data you collect and what conclusions you can draw based on those data.

To illustrate this point, let us take a particular research question. Perhaps you have been following the climate change debate and have noticed people making the argument that mitigating climate change may require us to sacrifice some economic growth. Suppose this makes you curious about the question: What exactly IS the relationship between emissions of carbon dioxide (CO2) and levels of economic development?

This may seem like a straightforward question. But for the purposes of doing a quantitative study, answering it requires us to answer a number of other questions first. Are we talking about one country, like the United States, at one point in time? Are we talking about the experience of one country over time? Over what time period? Or are we talking about comparing different countries? Or are we not talking about countries at all, but other levels of jurisdiction, like states, provinces, counties, prefectures, or municipalities?

To answer these questions, you should think carefully about your unit of analysis. One possibility is to compare different countries at one point in time, in which case your unit of analysis is: *all countries, year* X. In this case, you would like to collect country-level data for a particular year. Then any conclusions you draw on the relationship between CO2 emissions and economic development would pertain to all countries but, strictly speaking, only for that year.

For example, Figure 5.1 displays part of a spreadsheet that contains information on per capita gross domestic product (PCGDP) and carbon dioxide (CO2) emissions for almost every country in the world in the year 2011. These data were taken from *World Development Indicators*, a database collected and maintained by the World Bank (see the appendix to this chapter).

Per capita GDP, or GDP per person, is a common measure of economic development. Taking one of these countries, the spreadsheet shows that in 2011, Afghanistan had a per capita GDP of $622.4 and carbon dioxide emissions of 0.4 metric tons per capita. So any conclusions we draw on the relationship between PCGDP and CO2 based on these data would be understood to apply to all countries in 2011.

The data in Figure 5.1 consist of observations on per capita GDP and emissions for a number of different countries at one single point in time, the year 2011. This type of data—a series of observations for different units at one point in time—is known as *cross-sectional* data. Data can often take a different form: a series of observations for one unit at different points in time. When these points in time are consecutive, the data are known as *time-series* data.

	A	B	C	D	E	F	G
1	Country Name	PCGDP	CO2				
2	Afghanistan	622.4	0.4				
3	Albania	4437.8	1.6				
4	Algeria	5447.4	3.3				
5	Andorra	41630.1	6				
6	Angola	4745	1.4				
7	Antigua and Barbuda	12817.8	5.8				
8	Argentina	13392.9	4.6				
9	Armenia	3417.2	1.7				
10	Aruba	25353.8	23.9				
11	Australia	62216.5	16.5				
12	Austria	51123.6	7.8				

Figure 5.1 GDP and CO2 emissions by country, 2011.

Source: Author.

Figure 5.2, for example, shows time-series data from *World Development Indicators* on per capita GDP and per capita CO2 emissions for one country—Qatar—for the years 2000 to 2011. Here, the unit of analysis is *Qatar, annual, 2000–2011*. The conclusions that you draw would be understood to be for Qatar, for this particular time period.

Notice that both units of analysis enable us to get at the relationship that we are interested in. This is useful, because data can come in a wide variety of forms with different units of analysis. So if data are not available in one form, they may be available in a different form, allowing you to still investigate your research question. The message here is: Don't get discouraged if your first choice of data is not available. To update an old saying that I am not terribly fond of, there is more than one way to skin an eggplant.

However, as you may have noticed, you will have to keep in mind your units of analysis when you draw your conclusions. Conclusions based upon the cross-country data in Figure 5.1 might not be valid for other years. Similarly, conclusions based upon the data for Qatar in Figure 5.2 may not be valid for other countries. It is always a good idea to keep in mind your unit of analysis when you are interpreting the results of a data analysis.

Units of observation

These spreadsheet fragments also show the other concept you need to know: the unit of observation. Many students find it a bit tricky to distinguish the unit of observation from the unit of analysis, since both are about, and defined in terms of, the object of study. But whereas units of analysis refer to the object of the analysis, units of observation refer to the level at which the data are collected.

To understand the difference, go back to Figure 5.1. As we said before, the unit of analysis here is countries, in the year 2011. Every one of the rows in the spreadsheet represents an observation on some country in 2011. The unit of observation

	A	B	C	D
1			PCGDP	CO2
2	2000		29914.8	58.5
3	2001		28666.6	49.5
4	2002		30748.5	44.9
5	2003		35644.4	54.1
6	2004		44051.7	60.6
7	2005		54228.8	62
8	2006		62920.6	57.4
9	2007		69167	55.3
10	2008		74189.3	48.6
11	2009		59935.5	44.8
12	2010		76413.2	42.6
13	2011		99431.5	44

Figure 5.2 GDP and CO2 emissions for Qatar, 2000–2011.

Source: Author.

is the specific level at which the data are defined. So the entries in columns B and C are understood to be values of PCGDP and CO2 for countries in 2011, which is the unit of observation. So units of observation are less about the object of study and more about the definition of the data you are using to capture what is going on with the object of study.

If units of analysis and units of observation seem really similar, that is because they are. In fact, sometimes they are identical, as they are in Figure 5.1. However, they need not be. One important way they can differ is that your unit of analysis may be at a different level of aggregation from your unit of observation.

For example, in your research, you may actually be interested in understanding how the relationship between economic development and CO2 emissions differs between developing and developed countries, or across different continents, or between different free trade zones. In all these examples, the comparison you are interested in is between different groups of countries: e.g., developing vs. developed. However, the unit of observation for your analysis may still be country-level, as it is in Figure 5.1.

The structure of a quantitative database

Another feature of the spreadsheet data in Figure 5.1 is the specific format of the data: every column is a different variable, and every row is a different observation on the variables. That is, every country in the spreadsheet has the same configuration of information on the two variables: per capita GDP in column B and CO2 emissions in column C. This means that column B is reserved for all of the data on per capita GDP and column C is reserved for all of the data on CO2 emissions. Generally speaking, this illustrates the format that all quantitative databases need to be in for analysis. They need to be arranged in a so-called *matrix* format: rows and columns of observations on variables.

To understand exactly why we require this particular format, let us consider more carefully the question of the relationship between the level of a country's economic development and its level of CO2 emissions. In Figure 5.1, each row is two pieces of information—country-level PCGDP and CO2—for one country. If we want to characterize the relationship between PCGDP and CO2 for all countries, we need to know how those variables move in relation to each other. If it happens to be the case that countries with low PCGDP also tend to have low emissions and that countries with high PCGDP tend to have high emissions, then we can conclude that there is a positive relationship. But to do this, we need to group all of the information on the different variables by country.

To see this graphically, let us create a scatterplot, as in Figure 5.3. In this scatterplot, which will be discussed more in Chapter 6, each one of these dots represents a different country, where that country's PCGDP is being measured on the horizontal axis and that country's CO2 emissions are being measured on

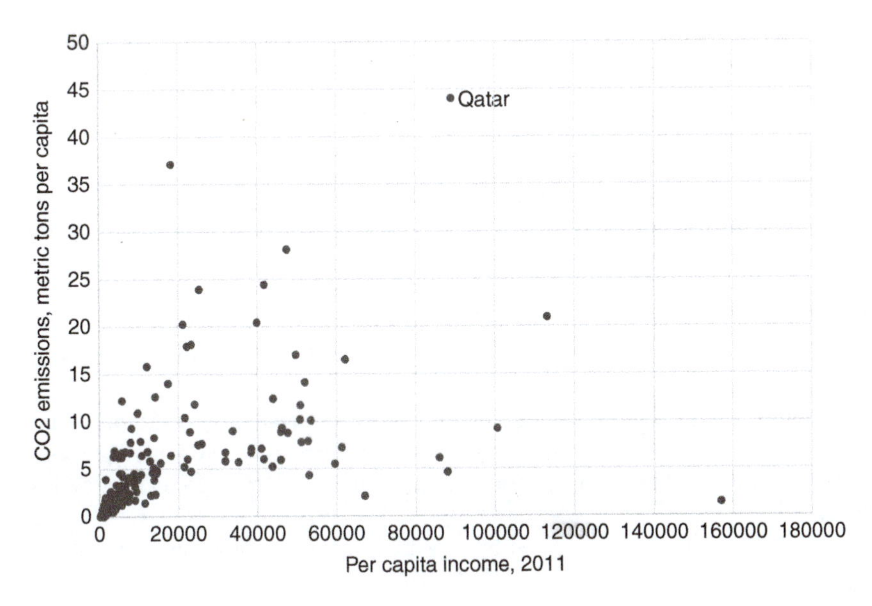

Figure 5.3 CO2 emissions vs. per capita income, 2011.

Source: Author.

the vertical axis. For example, the Middle Eastern country Qatar is the highest dot, which shows it has a per capita income of a little over $89,000 and by far the most annual CO2 emissions of any country—roughly forty-four metric tons per capita.

Associating every variable with each other through the same observation permits us to observe how different variables move together. In this scatterplot, you have a pattern of mostly high-GDP, high-emissions countries like Qatar, Liechtenstein, and the United States and low-GDP, low-emissions countries like many African countries. This suggests a positive relationship between GDP and emissions.

Measurement error

Whenever you are working with data, it is useful to keep in mind its potential limitations, in terms of how much useful information it is providing. One common issue with many forms of data has to do with the way data are measured. For a variety of reasons, data measurement may be inaccurate, which has important implications for what we can infer from it about the real world.

To understand this issue, just think about the numbers in the spreadsheet in Figure 5.1 and ask yourself the question: How confident am I in those numbers?

Consider, for example, that entry in column C that indicates that Afghanistan had 0.4 metric tons of CO2 emissions per capita in 2011. Coming up with that number required the World Bank to perform the following calculation. It had to take total CO2 emissions for the entire country during the entire year and divide that number by total population:

Per capita CO2 emissions = *CO2 emissions/population*

Constructing that number required the World Bank to make assumptions about the total CO2 emissions and total population of Afghanistan in 2011, since there is no way they could know the true, in-the-world values of those two pieces of information for certain. Think about how hard it would be to measure every single actual emission of CO2 everywhere in the country for an entire year! The exact amount of CO2 generated by every industrial plant burning fossil fuel? Every automobile tailpipe?

Similarly, how easy would it be to know the exact population of Afghanistan, with home births, unrecorded deaths, imperfect hospital records, immigration, porous borders, and areas of the country where it is dangerous for census takers to travel?

No, this number was generated by making a whole lot of assumptions about things it would be literally impossible for the World Bank to know for sure. In other words, they are guesses: maybe reasonable guesses, but guesses nonetheless. When the numbers that appear in your database are off for these reasons, we say that they are subject to *measurement error*.

For many environmental variables, measurement error is an unfortunate fact of life. When you encounter data from published sources on the number of endangered species in a country, you should keep in mind that there is no way those numbers could reflect the true number of species that are in danger of becoming extinct. When you see data on the volume of groundwater supplies, again, those numbers will not reflect the actual, underground reality. The same goes for air- and water-pollution measurements, energy supplies, toxic chemical emissions, you name it.

An important distinction: Random vs. systematic measurement error

The fact that data on so many environmental (and other!) variables are subject to measurement error does not, however, mean that it is useless to perform analysis of environmental data. Even imperfectly measured, it may still be able to tell us a lot. One important question is whether the measurement errors are *random* or *systematic*.

When measurement error is random, this means that it does not alter the average values of the variables you are trying to measure. Some of the sources of measurement error might cause the estimate to be high, others might cause it to be low. But when the measurement error is random, these upward- and downward-biasing errors balance out. Random measurement error does tend to increase the uncertainty in your measures of a variable, but it does not cause them to be systematically too high or too low.

Systematic measurement error, on the other hand, does result in measures of variables that are systematically either too high or too low. For example, if the World Bank did in practice rely on census takers and included in its population estimates only people they managed to actually contact, its population estimates would be too low since it is a real, perhaps insuperable challenge to contact literally everyone. Furthermore, it would tend to particularly undercount the number of residents in those areas of the country where it is dangerous to travel.

In order to deal with measurement error, it is probably useful to consider the possibility that both kinds may be present in your data. In some cases, it may be useful to investigate how the data were generated so you can think about whether there are any obvious sources of systematic error, as in the population example.

For example, for some studies, you may be generating your own data for a quantitative analysis by collecting survey information. In this case, you may encounter the measurement error issue in a different guise.

When you conduct a survey, you are posing questions and your data consist of the responses. What you are trying to ascertain are true attitudes or beliefs on specific issues. Your success in obtaining accurate responses will depend upon, among other things, the formatting of the survey and the wording of the questions.

Measurement error may occur if questions are poorly or confusingly worded, or if they are worded in such a way as to influence the responses. If you are generating your own quantitative data, for example through surveys, there are also steps you can take to try to minimize both kinds of error. These are covered more completely in Chapter 16.

Data collection: Sampling issues

So, we do quantitative data analysis in order to draw conclusions regarding what is going on in the world. When our scatterplot of CO2 emissions vs. per capita GDP exhibits a positively sloped pattern, we use that to conclude something like: "countries that are more economically developed also tend to produce more CO2 emissions." That is, we are making an *inference* about the relationship between economic development and emissions.

A key issue in data analysis is the extent to which an inference is actually warranted, something we can count on as being true or at least supported convincingly by evidence. It turns out that valid inferences depend crucially on our ability to take a *random sample*.

The importance of random sampling

Let us begin by making sure we know what is meant by a random sample. A random sample is one that is chosen in such a way that every individual in a population has an equal probability of being selected for inclusion in a sample (see Figure 5.4). For this reason, random sampling is sometimes referred to as *probability sampling*.

Figure 5.4 Random sample generator.
Source: Shutterstock.

To make this concept as intuitive as possible, imagine a barrel filled with ping-pong balls. This barrel has a crank that allows an operator to rotate the barrel, which randomizes the ping-pong balls inside. After rotating the barrel for a while, you close your eyes and select a ball from the barrel at random. By following this procedure, every ball in the barrel should have an equal probability of being chosen. This is the intuition behind random sampling.

To see how this principle applies in the real world, suppose that you are interested in the relationship between CO2 emissions and the level of economic development. And also suppose you have settled on your unit of analysis, which is *countries, year 2011*. There is a population of countries out there; namely, every single country in the world. Your inferences on this relationship apply to this entire population. A random sample from this population would be one where every country has an equal probability of being sampled, like drawing ping-pong balls blindly from a barrel.

So how does random sampling contribute to producing valid inferences? By ensuring that any pattern in the population is reproduced in the sample. Though it may sound surprising that a random sampling process can do this, here is where randomness actually works in our favor.

To see the argument, consider Figure 5.5, which is a stylized version of Figure 5.3. Here are represented the CO2 emissions and PCGDP of every single country in the world. This means that the pattern we see here reflects the "true" relationship between emissions and economic development.

We want our inference to be as accurate as possible in capturing this reality. The problem is that, generally speaking, it is extremely hard, if not impossible, to collect evidence on every single country in the world. Even in the *World Development Indicators* database, there are missing data, so that Figure 5.3 depicts not all countries, but a subset of countries. This is the general issue of sampling.

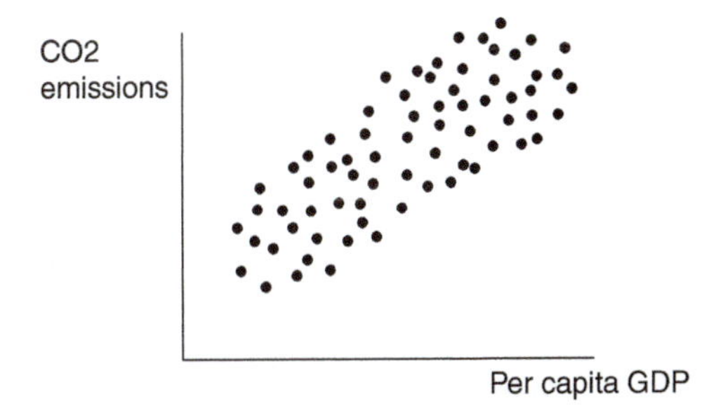

Figure 5.5 A population of countries.

Source: Author.

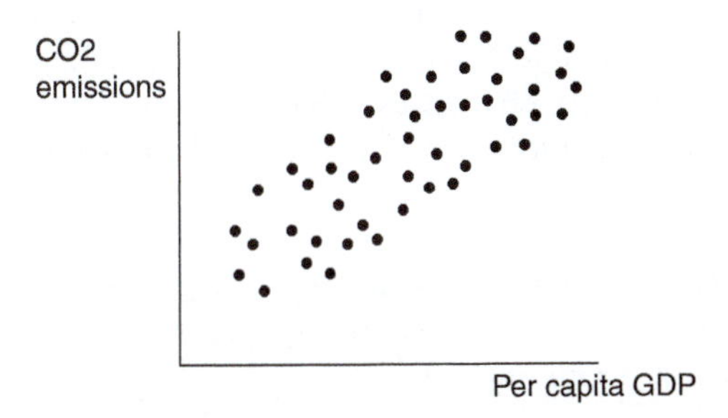

Figure 5.6 A random sample of countries.

Source: Author.

Because data on an entire population are generally not available, we settle for taking a sample, keeping our fingers crossed that the pattern in our sample accurately reflects the pattern in the population.

A random sample should accomplish exactly this. In Figure 5.6, for example, we see a random sample of countries taken from the population of countries in Figure 5.5. Notice that in outline form, the pattern in the sample looks the same as the pattern in the population. The only difference is that the pattern in the sample is sparser, with fewer observations, which makes sense since you are only sampling a subset of all of the countries. But the overall positive relationship looks the same. So one would be justified in using the pattern in this sample to make inferences about the pattern in the larger population. This is the fundamental argument for relying on random samples whenever possible.

The main problem with random sampling is that it is generally extremely difficult to pull off. As we have seen, to qualify as random sampling, every member of the population has to have an equal probability of being included in the sample. From a practical standpoint, this is often simply not possible.

Consider, for example, my sample of countries taken from the *World Development Indicators* database. As I mentioned earlier, data from some countries have been excluded from my sample. We do not know for sure why certain countries are lacking data, but we can perhaps guess.

To help us guess, here is the complete list of the countries missing CO2 emissions data in the *World Development Indicators* database in 2011: American Samoa, Channel Islands, Curacao, Guam, Isle of Man, Kosovo, Monaco, Northern Mariana Islands, Puerto Rico, San Marino, Saint Martin, Somalia, South Sudan, Tuvalu, and the Virgin Islands.

Do you have any guesses as to why the World Bank would be missing data for these particular countries? Mine is that these countries tend to be small and remote, and some are war-torn (Somalia, South Sudan). These factors would present obstacles to coming up with reasonable estimates of emissions. Which is to say that there are certain physical and political realities that make it less likely that certain types of countries will appear in this database. This fact makes it unlikely that this is a genuinely random sample.

More generally, there are typically many challenges to sampling in a completely random way from virtually any population you will encounter. Fortunately, under some conditions, there are ways to sample non-randomly but still enjoy the benefits of random sampling. These include *systematic random sampling, stratified random sampling*, and *cluster sampling*. These methods each involve an element of randomness in sampling, even though they do not, strictly speaking, fit the metaphor of blindly drawing balls from a rotating barrel.

Systematic random sampling

Under systematic random sampling, the researcher numerically orders a target population and then samples from this population at some regular numeric interval. The size of the interval depends upon the desired sample size (Lohr 1999, p. 159).

It is probably easiest to see this with an example. Suppose that you are interested in conducting a survey of students at your college on their attitudes toward global warming. However, you do not want to incur the time and expense of surveying every single student. You could take a systematic random sample by obtaining a complete list of student names, ordering them in some randomized way, and then assigning each student a number. Then, depending upon the desired sample size, you start at some arbitrary point in the list and sample every Xth student. So, if there are 10,000 students at the college and you want a sample of 100 students, you would choose an interval of 100, sampling every 100th student on the list in order.

In the case of the countries in our database, *World Development Indicators* lists 214 countries. If you wanted a systematic random sample of, say, fifty countries, you would first set up a numerical order of these 214 countries where each country is assigned a number. In this case, it would probably be safe to use an alphabetical listing of the countries. You would then set an interval length of four and have a random number generator choose a starting number for you. If the random number generator chose, for example, the number 48, then you would sample the countries numbered: 48, 52, 56, 60, 64, 68, 72, etc.

In both of these examples, the sampling rule does not seem random: after all, you seem to be sampling in an intentional, systematic way. Furthermore, it does not seem as if the probability of choosing any member of the population is equal. In the second example, once the random number generator gives you the starting number 48, the probability that country number 51 will appear in your sample is zero. However, the sampling rule is random in the sense that the choice of starting number is chosen in a random way. Given a randomly chosen starting number, every country does in fact have an equal probability of being included in the sample.

The simplicity of the method of systematic random sampling contributes to its popularity as a practical way to implement random sampling. It should be noted that carrying it out requires having a list of the members of the entire population. This may be possible for certain populations, such as every country in the world, every student enrolled in your college, or every employee of a company. However, it may not be possible for many others, such as all generators of CO2 emissions or chemical toxic releases, or all agricultural emitters of nutrient loading. For these latter populations, you will need to rely on other ways to obtain randomness.

It is also important that your sampling decision rule not be inadvertently correlated with whatever characteristic you are trying to collect data for. In the above CO2 emissions example, if it turned out to be the case that every fourth country in your list just happened to be a low-income developing country, your sample would not be a fair representation of all countries, as it would be excluding higher-income developed countries. In this particular case, this doesn't seem likely and probably isn't. However, you should always keep the possibility in mind when doing your own study.

Stratified random sampling

Another type of (mostly) random sampling is something called *stratified random sampling*. This type of random sampling is used when your population contains sub-populations that you are interested in. Stratified random sampling is used to make sure you can make valid inferences about the sub-populations (Lohr 1999, p. 95).

Consider again the earlier example of sampling students in your college, but now suppose you are interested in comparing the attitudes of students in the different classes—first-years through seniors. When you take a random sample of 100 students, there is the danger that random sampling will not give you a sample with the actual proportions of students in the different classes. Thus, in a way that you think may matter, your sample will not be representative of the population you are interested in.

For example, suppose there are 10,000 students in your college divided up equally among the four classes, 2,500 in each. For a sample of 100 students that is representative of this class breakdown, you would ideally like to have twenty-five from each class. However, there is no guarantee that a completely random sample will yield those numbers.

For example, I used a random number generator to generate three samples of 100 students, the results of which are shown in Figure 5.7. As you can see, the results varied pretty dramatically from sample to sample, which is exactly what you would expect from a random sampling process.

	1	2	3
First-years	26	21	23
Sophomores	29	23	27
Juniors	16	29	31
Seniors	29	27	19

Figure 5.7 Results of three random samples of 100 students, class breakdown.

Source: Author.

However, the more important point here is that sometimes the numbers varied quite a bit from an even 25–25–25–25 split across the classes. In the first sample, we would have ended up with only sixteen juniors! So by following a purely random sampling process, we would have had a sample that significantly underrepresents juniors.

Stratified random sampling addresses this issue of disproportionate representation by first dividing up the population into the relevant sub-populations, or *strata*, and then sampling randomly from each one. In this example, you would have taken each of the classes and sampled randomly within each class. The metaphor here is four rotating barrels instead of just one, each one filled with different colored ping-pong balls. So you are still taking advantage of random sampling, but now you can make sure you get twenty-five students from each class.

Stratified random sampling can be used whenever you have well-defined strata that you want to make sure are included and adequately represented in your sample. In the above survey, you might have been interested in differences in climate attitudes based on gender, or ethnic group, or religious affiliation. If so, you could have created these strata and then taken a random sample from each one.

You should also keep in mind that you can combine different population characteristics when you are creating your strata. For example, in addition to distinguishing among students in different class years, you could have also distinguished by, say, gender. So instead of creating merely four strata for the four class years, you could have created eight strata: first-year women, first-year men, sophomore women, etc. Here, you would go ahead and take eight random samples, one from each stratum.

There are a couple of things to keep in mind if you are considering doing a stratified random sample. First, stratified random sampling is particularly useful if one or more of the strata you are interested in is relatively small. For example, if you are interested in whether climate attitudes differ based on ethnic group, some of your strata (perhaps African-Americans) might be a small percentage of the overall student population. When this is the case, there is a real danger that straight random sampling will yield few if any observations from those sparsely populated strata. Stratified random sampling at least ensures that you can get a minimum number of responses from these strata.

Second, to do stratified random sampling, it is important to be able to classify each of your observations as belonging to one, and only one, stratum. This means that you need to have clearly defined strata. For many colleges, the strata "Sophomores" and "Senior women" are pretty clearly defined, despite issues of part-time students, and varying degrees of progress toward graduation because of dropped classes, leaves of absence, and for-partial-credit independent studies and science labs. However, "Developed countries" and "Developing countries" are probably too ambiguous because it may not be clear where to set the dividing line. Before deciding to do stratified random sampling, you should convince yourself that you will be able to define sensible strata from which to sample.

Cluster sampling

Cluster sampling is yet another method of random sampling. The idea here is to rely on data that are clustered together in such a way as to make collection more convenient. Though it is not, strictly speaking, random sampling in the rotating barrel sense of the term, it relies on elements of randomness. And under the right conditions, it can approximate a random sample while making data collection a lot easier (Lohr 1999, p. 131).

In the interests of clarity, let us illustrate cluster sampling using the climate change survey example. You are interested in collecting data on climate change attitudes on your campus, but you are a bit daunted by the prospect of taking a probability sample from the entire roster of 10,000 enrolled students. Under a cluster sampling strategy, you would randomly choose a set of potential respondents who happen to be clustered together in a convenient way, and sample all of them.

For example, suppose that there are twenty residence halls on your campus. A cluster sampling strategy might randomly select one or a handful of these residence halls and survey everyone who lives in them. The number of halls you choose will depend upon how large you want your sample to be. Similarly to systematic sampling, the randomness in cluster sampling comes from the random way in which the halls themselves are chosen. To ensure randomness, you could assign a number to each residence hall and use a random number generator to pick your residence halls for you.

The big advantage of cluster sampling is convenience. Rather than having to sample from all parts of campus, you can concentrate your efforts in a particular, perhaps narrowly confined area. This may help you dramatically reduce the amount of time and effort you have to expend to collect your survey data.

A potential serious downside of cluster sampling is the danger that your sample of residence halls chosen in this way may not be representative of students in general. For example, if you decide to pick two residence halls at random, they may just turn out to be the two residence halls that have traditionally housed first-year students. Cluster sampling works best if the clusters themselves are relatively homogeneous. For example, if your interest was in the climate change attitudes of residents of a suburban neighborhood, a cluster sampling strategy that might work would be to select blocks of particular streets at random.

A *word on non-random sampling*

There are times in environmental research when one may want to collect and use data that cannot be described as randomly sampled. As we have seen, a key virtue of random sampling is that it permits us to make inferences about a larger unobserved population, because a random sample preserves the pattern to be found in that population. There is no guarantee that a non-random sample will do the same thing. If not, then what would be the point of collecting a non-random sample?

The answer has to do with the objectives of your research and in particular, what you are using the data for. It turns out that quantitative researchers often have different objectives and different uses of data than qualitative researchers. In quantitative research, the primary objective is generally inference about a variable or relationship among variables in an unobserved population. For valid inferences, random sampling is crucial. This is why quantitative researchers have devised all of these methods—random sampling, systematic random sampling, stratified random sampling, and cluster sampling. All of these are designed to allow us to reproduce and understand what is going on in a population.

Qualitative research, on the other hand, is not so much about making inferences about variables and relationships among variables. As we have seen, it often has more to do with understanding underlying processes and mechanisms, or about the attitudes, beliefs, and meaning ascribed by people to environmental issues.

The sorts of things that qualitative researchers do—case studies, observer-participant research, analysis of literary discourse, social construction of environmental issues—often rely not so much on data but on broader forms of evidence. But when they do use data, it is often to understand things—people, attitudes, interpersonal communication—in and of themselves, as opposed to generalizing to larger populations. This makes it less important that data be sampled randomly.

As we shall see in the later section on qualitative analysis, qualitative researchers have also devised a battery of sampling techniques—methods like convenience sampling, snowball sampling—that in no way, shape, or form could be considered random sampling methods. Given the often different nature of their enterprise, these non-random sampling methods serve their purposes just fine. However, in those instances where they do want to make inferences about a larger population, the use of non-random sampling means that any such inferences must be made with caution.

Some practical issues of collecting and managing data

When doing quantitative research, you will encounter a whole slew of issues relating to data collection and management. You will be glad to hear that with the proliferation of the internet, data collection for doing environmental research is much easier nowadays than it was even ten or fifteen years ago. There are many excellent on-line sources of environmental data, a few of which are listed in the appendix to this chapter.

When working with environmental data, you will find it useful to use software to organize, manage, and analyze your data. Here you will find a wealth of resources in the form of spreadsheets, databases, and statistical software packages. As you will be able to see by perusing the on-line data sources in the appendix, much data is available in spreadsheet format, commonly Excel. So much of this discussion will focus on Excel.

This is not designed to be a user's guide to Excel, but rather general suggestions you may find useful when working with environmental data in Excel. If you do not yet have a working familiarity with Excel, I strongly encourage you to develop at least some basic Excel skills. You can do this through formal course instruction and, in addition, you will find a great many useful resources for learning Excel skills on the internet.

General considerations

To begin with, consider Figure 5.8, which reproduces Figure 5.1. This is an Excel spreadsheet, which contains data on two variables for 191 countries. In general, Excel permits you to work with very large data sets, as Excel spreadsheets can contain millions of rows and thousands of columns. This is more than enough for the data storage needs of most research projects, though extremely large data sets

	A	B	C	D	E	F	G
1	Country Name	PCGDP	CO2				
2	Afghanistan	622.4	0.4				
3	Albania	4437.8	1.6				
4	Algeria	5447.4	3.3				
5	Andorra	41630.1	6				
6	Angola	4745	1.4				
7	Antigua and Barbuda	12817.8	5.8				
8	Argentina	13392.9	4.6				
9	Armenia	3417.2	1.7				
10	Aruba	25353.8	23.9				
11	Australia	62216.5	16.5				
12	Austria	51123.6	7.8				

Figure 5.8 GDP and CO2 emissions by country, 2011.

Source: Author.

present challenges in other ways, especially when you are cleaning and debugging a data set prior to analysis.

Tip: rows for observations and columns for variables

The important point here is that these data are in the required database format mentioned earlier: rows of observations on columns of variables. Every row has a *row header*—the name of the country—and every column has a *column header*—the name of the variable. These are useful for organizational purposes: to help keep the data straight so you can interpret each number in the spreadsheet. They will also be helpful for a less obvious reason: to serve as variable labels for charts and graphs and, later on, for when you import your data into statistical packages such as R, STATA, SAS, or SPSS for analysis.

Data collection

When doing quantitative research, your data will usually come from one of two sources. Either it will have been generated by someone else—say, a government agency—or you will have generated it yourself—say, through administering a survey or conducting an interview.

If you generated the data yourself, you will most likely be manually recording the data in a spreadsheet. Here, it probably goes without saying that you should take extreme care to enter the numbers accurately. However, even if you do, be prepared to have to "debug" the data for inaccuracies. Even if you entered the data completely accurately, some of it may be unusable because survey respondents misinterpreted your questions, or simply incorrectly entered their responses. This is par for the course with many surveys.

If your data were generated by someone else, nowadays you will likely be retrieving it from the internet, probably from a particular web page on a web site. Sometimes you will be lucky and there will be a clickable link that allows you to download a spreadsheet directly. Or the data will at least be in spreadsheet format, which allows you to copy and paste the relevant variables to your own spreadsheet. This is often the case with government agencies whose mandate is the collection and dissemination of information. In this case, you can retrieve the data you need directly, with relatively little bother.

Tip: Be prepared for challenges in extracting on-line data

In many cases, however, you will not be so lucky, and the data will appear in other machine-readable formats, such as PDF or XTML. Here, recovering the data is harder but not impossible. The brute force way would be to simply manually record the values, reading them directly off your computer screen. However, this is probably a reasonable way to proceed only if you require a small amount of data. For larger data sets, you will probably have to resort to a technique called *data scraping*.

Data scraping refers to the process of extracting machine-readable content from websites. This is done either by using scraping tool software or writing a piece of computer code, which take the data and transform it into a format suitable for analysis. Either way, the process is a bit involved so that you may want to rely on someone else to scrape the data for you. At my college, for example, the folks at Information Technology Services provide assistance for data scraping on student research projects. They are also aware of any potential legal issues associated with data scraping, for which there are currently a number of unanswered questions.

Data management

Once you have the data in hand and securely in your spreadsheet, there are a number of issues you will confront regarding ways to efficiently and safely manage your data in preparation for performing your analysis. The basic issue is to make sure you have an accurate and complete set of variables.

Tip: debug your data, systematically if you can

I mentioned earlier that your data set may need to be "debugged." By this, I meant that you need to do what you can to ensure that the numbers are real: that they really do reflect the true values of your variables. If, for example, your PCGDP column contained a value of 1,000,000,000 in a particular cell, you could be pretty well assured that that number was wrong.

This whole issue of debugging came up in the *North Shore Climate Change* study. Recall that as part of the study, we surveyed tourists on the north shore of Lake Superior in northern Minnesota regarding the amounts they spent on various categories of items such as restaurants, lodging, and gasoline. For this, they were handed iPads and asked to type in their answers.

When we looked at the results later, the numbers seemed reasonable for the most part. However, a few seemed implausibly high or low. One respondent, for example, typed in that he had spent $100,000 for three nights lodging in a hotel. This response was dropped from our sample.

In some cases, it may be difficult to know whether a response is "real" or not. Dropping the $100,000 response was an easy call, but there were others where it was less clear. For these cases, we needed a decision rule for inclusion that was consistently applied to all observations. So, for example, we adopted the rule that a response of more than $500 per person per night on lodging was implausibly high and was to be omitted. Our rules were chosen based on common sense, but also informed by what we could find out about the range of actual going rates for hotel rooms in the area.

Tip: Annotate your variables

In the small data set shown in Figure 5.8, it is easy to keep the variables straight: what the labels mean and how the variables are defined. However, this can become a challenge in a larger data set with many variables. One nice feature of Excel is that you can add explanatory text using the *Comment* feature. So suppose you wanted to make sure you remember what "PCGDP" means. To annotate a variable, first click on the variable name PCGDP in cell B1. If you then click on *Review* and then click on *Add comment*, you can then type in explanatory text. Then, whenever you click on that cell in the future, your explanatory text will appear, reminding you of what the variable is and how it is defined.

Tip: Keep a backup file of your original data

If your study progresses like many studies do, you will find yourself modifying your data set in various ways, including: adding data, omitting observations, manipulating variables, and using formulas to create new ones. It is a good idea to keep a "clean" copy of your original data set, the one that you had originally downloaded or scraped, or that contained all of the raw responses to your survey. This is because mistakes can be made along the way: observations accidentally deleted, incorrect formulas applied.

So when you are beginning to work with your data, my advice is to create a working copy of the original data set and do all of your data manipulation only on the working copy. Keeping the original data set provides you with insurance, so that it is always possible to reconstruct what you did. And feel free to make a series of working copies as your work progresses so that if you do make mistakes along the way, you will not have to entirely reinvent the wheel.

Box 5.1 Checklist: Tips for data collection/management

- ✔ Be prepared for challenges in extracting on-line data.
- ✔ Debug your data, systematically if you can.
- ✔ Annotate your variables.
- ✔ Keep a backup file of your original data.

Conclusions

Working with quantitative data requires that you keep a number of things in mind. The data need to be collected carefully, with as much attention as possible paid to trying to obtain a random sample. You should also keep in mind the limitations of the data, in terms of how complete they are, and how carefully measured. And if you believe there may be measurement error, is it the relatively innocuous random kind or the more problematic systematic kind?

Once you have satisfied yourself on all these scores, it is crucial that the data be structured correctly in preparation for analysis: rows of observations on columns of variables. And then finally, there are a number of broad challenges relating to how you manage your data. All of these are part of being a careful quantitative researcher.

Being attentive to them will go a long way toward being able to make valid inferences, in which case your research experience is likely to be a successful and rewarding one.

Exercises/discussion questions

(1) In which of the following cases would you believe that there is likely to be (problematic) systematic, as opposed to (harmless) random, measurement error?

- Estimating relative numbers of endangered species across counties in your state by measuring the relative size of areas of their preferred habitat (as defined by objective scientific studies).
- Estimating the relative size of fish populations in two similar large lakes by measuring the size of total fish catches from the two lakes at the end of a randomly chosen day.

(2) Consider the three types of random sampling: systematic, stratified, and cluster. Which, if any, do you think would be appropriate to use in each of the situations listed below? If you think more than one would be suitable, explain why. If you think there is more than one, which one would you use?

- A survey of students at your college regarding support for removing trays from the food service in order to reduce food waste.
- A survey of residents in your neighborhood regarding support for zoning to curb local development.
- A survey of the residents of New York City regarding support for a citywide ban on the sale of large soft drinks at restaurants and movie theaters (for details, see Grynbaum 2012).
- A survey of US citizens regarding support for a carbon tax.

(3) Suppose your college is considering switching to a new food service that emphasizes more natural, organic, and locally grown produce than the existing food service. However, switching to the new food service would lead to an increase in student fees of $50 per semester. You are interested in assessing overall support among students at your college for switching to the new food service. You are considering employing cluster sampling by surveying everyone on your residence hall floor. How likely is it that this would yield a sample that would accurately reflect overall support among the general student body?

(4) In the section on "debugging" data, there was a description of a decision rule adopted in the *North Shore Climate Change* study to omit all responses of more than $500 spent per person per night on lodging as being implausibly high. Suppose you surveyed residents in your neighborhood regarding support for local zoning restrictions, and one question asked respondents to state their annual household income levels. What decision rule would you use to weed out implausible responses?

Additional resources

Bluman, Allan G. *Elementary Statistics: A Step by Step Approach* (2nd ed.). Dubuque: Brown, 1995.

Chapter 15 has a clear, useful discussion of principles of sampling.

Johnson, Robert. *Elementary Statistics* (4th ed.). Boston: Duxbury, 1984.

Good, clear discussion of basic statistical concepts and techniques. Chapter 1 is a good, brief introduction to data and sampling.

Lohr, Sharon L. *Sampling: Design and Analysis*. Pacific Grove: Duxbury, 1999.

Comprehensive, intermediate-level discussion of various methods of sampling.

Salkind, Neil J. *Statistics for People Who (Think They) Hate Statistics*. Thousand Oaks: Sage, 2000.

A fun and highly accessible treatment of various statistical concepts and techniques. Check out chapter 18: The Ten Commandments for Data Collection.

Appendix: Sources of environmental data

Here is an annotated list of some important on-line sources of environmental data. You may find them useful for doing your own environmental research.

(1) US Environmental Protection Agency, *AirData*, https://www.epa.gov/outdoor-air-quality-data
Contains air quality data for locations throughout the United States.

(2) IUCN, *Red List of Threatened Species*, http://www.iucnredlist.org/about/introduction
Contains country-level information on endangered and threatened species.

(3) NOAA: National Centers for Environmental Information, *DataAccess*, https://www.ncdc.noaa.gov/data-access
Contains a variety of data on weather and climate variables.

(4) *SHELDUS* database, Hazards and Vulnerability Research Group, University of South Carolina, http://hvri.geog.sc.edu/SHELDUS/
Contains US county-level data for a variety of natural hazards including thunderstorms, hurricanes, floods, and tornadoes.

(5) US Environmental Protection Agency, *Toxic Release Inventory*, https://www.epa.gov/toxics-release-inventory-tri-program
Contains information on local releases of various toxic chemicals for the entire United States.

(6) US Geological Survey, *WaterData*, http://waterdata.usgs.gov/nwis
Contains information on local water resources data for the United States.

(7) World Bank DataBank, *World Development Indicators*, http://databank.worldbank.org/data/reports.aspx?source=world-development-indicators
Useful source of country-level data on a variety of environmental measures.

References

Grynbaum, Michael M. "New York Plans to Ban Sale of Big Sizes of Sugary Drinks," *New York Times*, May 30, 2012.

Lohr, Sharon L. *Sampling: Design and Analysis*. Pacific Grove: Duxbury, 1999.

"Unit of Analysis," *Research Methods Knowledge Base*, October 20, 2006, https://www.socialresearchmethods.net/kb/unitanal.php

"World Development Indicators," World Bank DataBank, http://databank.worldbank.org/data/ reports.aspx?source=world-development-indicators

6 Basic quantitative methods and analysis

Introduction

As we have seen, in environmental studies the quantitative approach is primarily concerned with quantifying the relationship among variables and testing hypotheses generated by theories. The vast majority of quantitative studies use statistical methods for their analyses. Over the next three chapters, we will be describing and illustrating a number of concepts and tools for doing statistical analysis. This chapter is devoted to basic statistical ideas and methods. Chapter 7 turns to some more advanced concepts and methods, while Chapter 8 discusses spatial analysis, a relatively new area of quantitative inquiry.

You should keep in mind that statistics is a rich and complex area so that in the next three chapters, we will only be scratching the surface. The discussion is intended to be not so much a detailed discussion of statistical methods, but rather to serve as a guide and complement to other books and on-line resources that develop the theory and practice of these methods in much more detail. At the end of each of the next three chapters, I provide an annotated list of recommended additional resources.

Why statistical methods?

When researchers in the social sciences use statistical methods, they are assuming something fundamental about human behavior; namely, that there is an important element of unpredictability. When humans interact with each other and with the environment, you really do not know how they are going to behave.

This is not entirely true. Economists argue that human behavior is a predictable response to incentives of various kinds. Sociologists argue that human behavior is embedded in culture—the cultural beliefs and expectations of a society—which are important determinants of how people behave. But all of our models and frameworks for understanding human behavior are incomplete. Despite our best efforts to predict people's behavior, at least some of what they do will continue to surprise you or, at least, remain something of a mystery.

Figure 6.1 Randomness.

Source: Shutterstock.

This is why statistics has come to be widely used as a tool for understanding human behavior, and why it comprises the fundamental basis for the quantitative approach in environmental studies. What statistics does is to provide a methodology, and a set of concepts and tools, to help us model, explain, and predict human behavior.

Central to the statistics methodology is the notion of *randomness*, which is when there is no pattern or predictability in events. This idea is exemplified by the roll of a pair of dice. When you roll dice, you never know in advance which sides are going to wind up facing upwards (Figure 6.1). We say that the outcome is unpredictable, because there are random influences that affect how the dice roll and how they end up.

Similarly, if it starts raining for shorter but more intensive periods of time under ongoing climate change, we cannot fully predict how tourist visits to North Shore state parks will be affected. Or when a country develops economically, you never know for sure what will happen to the level of pollution that economy will generate (the notion of the environmental Kuznets curve, which we encountered in Chapter 4). In these and many other examples, you may have some inkling of what will happen, maybe even some theory-based predictions, but you just never know for sure.

What statistics does is to take this notion of randomness and run with it. It identifies factors and variables that will be subject to randomness. It creates little models of what it thinks the randomness exhibited by these factors and variables looks like. It uses tools to analyze the patterns of randomness. And it helps us interpret what is going on, in terms of the behavior of individual variables or the relationship among variables.

What sorts of questions might you ask of your data?

Assuming you have formulated a general research question and collected data to try to answer it, the next step is to think about what it might be useful for you to know. For this, it will help to keep in mind the goal of many environmental research projects: to determine if variables are related to each other and, if so, the nature of this relationship. So suppose this is your goal. What would you want to know that the data might reveal?

This question is extremely broad, so let us think about it within the context of a particular data set. When you do your own study, you should think about how this discussion relates to your own data.

The data we will use are from the *North Shore Climate Change* study. A sample of this data file is shown in Figure 6.2. Here we see the beginning of a spreadsheet containing data collected for the climate change project. Each of the rows in this spreadsheet contains a daily observation on a series of variables for one state park. For example, row 2 tells us that on May 1, 2002, there were 148 visitors to Cascade State Park, on which date the average temperature was 40 degrees, the heat index was 46.39 degrees, it did not rain, and so forth.

If you could scroll down further, you would see more data on all of these variables for the summer months (May through September) for Cascade through the end of 2014. This would then be followed by observations starting on May 1, 2002 for the next state park, Crosby-Manitou, and so forth. So these data are organized in the way described in Chapter 5—a series of observations on a series of variables.

Suppose your research question is: How are North Shore state park visitations influenced by weather conditions? Here are some questions it might be useful to try to answer with these data, and some sense for how statistics can help us answer them:

- *How many people visit the parks each day?* Answering this would give us a sense for how quantitatively important the issue is. If the numbers are really small, it might even be worth investing your time and energies in a different project. With randomness, there will be no one answer, so we will have to rely on statistical tendencies.
- *How much do visitations vary from day to day?* Answering this question is crucial. If the answer is very little, statistical analyses will likely tell us very little about factors that affect visitations. Statistics can give us measures of variability, which describe how much randomness there is.
- *Does the number of visitors vary from park to park? How much? Is there a significant difference?* Answering these questions might tell us whether different parks have different experiences, or need to be treated differently in the statistical analysis. It might also alert us to look for factors that might explain the differences.
- *What is the probability that X people will visit a park?* Answering this question will tell us how likely different outcomes are. Statistics provide ways to model randomness in order to calculate these probabilities.
- *How is the number of visitors affected by changes in temperature? Rainfall?* Answering these questions provide us insights into the nature of relationships among variables: whether there is a relationship, how strong, and so

Date	Park	Visitation	Temperature	HeatIndex	Precipitation	ERC	Weekend
5/1/2002	Cascade	148	40	46.39	0	16	0
5/2/2002	Cascade	221	37.5	32.13	0	15	0
5/3/2002	Cascade	68	36.5	45.28	0	18	0
5/4/2002	Cascade	208	35.5	45.47	0.27165354	11	1
5/5/2002	Cascade	76	42	43.1	0.1496063	20	1
5/6/2002	Cascade	134	42	39.49	0.01181102	17	0
5/7/2002	Cascade	129	39	41.1	0.2519685	22	0
5/8/2002	Cascade	175	38	35.99	0.7007874	10	0
5/9/2002	Cascade	193	35.5	35.68	0.07874016	5	0
5/10/2002	Cascade	128	41	51.05	0	11	0
5/11/2002	Cascade	148	45.5	48.96	0.31889764	18	1
5/12/2002	Cascade	199	45	40.43	0.11811024	2	1
5/13/2002	Cascade	77	40	48.95	0.09055118	10	0
5/14/2002	Cascade	301	44.5	44.91	0	16	0
5/15/2002	Cascade	247	38.5	67.8	0.01181102	18	0
5/16/2002	Cascade	233	47	67.82	0	20	0
5/17/2002	Cascade	340	36.5	45.66	0	22	0

Figure 6.2 Data from climate change project, MN North Shore state parks.

Source: Author.

forth. Statistical analysis will help us distinguish between what is systematic variation and what is random noise.

- *How confident can I be in the answers to these questions?* With randomness, there is always a question of whether observed variation or covariation is due to systematic or random influences. Answering this question might help us tell which it is. Statistics provide ways to help us answer this question.

Describing random variables

With these questions in mind, let us return to the notion of randomness as describing a particular activity, process, or behavior, which then takes on the character of a *random variable*. Though the term random variable has been applied to a lot of things, in this discussion we will mostly be using it to describe either human behavior or environmental outcomes. These might include North Shore state park visitations, temperature rises under ongoing climate change, or levels of pollution generated by economies.

Notice one thing that all of these examples have in common. They are all stated in such a way that you can put a number on them: the number of visitors, or the number of degrees that temperatures rise, or parts per million (ppm) ambient concentration of some particular pollutant or group of pollutants. This signifies that the notion of a random variable generally refers to a variable that can take on different numerical values. I suppose one could think of the flight of a hummingbird as being a random variable, but since it is not something you can assign a number to, we will not be concerned with it here.

Defining random variables in this way opens up the possibility of applying a whole host of tools and concepts for analysis. Let us begin with a very important set of tools: ones that we use for *data visualization*. For the purposes of interpreting what is going on in particular contexts, it often really helps to actually see how a random variable is behaving.

Data visualization

For this discussion, we will use a particular example of a random variable: the number of visitors to one of the state parks on the North Shore. To begin to visualize the data, let us consider the *Visitation* data in our data set for one of the parks, Gooseberry Falls State Park (*GFSP*). Referring back to Table 6.1, here we are extracting just the observations in column C for those rows corresponding to GFSP.

First, to visualize the behavior of this particular random variable, we will create what is known as a *histogram*. A histogram displays the frequency with which a variable takes on values in different intervals. To illustrate, the histogram in Figure 6.2 has split up the entire range of values of visitations to GFSP into intervals of approximately 300 each (the width of the vertical bars) and then counted the number of times actual daily visits falls into each interval. So, for example, the tallest bars indicate that there were slightly more than 150 days when the number of visitors to the park fell into those particular intervals.

The nice thing about histograms is that they provide a lot of useful information about the behavior of a variable in a compact, easy-to-see snapshot. For example, Figure 6.3 shows us the historical range of numbers of daily visitors, as well as the typical numbers of daily visitors. The number of daily visitors generally falls between 1,000 and 5,000, and it is extremely rare for the number to exceed 7,000 or so.

As an example of how this information might be practically useful, park officials could use this histogram when deciding whether an expansion in park facilities is warranted by visitor numbers. If current facilities could

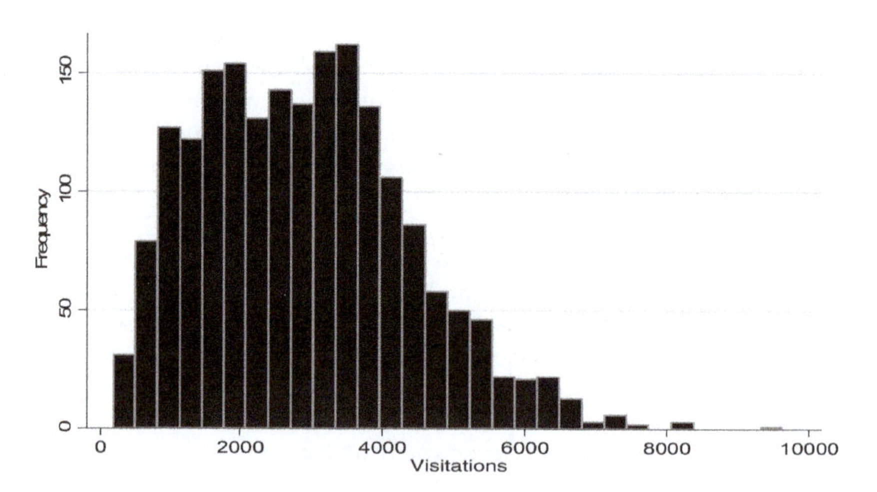

Figure 6.3 Histogram of daily visits, Gooseberry Falls State Park, summer months, 2002–2014.

Source: Author.

comfortably handle, say, 7,000 visitors per day, this information would suggest little need for expansion. However, if the current capacity was at, say, 4,000, the officials might see a significant need for expansion, since there have been many days when the park received more than 4,000 visitors, sometimes considerably more.

Another useful visualization tool is the *scatterplot*. This is useful when you are trying to get a rough idea of the relationship between two variables. In Figure 6.4, for example, we have created a scatterplot of the relationship between daily visits and daily temperature at GFSP. Each one of the dots represents a daily observation on two pieces of information: the number of visitors at the park and the temperature that day. The upward shape of the scatterplot suggests there is a positive association between park visitors and temperature. The warmer it is, the more people tend to come to the park.

I should point out one important feature of this scatterplot. It tells us that there is a "loose" relationship between visitations and temperature, indicated by the vertical thickness of the spread. For any given temperature, we observe many different values of visitations. If there was a non-random, or deterministic, relationship between the two variables, we would expect there to be one value of visitations for each temperature level. In actuality, the scatterplot reveals there are many. This suggests that there may be other, possibly random, influences on visitations.

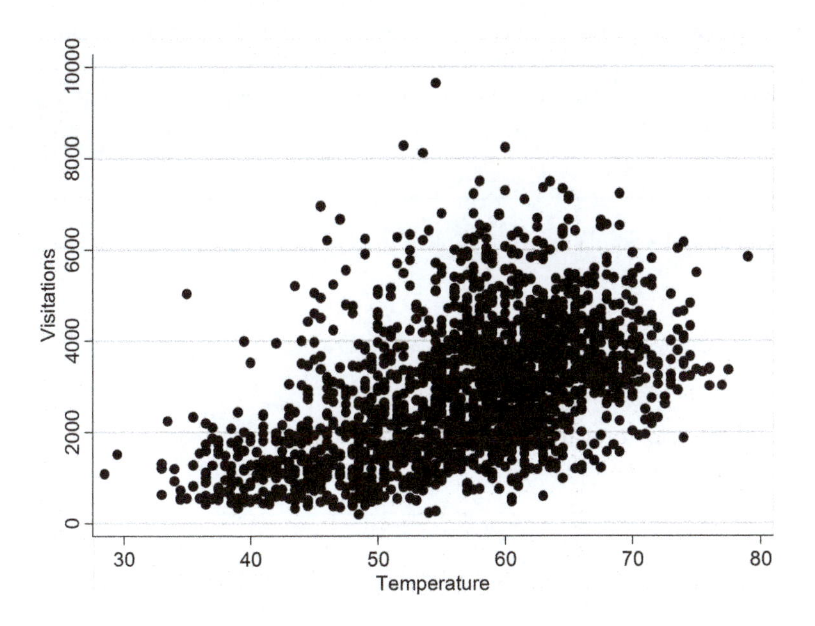

Figure 6.4 Scatterplot of daily visits and daily temperature, Gooseberry Falls State Park, summer months, 2002–2014.

Source: Author.

Statistics for describing randomness

As helpful as visualization tools are, there are many things they cannot tell us that we might like to know. The histogram in Figure 6.3 is not very precise in telling us *how many* visitors we should expect at the park on an average summer day. The scatterplot in Figure 6.4 is not very precise in telling us *how many* more visitors to expect when it gets warmer.

In general, there are three important things we might want to know about random variables: how large they are, how much they vary, and how they co-vary with other variables. These are captured in measures of *central tendency*, measures of *dispersion*, and measures of *correlation*.

Measures of central tendency

One thing it is often extremely important to know about random variables is how large they are: how many visitors, how many degrees warmer the world will be, how much pollution, and so forth. With random variables, however, there is no one answer because they are subject to randomness. Random influences sometimes make them larger, sometimes make them smaller. A measure of central tendency is about how large they are *on average*.

One extremely important measure of central tendency is the *sample mean*, which simply adds up all the values that a random variable takes in a data sample and divides by the number of observations on that random variable. To introduce a little notation, suppose you have collected a sample of thirty observations on daily temperature for the month of June 2014. Let X_1, X_2, X_3, X_4, ... X_{30} be the values of these observations. The sample mean estimator formula is then: *m (sample mean)* = $\Sigma X_i/30$.

Box 6.1 General formula for the sample mean

$$\text{m (sample mean)} = \sum \frac{X_i}{N}$$

where

X_i = ith observation on variable X,
N = number of observations

Another important measure of central tendency for a random variable is the *sample median*. The sample median is found by taking all of the observations in your sample, placing the values in increasing order, and then finding the value right at the midpoint. So, for example, if you had collected precipitation data for the third week of June 2014, perhaps they would look like this: Sun: 0.0; Mon: 0.2; Tue: 0.1; Wed: 0.0; Thu: 1.6; Fri: 0.2; Sat: 0.0. In this case, the sample median is

0.1, because on exactly three of the days, rainfall is less and on exactly three of the days, rainfall is more.

Notice that in this example, the sample mean of rainfall is: (0.0 + 0.2 + 0.1 + 0.0 + 1.6 + 0.2 + 0.0)/7 = 0.3. The question you might ask yourself is: In this case, which number better represents "average" conditions, the sample mean (0.3) or the sample median (0.1)? Many people might argue that the median of 0.1 is more like an average day, since in six out of the seven days, there is little or no rain. The heavy rainfall on Thursday is a so-called *outlier*, which pulls the sample mean up. This is why the median is sometimes used to represent average conditions: it is less affected by the presence of outliers in your data.

Measures of dispersion

In addition to needing to know the average magnitude of a random variable, it is often useful to know how much the variable fluctuates, or varies. For this, we have the important notion of the *standard deviation*. This is a concept that describes the inherent variability of a random variable. The larger it is, the greater is the average variability of the variable; that is, the more "dispersed" are the values.

To calculate the standard deviation of a random variable in a sample, you apply the formula in Box 6.2. This formula tells us that the standard deviation *s* will tend to be large when there is more variation in X. The greater the variability in the variable, the greater the average differences between the observation values and the sample mean will be: $(X_i - m)$. When you take these differences, square them, and sum them over the entire sample, this formula will then tend to produce a larger number.[1]

Box 6.2 General formula for the standard deviation

$$s = \sqrt{\left[\sum \frac{(X_i - m)^2}{(N-1)}\right]}$$

where

X_i = ith observation on variable X,
m = the sample mean, and
N = number of observations

Measures of correlation

This third type of measure is used to characterize how different random variables move together. There are three possibilities here. They tend to vary in the *same* direction, they tend to vary in *opposite* directions, or they tend *not to vary together*. These are the cases of *positive*, *negative*, and *zero* correlation, shown in Figure 6.5. So for the data shown in Figure 6.4, visitations and daily temperatures are exhibiting positive correlation.

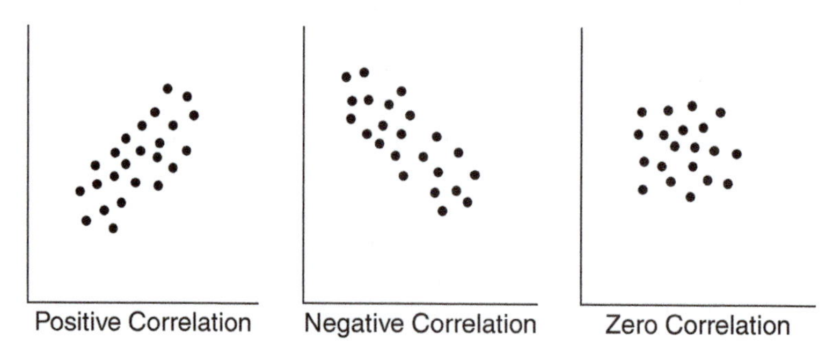

Figure 6.5 Positive, negative, and zero correlation.

Source: Author.

As a measure of the way variables move in relation to each other, correlation is measured using the so-called *correlation coefficient*. So suppose there are two variables, X and Y. Then the formula for the correlation of X and Y is shown in Box 6.3. Defined in this way, the correlation can take on values in the range between –1 and 1. For some intuition for this formula, see the appendix at the end of the chapter.

Box 6.3 General formula for the correlation of two variables X and Y

$$\rho = \sum \left[\frac{\left[\frac{(X_i - m_x)}{s_x}\right]\left[\frac{(Y_i - m_y)}{s_y}\right]}{(N-1)} \right]$$

where

X_i = ith observation on variable X,
Y_i = ith observation on variable Y,
m_X = sample mean of X,
m_Y = sample mean of Y,
s_X = standard deviation of X,
s_Y = standard deviation of Y, and
N = number of observations

Estimation and inference

Now that we have seen a few ways to represent and measure randomness in environmental variables, let us think about using this information to draw inferences about what is happening in a target population.

To clarify, you may have noticed that all of the discussion in the last section was about working with data contained in a sample drawn from a population. We now know how to characterize the behavior of the sample data. The question is:

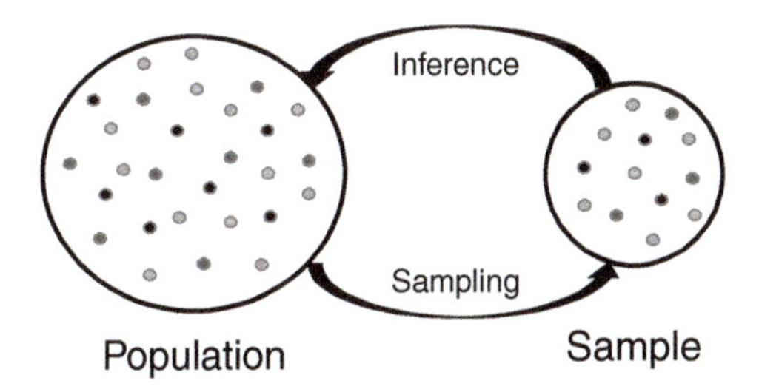

Figure 6.6 Sampling and inference.

Source: Author.

What can we infer about the population from which it is drawn? (See Figure 6.6.) In this discussion, we will assume you have carefully followed all the principles of good sampling discussed in Chapter 5. This means that you now have a sample that faithfully represents the population in all important ways.

The first step is to assume there is some particular characteristic of the population you are interested in knowing more about, perhaps providing a number for. In our climate change example, it might be the percentage of visitors to the North Shore who stay overnight. Or it might be average daily precipitation over some historical period. Or it might be the effect that temperature increases have on park visitations. In all of these examples, the characteristic—the percentage of visitors, the average precipitation, the change in park visitors—is unknown because the population is unobserved. This characteristic is called a *population parameter*.

A general objective of much statistical research is to come up with an estimate of the value of a parameter. We generally do this by taking the data in our sample and applying a rule, which yields a particular number. We saw several examples of this in the last section. The formulas for the sample mean, standard deviation, and correlation are all mathematical rules, or *estimators*, that turn sample data into particular numbers, called *estimates*. These estimates are used to make inferences about the population from which the sample is drawn.

So suppose we wanted to estimate average daily temperature on the North Shore during the summer. When I say "average" here, let me use the statistical notion of an expected value, which loosely speaking takes all possible outcomes and weighs them by how likely they are to occur. Introducing some notation, if we use X to represent "daily temperature during the summer," then E(X) is the expected value of daily summer temperatures.

I hope it is clear why E(X) is a parameter. "Summer" is a general term that applies to any three-month period June through August in any year, not just the ones in any sample we could collect. North Shore summer temperatures vary depending upon location and time of day, making it next to impossible to set up enough temperature gauging stations to determine a true expected value. And no matter how precise our thermometers are, there will be errors in our temperature measurements. All of these add up to our never knowing for sure what the average North Shore summer temperature really is.

Because all of these logistical and informational challenges are really difficult to overcome, we settle for less. We use one or a handful of temperature gauging stations. We measure temperatures as precisely as we can, knowing that the measurements will not be perfect. And we assume that the summers we collect data for are representative of "summers" in general, knowing that there is no way to know this for sure. We do all of this to construct an estimate of average summer temperatures: perhaps a really good guess, but a guess nonetheless.

So when we calculate a sample mean for a random variable using data in a sample, we use it to estimate the *true* expected value of that variable in the population from which the sample was drawn. Similarly, we calculate a standard deviation based on sample data in order to estimate the true standard deviation in a population. And we calculate a sample correlation among random variables in order to estimate the true correlation among those variables in a population. All of this allows us to draw inferences about how to describe what is going on in the population.

Bottom line: Statistical analysis typically involves collecting data in a sample drawn from an unobserved population, in order to come up with an estimate of some unknown characteristic of that population (a so-called *parameter*). The estimate is calculated by applying a mathematical formula (a so-called *estimator*) to the sample data.

More on characterizing random outcomes: Probability distributions

If you think about what we were just saying about inference from a sample to a population, it seems to imply that patterns discerned in the sample should reflect patterns in the underlying population. This goes not just for our measures of central tendency, dispersion, and covariation. Indeed, the entire pattern of observations in the sample should give us an idea of what the pattern looks like in the population.

For example, consider Figure 6.7, which reproduces Figure 6.3. Here, we see a histogram of the observations on daily park visitations at GFSP for our sample: the summer months from 2002 to 2014. This "hill-shaped" pattern of observations in these data is actually quite common. This fact opens the door for us to use a wide variety of statistical methods and tools to analyze behavior of various kinds.

The first step is to model the randomness in this variable. This is done by creating a *distribution function* for the variable in the population (see Figure 6.8). This distribution function looks an awful lot like the histogram of the visitation data. The main difference is that the distribution function has "smoothed out" all of the rough edges in the histogram. This is done purely for purposes of analysis: the rough edges really do not matter very much, and assuming that they don't matter frees us up to use a lot of statistical tools. This particular bell-shaped distribution is known as a *normal distribution*.

One important way we can use the normal distribution is to calculate probabilities that the random variable will take on different values. This is because

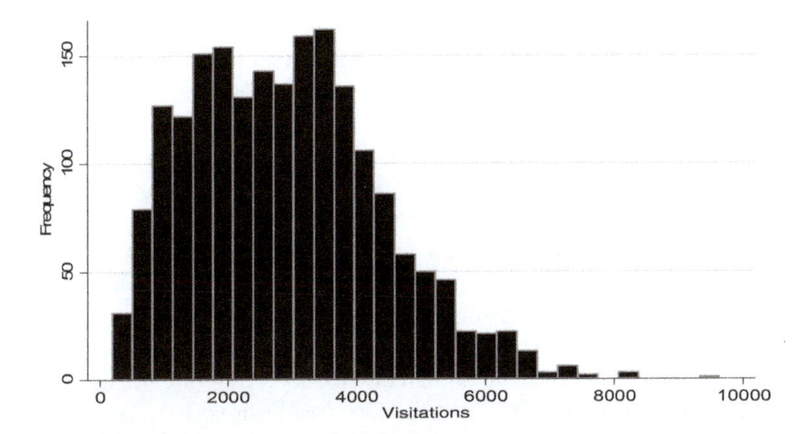

Figure 6.7 Histogram of daily visits, Gooseberry Falls State Park, summer months, 2002–2014.

Source: Author.

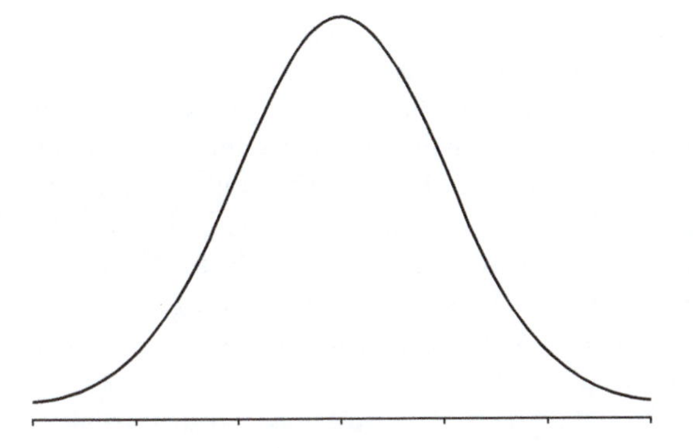

Figure 6.8 Normal distribution.

the shape of the distribution reflects the probability of different outcomes. Those outcomes where the distribution is highest—that is, right in the center of the distribution—are most likely to occur. Those outcomes that are far away from the center where the distribution is lowest—in the "tails"—are least likely to occur.

This is why, in the histogram of GFSP visitations, we observe many summer days where visits are between 2,000 and 4,000, and hardly any days above 7,000 or so. If, for example, there are hardly ever any days in the underlying population where there are more than 7,000 visitors, and our sample is representative of the population, we should not be surprised if few days with more than 7,000 visitors show up in our sample.

It turns out that we can actually be quite specific about the probabilities of different outcomes for random variables that happen to be normally distributed. This is because the probability of any set of outcomes equals the area under the distribution over that range of outcomes. If we can calculate the area, we can calculate a probability.

So, for example, in Figure 6.9, the probability that visitations will take on values between A and B is equal to the area marked P. So if A is 1,500, B is 2,500, and P is, say, 0.23, this says that the probability is 23% that there will be between 1,500 and 2,500 visitors on a given day at GFSP. This 23% number is also basically equal to the percentage of days in which the number of visitors will fall within this range.

Practically speaking, it may be useful for you to be able to actually calculate the probability of a range of outcomes of a normally distributed random variable. Here, we will see one way to do it, using tabular information. You should also be aware that there are software packages and on-line calculators that can calculate these probabilities for you.

First, I need to emphasize that the normal distribution is not one single distribution, but rather an entire family of distributions (see Figure 6.10). As you can see, these distributions can vary with regard to central tendency (where they are located on the X axis), dispersion (how spread out the possible outcomes are), or both. More formally, normal distributions may differ with respect to expected value and standard deviation. Distributions A and B have the same expected value but different standard deviation. Distributions B and C have the same standard deviation but different expected value. And distribution D has both a different expected value and a different standard deviation from all the rest.

One implication of this, of course, is that the probability of any particular range of outcomes depends upon *which* normal distribution characterizes your variable. In Figure 6.10, it is obvious that the probability of taking on a value between –1 and 1 is going to differ if the random variable is described by distribution A rather than distribution C. In order to calculate probabilities of outcomes, therefore, we need to specify which normal distribution we are using.

It has become a convention, when calculating probabilities of different ranges of outcomes, to use one particular member of this family: the so-called *standard*, or *unit*, normal distribution. The standard normal distribution is the distribution that has an expected value (μ) of zero and a standard deviation (σ) of one. In Figure 6.10, this is distribution B.

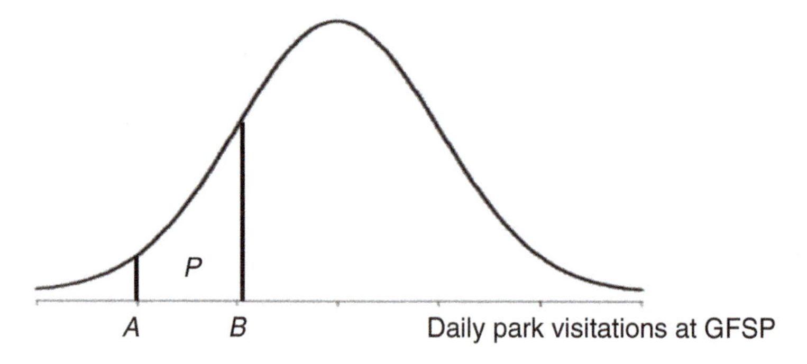

Figure 6.9 Probability of a set of outcomes for a normally distributed random variable.

Source: Author.

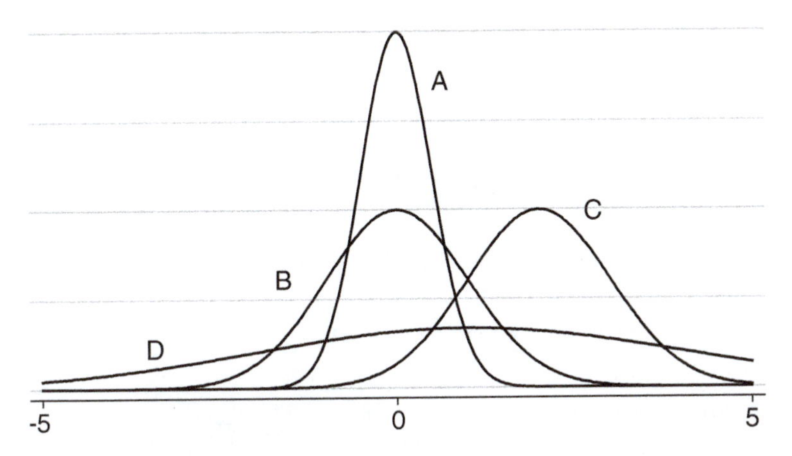

Figure 6.10 The family of normal distributions.

Source: Author.

To calculate probabilities of different outcomes for a random variable subject to a standard normal distribution, we could use a table as shown in Table 6.2. The entries in this table are equal to the shaded area, and thus represent probabilities that this random variable falls into the interval from zero to the value Z (the so-called Z *score*). So, for example, when Z = 1.50, the probability is 0.4332. That is, the probability is 43.32% that a standard normal random variable falls into the interval between zero and 1.5.

One important Z value is 1.96. Table 6.1 tells us that the probability associated with this Z score is .4750. This means that the area above the interval from –1.96 to 1.96 is (2 × .4750), or 0.95, since the normal distribution is symmetric. This is a useful fact, because it says that for a standard normal random variable, roughly 95% of all outcomes fall within two standard deviations of the expected value (remember that the standard deviation of a standard normal random variable is one). We will exploit this fact in the next section when we start talking about statistical inference procedures like constructing confidence intervals and testing hypotheses.

Even though many random variables are normally distributed, we will rarely be so fortunate as to be working with one that take on a *standard* normal distribution. So how do we calculate probabilities of outcomes in this case? It turns out that this is relatively straightforward to do.

To see how, let us introduce some additional notation. Suppose X is a (not necessarily standard) normally distributed random variable, with unknown expected value of μ and standard deviation of σ. We will denote this as follows:

$$X \sim N(\mu, \sigma)$$

Here, the symbol "~ N" is read as "is distributed as normal," and the two terms in parentheses represent the parameters of the distribution: expected value of μ and

Table 6.1 Table of probabilities for a standard normal random variable

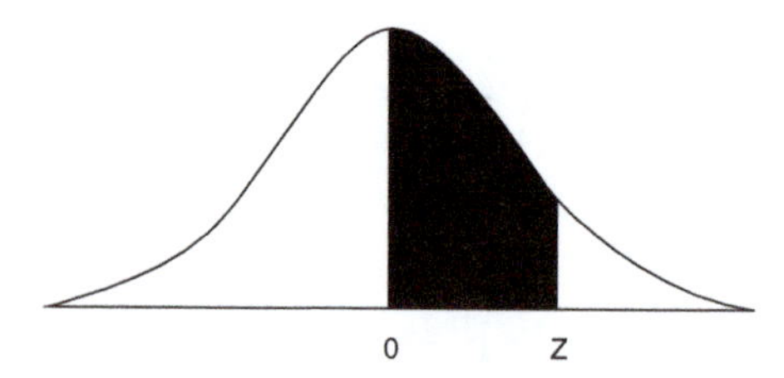

This table presents the area between the mean and the Z score. When Z = 1.96, the shaded area is 0.4750.

Areas under the Standard Normal Curve

Z	0.00	0.01	0.02	0.03	0.04	0.05	0.06	0.07	0.08	0.09
0.0	0.0000	0.0040	0.0080	0.0120	0.0160	0.0199	0.0239	0.0279	0.0319	0.0359
0.1	.0398	.0438	.0478	.0517	.0557	.0596	.0636	.0615	.0714	.0753
0.2	.0793	.0832	.0871	.0910	.0948	.0987	.1026	.1064	.1103	.1141
0.3	.1179	.1217	.1255	.1293	.1331	.1368	.1406	.1443	.1480	.1517
0.4	.1554	.1591	.1628	.1664	.1700	.1736	.1772	.1808	.1844	.1879
0.5	.1915	.1950	.1985	.2019	.2054	.2088	.2123	.2157	.2190	.2224
0.6	.2257	.2291	.2324	.2357	.2389	.2422	.2454	.2486	.2517	.2549
0.7	.2580	.2611	.2642	.2673	.2704	.2734	.2764	.2794	.2823	.2852
0.8	.2881	.2910	.2939	.2967	.2995	.3023	.3051	.3078	.3106	.3133
0.9	.3159	.3186	.3212	.3238	.3264	.3289	.3315	.3340	.3365	.3389
1.0	.3413	.3438	.3461	.3485	.3508	.3531	.3554	.3577	.3599	.3621
1.1	.3643	.3665	.3686	.3708	.3729	.3749	.3770	.3790	.3810	.3830
1.2	.3849	.3869	.3888	.3907	.3925	.3944	.3962	.3980	.3997	.4015
1.3	.4032	.4049	.4066	.4082	.4099	.4115	.4131	.4147	.4162	.4177
1.4	.4192	.4207	.4222	.4236	.4251	.4265	.4279	.4292	.4306	.4319
1.5	.4332	.4345	.4357	.4370	.4382	.4394	.4406	.4418	.4429	.4441
1.6	.4452	.4463	.4474	.4484	.4495	.4505	.4515	.4525	.4535	.454$
1.7	.4554	.4564	.4573	.4582	.4591	.4599	.4608	.4616	.4625	.4633
1.8	.4641	.4649	.4656	.4664	.4671	.4678	.4686	.4693	.4699	.4706
1.9	.4713	.4719	.4726	.4732	.4738	.4744	.4750	.4756	.4761	.4767
2.0	.4772	.4778	.4783	.4788	.4793	.4798	.4803	.4808	.4812	.4817
2.1	.4821	.4826	.4830	.4834	.4838	.4842	.4846	.4850	.4854	.4857
2.2	.4861	.4864	.4868	.4871	.4875	.4878	.4881	.4884	.4887	.4890
2.3	.4893	.4896	.4898	.4901	.4904	.4906	.4909	.4911	.4913	.4916
2.4	.4918	.4920	.4922	.4925	.4927	.4929	.4931	.4932	.4934	.4936
2.5	.4938	.4940	.4941	.4943	.4945	.4946	.4948	.4949	.4951	.4952
2.6	.4953	.4955	.4956	.4957	.4959	.4960	.4961	.4962	.4963	.4964
2.7	.4965	.4966	.4967	.4968	.4969	.4970	.4971	.4972	.4973	.4974
2.8	.4974	.4975	.4976	.4977	.4977	.4978	.4979	.4979	.4980	.4981
2.9	.4981	.4982	.4982	.4983	.4984	.4984	.4985	.4985	.4986	.4986
3.0	.4987	.4987	.4987	.4988	.4988	.4989	.4989	.4989	.4990	.4990
3.1	.4990	.4991	.4991	.4991	.4992	.4992	.4992	.4992	.4993	.4993
3.2	.4993	.4993	.4994	.4994	.4994	.4994	.4994	.4995	.4995	.4995
3.3	.4995	.4995	.4995	.4996	.4996	.4996	.4996	.4996	.4996	.4997
3.4	.4997	.4997	.4997	.4997	.4997	.4997	.4997	.4997	.4997	.4998
3.6	.4998	.4998	.4999	.4999	.4999	.4999	.4999	.4999	.4999	.4999
3.9	.5000									

Source: Adapted with permission from *Statistical Methods* by George W. Snedecor and William G. Cochran, sixth edition © 1967 by The Iowa State University Press. Ames, Iowa. p. 548.

standard deviation of σ. This notation means, of course, that we could indicate a *standard* normally distributed random variable Y as: $Y \sim N(0, 1)$.

It turns out that if X is distributed in this way, the following random variable is standard normally distributed:

$$\frac{(X - \mu)}{\sigma} \sim N(0, 1)$$

What this says is that you can convert any normally distributed random variable to standard normal by subtracting its expected value and then dividing by its standard deviation. This is an important and extremely useful rule, so let me emphasize it in the a bottom line.

> **Bottom line:** Any normally distributed random variable can be converted into a standard normally distributed random variable by first subtracting its expected value and then dividing by its standard deviation.

To return to our GFSP visitation example, suppose that we wanted to calculate the probability that park visitations fell into the range of 2,000 to 6,000 visitors. Suppose also that we know that daily visitations to GFSP, denoted as X, is normally distributed in the population with expected value of 4,000 and a standard deviation of 1,000.

$$X \sim N(4{,}000, 1{,}000)$$

How do we calculate this probability?

Step one: Make a probability statement about the event we are interested in:

$$\text{Probability } [2{,}000 \le X \le 6{,}000] = P$$

The way to read this statement is that the probability of the event inside the brackets—that is, that X falls into the range from 2,000 to 6,000—is equal to P, a probability value between zero and one.

Step two: Transform all sides of this inequality so as to convert X to a standard normal random variable:

$$\text{Probability } [-2 \le (X - 4{,}000) / 1{,}000 \le 2] = P$$

Here, we have transformed the original probability statement into one about the probability that a standard normal random variable will take on particular values: the range between negative two and two. Notice that we are applying the same operations to all sides of the inequality, which leaves the probability P unaffected. At this point, it is safe to consult the standard normal table in Figure 6.2, which tells us this probability P is (2 × 0.4772), or 0.9544. This is then the probability that park visitations will be between 2,000 and 6,000 per day.

Notice that in this example, the range of values from 2,000 to 6,000 is exactly those values that lie within two standard deviations of the expected value (here, the standard deviation is assumed to be 1,000). And, lo and behold, there is that roughly 95% probability value again. So the takeaway message here is that it doesn't matter whether we are talking about a standard normal or non-standard normal distribution. In either case, the region of values spanning two standard deviations from the center will contain roughly 95% of the available probability.

How good are our guesses? Statistical inference

At this point, let us go back to our earlier discussion of estimation and think a bit more about the answers we get. For example, I went ahead and calculated that the sample mean of daily visitations for Gooseberry Falls State Park during the 2002–2014 period was 2,895.4. This is my estimate for the expected value of GFSP daily visits, what is sometimes called a *point estimate*. The question is: How confident am I in this number? How certain can I be that it gives me a good idea of the true expected value?

In statistics, there are two distinct but complementary ways of going about answering these questions. We can construct confidence intervals, or we can perform hypothesis tests. Let us examine each of these procedures in turn.

Constructing confidence intervals

The idea behind confidence intervals is to be able to state how confident we are that our estimates do indeed give us a good idea of the true value of the parameters we are trying to estimate. Furthermore, we can be very precise in what we mean when we say "confident."

Intuitively, confidence intervals are ranges of values that we interpret, with a certain level of confidence, as containing an unknown parameter. We construct confidence intervals essentially because it is hard to know how much to trust point estimates. They are, after all, one single number that we have constructed from a random sample. The randomness in the sampling process means that it is extremely unlikely that our guess will be exactly correct. To deal with this problem, we construct confidence intervals *around* our point estimates (Figure 6.11). Essentially, the confidence interval tells us if we are close.

To illustrate, consider our sample mean estimate of 2,895.4, which you should now be viewing with suspicion because you know that it is almost surely wrong. Let us use it to construct a confidence interval for μ to see if we are even close.

To construct a confidence interval for μ, you first need to choose a level of confidence. Here you are faced with a bit of a dilemma, which is illustrated in

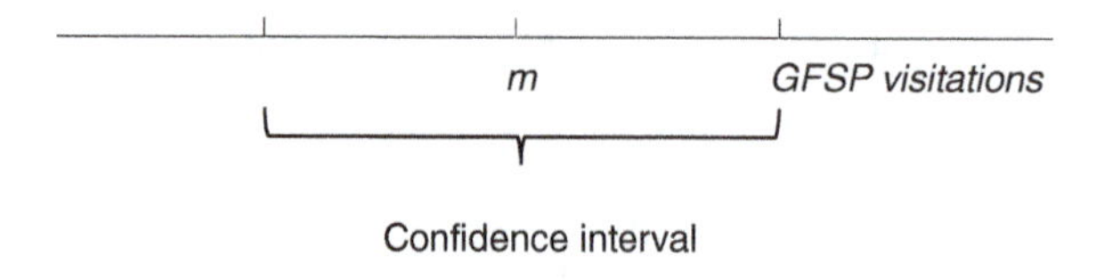

Figure 6.11 Confidence interval for true unknown expected value μ.

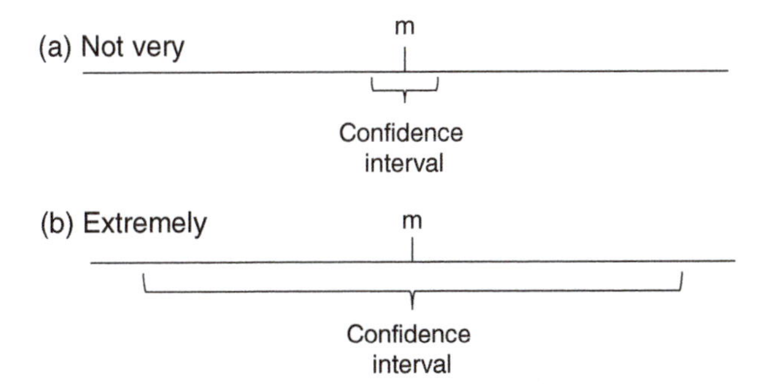

Figure 6.12 How confident do you want to be?

Figure 6.12. On the one hand, we would like to be confident that our interval contains μ. Choosing a larger interval, as in (b), allows us to be more confident that our interval has captured the parameter. However, the downside of choosing a larger interval is that our conclusions about the parameter μ will be less useful. For example, you could say with complete and utter confidence that the true expected value μ falls between $-\infty$ and $+\infty$, but obviously, this would not do you much good. It is more useful to be able to say it falls into a small range, as in (a). But you just can't be as confident that this will be true.

As a compromise, and what is a convention in much statistical work, researchers often use a 95% confidence level. To see exactly what this means, consider Figure 6.13, which illustrates an important fact about our sample mean estimate: that it is a random variable, subject to a probability distribution. This makes sense, if you think about it. Given random sampling from the population, the sample mean estimate will vary from sample to sample. The random sampling process imparts randomness to the sample mean estimate.

This means, of course, that we can calculate probabilities of different values of the sample mean, if we know its probability distribution. Figure 6.13 depicts the distribution as normal, and it turns out that there are good reasons for this, as long as the variable visitations is itself also normally distributed.

Assuming then, that the sample mean is normally distributed, we can calculate probabilities that it will take on certain ranges of values, as we saw in the last section. Specifically, we know from that previous discussion that for normally distributed random variables, 95% of the probability will lie within roughly two standard deviations of the center (see Figure 6.14).

Now, let's interpret the image in Figure 6.14. It says that the probability is 95% that the random variable m falls into this range of values around the expected value μ. Using the probability statement notation from the last section, let us write this interpretation as follows:

$$\text{Probability } [\mu - 2s < m < \mu + 2s] = 0.95$$

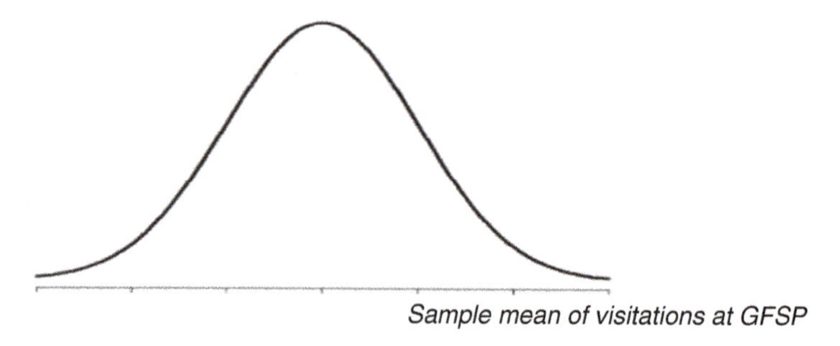

Figure 6.13 Sample mean as a random variable.

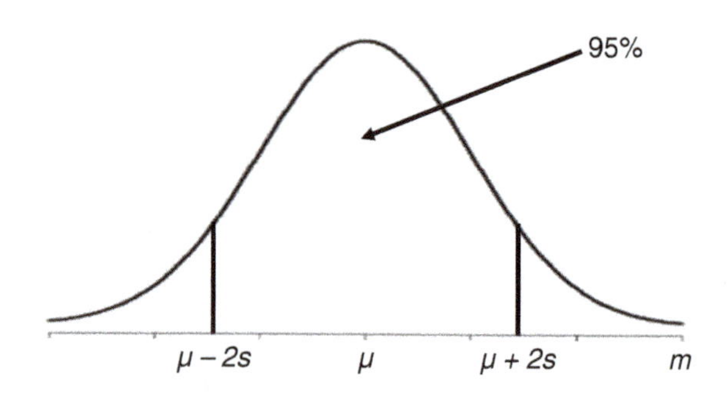

Figure 6.14 Outcomes of m likely to occur 95% of the time.

With a little rearranging, it is easy to show that this is equivalent to the following statement:

$$\text{Probability } [m - 2s < \mu < m + 2s] = 0.95$$

This last statement is for all intents and purposes a statement of the 95% confidence interval; namely, the interval within two standard deviations of the sample mean.

So in our case, the standard deviation of the sample mean of park visitations was 33.43, so this expression becomes: 2895.4 ± 66.86, or (2828.54, 2962.26).

So what have we just shown? That the probability is 95% that the true expected value of park visitations falls into this particular confidence interval? Not quite. When we think about it, there are two possibilities: either this interval contains the true expected value, or it does not. So what does 95% mean?

To interpret what this interval is telling us, let us go back to the important idea that this interval was based on one sample out of many possible ones, all drawn from the same population. If we were to repeat the experiment again, it would yield a different point estimate, but also a different confidence interval, because of the randomness of the sampling process (see Figure 6.15). Depending upon what μ actually is, it could be contained in one interval, the other interval, both, or neither.

Now imagine taking 100 samples, from each of which you estimate a (different) sample mean and a different confidence interval. Just like before, some of

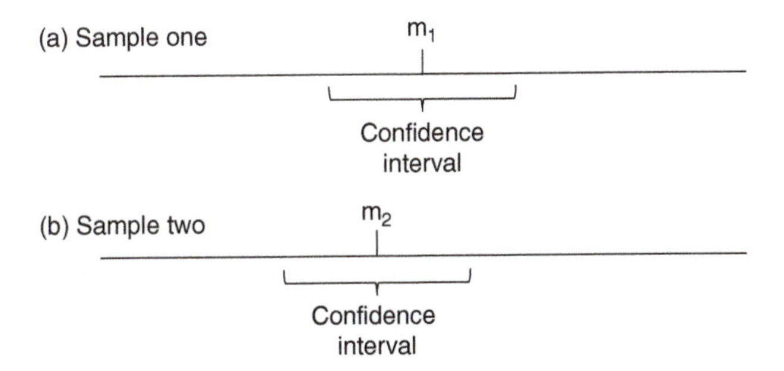

Figure 6.15 Variation in the confidence interval across different samples.

these confidence intervals may contain the true expected value, but some may not. When we say 95%, we do not mean that there is a 95% probability that any particular interval will contain the true expected value, as we are tempted to do. Rather, the correct interpretation considers *all* of these possible samples: out of all of them, 95 out of 100 will contain the true expected value, and the others will not. This is how you should think about the confidence interval.

Now that we have seen what a confidence interval is and how to go about calculating it, let us step back for the larger picture. We started this discussion with a simple point estimate of the unknown expected value of daily park visitations. This gave us a guess as to the true value, but it was only a guess. We constructed a confidence interval for the unknown expected value in order to see how much to trust this guess. If 95 out of 100 intervals like the one we constructed on the basis of our sample contain the true expected value, we feel like we have gotten a pretty good idea of that value.

Hypothesis testing

Let us now turn to an extremely important topic: the notion of testing a hypothesis. One of the real strengths of the statistical approach is that it provides us with a structured and rigorous methodology for hypothesis testing. Let us illustrate the approach, again using the context of the *North Shore Climate Change* study.

When you test a hypothesis, you need to be very specific about precisely what you are testing. For example, let us again think about my estimated sample mean for GFSP visitations of 2895.4. Rather than using it to construct a confidence interval for μ, we could use it to test a hypothesis *about* μ. A common hypothesis to test would be whether it equals a particular value.

So say, for example, that we wanted to test the hypothesis that μ is equal to 3,000; or, in words, that on average, GFSP receives 3,000 visitors per day. This forms the so-called *null hypothesis* for our test. Introducing some notation, let us call the null hypothesis H_0. The alternative hypothesis is that the null hypothesis is not true; namely, that it is not equal to 3,000: denote this as H_1. Box 6.4 shows the set-up for our hypothesis test.

Box 6.4 Setting up a hypothesis test: the null and alternative hypotheses

$$H_0: \mu = 3{,}000$$

$$H_1: \mu \neq 3{,}000$$

Now here is an important point of interpretation. When we perform a hypothesis test, we make the assumption that the null hypothesis is true. The question is: Given that it is true, is our sample statistic (here, the sample mean = 2985.4) highly unlikely? If it is, then we conclude that the null hypothesis cannot be true. In this case, we reject the null hypothesis.

In order to determine whether our sample statistic is highly unlikely, we create an interval of values around the hypothesized value that contains so much of the available probability. How much probability depends upon the level of significance of the test. So if we wanted to perform a hypothesis test at a 5% level of significance, we would choose the interval that contains 95% of all of the probability. As we have seen, for a normal distribution this interval is the expected value plus or minus two standard deviations. This becomes the so-called *acceptance region* for our test. All other values constitute the *critical region*.

So, for example, in Figure 6.16, the interval from 3,000 plus or minus two standard deviations contains roughly 95% of all of the probability. If 2985.4 does not fall into this interval, then we conclude at a 5% level of significance that it is highly unlikely that this distribution would have generated the test statistic. This leads us to reject the null hypothesis: the test statistic of 2985.4 is inconsistent with the null hypothesis.

Conclusions

To conclude, let's return to the questions we posed toward the beginning of this chapter.

- How many people visit the parks each day?
- How much does this vary from day to day?

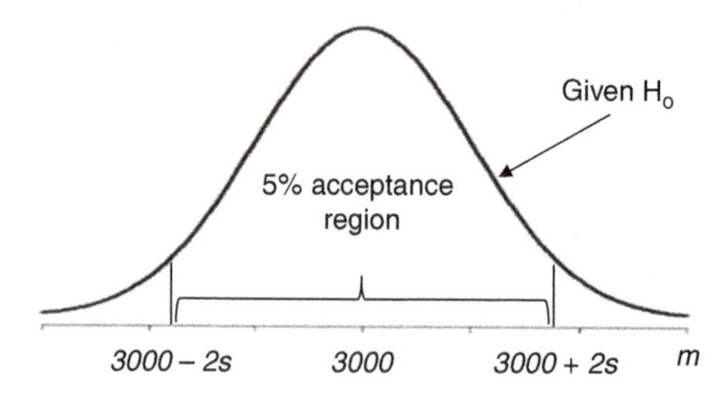

Figure 6.16 Testing the null hypothesis.

- Do the number of visitors vary from park to park? How much? Is there a significant difference?
- What is the probability that X people will visit a park?
- How is the number of visitors affected by changes in temperature? Rainfall?
- How confident can I be in the answers to these questions?

In this chapter, we have illustrated how simple statistics may be used to answer these questions. When you conduct your own study, I encourage you to think about the specific questions that you would like to answer that might be amenable to convenient statistical summary, like these ones are. The answers could you tell you a lot about a number of issues of practical importance. These include: the quantitative importance of environmental issues, simple relationships among variables, and useful guidance you might be able to give to environmental managers and policymakers.

One thing to notice here is that the tools presented have been, for the most part, simple ways to represent variables and the relationship among variables. They are not really suited to capturing the sometimes complex relationships among environmental variables that we experience in the real world. In Chapter 7, we go a short way down that road to develop somewhat more advanced quantitative tools of analysis, in order to give you a better sense of the analytical power of the quantitative approach.

Exercises/discussion questions

For these exercises, you will be using the data in Table 6.2 on daily average temperatures and daily visitors at Gooseberry Falls State Park for July of 2014.

(1) Calculate the mean, median, and standard deviation of visits and average temperatures during this month. Compare the mean and median temperatures. Which do you think is more representative of average temperatures during that month? Why?

(2) Calculate the correlation coefficient between visitations and average temperature. Do visits tend to increase when the days are warmer?

(3) Suppose that GFSP daily visitations, denoted X, are normally distributed in the following way:

$$X \sim N(4000, 1000)$$

Use the information in Table 6.1 to calculate the probability that visitations to GFSP fall between 2,000 and 2,500 per day.

(4) Use the sample mean you calculated in problem (1) to construct a 95% confidence interval for the expected daily temperature in July.

(5) Verify that: (a) Probability $[\mu - 2s < m < \mu + 2s] = 0.95$ and (b) Probability $[m - 2s < \mu < m + 2s] = 0.95$ say the same thing.

(6) Using your estimated sample mean, test the hypothesis, at a 5% significance level, that expected daily visits in July equals 5,000.

Table 6.2 Average daily temperatures, daily visitations, Gooseberry Falls State Park, July 2014

Date	*Visitors*	*Temp*
7/6/2014	4319	74.93
7/7/2014	3616	71.51
7/8/2014	3847	64.49
7/9/2014	2552	61.52
7/10/2014	3501	66.56
7/11/2014	3381	67.46
7/12/2014	5897	68
7/13/2014	4343	61.52
7/14/2014	2514	57.47
7/15/2014	3279	62.06
7/16/2014	3539	59.99
7/17/2014	3556	66.02
7/18/2014	4316	68
7/19/2014	5527	69.98
7/20/2014	4725	74.93
7/21/2014	3753	79.97
7/22/2014	3340	76.46
7/23/2014	3730	65.48
7/24/2014	3797	66.47
7/25/2014	4266	66.56
7/26/2014	4263	74.93
7/27/2014	3636	67.64
7/28/2014	3896	64.94
7/29/2014	4427	66.02
7/30/2014	4056	64.04
7/31/2014	3892	68.54

Additional resources

Berry, Donald A., and Bernard W. Lindgren. *Statistics: Theory and Methods*. Belmont: Wadsworth, 1996.

Intermediate-level treatment of statistical concepts and techniques, for students who are more mathematically inclined. Many examples and exercises that complement and illustrate the concepts nicely.

Bluman, Allan G. *Elementary Statistics: A Step by Step Approach* (2nd ed.). Dubuque: Brown, 1995.

Good introductory statistics textbook. Many useful examples and exercises.

Byrkit, Donald R. *Statistics Today: A Comprehensive Introduction*. Menlo Park: Cummings, 1987.

Exactly what its title suggests: a comprehensive introduction to statistical concepts and methods, complete with many useful exercises and applications.

Lock, Robin et al. *Statistics: Unlocking the Power of Data*. Wiley: Hoboken, 2013.

Excellent, user-friendly introduction to statistical analysis. Many useful applications and exercises.

Salkind, Neil J. *Statistics for People Who (Think They) Hate Statistics*. Thousand Oaks: Sage, 2000.

A fun and highly accessible treatment of various statistical concepts and techniques. Highly recommended, particularly if you find statistics intimidating.

Appendix: Some intuition for interpreting the correlation coefficient formula

Consider the formula for the correlation coefficient given in Box 6.3 and reproduced here. Notice that the number you calculate for the correlation could be either negative, positive, or zero. When will it be positive? The answer is: *When the numerators of the terms multiplied together—*$(X_i - m_X)$ *and* $(Y_i - m_Y)$*—tend to have the same sign.* That is, when larger-than-average values of one variable tend to be associated with larger-than-average values of the other variable and when smaller-than-average values of one tend to be associated with smaller-than-average values of the other. So positive covariation is indicated by positive estimated correlation values. And the more closely correlated the variables are, the closer the correlation will be to one.

Box 6.5 General formula for the correlation of two variables X and Y

$$\rho = \sum \left[\frac{\left[\frac{(X_i - m_x)}{s_x} \right] \left[\frac{(Y_i - m_y)}{s_y} \right]}{(N-1)} \right]$$

where

X_i = ith observation on variable X,
Y_i = ith observation on variable Y,
m_X = sample mean of X,
m_Y = sample mean of Y,
s_x = standard deviation of X,
s_Y = standard deviation of Y, and
N = number of observations

Similarly, the estimated correlation will tend to be negative when the terms multiplied together—$(X_i - m_X)$ and $(Y_i - m_Y)$—tend to have the *opposite* sign. This occurs when *smaller*-than-average values of one variable are associated with *larger*-than-average values of the other variable. So negative covariation is indicated by negative estimated correlation values. Here, the more closely correlated the variables are, this time in the negative direction, the closer the correlation will be to –1.

Finally, zero covariation is indicated when the terms multiplied together are no more likely to have the same sign as the opposite sign. In this case, the positive terms cancel out the negative terms, resulting in an estimated correlation of zero.

Note

1 We also have the notion of the *sample variance*, an alternative way to represent the dispersion of a random variable. It is calculated simply by taking the standard deviation and squaring it.

7 More advanced methods of quantitative analysis

Introduction

In the last chapter, we discussed a number of basic statistical concepts that often arise in quantitative studies of environmental issues. Let us now develop that discussion in more depth. In this chapter, we will focus on how to characterize the relationship among variables. As we have seen, the relationship among variables lies at the heart of many environmental issues. Thus, it is not surprising that characterizing exactly how variables relate to each other is the objective of many studies of the environment, both quantitative and qualitative.

The question of determining how variables are related goes far beyond drawing scatterplots or calculating the measure of correlation we encountered in Chapter 6. Doing these things, though often important and useful, is only the first step in a quantitative study of the relationship among variables for an environmental issue. So, for example, suppose we wanted to really understand how visitations to North Shore state parks will be affected by increases in temperatures under ongoing climate change. A number of questions arise:

1. How do we know that an estimated relationship is not being generated by random noise?
2. How do we quantify the relationship between visitations and temperatures?
3. How trustworthy are our estimates of the relationship?
4. Is the relationship between visitations and temperatures linear?
5. How do we know it is temperatures that are affecting visitations and not something else?

The remainder of this chapter will be devoted to addressing a number of issues that commonly arise when one does a quantitative study of the environment. It will do this by focusing on the above questions as an organizing framework for the discussion.

How do we know that an estimated relationship is not being generated by random noise?

Whenever we do statistical analysis, we have to consider the possibility that things are not always what they seem to be. That is, patterns in data may not actually reflect anything systematic going on, but rather may be being generated by random processes. If so, there is absolutely no reason why you would expect the same pattern to be observed in the future.

As a simple example, consider the flipping of a coin. If you were to flip the coin five times, it is entirely possible you might get five "heads." Should you conclude that the coin is rigged? Not necessarily, because it is quite possible that a fair coin flipped five times might come up heads every time. The question is: How do you *know* the coin is not rigged?

One way would be to just keep on flipping the coin. Five heads in a row you can chalk up to the vagaries of random flipping. Ten heads in a row, however, should start to arouse your suspicions. Fifty in a row should leave you little doubt that the coin is not fair. The more observations you have, the more convinced you can be that any patterns you observe really are patterns, and not generated by random noise.

For an environmental example, consider the data in Figure 7.1, which is based upon the same data that generated Figure 6.3 in the last chapter. The difference is that the scatterplot in Figure 7.1 was created from a very small sample—ten observations—from that data set. These data do not suggest any sort of relationship between park visitations and temperatures.

Now consider what happens to the pattern when we take larger samples of observations from the exact same park, same summer months, same time frame. In Figure 7.2, we show scatterplots for samples of 50, 100, and 1935 observations. The scatterplot on the right-hand side uses the entire sample for the overall period and thus reproduces the scatterplot in Figure 6.3. As we take more observations, the pattern gets filled out and the true pattern becomes more and more apparent.

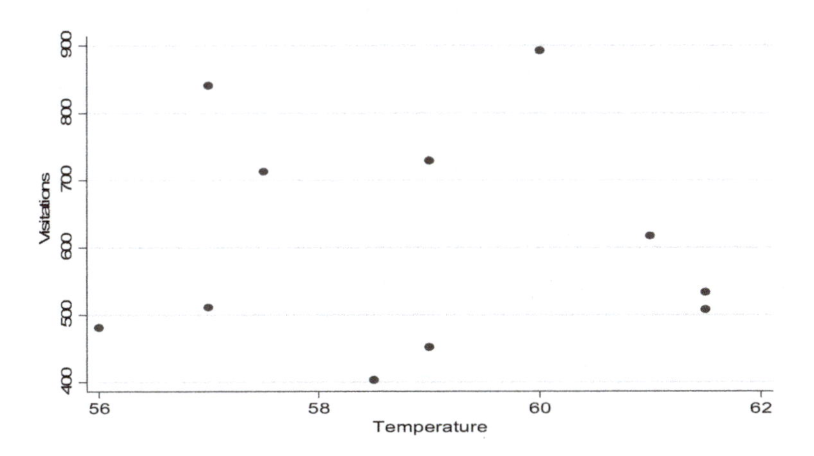

Figure 7.1 Scatterplot of daily visits and daily temperature based on ten observations, Gooseberry Falls State Park, summer months, 2002–2014.

Source: Author.

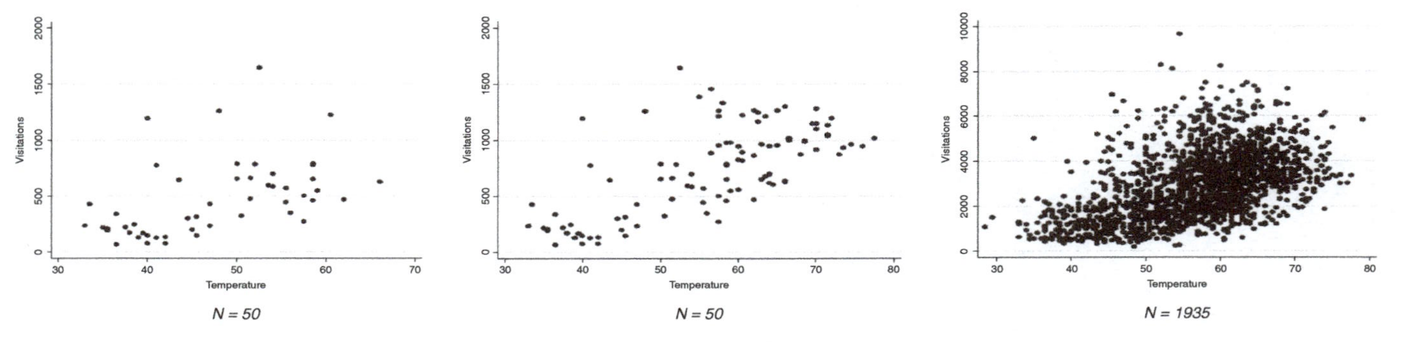

Figure 7.2 Scatterplots of daily visits and daily temperature, GFSP, different sample sizes.

Source: Author.

Figure 7.3 Random influence on park visitations.

Source: Shutterstock.

These figures illustrate an extremely important principle of statistical analyses in general: the importance of large samples if you really want your analysis to reveal what is going on in the population. When you take a tiny sample, you make it much more likely that the overall pattern in the data will reflect the randomness of the sampling process.

For intuition, consider the following. If visitations are subject to some randomness (for example, as shown in Figure 7.3), we can all imagine occasional days when the visitation/temperature relationship does not fit the general pattern. Perhaps on a warm day, there just happens to be a traffic accident that blocks the main road to the park, resulting in few visitors that day.

Or perhaps a long-planned major public event in the park just happens to fall on a cold day, but people are committed so they dress warmly and come anyway. These sorts of things are bound to happen in any sample you might take. Taking a large sample means you have more observations that "balance out" random influences, allowing us to observe the actual overall pattern.

> **Bottom line:** When possible, it is preferable to use large samples, in order to minimize the influence of random factors and better allow us to discern the true systematic patterns in the data.

How do we quantify the relationship between visitations and temperatures?: The basics of two-variable regression analysis

Creating a scatterplot or calculating a correlation coefficient can be suggestive of a positive, negative, or zero relationship between two variables. However, they

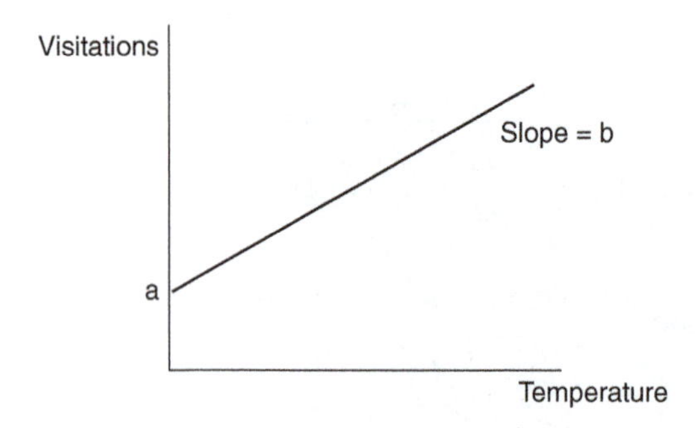

Figure 7.4 Best-fit line, interpreted.

do not enable us to actually quantify the relationship, which is often quite useful. This is one reason you might consider doing a regression analysis, which both quantifies how the variables are related and can tell us whether the relationship is statistically significant.

Consider, for example, the relationship between visits to GFSP and daily temperatures. The pattern in the data shown in the right-hand side graph in Figure 7.2 suggests that there might be a systematic positive relationship: as temperatures increase, visitations tend to also. In order to precisely quantify this relationship, statisticians often recommend taking a "best-fit" line to the data. You can think of this best-fit line as being the one that best captures the relationship among the variables.

Figure 7.4 shows the best-fit regression line to the GFSP data. This line cuts right through the heart of the pattern. It is not surprising that almost all the observations do not fall right on the regression line. The fact that they are scattered around the line in a cloud reflects random influences on visitation behavior. Sometimes, the number of visits on a given day will exceed what you expect given the temperature that day (unexpectedly cold temperatures on the day of long-planned public events). Other times, visitations will fall short (traffic accidents blocking the main road to the park).

This regression line turns out to have a very specific interpretation in terms of quantifying the relationship between visitations and variables. This best-fit line is of course linear, and, thus, it may be represented algebraically with the equation for a line: $Y = a + bX$. In this equation, the variable Y is a linear function of the variable X, where a is the intercept and b is the slope.

Using this formula, the best-fit regression line for the relationship between park visitations and daily temperature may be written as:

$$Visitations = a + b\ Temperature$$

Figure 7.5 shows the graphical interpretation of the best-fit line. Notice all of the information contained in this line. First, it shows us how visitations are predicted

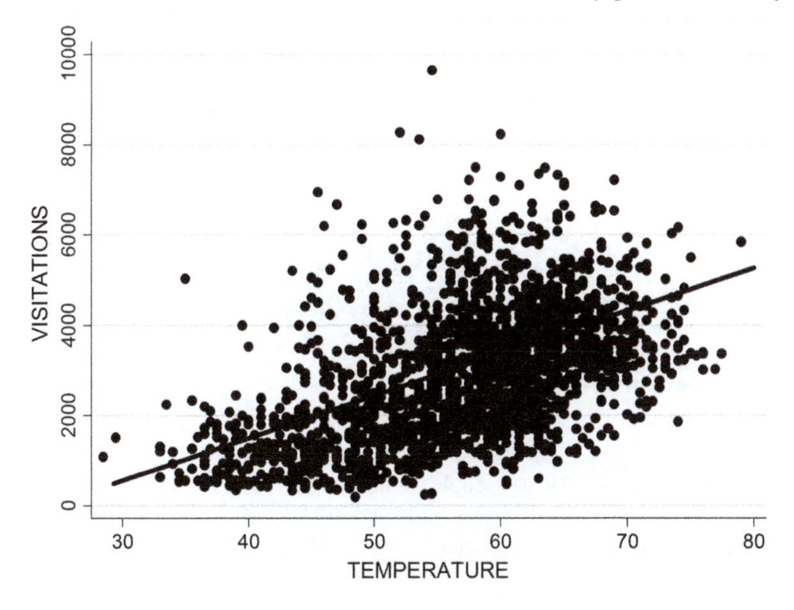

Figure 7.5 Best-fit regression line to GFSP data.

Source: Author.

to vary as temperature varies. This vital piece of information is given by the slope of the line b, which tells us that when temperature increases by one unit (here, one degree Fahrenheit), visitations are predicted to increase by b. The slope thus provides a measure of how visitations and temperatures vary together.

Second, this line can give us a prediction for how many visitors there will be when the temperature takes on any value. Predicted visitations could be found simply by taking whatever temperature value you are interested in and plugging it into the equation for the best-fit line. So, for example, the predicted number of visitors when the temperature is 60 degrees is found by multiplying 60 by the slope coefficient b and adding the intercept a:

$$\textit{Predicted visitations} = a + b*60$$

Now that we know how to interpret the results, let us go out and estimate the best-fit line. The results of an estimation of this best-fit line are shown in Figure 7.5. These estimates were calculated using the statistical software package *STATA*. Apparently, the values of a and b that best describe the data are: $a = -2029.80$ and $b = 86.47$.

Let us interpret these results as we did before. First, the value $b = 86.47$ tells us that for every one degree increase in temperature, visitations are predicted to increase by 86.47 visitors per day. Second, if the temperature is 60 degrees, the predicted number of visitors per day is: $-2029.80 + 86.47(60) = 3158.4$. You can see this in Figure 7.6 by following the vertical black line up from (Temperature = 60)

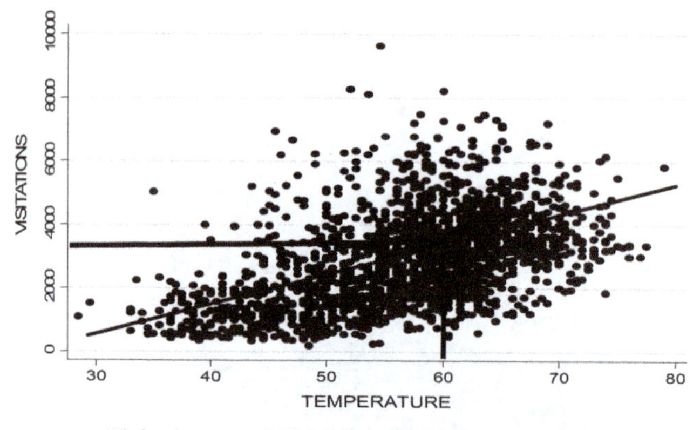

Visitations = –2029.80 + 86.47 Temperature

Figure 7.6 Prediction, using best-fit regression line to GFSP data.

Source: Author.

to the best-fit line and then over to the vertical axis, where you can read off the number of predicted visitations.

> **Bottom line:** We can use two-variable regression analysis to make very specific predictions for how a variable Y is affected by another variable X. These include both: predicted *levels* of Y for all values of X, and predicted *changes* in Y as X changes.

How trustworthy are our estimates of the relationship I?: The important notion of validity

In quantitative research, we always have to be concerned about two key questions: Are our conclusions *credible?* And are they *generalizable?* That is:

- *Credibility*: Are we drawing the correct conclusions from our evidence?
- *Generalizability*: Do our results apply in other parts of a population?

The answers to these questions are bound up in the concept of *validity*. Let us begin to understand this concept: how it is defined in quantitative research and why it is important. As it turns out, the answers to these two questions are about two types of validity: *internal validity* and *external validity*.

Internal validity

When researchers think about what makes conclusions credible, perhaps the first question they ask is: Are the conclusions warranted by the evidence presented?

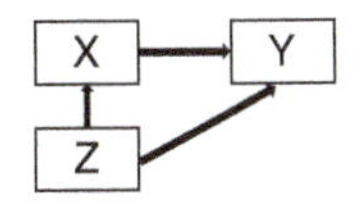

Figure 7.7 Spurious causality.

Source: Author.

This is the question of internal validity. When they think about the answer to this question, one issue that commonly arises is the issue of causality.

Specifically, the question is: If a study finds a relationship among variables, is it fair to interpret it as a *causal* relationship? For example, consider our simple two-variable regression analysis, where we found a positive relationship between daily visitations and daily temperatures. One is tempted to interpret that finding as evidence of a causal relationship, because it makes intuitive sense that warmer weather would bring more tourists out to the parks.

However, this conclusion may not be valid if there are other factors not being considered in your analysis that are affecting both variables. In this case, your variables may seem to be causally related when, in fact, it is these other unconsidered factors that are really responsible for the finding of correlation. In this case, we say the causal relationship is *spurious*.

So, consider our finding that park visitations go up when it is warmer. Should we conclude that warmer temperatures cause people to visit the parks more? Perhaps not. It may be the case that it is actually rain that discourages people from visiting parks, and it just so happens that rain tends to occur on cooler days. It may *look* like warm weather brings people out to the parks, when it is merely the fact that on those days, it tends not to rain. In this case, we would say that rain is a *confounding* variable and that not considering it poses a *threat* to the internal validity of our conclusion.

The general argument is illustrated graphically in Figure 7.7, where Y is a variable whose behavior we are trying to explain and our research design poses X as the causal factor. Based on our empirical analysis, which shows a positive correlation between X and Y, we conclude that X causes Y. However, in fact what is really going on is that Y is being caused by Z, which just happens to be correlated with X. By not considering Z, we draw the spurious conclusion that X is causing Y. In this case, our conclusion that X causes Y lacks internal validity.

Bottom line: The internal validity of a conclusion can be threatened by not accounting for other factors that may be causing the estimated relationship among your variables.

External validity

In quantitative research, external validity is about whether your conclusions, based upon the observations in your sample, are true for the larger population from which you drew the sample. As you can probably guess, the issue of random sampling is key here. As we have seen, if you fail to sample randomly, the pattern in your sample may not accurately mirror the underlying population. In this case, your conclusions concerning the relationship may lack external validity.

As a simple example, suppose you are interested in doing a study of support for policies that would effectively mitigate climate change. For this study, you decide to survey students randomly at your university. The question is: Would your findings regarding the level of support for these policies generalize to the larger population of all US citizens? Here, the answer is quite possibly not, perhaps because more highly educated respondents might tend to be more supportive of such policies.

More generally, a big threat to external validity is choosing a decision rule for sampling that inadvertently introduces bias into your sample. By this, I mean that your decision rule causes you to select a sample that differs from your population in some systematic way, and this throws off your estimates. In quantitative research, this is known as *sample selection bias*.

Let me explain sample selection bias with a simple example. Suppose you are a high school math teacher with a class of forty students. You have written two exams, A and B, that you believe are similar in difficulty, but you would like to test whether this is true. You decide to administer them to students and see if the scores are lower on one of them. So you make twenty copies of each exam and on the day of the exam, you hand out exam A to the first twenty students to show up and exam B to the remaining twenty students. *Before proceeding, can you see the potential sample selection bias issue?*

The potential problem here is that the students who show up early may be more motivated, or more organized, than the rest. In either case, you might expect their scores to be higher on average *even if the two tests were equally difficult*. Suppose you examine the test scores and find that the scores are higher on exam A. On this basis, you conclude that exam A is the easier exam. But this conclusion may not be warranted: it may simply be that the more motivated, more organized students were the ones that took it.

Bottom line: The external validity of a conclusion can be threatened by inadvertently using a non-random sampling rule that is itself correlated with the variables in your analysis (*sample selection bias*).

How trustworthy are our estimates of the relationship II?: Statistical inference again

Now that we understand the companion concepts of internal and external validity, let us return to our visitations analysis again and ask the important question: How much can I trust those results to tell me the true relationship between visitations and temperature? Here, we will assume that we have a theoretically defensible model, we have not overlooked or incorrectly defined any key variables, and we have done a careful job of collecting a reasonable random sample. That is, we will not be concerned about issues of validity.

Recalling our earlier results, our estimated best-fit line strongly suggests that more people tend to visit the park when it gets warmer. However, from the discussion in Chapter 6, we know that our estimate of b is subject to randomness. We get an estimate of 86.47 from the particular sample that we happened to choose: one particular set of ping-pong balls that were drawn randomly out of the barrel. What would happen if we choose a different sample, a different set of ping-pong balls? We might very well get a different estimate. Indeed, it is possible that the new estimate will be completely different from the first one. This possibility should not fill us with confidence in the reliability of our estimate of 86.47, unless we can support it in other ways.

To give us more confidence in the reliability of our estimates, let us return to two extremely important procedures that we discussed in Chapter 6: confidence intervals and hypothesis testing.

Confidence intervals

In Chapter 6, we constructed a confidence interval for an unknown expected value using a sample mean. The principle of constructing a confidence interval, however, applies to many situations where you are interested in estimating a parameter. When you perform a two-variable regression and select a best-fit line, you are implicitly trying to estimate an unknown parameter that describes the relationship among variables in the population. Our estimated b is our guess as to the value of this true slope parameter. Let us call the slope parameter β.

The idea behind constructing a confidence interval for β using b is basically the same as when constructing a confidence interval for an unknown expected value using a sample mean. The confidence interval for β is centered on b, with the width of the interval depending upon the standard error of b and the confidence level for the interval. As before, let us construct a 95% confidence interval.

To construct the confidence interval, we will need the rest of the regression output, which is shown in Box 7.1. If you have not seen regression output from statistical software before, this box reports output that is pretty standard for statistical packages. Notice the second column labeled *Coefficient*, which reports the estimates of a (–2029.796) and b (86.47025). To construct the confidence interval, we will focus on the boldfaced output in the row for *Temperature*.

Box 7.1 STATA regression output. Visitations model, GFSP

Visitation	*Coefficient*	*Standard error*	*t*	*P>t*	*[95% Confidence interval]*	
Temperature	**86.47025**	**3.385025**	**25.54**	**0.000**	**79.83157**	**93.10894**
Constant	–2029.796	194.7052	–10.42	0.000	–2411.65	–1647.941

Source: Author.

If you skip to the end of the row, you can see that STATA has calculated a 95% confidence interval for β already: [79.83157, 93.10894]. How did it get this? In essentially the same way as we calculated the confidence interval for the expected value using the sample mean in the last chapter: by calculating a band around b that is essentially two times the standard error of b in both directions, positive and negative, like so:

$$95\%\ \textit{confidence interval for}\ \beta\text{: } b \pm 2 * \textit{standard error of } b$$

Here, STATA has calculated the standard error of b for us: 3.385025. So the 95% confidence interval is 86.47025 ± 2 * 3.385025. If you calculate this interval by hand, you will find that it is very close to the 95% confidence interval provided by STATA. Why it is not *exactly* the same interval is an esoteric point that need not concern us here.

What does this confidence interval tell us? Recalling the discussion from the last chapter, it should be interpreted as follows: in 95 out of 100 repeated samples, the interval constructed in this way will contain the true β. If the interval was extremely large, we could not be terribly confident in our estimate: this would suggest that our next estimate could be quite different. However, because the interval in this particular case seems relatively narrow—plus or minus roughly 6.8 visitors for every extra degree of temperature—we can conclude with reasonable assurance that our b estimate of 86.47 is fairly reliable.

Bottom line: The confidence interval provides a measure of the reliability of an estimate of the relationship among variables. It tells us, at a given level of confidence, how much variability there is in our estimates, across repeated samples.

Hypothesis tests

In Chapter 6, we also encountered the notion of testing a hypothesis. The question is: How can we use this notion to determine whether our estimate is reliable?

To begin to answer this question, think about what we are trying to infer about the underlying relationship between visitations and temperatures in the population. One important issue is whether there really is a relationship at all. That is, when temperatures change, do visitations also tend to change?

Notice that if the answer is no—that temperature changes have no effect on visitations—this implies something very specific about the value of β: that it is equal to zero. Figure 7.8 illustrates this case. Where the slope of the function is zero, visitations do not change when temperatures change. That is, visitation behavior does not seem to be affected by changes in temperatures.

This fact suggests the following hypothesis test: test to see whether or not β is equal to zero. If it is not, then we can reject the hypothesis that there is no systematic relationship between visitations and temperatures.

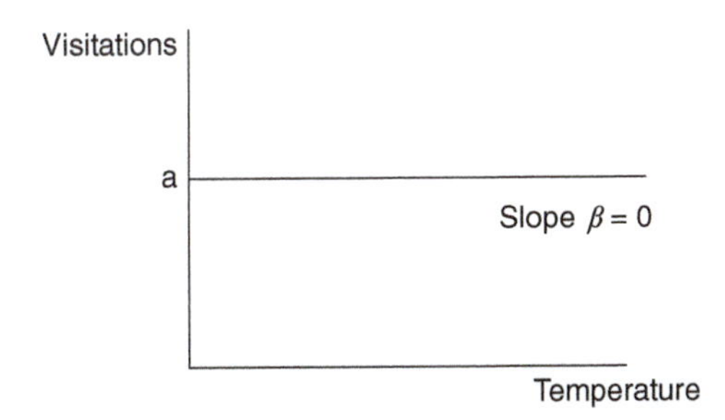

Figure 7.8 The case where temperature changes have no effect on visitations.

Source: Author.

As before, we begin by setting up the null and alternative hypotheses, which are both about the value of β. The null hypothesis is that β equals zero, the alternative hypothesis is that it does not equal to zero:

$$H_0: \beta = 0$$

$$H_1: \beta \neq 0$$

The question is whether your estimated statistic b seems consistent or inconsistent with the null hypothesis. It may seem hard to believe that we would have come up with an estimate of $b = 86.47$ if it were really the case that $\beta = 0$. However, by now you are probably asking yourself the right question: What is the standard error of our estimate?

If the standard error of b is small compared to the estimate of b, then it is hard to imagine coming up with a much different value if we were to sample again. In this case, it is easy to believe that our estimate is inconsistent with the null hypothesis that $\beta = 0$. However, if the standard error is large compared to b, we could easily see coming up with a very different value of b based on another sample. Perhaps it would be a lot closer to zero. It might even be negative. In this case, it would be a lot harder to feel comfortable with rejecting the null hypothesis.

Now that we have the intuition behind the test, let's talk procedure. We have already set up the null and alternative hypotheses. Assuming the null hypothesis is true, let us set up the acceptance region for the test. Here, it will be centered at zero since that is the hypothesized value under the null hypothesis. And then the acceptance region will be roughly two standard deviations on both sides of zero (see Figure 7.9).

Here, with the standard error of b being roughly 3.385, the 95% acceptance region for this test is roughly twice that, in both directions from zero: (–6.77, +6.77). Our estimated b value of 86.47 is nowhere close to lying in this acceptance region. Thus, it is highly improbable that this distribution, which assumes

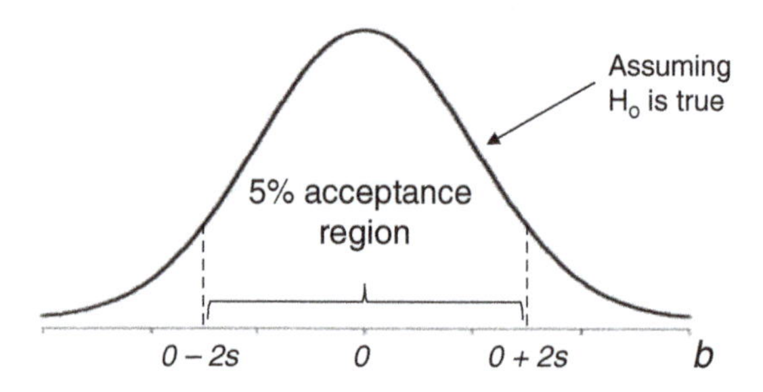

Figure 7.9 Hypothesis test for β = 0.

Source: Author.

β = 0, would have generated it. We can reject the null hypothesis and conclude that changes in temperature *do* systematically affect visitations.

Notice one more thing about this hypothesis test. The estimate *b* falls outside of the acceptance region whenever it is greater than twice its own standard deviation, in absolute value. This fact makes it quite easy to test the null hypothesis that β = 0: simply inspect *b* and compare it to its own standard deviation. If *b* is more than twice as great (again, in absolute value), then we can reject the null hypothesis and conclude there is a systematic relationship, at a 5% level of significance.

One nice thing about this is that software packages make it really easy for you to perform this test. If you go back and inspect the STATA output in Box 7.1, you will see numbers in the fourth column that has the heading "t." This column lists the so-called *t-ratio* for each variable (as well as the constant *a*), which is defined as the estimated coefficient divided by its own standard error (you can verify this by taking each number is the second column and dividing it by the corresponding number in the third column).

The above rule says that whenever a t-ratio exceeds two in absolute value, we can reject the null hypothesis that the parameter β equals zero and conclude that the variable is statistically significant at a 5% level of significance, roughly speaking. Since this rule is not exact (though it is pretty close!), we will call it the "rough" rule for statistical significance, as stated in Box 7.2.

Box 7.2 Rough rule for statistical significance, 5% significance level

Whenever the following condition is satisfied:

$$\left|\frac{b}{se(b)}\right| > 2$$

we can reject, at a 5% level of significance, the null hypothesis that the parameter β equals 0. In this case, we can conclude that the variable is a systematically important influence on the variable whose behavior we are trying to explain.

Source: Author.

In Box 7.1, the t-ratio for *Temperature* is 25.54, meaning that it easily satisfies this rule (this t-ratio indicates that the coefficient is more than 25 times as large as its own standard error!). This means that we can be extremely confident that temperature and visitations are systematically related. A cursory inspection of the t-ratio column can thus tell us quickly whether a variable is systematically important in influencing another variable.

Bottom line: We can use confidence intervals and hypothesis tests as supportive procedures when we are trying to assess how reliable our estimates are. The smaller are the confidence intervals, the more confident we can be that our estimates are *reproducible*: that they would not change dramatically if we were to repeat the entire procedure again with a new randomly chosen sample. The farther away our estimates are from the acceptance region of a hypothesis test, the more confident we can be that the hypothesized value cannot be the true one. This can be particularly useful if we are interested in testing the hypothesis that a coefficient on an explanatory variable is zero; namely, whether or not the variable has a systematic impact on another variable.

Is the relationship between visitations and temperatures linear?: Functional specification

One issue that commonly arises in regression analysis may have already occurred to you: How do we know that there is a *linear* relationship between the variable we are interested in and the variables that we think may systematically affect it? In all of the models we have been considering so far, the relationship among the variables is assumed to be a straight line. So that, for example, when temperature increases by one degree, the effect on visitations is the same, regardless of the temperature level. But what if this is not the case?

This discussion will not be able to address all of the possibilities for non-linear models, but let us focus on two common and important strategies: *log-linear* models and *quadratic* models.

Log-linear models

For intuition, consider the variable temperature. In the model in Box 7.1, whenever temperature increases by one degree, visitations are predicted to increase by 86.47 per day. And, again, this is the case regardless of how cold or how hot it is. But what if it gets extremely hot, uncomfortably hot? Is it reasonable to assume that more and more people will keep coming to the park in equal numbers?

One possibility is that, as it gets warmer and warmer, additional visitations will start to tail off. Figure 7.10 illustrates this possibility. When it is relatively cool, an extra degree of temperature induces many extra people to visit the park. This

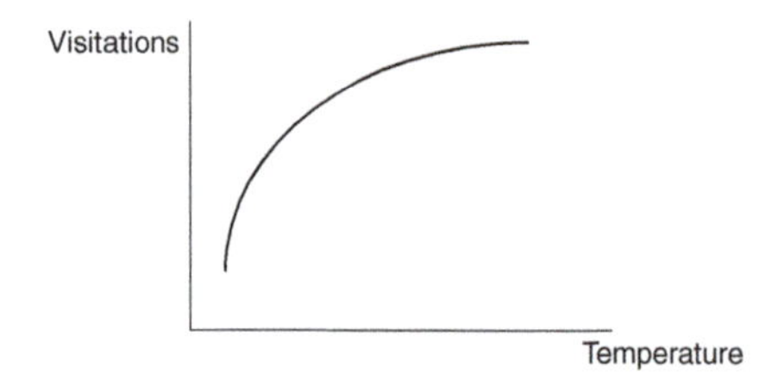

Figure 7.10 Non-linear relationship between visitations and temperature.
Source: Author.

is reflected in the relatively steep slope of the visitations function at temperatures near the vertical axis. However, as we move farther and farther away from the vertical axis, the function flattens out. This reflects the fact that when it is hot, an extra degree of temperature will not be nearly as enticing to visitors.

Suppose we believe this is the case. How do we allow for this possibility in our regression model?

One common way is to model the relationship not as linear in the variables but rather, as *multiplicative*, in the following form:

$$Visitations = a\ Temperature^{b}$$

Where, again, *a* and *b* are constants: *a* is the coefficient on *Temperature* and *b* is an exponent.

One nice thing about this multiplicative function is that it allows for a wide range of types of relationships between visitations and temperature, depending upon the value of *b*. Figure 7.11 illustrates what the relationship looks like if *b* assumes different values. For example, in the upper left-hand side panel, $b = 0$ and changes in temperature have no effect on visitations. In the adjacent panel, *b* falls between 0 and 1 and the relationship is positive but increases at a decreasing rate. The remaining three panels illustrate what the relationship looks like for values of *b*: equal to one, greater than one, and less than zero.

So if our intuition is correct and people start staying away as it gets increasingly hot, we might expect the data to reflect a pattern like the second panel. In this case, *b* would be between 0 and 1.

Another nice thing about the multiplicative function is that it is fairly straightforward to run a regression that allows for all of these different possibilities. Notice in particular what happens to the multiplicative function if you take the natural logarithm of both sides:

$$\ln Visitations = \ln a + b \ln Temperature$$

This transformed function is linear: not in the variables, but rather in the *natural logarithms* of the variables. Because of this feature, this new function is sometimes referred

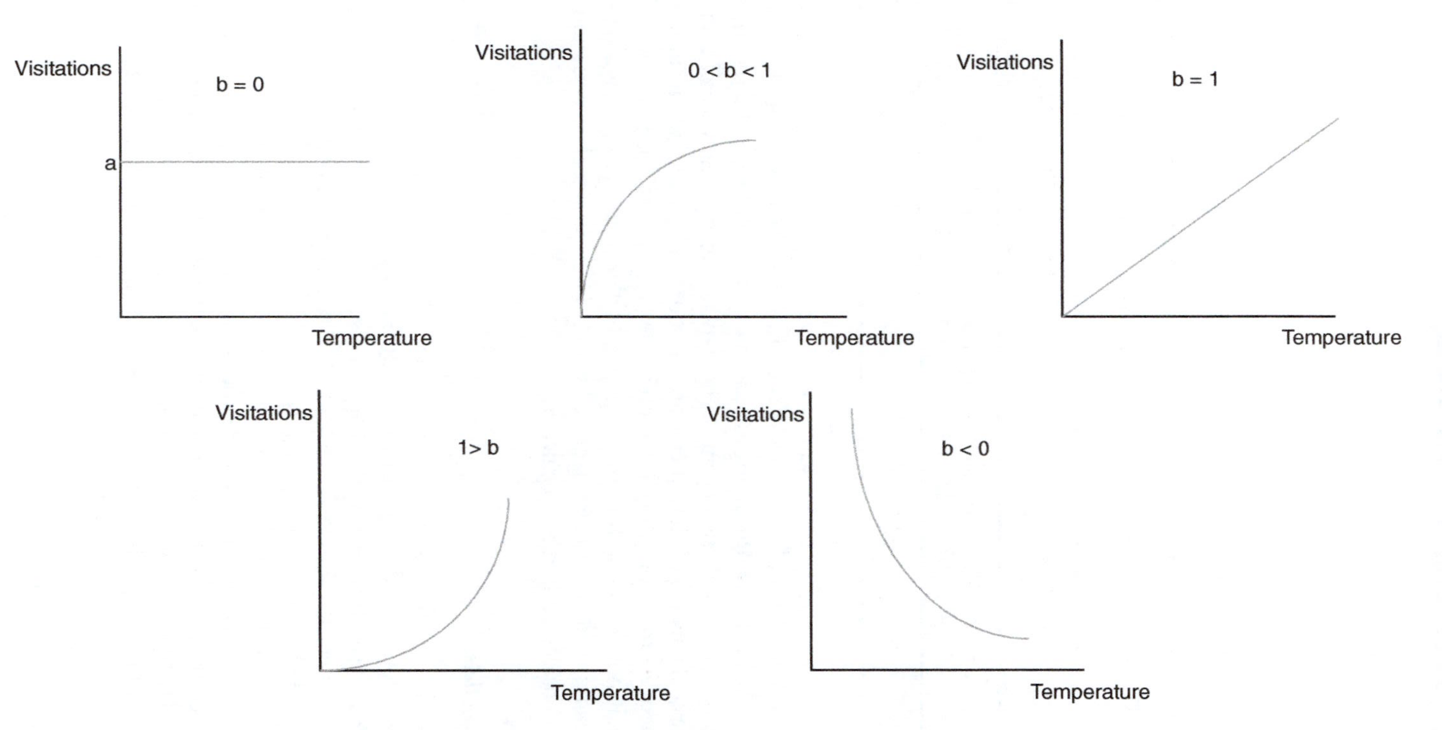

Figure 7.11 Multiplicative visitations function, various values of b.

Source: Author.

to as a *log-linear* model. This means that it would be easy to do a regression analysis, first by transforming your variables and then running your regression as always.

To be clear, to perform an estimation of this log-linear model, you would first take each of your variables—*Visitations* and *Temperature*—and create two new variables, the natural logarithm of each one. Then simply regress one on the other. The results of a simple two-variable regression of *lnVisitations* and *lnTemperature* are reported in Box 7.3.

Box 7.3 STATA regression output, log-linear visitations model, GFSP

Visitation	*Coefficient*	*Standard error*	*t*	*P>t*	*[95% Confidence interval]*	
Ln(Temperature)	2.11394	.0770306	27.44	0.000	1.962868	2.265011
Constant	−1.074938	.3239853	−3.32	0.000	−1.710335	−.4395415

Source: Author.

To interpret these results, you may want to refer back to Figure 7.11. It is interesting that the coefficient on *lnTemperature* is slightly over two, meaning that the function is increasing at an increasing rate, as in panel four. We can also tell that the coefficient is extremely significant, as its standard error is really small compared to the coefficient. This interpretation does not comport with our intuition regarding how we think people will respond to even higher temperatures when it is extremely hot. This non-intuitive result might clue us in that there is something else going on that might be captured with a different model specification. Let us now consider a different specification.

Quadratic models

An additional possibility is that at some point, the temperature may get hot enough that people decide to go to the beach instead, or choose some indoor activity like going to the movies, or perhaps even stay home. After all, who wants to go outside when it is miserably hot? So when it gets hot enough, visitations might actually fall, as shown in Figure 7.12.

The problem with all of the models we have seen so far in this chapter is that they cannot capture this type of relationship. For example, when we simply include *Temperature* as an explanatory variable, we build in an assumption about the relationship between visitations and temperature. As temperatures increase, visitations are predicted to either increase or decrease. If the coefficient on *Temperature* is positive, the model predicts visitations will increase. If the coefficient is negative, the model predicts visitations will decrease. In that model, we can have one or the other, not both. The assumption of either a positive linear or negative linear relationship is built into the model specification.

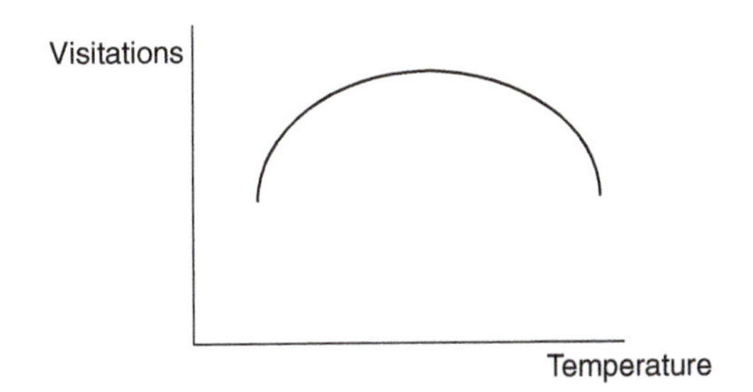

Figure 7.12 A (plausible) non-linear relationship between visitations and temperature.

Source: Author.

Similarly, if you inspect all of the possible relationships in the log-linear model in Figure 7.11, you will notice that they all involve either an increasing or decreasing relationship between visitations and temperature, again not both.

So what do we do if we believe that in reality, park visitations increase for a while over a range of values of temperature and then decrease when it starts to get uncomfortably hot?

Probably the simplest strategy is to consider quadratic functions, which you may recall take the following general form:

$$Y = a + b\,X + c\,X^2$$

Here, we say that the variable Y is a quadratic function of the variable X. In our case, we could simply apply this functional specification to model visitations as a quadratic function of temperature:

$$Visitations = a + b\ Temperature + c\ Temperature^2$$

In this model, the shape of the function depends upon the values of *b* and *c* and, in particular, whether they are positive or negative. Figure 7.13 illustrates the various possibilities. For example, the far left-hand side panel reflects the case where *b* is positive and *c* is negative. In the next panel, *b* is negative and *c* is positive. The last two panels reflect the cases where *b* and *c* are either both positive or both negative.

You will recall that this same issue of non-linearity appeared when we introduced the notion of the environmental Kuznets curve in Chapter 4. There, the proposed solution was the same: estimate a quadratic function.

The difference between that case and this one is in the predicted values of the *b* and *c* coefficients. The theory of the environmental Kuznets curve suggests a U-shaped relationship between environmental quality and economic development. This implies that the coefficients *b* and *c* will be negative and positive, respectively.

In the present example, since we would expect fewer park visitors on really hot summer days, we expect the relationship between park visitations and

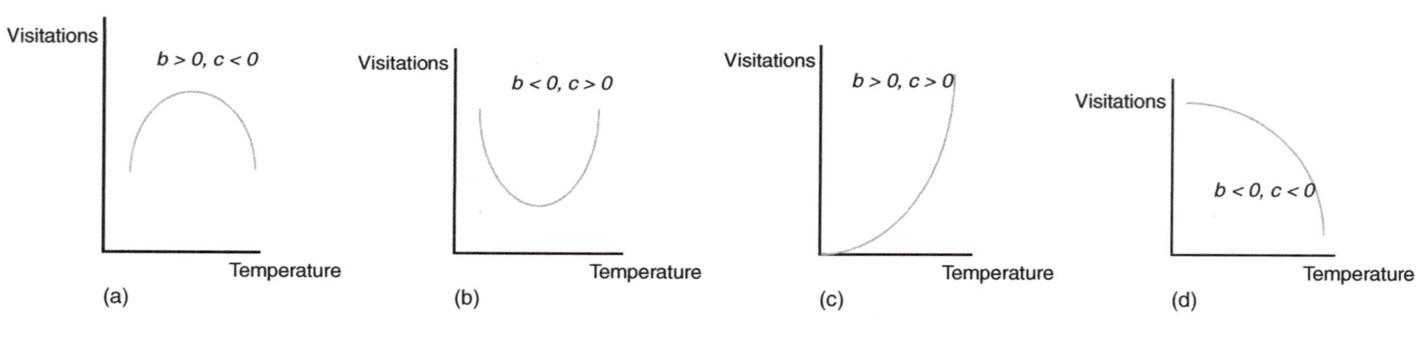

Figure 7.13 Quadratic Visitations function, various values of b and c.

Source: Author.

temperatures to be "hill-shaped." This would imply that the coefficients b and c will be positive and negative: precisely the opposite from before.

As with the log-linear model, it is easy to perform a regression analysis on the quadratic model. Again, the procedure is to first transform your variables and then run a regression. Here you create a new variable called $Temperature^2$, simply by taking your *Temperature* variable and squaring it. This new variable serves as the quadratic term in your regression model. You then add this new variable to your previous linear model. The results of this regression are reported in Box 7.4, where the coefficient on *Temperature* represents b and the coefficient on $Temperature^2$ represents c.

Box 7.4 STATA regression output, quadratic visitations model, GFSP

Visitation	*Coefficient*	*Standard error*	*t*	*P>t*	*[95% Confidence interval]*	
Temperature	161.5311	30.86907	5.23	0.000	100.991	222.0712
Temperature^2	–.6945861	.2330207	–2.98	0.003	–1.151584	–.2375883
Constant	–4795.482	1010.93	–4.74	0.000	–6778.108	–2812.836

Source: Author.

As you can see, the coefficient on *Temperature* is positive and significant, while the coefficient on *TempSquared* is negative and significant. These results strongly suggest a "hill-shaped" relationship between visitations and temperature, as in the first panel in Figure 7.12. These results comport with our intuition that when it gets hot enough, people are discouraged from visiting the park.

Bottom line: In many real-world situations, there may be reason to believe that the relationship among variables is not linear. If so, log-linear and quadratic functions may come in handy. They are easy to use and together, they allow us to capture a wide range of non-linear relationships.

How do we know it is temperatures that are affecting visitations and not something else?: Multiple Regression

Let us now return to the notion of internal validity. One serious problem with the simple visitations/temperature model is that it is overly simplistic in not accounting for other factors that might also affect park visits. These include: other *climatic* factors such as rain, flooding, and wildfires; *economic* variables such as income, gas prices, and unemployment; and *structural* factors such as holidays and weekends. To the extent that these other factors are important, the results of the simple two-variable regression may lack internal validity. That is, we may be mistaken in concluding that temperatures are affecting park visits.

However, there is another problem that arises if you don't take these other factors into account. The estimated coefficient on *Temperature* will not be reliable. That is, it won't even give you a good idea of the actual relationship between temperatures and park visits. The reasoning here is a bit esoteric, but since the issue is extremely important, let us discuss it briefly.

Suppose you were to estimate the visitations/temperature model but it turns out that you have omitted another systematically important variable that happens to be correlated with temperature. In omitting this other variable, you are in effect having your *Temperature* variable do "double duty": it is not only capturing the effect of temperatures on visitations, it is also capturing the effect of the other variable. The problem is that you will be misinterpreting its coefficient as capturing the effect of temperature alone, when in fact it is capturing both. This gives you a misleading picture of the true effect of temperature changes.

In the jargon of statistics, we say that the coefficient on *Temperature* is *biased*: it will not accurately reflect β, the true effect of temperatures on park visitations. This problem, which is called *omitted-variables bias*, is extremely common in regression analysis and needs to be guarded against.

> **Bottom line:** When you omit a systematically important variable from your regression model, this will bias the estimated coefficients of all included variables that are correlated with the omitted one (problem of *omitted-variables bias*).

How do you guard against omitted-variables bias? The short answer is to be extremely careful when you are constructing your model, making sure you consider all of the variables that are likely to be important. In doing this, you will receive guidance from your theoretical model. If it is doing its job, your model will help you to identify important factors and generate testable hypotheses. As we have seen, this is an important function of theory under the quantitative approach.

To see concretely how this is done, let us consider the model of visitations a bit more carefully in terms of theory. One way to think about people coming to visit state parks like GFSP is from an economic perspective. They are making decisions about whether to visit state parks based on costs, the amount of income they have to spend, alternative uses of their time and money, and the "quality" of the park-going experience. All of these factors are readily modeled using a simple economic model of demand (for example, see Richardson and Loomis 2004, p. 84).

According to this model, their likelihood of going to a state park (their demand for the park experience) will increase whenever any of the following occur: a reduction in the cost of a visit; an increase in their income; a reduction in the cost and attractiveness of alternatives; or an improvement in the quality of the park-going experience. A complete model will try to account for as many of these factors as it can.

An important distinction: Continuous vs. categorical variables

Before considering a specific model that more completely captures all of these different factors, we first need to draw an important distinction between so-called *continuous* and *categorical* variables.

Continuous variables are ones that can take on essentially any value over the range of values it is possible to take. For example, over the course of a year, the temperature in my home state of Minnesota can be any number between roughly –50 and 100 degrees Fahrenheit (thank goodness the range is not wider than that!). This is not exactly a purist's definition of continuous, but let us not worry about that.

Categorical variables, on the other hand, are ones that can assume only a handful of categories of values. For example, it is either snowing or it is not. One is either old enough to vote or not. It is either night or day. One could belong to any of a handful of environmental organizations. In each of these cases, the variable varies in a discrete way, with only a limited number of possibilities.

In these examples, the number of categories is usually two (though not always). When there are two categories, it is often useful, for the purpose of doing a regression analysis, to create a numerical variable that captures the different categories with values of 0 or 1. So, taking the voting variable as an example, you could create a variable that equals 1 if a person is old enough to vote and equals 0 if not.

To see how we might use a categorical variable in a regression model, consider the following (slightly) expanded version of the basic visitations model:

$$Visitations = a + b\ Temperature + c\ Weekend$$

In this expanded model, we will define *Weekend* as a categorical variable: either a particular day falls on a weekend, or it does not. Here, let *Weekend* be equal to 1 if the day falls on a weekend (that is, either Saturday or Sunday) and equal to 0 if it does not.

Notice that adding this categorical variable to the model creates two visitation models: one for weekend days and another for non-weekend days. When it is not a weekend, the *Weekend* variable equals zero and the last term disappears, leaving the original model:

$$Non\text{-}weekend\ Visitations = a + b\ Temperature$$

However, on weekends, the *Weekend* variable equals one and then the model becomes:

$$Weekend\ Visitations = (a + c) + b\ Temperature$$

In this last equation, the term involving c has become a constant and so I have simply added it to the other constant in the model a.

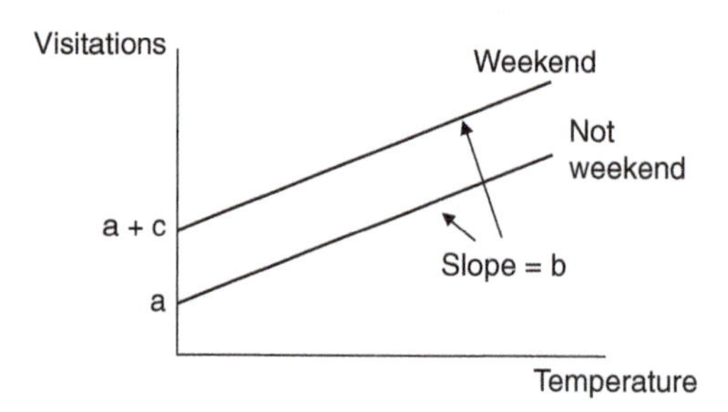

Figure 7.14 Basic visitations model with *Weekend* categorical variable.
Source: Author.

Notice that the two models are parallel vertical displacements of each other. They both have the same slope *b*, but they are separated by the vertical distance equal to *c*, the coefficient on the *Weekend* dummy variable (see Figure 7.14).

To see how well this new model is working, consider the regression output in Box 7.5 for the model that also includes the *Weekend* categorical variable. First, notice the extremely significant coefficients on both *Temperature* and *Weekend*, as evidenced by the extremely large t-ratios. These results tell us that daily visits are systematically affected by both temperatures and whether or not it happens to be a weekend day.

Box 7.5 Regression output, simple visitations model plus categorical variable

Visitation	*Coefficient*	*Standard error*	*t*	*P>t*	*[95% Confidence interval]*	
Temperature	71.43853	2.582079	27.67	0.000	66.37458	76.50248
Weekend	1511.781	55.90479	27.04	0.000	1402.141	1621.421
Constant	–2376.188	177.5343	–13.38	0.000	–2724.366	–2028.009

Source: Author.

Interpreting the coefficients, we see that visitations tend to increase as temperatures increase: for every one degree increase in temperature the model predicts that visitations will increase by 71.44 per day. Also, notice that visitations are higher on weekends, as evidenced by the coefficient *c* being positive (and highly significant!). This would certainly accord with our intuition that visitations will tend to be higher on weekends. Specifically, the model predicts that there would be 1511.78 more visitors on an average weekend day. The 95% confidence intervals for both coefficients are quite small relative to the magnitude of the coefficients, suggesting that the estimates are fairly reliable.

Bottom line: Categorical (dummy) variables can be used to capture influences that vary discretely; that is, ones that only take on a few discrete values. The coefficient on the categorical variable is interpreted as the change in the predicted *level* of the variable whose behavior you are trying to explain.

More complete multiple regression

The model estimated in Box 7.5 is an example of a multiple regression model. This simply means that there is more than one explanatory variable. In that model, there is one continuous variable (*Temperature*) and one categorical variable (*Weekend*), but a multiple regression model can contain any number of continuous and/or categorical variables. That model was more intended to illustrate the use of categorical variables than to model the determinants of visitations in any complete way.

For a more complete model based in theory, let us return to the demand framework we were considering earlier. Consider, for example, the following model, which is not comprehensive but models a number of additional factors that a demand model suggests might matter.

$$Visitations = a + b\ Temperature + c\ Precipitation + d\ PCIncome + e\ Weekend$$

So in addition to temperatures and peak weekend periods, this expanded model includes (daily) precipitation and a measure for per capita state income (a measure of general economic conditions in the state). Thus, this model controls for another climate variable that plausibly affects the quality of the park-going experience; economic conditions; and a structural variable that captures possibly greater demand on weekends.

The results of a multiple regression analysis of this model are reported in Box 7.6. These results show that all of these variables seem to have systematic impacts on visitations at GFSP. As before, visitations are higher on weekends and when it is warmer. We now see, however, that other factors matter as well. The negative coefficient on *Precipitation* indicates that visitations tend to fall when it rains, a sensible result. We also see that visitations tend to increase when economic conditions are better, as evidenced by the positive coefficient on *PCIncome*. This, too, comports with our intuition. We can be pretty confident in all of these conclusions because the t-ratios exceed two in absolute value and therefore pass the rough rule for statistical significance.

Box 7.6 Regression output, more complete visitations model

Visitation	*Coefficient*	*Standard error*	*t*	*P>t*	*[95% Confidence interval]*	
Temperature	71.3012	2.543032	28.04	0.000	66.31385	76.28859
Precipitation	−576.393	79.79676	−7.22	0.000	−732.8898	−419.8963
PCIncome	.0576479	.0189218	3.05	0.000	.0205386	.0947573
Weekend	1511.033	55.05748	27.44	0.000	1403.054	1619.011
Constant	−4995.977	902.6104	−5.54	0.000	−6766.169	−3225.785

Source: Author.

Just one more point about the multiple regression model, and for this, let us return to our earlier discussion of non-linear relationships. In particular, we saw some evidence earlier that suggested a non-linear relationship between park visitations and temperature. At very high temperatures, visitations may actually fall, presumably because torrid conditions reduce the quality of the park-going experience.

That finding was arrived at in the context of a simple model in which visitations were assumed to be influenced by temperatures alone. You should bear in mind that non-linear relationships may also be incorporated into a more complete multiple regression model, which includes other determinants of visitation behavior.

So, for example, consider the regression output in Box 7.7. This model includes the same explanatory variables as in the previous model, except that we have added the variable *Temperature*^{2}. Notice that the same pattern of non-linearity emerges here in the more complete model: a positive coefficient on *Temperature* and a negative coefficient on *Temperature*^{2}. So this tells us that even controlling for other important variables, the result that visitations are discouraged at extremely high temperatures can be found in the data.

Box 7.7 Regression output, more complete visitations model, non-linearity in temperature

Visitation	*Coefficient*	*Standard error*	*t*	*P>t*	*[95% Confidence interval]*	
Temperature	179.5513	25.87619	6.94	0.000	128.8031	230.2994
Weekend	1513.654	54.82527	27.61	0.000	1406.132	1621.177
Precipitation	−591.4737	79.53602	−7.44	0.000	−747.4591	−435.4883
PCIncome	.0574852	.0188409	3.05	0.002	.0205346	.0944357
Temperature^2	.8211031	.1953353	−4.20	0.000	−1.204193	−.4380132
Constant	−8474.307	1221.661	−6.94	0.000	−10870.22	−6078.396

Source: Author.

Conclusions

This chapter has presented and described some more advanced concepts and techniques that are commonly used in quantitative analysis of environmental issues. I hope that it is clear that this chapter was not meant to be comprehensive in its treatment. Even combined with the discussion in Chapter 6, we could not hope to cover or even do justice to the enormously rich set of statistical tools that are available for performing quantitative analyses.

However, I hope that by now you have a better sense of how the quantitative approach enables us to answer two important questions: (1) What is the quantitative nature of the relationship among variables? and (2) How do we go about testing hypotheses regarding these relationships? Being able to answer these two questions within particular settings is the primary focus of much quantitative research on the environment. The concepts and techniques that we have presented here are powerful tools that can be used to gain insight into a wide range of environmental issues.

Moving forward, you are strongly encouraged to use this material as a starting point for your own quantitative research. This means that once you have identified a research question that you think is amenable to quantitative analysis, think about how the arguments presented here apply to your own specific question. And your own research project may have to dig deeper, applying additional concepts and techniques that we have been unable to cover here. Consider yourself to be at the beginning of a journey to learn and master quantitative techniques of analysis, which if you are interested enough can be a life-long process.

Exercises/discussion questions

(1) Studies have found that children who play outdoors express more interest in protecting the environment (Hindustantimes 2017). Discuss the internal validity of concluding that there is a causal relationship.

(2) Comment on the external validity of surveying students at your university to draw conclusions on the following issues, for the specified population:

- Issue: Support for endangered species protection; Population: US citizenry.
- Issue: Opposition to free trade; Population: Local residents.
- Issue: Support for local dedicated bike trails; Population: Local residents.

(3) Consider the example in the chapter of trying to determine whether two math exams are equally difficult. Can you think of a sampling procedure that would effectively address the issue of sample selection bias and allow you to draw the appropriate conclusion?

(4) You are trying to gauge the overall level of interest in adopting a particular program of voluntary energy conservation measures in your freshman residence hall. For this, you propose to survey residents in the hall, in which you ask them the yes-or-no question: *Would you participate?* Consider each of the following ways to sample residents. In each case, would you expect there to be sample selection bias?

- An in-person cluster sample of all residents living on the first floor.
- Taking an alphabetized list of all residents and e-mailing every fourth person on the list.
- A questionnaire handed out at an ice-cream social during New Students Week.

(5) Consider the output in Box 7.1. You want to test the hypothesis that a one-degree increase in temperature increases park visits by fifty visitors per day.

- State the null and alternative hypotheses in the format given in the text.
- Assuming a 5% significance level, calculate the acceptance region and critical region for the test.
- Perform the test.

(6) Consider the output in Box 7.3. Calculate the predicted number of visitors when it is 70 degrees.

(7) For each of the following examples, consider whether you think the relationship may be considered linear. If not, which of the non-linear functions would be appropriate?

- 100-yard dash time as a function of age.
- Market value of a house as a function of the age of the house.
- Winter tourism on the North Shore as a function of snow depth.

(8) Consider the output in Box 7.4. What is the predicted number of visitors when it is 70 degrees? 90 degrees? *Extra credit challenge*: At what temperature does the model predict that visitors will be at a maximum?

(9) Consider the output in Box 7.5. What is the predicted number of visitors on a Friday when it is 80 degrees? On a Sunday?

(10) In each of the following cases, would you expect there to be omitted-variables bias?

- Lifetime earnings as a function of IQ.
- College GPA as a function of SAT score.
- College GPA in math courses as a function of SAT math score.

(11) For the purposes of doing a regression analysis, which of the following variables would you treat as continuous, and which would you treat as categorical?

- Eligibility to drink alcohol, legally.
- The seasons of the year.
- MPAA movie ratings.
- The number of your siblings.

(12) Consider the output in Box 7.6 and, in particular, the estimated coefficient on temperature. Would you expect this estimate to suffer from omitted-variables bias?

Additional resources

Berry, Donald A., and Bernard W. Lindgren. *Statistics: Theory and Methods*. Belmont: Wadsworth, 1996.

Chapter 15 provides a good clear discussion of regression analysis, if you are mathematically inclined.

Byrkit, Donald R. *Statistics Today: A Comprehensive Introduction*. Menlo Park: Cummings, 1987.

Intermediate-level discussion of statistical concepts and methods, complete with many exercises and applications. Chapters 13 and 14 provide a good discussion of regression analysis.

Foster, Jeremy, Emma Barkus, and Christian Yavorsky. *Understanding and Using Advanced Statistics*. London: Sage, 2006.

Nice, relatively non-mathematical introduction to more advanced statistical tools and approaches. Highly recommended if you are interested in what comes after multiple regression analysis.

Fox, John. *An R and S-Plus Companion to Applied Regression*. Thousand Oaks: Sage, 2002.

A useful, statistical software-oriented approach to data analysis, which illustrates many of the practical nuts-and-bolts steps involved in carrying out the analysis when working with statistical software.

Kahane, Leo H. *Regression Basics*. Thousand Oaks: Sage, 2001.

A very clear, brief introduction to regression analysis.

Note

1 This 0–1 categorical variable is sometimes called a *dummy* variable.

References

"Kids who Love Nature and Play Outdoors More Likely to Protect Environment," *Hindustantimes*, March 18, 2017, http://www.hindustantimes.com/health-and-fitness/kids-who-love-nature-and-play-outdoors-more-likely-to-protect-environment/story-JRWNWFIEORrM44SplzKAnM.html

Richardson, Robert B., and John B. Loomis. "Adaptive Recreation Planning and Climate Change: A Contingent Visitation Approach," *Ecological Economics* 50(2004): 83–99.

8 Spatial analysis and GIS

Introduction

Let us now turn to yet another tool for quantitative analysis of environmental issues that has emerged in recent years: *spatial analysis*. Spatial analysis involves using various tools and databases in order to characterize spatially distributed variables as well as the relationship among these variables. Its particular value in studying the environment comes from the fact that many environmental issues have a spatial component. Spatial analysis uses information on spatial variation to allow us to characterize the spatial extent of environmental problems and the spatial relationship among variables.

It turns out that these capabilities allow us to answer a number of important research questions regarding the environment. Examples of such questions include:

- Are environmental conditions improving over time? How do they vary from location to location?
- How has climate change affected water availability and streamflows?
- Who bears the costs of environmental contaminants?
- How can we most effectively manage our national parks?
- How much do people value environmental amenities?
- What is the environmental impact of the spread of invasive species?

Each of these particular questions has been the focus of a recent study involving the use of spatial analysis. We will be returning to several of these questions later in the chapter.

To be clear, this chapter is not intended to provide a complete discussion of how to do a spatial analysis. This turns out to be a rather complex undertaking that involves working with spatial data and learning software for spatial data analysis such as ArcGIS. If you have chosen a research question that seems conducive to spatial analysis, you will have to acquire further training in the concepts and techniques of spatial analysis.

The spatial nature of many environmental issues

As a tool for studying the environment, spatial analysis capitalizes on two important factors. The first is that all environmental issues have a spatial dimension. For example, deforestation is about reduction in forest cover and potential loss of habitat in some particular region. Climate change is about the dispersion of greenhouse gases around the globe. The problems of air and water pollution are about the emissions of various contaminants that affect others in a city, neighborhood, watershed, and so forth.

Whenever there is a spatial component to an environmental issue, this raises the possibility of an analysis based upon spatial variation. And sometimes the result of this analysis can yield remarkably useful insights.

To illustrate this point, consider the famous case of John Snow. Snow was a physician who lived in London in the mid-nineteenth century. At the time, London was suffering from a terrible outbreak of cholera and nobody really knew why. The prevailing theory was that cholera was transmitted by foul-smelling air (called *miasma*) from industrial processes such as the tanning of animal hides and the boiling of soap. But if this was true, nobody could understand why it was that only certain people were dying of cholera. Snow, however, suspected that cholera was caused not by bad air, but rather by contaminated water (Tufte 1997; Ball 2009).

In order to solve the mystery, Snow took it upon himself to walk around London and record on a map the location of every cholera death. By observing the overall spatial pattern of deaths and collecting other information, he was able to isolate the apparent cause: one particular contaminated well.

Figure 8.1 shows a copy of part of Snow's map of the cholera incidents. In the center of the map is the well (marked "Pump") from which contaminated water was being pumped. The black bars indicate the number of deaths at each address along the nearby streets. On the basis of his evidence, Snow was able to convince local officials to remove the handle from the pump to keep people from using the well. The cholera outbreak soon subsided.

Today, Snow is hailed by many as a hero and one of the fathers of epidemiology for discovering the cause of cholera: water-borne bacteria, not foul-smelling air. But the important point here is that he was among the first researchers in history to perform a spatial analysis in order to gain insight into an environmental problem.

To convey a better sense for how spatial analysis might be used to address contemporary environmental problems, let us consider three recent examples of scholarly studies that have used spatial analysis.

National park planning in Victoria, Australia

In a recent study, the researchers Greg Brown and Delene Weber were interested in using spatial analysis to improve national park management in Australia (Brown and Weber 2011). Their study involved conducting a survey that asked park visitors a series of questions regarding their park experiences as well as some personal information.

Figure 8.1 Part of John Snow's cholera map.

Source: Wikimedia commons.

As part of the survey, which was conducted on-line, respondents who had visited the parks were able to place markers on a map of the parks that indicated two things: (1) what sorts of experiences they had (e.g., wildlife viewing, overnight camping), and (2) what sorts of environmental impacts they had observed (e.g., degraded trail or campsite conditions, trash) in specific park locations. These responses could then to be used to identify specific locations that were subject to particularly heavy use, and environmental "hotspots" where environmental impacts were particularly severe.

Impacts of toxic atmospheric releases in southern California

As another example of the spatial nature of environmental problems and the potential value of the analysis of spatial patterns, consider a recent study by the sociologists Manuel Pastor, James Sadd, and Rachel Morello-Frosch (Pastor et al. 2004).

You may know that the Environmental Protection Agency (EPA) keeps track of manufacturing facilities, or so-called *toxic release inventory (TRI) facilities*, that emit significant amounts of toxic chemical substances into the atmosphere. In their study, Pastor and his co-authors used publicly available spatial data to investigate whether the siting of toxic air release facilities in southern California was differentially affecting different groups of people living in the area.

Working with maps of the locations of TRI facilities and location-specific demographic census data, the authors were able to document a correlation between the location of facilities and concentrations of various ethnic groups. According to their analysis, toxic contaminants were being borne most heavily by certain groups, especially Latinos. They concluded that there might be some previously overlooked issues of environmental justice in the siting process.

Lead contamination in Syracuse, New York

As a final example, consider a study by the researchers David Griffith and several co-authors that used spatial analysis to examine lead contamination in Syracuse, New York (Griffith et al. 1998). These researchers wanted to know whether a spatial analysis could provide any insight into the extent of lead contamination, the sources of this contamination, and who was being affected. Their specific focus was very young children under the age of five.

Using maps of Syracuse and hospital records for cases of elevated pediatric blood-lead levels over a three-year period, they discovered a pronounced spatial pattern of elevated blood-lead levels, particularly in African-American and Hispanic neighborhoods.

Their analysis also provided insight into the likely causes of lead contamination. First, they did not find strong evidence of elevated blood-lead levels near major traffic arteries. Second, they found strong evidence that the incidence of elevated blood-lead levels was highest among children around the age of two. On the basis of these findings, they concluded that lead exposure was likely mostly attributable to lead-based paint (which was most likely to be ingested by young toddlers) and less attributable to the use of leaded gasoline, which had been phased out of use starting in the 1970s.

Geographic information systems (GIS)

The fact that so many environmental issues have a spatial dimension provides an opportunity for researchers to study environmental problems by analyzing spatial patterns. However, taking advantage of this opportunity requires the technical capability to analyze these patterns. The second important reason for the recent surge in the use of spatial analysis to study the environment is an explosion of enormous amounts of spatial data of various kinds, along with the development of powerful tools to analyze these data. This has all come together in the new and booming field of *geographic information science*.

The term geographic information science refers to the systematic study of information contained in geographic databases. These databases are contained within computer-based systems that capture and store geographic information and then provide tools to manipulate, analyze, and display the information visually. Systems that do all of these things are called *geographic information systems*. Both "geographic information systems" and "geographic information science" can be, and often are, represented with the same acronym GIS. In this discussion, we will use GIS to refer to geographic information systems, which is probably the more common usage.

Geographic information systems have been created, in essence, so that researchers can apply quantitative techniques to what have historically been non-quantitative spatial data. Spatial data have, of course, historically been represented on maps of various kinds and that remains true to this day. Until fairly recently, however, maps were drawn almost exclusively on paper, which presented major challenges to performing a rigorous spatial analysis of the data.

Consider, for example, the difficulties experienced by John Snow in doing his spatial analysis of cholera outbreaks in 1854 London. He had to trudge around the streets of the city identifying every location where a cholera death occurred. He then went back home, took out a map of London and marked each of the locations in ink. Standing back and looking at the map confirmed the spatial concentration of deaths around the contaminated well.

But to corroborate his suspicions, he then went out and collected voluminous hospital and public health records on the timing of the deaths and whether the victims had in fact drunk water from the well. Performing this analysis required Snow to undergo an incredibly laborious and time-consuming process.

Nowadays, many maps exist in electronic format, which has made access to spatial data much easier and has hugely expanded the boundaries of what we can do, for a couple of related reasons.

First of all, access to a great deal of spatial information is only a couple of clicks away on your computer. For example, I just spent a couple of minutes in Google Earth locating an image of my college (Figure 8.2). Here, you can see every physical feature of the college, including the football stadium on the left near the river and two artificial lakes on the upper right. And, again, accessing this image and downloading it onto my computer took almost no time at all.

As another example, I was recently looking for historical information on water projects in the western United States and came across the map shown in Figure 8.3. This is a map of a proposed dam in the northern part of California on the Trinity River. This map was created using digitized GIS data.

Second, once we have spatial data like this in electronic form, there are a whole lot of things we can do with it. The past twenty years or so have seen an explosion of creative energies devoted to creating computer applications to work with spatial data. Furthermore, we can now take all sorts of data—environmental, economic, political, social, and cultural—and display it spatially. These two developments have paved the way for social scientific analyses of spatial data on a wide range of environmental issues.

Figure 8.2 Google Earth image of Carleton College.

Source: Google.

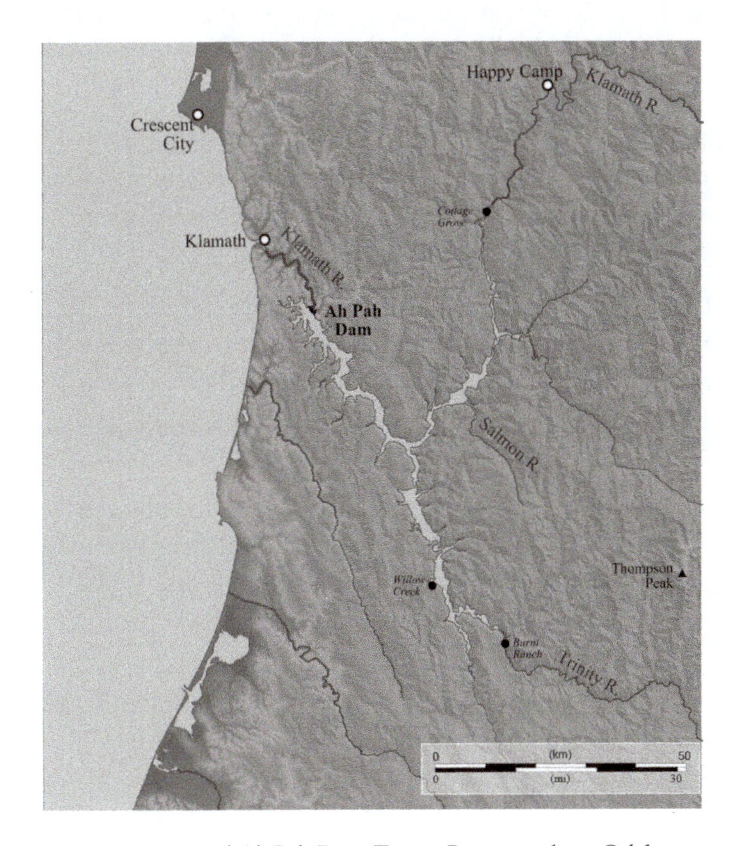

Figure 8.3 Proposed Ah Pah Dam, Trinity River, northern California.

Source: Wikimedia commons.

Some fundamentals of spatial analysis

To begin with, recall a key objective of much environmental research: to characterize a functional relationship among variables. In the quantitative approach we have seen so far, this is done by collecting data on different variables and seeing how their numerical values are correlated by performing some sort of statistical analysis. The spatial approach is to take variables that vary across space and see how their spatial patterns are correlated.

To see the basic idea, consider the study that we saw earlier by Pastor and his co-authors on the siting of toxic release facilities in southern California. In Figure 8.4 is shown an (extremely!) stylized map of an area of southern California that is divided up into sixteen neighborhoods. Here, "W" denotes a white neighborhood and "L" denotes a Latino neighborhood.

Now suppose there happen to be three toxic release facilities in this area, and we know where they are located. In Figure 8.5, I have taken the map of the neighborhoods and added the information on the toxic release facility sites, which are denoted by asterisks. In this example, the facility sites all happen to be located within Latino neighborhoods, so that Latinos appear to be bearing all of the environmental costs associated with living near the facilities. This analysis could be the basis for critiquing siting decisions on environmental justice grounds, as Pastor and his co-authors concluded.

One of the challenging things about doing spatial analysis is that spatial patterns are not always clear-cut. Figure 8.6 shows another possible way the facilities

L	W	L	W
W	L	W	L
L	W	W	W
W	W	W	L

Figure 8.4 A stylized region with different ethnic neighborhoods.

Source: Author.

L	W	L	W
W	*L	W	L
L*	W	W	W
W	W	W	L*

Figure 8.5 One possible siting of toxic release facilities across ethnic neighborhoods.

Source: Author.

L	W*	L	W
W	L	W	L
L*	W	W	W
W	W	W	*L

Figure 8.6 Another possible siting of toxic release facilities.

Source: Author.

could be located in space. Here, one of the sites happens to be located in a white neighborhood. And so even though it *looks* like Latinos are bearing a disproportionate share of the siting costs (after all, there are fewer Latino neighborhoods and they contain more sites), the evidence taken as a whole is less conclusive of a race-correlated pattern of siting. Recalling the discussion of Chapter 7, in quantitative terms there may not be a statistically significant difference between the chances that Latino neighborhoods and white neighborhoods will have a site. We will return to this issue shortly.

The example provided in Figures 8.4 to 8.6 is extremely stylized in order to give you the basic idea behind (much) spatial analysis. In fact, actually performing spatial analyses is considerably more involved for a number of reasons. First and most obviously, most spatial data will not be taking these nice convenient rectangular shapes, because the world is a much messier place.

For example, consider Figure 8.7, which contains a map created by Pastor and his co-authors that shows the actual mapping of toxic release facilities across southern California (Pastor et al. 2004, p. 426). In this figure, the darker shaded areas contain greater percentages of "people of color." Pastor and his co-authors conclude that people of color are disproportionately bearing the costs of the siting decisions, because the sites appear to be concentrated in the darker areas.

This map was, of course, created using GIS. I will not explain all of the technical details regarding how this map was constructed, but there are a few things you should know.

Creating maps

A caveat on map-making

To begin with, it is worth mentioning that taking specific locations on the planet and creating maps is no easy task. What you are doing is taking locations that exist in three-dimensional space and representing them in a two-dimensional

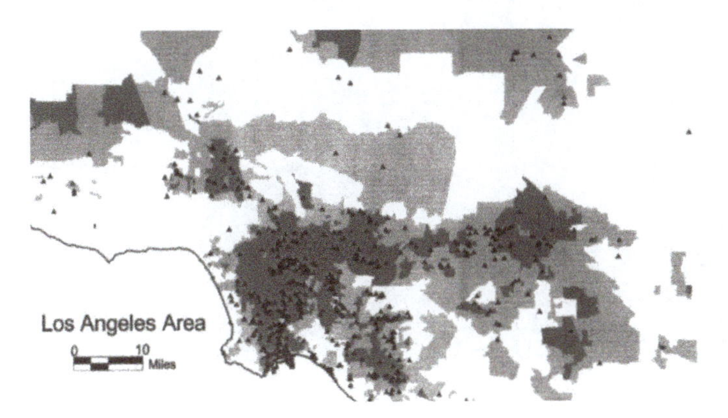

Figure 8.7 Toxic release facilities and ethnic neighborhoods, southern California, 2000.

medium, such as a Google Earth image that appears on your flat computer monitor. The question is how to do this and still provide a realistic sense of true locations and distances as they exist in the real world. Cartographers have been struggling with this issue for a long time.

For example, consider Figure 8.8, which shows a map of the world. In this map, the lines of longitude are shown as running in parallel. This method, pioneered by the Flemish cartographer Gerardus Mercator many years ago, was used for a long time because it helped ship captains stay on course when they were out at sea. Say you were out on the open seas and you wanted to reach a particular island. This map would show you that the island was precisely 23 degrees to the Northwest, and you could use your compass to guide you there.

The problem with this map is that it distorts distances to make objects seem bigger than they really are, especially at higher latitudes. For example, look at the size of Antarctica. On this map, it appears to be larger than all of the rest of the land masses put together, when it is actually quite small, comparatively speaking. Notice also the size of Greenland. This map makes it appear to be about as large as Africa. In actuality, Africa is more than *fourteen* times as large as Greenland!

Figure 8.8 Mercator-style map of the world.

Source: Wikimedia commons.

The reason Antarctica and Greenland look so large on this Mercator-style map is that lines of longitude are not parallel in the real world but converge on two points: the North Pole and the South Pole. At locations near the poles, different lines of longitude are really close together. By drawing them as parallel, this type of map takes tiny distances and shows them as huge.

Over time, map-making has become increasingly refined, so that we have become much better at accurately representing distances and locations on flat maps as they actually occur in the real world. However, it is useful to keep in mind that all two-dimensional representations of three-dimensional reality will contain some distortions. This includes maps created by GIS. However, for your purposes, you can consider GIS maps to be pretty accurate. And if you go on to take coursework in GIS, you will find that GIS allows you to work with maps in order to minimize distortions of distances and shapes (Delaney 1999, p. 44).

Bottom line: One of the practical challenges of GIS is to represent actual geographic features in the real world on two-dimensional maps. It is useful to keep in mind that any GIS map you will be working with will contain some distortions of real-world shapes and distances.

Vector and raster: Two general ways to create maps in GIS

So let us assume that GIS-created maps such as the earlier one of southern California are reasonably accurate. How exactly are these maps made? Answer: By using locational information; namely, information on the precise locations of every facility, as well as on the boundaries of all of the shaded areas.

Every place on earth is, of course, located at a particular latitude and longitude. The building where my office is located at my college, for example, lies at a latitude of 44.4608 degrees North and a longitude of 93.1560 degrees West, according to Google. Similarly, each one of the toxic release facilities in southern California is located at a particular latitude and longitude. GIS can take this information and display it visually, as in this map.

Drawing the boundaries of the shaded areas is a slightly tougher nut to crack, because these are not individual locations but entire *series* of locations (that is, every point on the boundary). However, it obviously does not present insuperable challenges to draw these boundaries, or Pastor et al. would not have been able to make this nice map. GIS can draw boundaries on a map in one of two ways: either using *vector* data, or *raster* data.

To understand vector and raster data, consider the somewhat less stylized shape of a set of neighborhoods depicted in Figure 8.9. Here, these six neighborhoods are irregularly shaped and butt up against each other in irregular ways. Suppose this was the way the neighborhoods were actually situated in real life.

Vector data consists of individual points on a grid, which may be connected using straight lines, or vectors. Given the locations A and B, for example, a GIS

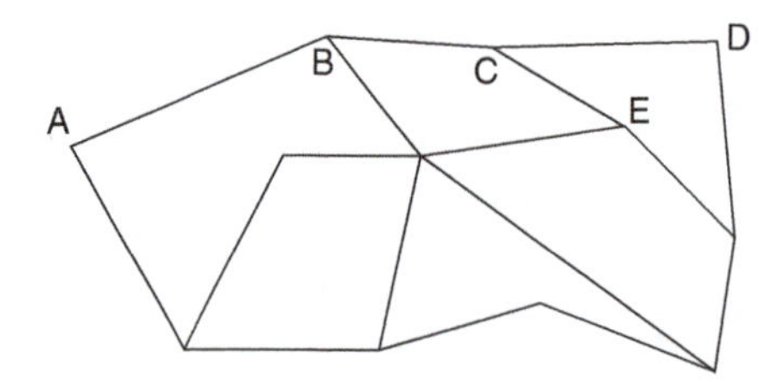

Figure 8.9 Six stylized neighborhoods.

Source: Author.

program using vector data could draw the boundary in between as a straight line between the two points. If the program had the locations of all of the vertices shown here—that is, C, D, E, etc.—it could create all of the boundaries and, thus, it could spatially represent all of the neighborhoods. Thus, vector data consists of points, lines, and polygons.

By contrast, raster data is comprised of pixels, kind of like the images created by a smart phone or digital camera. Using raster data, the program would create a grid of pixels and create the polygons as sets of pixels, grouped together on the basis of location on the map. For example, when Brown and Weber constructed their map of environmental hotspots in those Australian national parks, they used raster data where each cell was color-coded according to the number of environmental impact responses they received (Brown and Weber 2011, p. 11).

To summarize this discussion of raster and vector data, Figure 8.10 illustrates the basic difference between a vector and a raster data depiction of the real world. Both depictions are of a stylized landscape consisting of a river with a smaller tributary flowing into it from the north. In the left-hand side, vector depiction of the world, the sectors of this landscape are drawn in outline using vectors. In the right-hand side, raster depiction, the entire landscape is represented as a grid of pixels and the different sectors are shown as groups of different colored pixels (for more information, see DeMers 1997, pp. 97–115).

When you do a spatial analysis using a software package like ArcGIS, you will have the option of using either raster or vector data. In choosing which one to use, you may want to keep in mind that each type of data has certain advantages and disadvantages. On the one hand, vector data allow you to represent borders and polygons more faithfully than raster data: that is, more like how they actually appear in the real world. This is particularly true at levels of low resolution, where

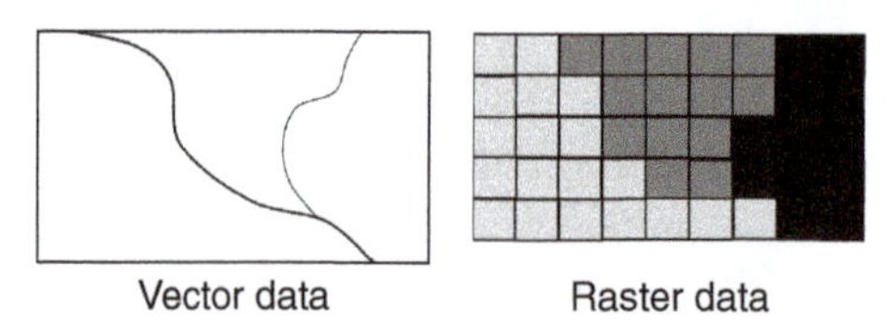

Figure 8.10 Vector vs. raster data.

Source: Author.

raster maps can start to look "pixelated," like images taken on a cheap smart phone if you blow them up to large poster-sized images.

On the other hand, vector data are less well-suited to representing data that can take on an entire continuum of values. For example, in their study, Brown and Weber wanted to provide a visual representation of the study area that showed environmental impacts of various intensities. They did this using raster data where various concentrations of environmental impacts were color-coded (Brown and Weber 2011, p. 11). This information would have been considerably harder to show effectively using vector data.

Bottom line: GIS permits you to represent spatial features on maps using either vector or raster data, each of which has advantages and disadvantages. Raster data can appear pixelated when magnified, but permit a finer gradation of color representations of various physical features.

Visual spatial correlation

This discussion of raster data and vector data explains the basic idea behind creating individual maps. However, it has glossed over one important issue: how you use maps to determine the spatial correlation among different variables. The toxic release facilities example made it sound like you could create, using either vector or raster data, one map with the boundaries of the different demographic areas and then just draw the location of the facilities on this map. In fact, there was something more complicated going on, which is a fundamental feature of GIS: namely, the creation and use of different overlapping maps.

In general, when you work with different variables in GIS, you create a map for each individual variable. For example, in the toxic releases example, you would have created one map for the different demographic areas, and then another map showing the locations of the toxic release facilities. And then, once you have these two maps, you create a composite map that basically superimposes these maps on each other. Each of the individual maps then becomes a *layer* in the composite map. But the layers are transparent, so that all of the information shown in each individual map can be seen in the composite map (DeMers 1997, pp. 320–47).

In this way, you can visually represent correlations among variables, such as between the location of toxic release facilities and residential concentrations of different ethnic groups.

One really nice feature of this layering approach is flexibility: it may permit you to investigate all sorts of different spatial relationships. This is because it is commonly possible to define many spatial layers. These would include physical features that are commonly found on maps, such as rivers, lakes, roads, streets, hills, and valleys. It could also include digital information from satellites, such as land cover, farmlands, and forests. And it could also include socioeconomic information collected by the government, such as population, income levels, and ethnic diversity. In many cases, all of these variables and more can be electronically mapped and made the subject of a spatial analysis.

Spatial correlation and spatial regression

The type of analysis we have just seen—overlaying layers representing different variables and visually inspecting maps for spatial correlations—can often tell us a lot about whether variables are correlated. However, visual inspection may often not provide a good sense for *how strongly* they are correlated. We saw this earlier, for example, in the stylized example of different ethnic neighborhoods depicted in Figures 8.4 to 8.6. Even in the detailed map of toxic release facilities in southern California shown in Figure 8.7, it is difficult to get a sense of how concentrated the facilities are in the ethnic neighborhoods. Simple visual inspection cannot always tell us what we need to know.

One of the nice features of GIS is its ability to create numerical measures of the strength of the relationship among spatially distributed variables, along with measures of statistical significance. These are done by performing *spatial correlation* and *spatial regression*.

Spatial correlation

As a starting point, it is useful to keep in mind that spatial correlation is very similar to the notion of correlation that we first encountered in Chapter 6. In both cases, the question is: How do different variables move in relation to each other? Adding the spatial dimension complicates how we calculate the relationship, but it does not change our interpretation of what it means for the variables to be correlated.

Suppose, for example, that you wanted to determine whether toxic release facilities were concentrated in particular ethnic neighborhoods. One strategy might be to simply compare the ethnic make-up of areas near the facilities to that of areas farther away.

Doing this would require that we define what it means for an area to be "near" a facility. One way to do this would be to locate every facility and draw a circle around it with a radius of a particular distance, say, one mile (see Figure 8.11). These circles would comprise areas "near" facilities. And then you could examine census data to see the percentages of households in each circle from different ethnic categories and compare these to the corresponding percentages in other areas.

Pastor and his co-authors did all this and found that neighborhoods near the facilities (that is, located within one mile) were over 41.9% Latino, compared to about 25% Latino in other neighborhoods. They concluded that there was suggestive evidence that Latinos were disproportionately bearing the burden of the siting decisions for toxic release facilities (Pastor et al. 2004, p. 425).

As another example, Brown and Weber were interested in visitor perceptions of environmental impacts in various national parks around Victoria, Australia (Brown and Weber 2011, pp. 9–10). They took survey responses regarding different types of impacts and located them on a map of the entire area. They found that around two-thirds of all reported impacts were located in one national park, suggesting that efforts to address impacts might target this park. Here, the relevant units of analysis were not one-mile-radius circles, but rather individual national parks.

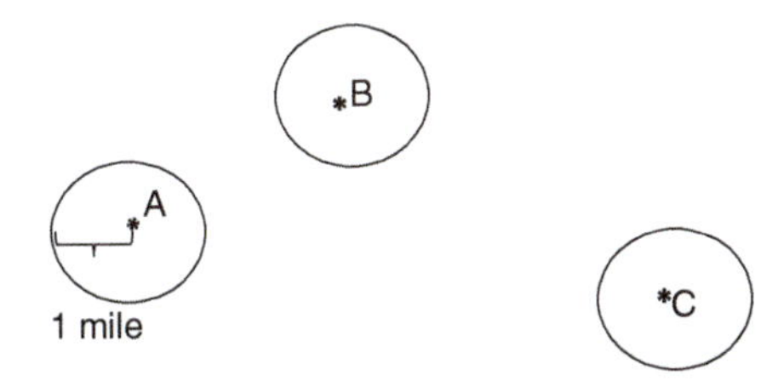

Figure 8.11 Areas "near" toxic release facilities.
Source: Author.

They then proceeded to break the responses down by type of environmental impact and found systematic differences across the parks. So, for example, one park had the highest reported percentage of degraded campsite impacts, while another had the highest percentage of impacts on local water quality. These findings suggested how park managers might set priorities for addressing impacts and permit them to effectively target different types of impacts.

Spatial regression

One takeaway message of this discussion is that the ability to quantify spatial impacts and spatial correlations may provide a clearer understanding of environmental problems than mere visual inspection of maps. However, simple statistics like percentages may not tell us what we need to know. This would especially be the case in complex situations where there may be many relevant factors.

Consider, for example, Pastor's conclusion that Latinos may be bearing a disproportionate burden of the siting of toxic release facilities. This conclusion was based on a simple correlation of the proportions of Latino vs. non-Latino populations in areas near to, versus far from, the locations of the facilities. The problem is that other factors besides ethnicity may also be important in determining whether a household lives near a facility.

One other systematic factor might be household income level. You might expect, for example, that low-income households might also tend to live near toxic release facilities. If this was the case, and if low-income households also tended to be Latino, then we may be incorrectly ascribing the burden to ethnicity rather than poverty. In other words, our conclusion that Latinos were disproportionately bearing the burden of the siting of toxic release facilities may lack internal validity.

In order to address this issue, you might want to perform an analysis of the role of ethnicity that controlled for other potentially important factors. It turns out that it is possible to do this by performing a regression analysis on spatial data that is very similar in many respects to the regression analysis we saw in Chapter 7.

The basic idea behind spatial regression is very similar to the basic idea behind non-spatial regression: to estimate a best-fit regression function to the data. So, for example, Pastor and his co-authors divided up the entire region of southern California into census tracts and created a variable for whether each census tract contained a toxic release facility. They then performed a regression analysis of this variable on the following set of explanatory variables:

- Percentage people of color;
- Percentage homeowners;
- (The natural logarithm of) median household income;
- Percentage manufacturing employees;
- (The natural logarithm of) population density; and
- A categorical variable for whether a particular census tract was located in an urban area.

Box 8.1 reports their estimated coefficients for each of these explanatory variables. All of these coefficients were highly significant at the one percent level.

Box 8.1 Basic spatial regression results

% People of color	1.867
% Homeowners	–0.691
LN median household income	–0.111
% Manufacturing employees	7.590
LN population density	–0.194
Urban	0.461

Adapted from Table 1, Pastor et al. 2004, p. 429.

The important thing here is to notice the resemblance of this regression output to the output from a standard, non-spatial multiple regression analysis. Each of the coefficients can be interpreted as the effect of a unit change in a variable, holding all other variables constant. Furthermore, the signs of these coefficients—positive or negative—indicate whether a particular variable has a positive or negative impact on the dependent variable; here, the siting decision.

So, for example, the positive coefficient on the "% People of color" variable indicates that census tracts where a toxic release facility is located tend to contain a greater percentage of people of color. Recall that when you run a multiple regression, the estimated coefficient for each explanatory variable is interpreted as holding all other included variables constant. Thus, the result on "% People of color" controls for the effects of all of the other included variables (here, including household income). This comprises one of the bases for their conclusion that facility siting decisions may be systematically related to ethnicity and, thus, that environmental justice may be an issue in the facility siting process.

If you understand the intuitions behind curve-fitting and interpretation of regression results, you might conclude on the basis of this discussion that there is little substantive difference between non-spatial and spatial regression analysis. After all, it seems as if the estimation procedures and interpretation of results are exactly the same. However, it would be misleading if we left it at that. When you do spatial regression, there is the added complication that some important statistical assumptions of the standard regression model may not be satisfied. If so, the reliability of your regression estimates could be called into question. The reasons for this are a bit technical, but let me try to give you some intuition.

The basic idea is that regression analysis generally requires that different observations in your sample be *statistically independent*. This means, loosely speaking, that the value of one observation provides you with no information about the value of any other observation in your sample.

This is the case, for example, when we draw ping-pong balls at random out of a rotating barrel. Each ball that we draw randomly out of the barrel tells us nothing about the value of the next ball, or any other ball that may come out of the barrel. Consider a barrel filled with red balls and blue balls. If we draw a red ball the first time we dip into the barrel, this tells us nothing about whether the next ball will be red or blue. This was the idea behind random sampling, which we first encountered in Chapter 5.

The reliability of regression analysis often depends upon whether or not the observations in your sample are statistically independent of each other. If they are not, then there is a good chance that your estimates will not be as reliable as they could be.

When you do spatial regression, the problem commonly arises that your observations are not independent. For intuition, recall the study by Daniel Griffith and his co-authors on lead contamination in Syracuse, New York.

Recall that in this study, the authors collected spatial observations on pediatric blood-lead levels in neighborhoods all over the city. If there was, in fact, spatial concentration of observations in certain specific neighborhoods, their observations would not have been independent. That is, a finding of elevated blood-lead levels in children in one household meant a higher likelihood of finding elevated blood-lead levels in other households in the same neighborhood. It is as if pulling a red ball out of the rotating barrel makes it more likely that the next one will be red. In Griffith's case, the observations in their sample were *spatially dependent*.

Spatial dependence is a common issue in spatial regression analysis. When it is present in your data, it may require you to perform a modified regression procedure. In Griffith's case, they performed tests that indicated spatial dependence was in fact present. Given the results of these tests, they then modified their regression procedure to control for the spatial dependence. The specific details of how this is done are highly technical and will not be addressed here. If you are interested in the spatial approach and decide to go on and take a course in spatial statistics, you will be able to see how this is done.

Conclusions

Spatial analysis is a booming field in environmental studies, thanks to tremendous recent advances in the technologies of mapping and computer-based tools for spatial analysis. This chapter has only provided a broad general overview to spatial analysis, describing some of its basic features and capabilities and providing some examples of specific studies done using spatial analysis. As I mentioned earlier, we have only been able to scratch the surface here. If you are intrigued by the notion of using spatial analysis to answer research questions of interest to you, you are encouraged to pursue further study in an entire course devoted to developing spatial analysis concepts, tools, and techniques.

Additional Resources

Delaney, Julie. *Geographical Information Systems: An Introduction.* Oxford: Oxford University Press, 1999.

A clear, non-technical introduction to fundamental GIS principles and methods. A really good place to start if you are brand-new to GIS.

DeMers, Michael N. *Fundamentals of Geographic Information Systems.* New York: Wiley, 1997.

An intermediate-level but relatively non-technical discussion of GIS methods.

Harvey, Francis. *A Primer of GIS: Fundamental Geographic and Cartographic Concepts.* New York: Guilford, 2008.

An excellent introduction to basic GIS principles. Emphasis on spatial representation and cartography, rather than statistics.

References

Aguirre, Jessica C. "The Unlikely History of the Origins of Modern Maps," *Smithsonian.com*, June 2, 2014, http://www.smithsonianmag.com/history/unlikely-history-origins-modern-maps-180951617/

Ball, Laura. "Cholera and the Pump on Broad Street: The Life and Legacy of John Snow," *The History Teacher* 43(November 2009): 105–19.

Brown, Greg, and Delene Weber. "Public Participation GIS: A New Method for National Park Planning," *Landscape and Urban Planning* 102(2011): 1–15.

Delaney, Julie. *Geographical Information Systems: An Introduction.* Oxford: Oxford University Press, 1999.

DeMers, Michael N. *Fundamentals of Geographic Information Systems.* New York: Wiley, 1997.

Griffith, Daniel A., Philip G. Doyle, David C. Wheeler, and David L. Johnson. "A Tale of Two Swaths: Urban Childhood Blood-lead Levels Across Syracuse, New York," *Annals of the Association of American Geographers* 88(December 1998): 640–65.

Pastor, Manuel, James L. Sadd, and Rachel Morello-Frosch. "Waiting to Inhale: The Demographics of Toxic Air Release Facilities in 21st Century California," *Social Science Quarterly* 85(June 2004): 420–40.

Tufte, Edward R. *Visual Explanations: Images and Quantities, Evidence and Narrative.* Cheshire: Graphics Press, 1997.

9 General principles of qualitative research

Introduction

The second main tradition in scholarly research is the qualitative approach, which is the subject of the next several chapters. We first encountered qualitative research in Chapter 3, where we provided a general description of the approach and contrasted it to the quantitative approach. Over the next several chapters, we will be examining the qualitative approach in much more detail. Or perhaps it would be more accurate to say that we will be examining a number of qualitative *approaches*, as there are many. By the end of Chapter 15, you should have a good idea of how to undertake research on environmental issues in a number of different ways, using a variety of different kinds of evidence.

It will be useful to keep in mind that the fundamental idea underlying the qualitative approach is basically the same as that underlying the quantitative approach. Both approaches require:

- A well-defined research objective (typically in the form of a clearly stated research question);
- Careful collection of evidence;
- Systematic processing and analysis of the evidence;
- Interpreting the results of the analysis based on well-defined criteria; and
- Drawing conclusions based on the evidence using your interpretive criteria.

All of these research components are included in both approaches in order to allow researchers to tell a consistent, coherent story in which the answer to their research question is supported by evidence.

At the same time, the two approaches differ in certain fundamental ways having to do with different assumptions about the nature of knowledge, the definition of admissible evidence, the objectives of the research, how the research is carried out, and the tools used to analyze the evidence. Whether you adopt a quantitative or qualitative approach to doing research will certainly depend upon your research question. But it will also depend upon more fundamental questions of methodology, such as how you think about knowledge and what you believe constitutes evidence.

What is qualitative research?

In order to begin to understand the qualitative approach, consider the modifiers "quantitative" and "qualitative." You may have guessed that these words come from the words *quantity* and *quality*. Some researchers have argued that the "quantity" in quantitative research refers to *quantifying* things, whereas the "quality" in qualitative research refers to the "*nature* of things" (Heyink and Tymstra 1993, p. 293). We have just seen how the quantitative approach quantifies variables and the relationship among variables. How does the qualitative approach help us characterize the nature of things?

Non-numerical data

Students encountering the distinction between quantitative and qualitative research for the first time commonly associate quantitative research with *numbers* and qualitative research with *words*. This is not a bad place to start, but it can be misleading. After all, quantitative studies use words in their argumentation, and many qualitative studies use numbers to describe variables, trends, and patterns. Focusing on numbers vs. words tends to blur the distinction between quantitative and qualitative research.

So, rather than focus on numbers vs. words, let us think about research *needs*. In order to perform the quantitative analyses described in the last three chapters, we require numerical data and, preferably, lots of it. Without numerical data, it is impossible to construct statistics to characterize variables and the relationship among variables. And lots of data help guard against drawing conclusions on patterns in the data that may not be warranted because they are caused, say, by a few random outliers. More generally, we require numerical data in order to use the statistical approach that is central to quantitative research.

But what if we have little, or even worse, *no* numerical data? Unfortunately, in studying the environment, we will encounter many instances where sufficient numerical data are simply not available. We will see one possible answer to this problem in Chapters 16 and 17: generate the data yourself, using surveys or interviews. However, this is not always an option, and besides, we may be interested in research questions that are simply not answerable using survey or interview data.

In this case, the idea behind much qualitative research is simple: use non-numerical data to support your research findings. Here, we may be expanding use of the word "data" beyond what you are used to. Even though a great deal of evidence used in qualitative studies contains little in the way of numbers, qualitative researchers often refer to the evidence as data. The rest of the discussion of qualitative methods will retain this convention.

What, then, would be considered qualitative data? These would include written texts of various kinds, such as government documents, court opinions, legislative bills and resolutions, news accounts, scientific studies, on-line blog posts, and tweets. It also includes oral texts such as speeches, oral presentations, interviews, and conversations. It also includes visual images, interpretive performances, voice intonations, body language, and the like. Many qualitative researchers would argue that all of these things and more can provide useful evidence in answering a research question.

All of this suggests a tradeoff that we have to negotiate when we are considering doing a qualitative study. The downside of the qualitative approach is that many of these types of evidence are not amenable to a statistical analysis. However, the upside is that many more types of evidence are now available to us. Depending upon the research question, it may be worthwhile to be able to call on other types of evidence, even if this means that we are not able to use the statistical tools in our researcher's toolbox.

> **Bottom line:** Qualitative research can call on a wide range of types of non-numerical evidence, which opens up possibilities for conducting research on topics not amenable to quantitative analysis.

Small numbers focus

The question then becomes: How do we use non-numerical data to answer a research question? Here, the answer depends in good part upon which qualitative approach you choose to take. But in much qualitative research, it comes down to choosing *one or a small number* of cases, examples, events, issues, and so forth, and studying them intensively (Mahoney and Goertz 2006, p. 230).

So, for example, you might be interested in understanding the politics of a particular event, like the 2015 Paris Climate Accord, the North American Free Trade Agreement (NAFTA), the 1990 Clean Air Act Amendments, or a local environmental referendum. Or you might be interested in the operation of a particular entity, such as the Environmental Protection Agency (EPA), the US Fish and Wildlife Service, or a grassroots environmental organization. Or you might be interested in the experiences of an individual person, urban neighborhood, or rural community in dealing with an environmental problem.

In each of these examples, there is a clear unit of analysis: the Paris Climate Accord, the EPA, a rural community, and so forth. So even though there may not be data that can be statistically analyzed (think of the matrix structure of data in spreadsheet format required for a statistical analysis), there may be many other kinds of non-numerical data that provide insight into an interesting environmental issue. It may be apparent to you that the central issue here is your choice of research question and whether it lends itself to analysis using numerical or non-numerical data.

> **Bottom line:** Qualitative research often focuses on a single instance, or a small number of instances, of an object of study.

Processes vs. outcomes

But it is not merely the opportunity for more intensive study of one or a small number of instances that the qualitative approach offers. Another practical distinction between the two approaches has to do with the focus of the analysis. As we discussed briefly in Chapter 3, quantitative studies tend to focus on *outcomes*, whereas qualitative studies tend to focus on the *processes* underlying those outcomes. In part, this distinction has to do with the different types of evidence that the two approaches use.

The numerical data used in quantitative studies typically pertain to realized outcomes: for example, how many tourists actually visit the parks and what the weather is like when they get there, as measured by variables like temperature and precipitation. Thus, when a quantitative analysis relies on numerical data, it is focusing on understanding the outcomes that the data embody, and how they are related.

But suppose we wanted to answer a different type of question, such as: What are the social factors that determine how tourists respond to changes in the weather? The simple quantitative analysis we did in Chapter 7 sheds little insight into this question, which is more about underlying beliefs, attitudes, and motivations. If you wanted to answer this question, you might well want to rely on non-numerical data, such as interviews, letters to the editor, minutes of town meetings, blog entries, and the like.

It turns out that a great many environmental research questions focus on processes and mechanisms, trying to understand them better. For example, you might be interested in the procedures used by the US Fish and Wildlife service when deciding which species should make the endangered species list. Or you might be interested in the attitudes of residents of rural areas of Norway toward climate change mitigation policies. Or you might be interested in the organizational dynamics within businesses that determine whether they adopt green practices such as recycling and green product design.

These are all specific research topics that we will encounter in later chapters, all of which have been tackled using the qualitative approach. And to emphasize the point, in each of these examples the focus is not on the actual outcomes themselves, but rather on the underlying process that generates those outcomes. So, for example, the question is not so much about which species make the endangered species list, but rather the process by which they get chosen.

> **Bottom line:** Qualitative research often focuses on gaining insights into underlying processes, mechanisms, and belief systems. This is in contrast to quantitative research, which typically focuses on outcomes.

Generating theory

Another feature of qualitative research that distinguishes it from quantitative research is the way it uses theory. We saw in earlier chapters that the quantitative approach uses theory to posit relationships or generate hypotheses that are then tested using data. This is the *deductive* approach championed by the positivists and post-positivists and formalized in the scientific method: starting with general principles and using them to infer outcomes in particular situations.

By contrast, qualitative studies commonly start with data and build theory from the ground up. This is the process of *induction*: moving from particulars to the general rather than the other way around (see Chapter 2; see also Creswell 2009, p. 175; Seaman and Gill 2016, p. 132). Sometimes theory is invoked to provide a framework through which to interpret data. But broadly speaking, qualitative research uses theory very differently from quantitative research. In qualitative studies, it is very rarely the case that hypotheses generated by theory are actually tested in any form that a quantitative researcher would recognize.

This feature of qualitative research provides flexibility in terms of carrying out the project. Starting with a body of data, researchers organize it, examine patterns, create categories, and develop interpretations of what they think is going on. Since they never know what they are going to find, the research plan is generally fluid and subject to change. The open-ended nature of qualitative research creates both an opportunity and a danger.

On the one hand, qualitative researchers are free to explore new avenues and unforeseen contingencies, with the result that they may serendipitously discover things they did not expect. New theories may emerge organically from this process.

On the other hand, there is the danger that the researcher may subconsciously conduct the research in such a way that confirms prior expectations, so that new findings may merely constitute self-fulfilling prophesies. An important part of doing good qualitative research is self-imposed checks on one's research, so that it is internally consistent, generalizable, and replicable. These are the notions of *validity* and *reliability*, which will be discussed shortly.

Bottom line: Qualitative research is largely an inductive approach to research, which starts with facts and evidence in order to generate new general understandings.

Strategies of qualitative inquiry

As it turns out, there are a variety of approaches to doing a qualitative study. Which approach you take depends upon your research objectives as well as the nature of the available data. In this section, we will briefly describe five distinct qualitative strategies. These by no means exhaust the available qualitative strategies, which also include *grounded theory* and *phenomenology* (Creswell 2009, p. 13; Seaman and Gill 2016, pp. 119–24). However, it is probably fair to say that the particular strategies we will focus on are the ones that are most widely used in study of the environment. Chapters 10 through 14 will develop each of these approaches in greater detail.

The case study

The *case study* is perhaps the most well-known qualitative strategy, with a long and well-established tradition in the social sciences, especially sociology and political science. What distinguishes the case study approach is its focus on one or a handful of instances, or *cases*, of some activity, event, organization, or process that one wishes to understand better. Sometimes the objective is merely to understand the case itself. For example, you might be interested in studying water management in your local watershed, or decision-making by the Environmental Protection Agency, or the political dynamics underlying the 2015 Paris agreement on climate change.

In each of these examples, there is one instance, and no necessary intent to draw conclusions on other watersheds, environmental agencies, or treaties. However, there is nothing in the case study approach that rules out using your findings to draw conclusions about similar instances and, in fact, this is often done. As we shall see, however, if we wish to do this, we will need to be careful about how we choose our case or cases, keeping in mind the larger universe of similar instances and how our cases relate to this larger universe. More on this in Chapter 10.

Ethnography

Another great qualitative tradition is the *ethnography* approach. Among the social sciences, ethnography has historically been most closely associated with cultural anthropology. However, in recent days it has come to be practiced in other fields, including sociology, history, and, most importantly for our purposes, environmental studies.

Generally speaking, ethnography is the study of cultures and the people who comprise those cultures. Because cultural factors can easily play a role in how people interact with their environment, some environmental researchers have found it fruitful to employ the ethnography approach. This commonly involves living within a community of people and experiencing their culture on a day-to-day basis. The practice of ethnography entails doing this in a structured, systematic way, which will be developed more in Chapter 11.

Actor-network theory

A third, more recently developed approach is *actor-network theory*. The basic strategy here is to treat environmental issues as comprised of a series of actors interacting within dynamic, evolving networks. Under this approach, the concept of an actor is very broad, including not only humans, but organizations, technologies, government agencies, and environmental variables. Actors interact across networks with varying intensities of connectedness, and networks themselves may evolve in response to outside influences or factors that affect the degree of connectedness among actors.

The actor-network approach is particularly suited to modeling and understanding changes in complex systems over time. Since this characterizes many environmental issues, a number of researchers have come to take this approach to model and try to understand environmental issues. The actor-network approach will be described in Chapter 12.

Environmental discourse analysis

Environmental discourse analysis is the interpretive study of texts in order to understand how people talk and think about the environment and their purposes in doing so. Generally, texts are written documents of various kinds, such as media accounts, newspaper editorials, government documents, committee reports, books, memoirs, blogs, tweets, and transcribed speeches. In these texts are contained written accounts of actions and events. These accounts are not neutral depictions, but rather narratives that tell a story, often with the intent of persuading others. By dissecting these narratives, we can tell a lot about the opinions, views, and political positions of the writers, which in turn provide insight into a number of environmental issues. Environmental discourse analysis is the subject of Chapter 13.

Action research

Action research is research in collaboration with non-specialists, with the express intention of informing effective action to solve real-world problems. Since action research is typically undertaken to address some local issue, collaborators are often local communities, neighborhoods, or local agencies. These collaborators are viewed as genuine partners in the research project, bringing knowledge and expertise to the collaboration that is considered just as useful as that brought by the researchers. In this sense, it may be the most democratic of all of the qualitative approaches. The action research approach is discussed in Chapter 14.

Qualitative data

Let us now return to the important question of evidence. As we have seen, whereas quantitative data are confined to being consistent sets of numerical observations on different variables, qualitative data can be a great many things. These include: observed behavior, expressed opinions, journals, diaries and memoirs, government documents, news accounts, artistic performances, blog entries, and so forth.

To understand why all of these things could be useful evidence for qualitative research, consider again one of the most important reasons to do a qualitative study. A *qualitative study may be called for when you are interested in characterizing processes, mechanisms, and belief systems*. Here, relevant factors might be: individual perceptions of the world, belief systems, or complex group dynamics.

It is not only that these things are difficult to quantify. It is that many other things can shed light on them. How people think, how they behave, what they communicate to others, and the ways in which they communicate—all of these can be relevant pieces of a complex puzzle. The types of qualitative data mentioned a moment ago can all help us put the puzzle together.

Collection of qualitative data

What this all means is that there will be a lot of different ways to collect qualitative data. For an ethnographic study, you may go out in the field and interact with members of a culture over an extended period of time. An action research study will also likely involve field work but may take a lot less time. Discourse analysis is more likely to involve on-line document collection, or visiting libraries, archives, or government document repositories. The data you need for case studies and actor network studies could be a wide range of things, collected in a lot of different ways.

For much qualitative research, however, there are two extremely important and commonly used methods for collecting data: conducting written surveys or oral interviews. Each involves targeting a set of potential respondents and asking them to respond to a series of questions. As a result, there is much overlap in the recommended way to do them in terms of things like sampling and the need to ask simple, clear, and non-leading questions.

However, each also presents slightly different challenges because of the different mediums—oral vs. written—in which they are conducted. Chapters 16 and 17 are devoted to detailed discussions of the principles of good surveying and interviewing.

Analysis of qualitative data

If you think about it, analysis of qualitative data presents a number of difficult challenges. For one thing, since it can come in all sorts of different forms, how does one compare and, potentially, reconcile all of the different pieces of data?

When we did a statistical analysis in a quantitative study, we were assuming that all of the observations were comparable. This made sense when we were comparing the number of visits to a state park on one day versus another day.

But can we, for example, really compare a factoid in a news account to an entry in a memoir? Can we really compare somebody's interpretation of their own behavior to others' interpretation of their behavior? In each of these cases, it may seem like we are trying to compare apples and oranges.

The issue of comparability is important because so much qualitative research relies upon data that derive from perceptions or personal opinions. But except, perhaps, for a study focused solely on describing one person's opinions and beliefs, qualitative studies will generally be taking multiple pieces of data from multiple perspectives. The task will then be to carefully consider and compare the different pieces of data to construct a coherent overall picture. The question is then: How?

The answer is essentially the same as for quantitative research: you weigh the preponderance of evidence. What story is emerging from all of your data, considered as a whole? In quantitative research, the preponderance of evidence is mostly a question of statistical results and how strong they are, measured in terms of things like standard deviations and t-ratios. The overall picture appears objectively clear and black-and-white.

When you do qualitative research, however, you often lack quantifiable measures of systematic importance and significance. As a result, you often find yourself making a lot of difficult judgment calls because of the challenges of comparing qualitatively different pieces of data. What do I do with a piece of data that seems inconsistent with the rest of my data? How much weight do I put on different pieces of data? At what point do I rethink my current story and modify it to accommodate the data that don't seem to fit?

None of this should be viewed as a drawback of qualitative research, a reason not to do it. It merely has to do with the nature of the question you have chosen to pursue, which is just less subject to quantification. The big advantage of doing all of this is that you can try to answer questions that are impossible to answer using quantitative methods.

Nevertheless, it does require systematic thinking about the data and good judgment. It also requires a willingness to not shoehorn the data into any preconceptions you may have, but rather to follow the data wherever they take you.

A relatively recent trend in some qualitative research is to try to make the analysis of qualitative data more regularized and systematic. This sometimes involves quantifying qualitative data to better discern themes and patterns. For example, some researchers who analyze text (such as in journals and diaries) may select and group certain words or phrases, and then count occurrences in the text to identify common themes and ideas.

This trend has been encouraged by the recent development of computer software packages that are designed specifically for analyzing qualitative data. For example, the qualitative software packages *NVivo* and *MAXQDA* allow users to input narrative text (such as you might use for an ethnographic study or a discourse analysis) and organize it using an open-ended coding system. This system affords users with the flexibility to combine words and phrases to create units of meaning, and to organize these units of meaning into themes for purposes of analysis. See Chapter 17 for a specific example using MAXQDA.

This trend towards greater quantification of qualitative data has not been embraced by all qualitative researchers. In the view of some, there is almost inevitably a loss of meaning that occurs when you take qualitative data and try to parse it in the ways the new methods and software packages permit you to do. Be aware, however, that depending on your research interests, some quantification and computer-assisted systematization may be useful options for you as a qualitative researcher.

Validity

In our earlier discussion of the quantitative approach, we encountered the notion of validity. In that discussion, we saw that this was a way to think about the credibility and generalizability of the conclusions of a quantitative study. It turns out that the issue of validity also appears in qualitative research, which will be described in this section. During the discussion of the various qualitative approaches in the chapters to come, we will discuss various ways of addressing the issue.

What is qualitative validity?

In qualitative research, validity also refers to the credibility and generalizability of the conclusions of a study. These are again expressed in the notions of internal and external validity, as discussed in Chapter 7. As we shall see, many of the ideas are very similar to the ones we discussed earlier concerning quantitative validity.

Perhaps the biggest difference, however, will be the extra care and attention we will pay here to the issue of measurement. Specifically, much qualitative research focuses on characterizing relationships where the concepts are difficult to measure (not that this is always simple in quantitative research! It is a matter of degree). In the practical implementation of a qualitative study, the issue often arises of whether or not the variables we are using are really getting at the theoretical concepts we are interested in understanding. This is the additional notion of *construct validity* (Yin 2009, pp. 40–1; Seale 2012, p. 529).

Internal validity

As with quantitative validity, the question of internal validity is all about ensuring that we are interpreting a finding correctly. This issue comes up frequently when we do an analysis aimed at determining the nature of the relationship among variables, in which we infer a causal connection from one variable A to another variable B. The question is whether such a causal inference is warranted. One reason it may not be is that there are *confounding variables*: for example, another, unconsidered variable C that is correlated with both variables A and B and that is itself actually responsible for a finding that A and B are related.

A simple example will illustrate the point being made here. Suppose we observe that people who drink more coffee tend to have more heart attacks. Would it be valid to conclude that drinking coffee causes heart attacks? Perhaps not, because there may be a third factor that is correlated with both.

For example, suppose it was the case that heart attacks are in fact caused by smoking cigarettes and that people who drink more coffee tend to smoke more. Without considering smoking behavior, it may look like drinking coffee is causing the heart attacks, when in fact it is smoking that is the real culprit. In this case, our conclusion that coffee drinking causes heart attacks lacks internal validity.

Bottom line: There is a danger of misinterpreting a finding of a relationship among variables as a causal one when you fail to consider other confounding variables that may in fact be responsible for the finding (internal validity).

Construct validity

Construct validity is essentially about giving yourself a reasonable chance of being able to actually find the causal relationship among your variables, if it exists. In order to accomplish this, you need to use variables in your empirical analysis that accurately embody the concepts, or so-called *constructs*, that you are studying. If your variables do not do this—that is, if they lack construct validity—then any relationships you discover in your data may not reflect the actual relationship you are interested in.

As a simple example, consider the concept intelligence. This is a concept that many researchers have been interested in characterizing and measuring, for a variety of reasons. Suppose you are interested in studying the effect of intelligence on some measure of life success, such as income or happiness. The question is: What variable will accurately measure intelligence?

Perhaps the most well-known measure of intelligence is the intelligence quotient, or IQ. You may be aware that IQ tests have been used for a long time to measure intelligence. You may also be aware that IQ tests are controversial: a number of people have argued that they do not measure intelligence well, or that they only measure one narrow aspect of intelligence (Kaufman 2009). This may be in part why there seems to be an extremely noisy relation between IQ scores and measures of life success (Jones 2016, pp. 4–5).

For a more extended illustration of construct validity, consider the common strategy in environmental economics of conducting so-called *contingent valuation* surveys in order to gauge the amount that people would be willing to pay for environmental protection. In these surveys, respondents are presented with a scenario (such as the clean-up of an oil spill or a policy to combat the effects of climate change), and then asked how much they would be willing to pay for the proposed measure to be implemented.

The idea is that the dollar amount that people state they would be willing to pay for such measures should reflect how much they would actually pay if presented with a real opportunity, such as in a market. The stated responses can then form the basis for a cost-benefit analysis of a particular policy, by providing a measure of benefit derived from the policy.

In this example, then, the construct is the personal willingness-to-pay of respondents, which you are measuring using the dollar amount that they state in a survey instrument. The question is: Will the responses have construct validity? That is, will their stated responses accurately reflect their true personal willingness-to-pay?

The economist Henrik Svedsäter set out to answer precisely these questions (Svensäter 2003), using a rather ingenious approach. He conducted a contingent valuation survey but was not content with simply taking the responses at face value and assuming they reflected respondents' willingness-to-pay. Instead, he explored the process whereby they formulated their responses, using a variety of qualitative tools.

For example, he used focus groups and follow-up debriefing questions to find out more about how they came up with their responses. In addition, when he presented respondents with a scenario (a policy to mitigate global warming), he asked them to think out loud when they were answering the question of how much they would be willing to pay. All of this was to gain insight into their thought processes as they were coming up with their willingness-to-pay number. In essence, Svensäter was looking inside the black box, hoping to shed light on the process whereby respondents arrived at their responses.

The results were revealing. A significant number of respondents volunteered that their responses had been about the environment in general and not global warming specifically. A number of respondents felt that it was inappropriate to put a "price tag" on protecting the environment, but then went ahead and gave a number anyway. Some respondents who were unsure of their responses appeared to seek confirmation from the interviewer that they were giving the "correct" answer. Some respondents were concerned with issues of fairness, including who was responsible for global warming, or what the appropriate tax system should be.

All in all, the considerations underlying the responses deviated pretty dramatically from any sort of statement of value and, therefore, personal willingness to pay, to combat global warming. All of this seemed to indicate that any conclusions based on the responses may have lacked construct validity.

Bottom line: The validity of a conclusion can be threatened by using variables that do not capture well the theoretical variables you are interested in characterizing (construct validity).

One final word on construct validity. You should probably not interpret this discussion as suggesting that similar issues do not arise when you do quantitative research. Indeed, this discussion suggests that construct validity is similar to the notion of measurement error, which was discussed at length in Chapter 5. This is true, and it is reflected by the fact that some discussions of construct validity call it measurement validity. The fact that we chose to single it out as a component of validity here reflects the emphasis placed on it by many discussions of the qualitative approach.

External validity

As with quantitative research, the issue of external validity in qualitative research is also about generalizability. The question here is: Are the findings of your study generalizable to other contexts? These would include other times, settings, and people. If the answer is no, then we say that the findings lack external validity.

There are a number of possible reasons why studies may not have external validity. Here, we will focus on two common reasons: so-called *selection threats* and *setting threats*.

Selection threats

Sometimes, the external validity of a study may be threatened merely by the way that participants in the study are selected. The problem is essentially that the chosen participants may differ in some important, and often not obvious, ways from people that you may want to draw conclusions about in other settings. The issue of selection threats is thus similar to the problem of *sample selection bias* that we encountered earlier when we were discussing the quantitative approach. In both cases, the choice of sample makes it problematic to generalize to a broader context.

As an example, suppose a pharmaceutical company wanted to test the efficacy of a new medication to treat clinical depression. It would like to know, of course, whether the medication would be broadly effective in all settings, with all sorts of different kinds of people. However, suppose it tests the new medication by asking for volunteers.

The problem is that volunteers may have particularly strong reasons for wanting to treat their depression: perhaps they have loved ones who are particularly affected by their mood swings, or they are just more pro-active in general. It is not clear whether findings of the efficacy of the medication among this self-selected group will generalize to the wider population.

Bottom line: The external validity of a conclusion can be threatened by using methods for selecting study participants who differ from members of a targeted setting (selection threats to external validity).

Setting threats

Setting threats occur when there are specific things about the setting in which a study is done that make it unlikely that the conclusions can safely be generalized to other settings. For example, suppose an elementary school is considering whether to adopt a new method for teaching arithmetic. In order to test the new method, it brings in a person with special testing expertise to administer the test to a selected class of students.

The problem is that the students may recognize the special testing circumstances and may exert extra effort to do well on the text. It is not clear that finding that the new method works well in this setting can be safely generalized to everyday classroom situations.

As another example, consider the question of whether or not children who witness violent behavior (say on TV or in the movies), or who play violent video games, tend to exhibit more aggressive, or even violent, behavior themselves. Some studies have been done that suggest that the answer may be yes.

Box 9.1 The Bandura experiment

In the early 1960s, the Stanford psychologist Alfred Bandura conducted a famous experiment with seventy-two preschool-aged children. In this experiment, some of the children witnessed an adult quietly playing with toys, while others witnessed the adult punching an inflatable clown doll. They were then presented with a situation where they had to deal with the frustration of not being allowed to play with some nice toys.

The ones who witnessed the clown-punching were more likely to express their frustration by punching a clown doll of their own. Bandura concluded that watching aggressive behavior tends to make children more aggressive, because they pick up on social cues to guide their behavior (Toppo 2015).

One famous study, for example, found that preschool-aged children that witness aggressive behavior in a controlled experimental situation were more likely to respond to a frustrating situation by displaying aggressive behavior themselves (see Box 9.1). The question of external validity is whether this finding would be generalizable to other settings, such as at home or on the playground. Based on subsequent studies, this question remains an open one (Toppo 2015).

Bottom line: The external validity of a conclusion can be threatened by conducting research in an artificial setting that does not reflect real-world conditions (setting threats to external validity).

Reliability

In qualitative research, reliability refers to replicability. The question is: Can the findings of a study be replicated? That is, would a similar study, following the same procedures, likely yield the same results? If they would, then we can say that conclusions are *reliable*, or *have high reliability* (see Yin 2009, pp. 40, 45; Seale 2012, p. 528). Box 9.2 contains some standard definitions of reliability.

Box 9.2 Definitions of reliability

Reliability is:

"demonstrating that the operations of a study … can be repeated, with the same results" (Yin 2009, p. 40).

"concerns the consistency with which research procedures deliver their results" (Seale 2012, p. 528).

"is the consistency of a measure; a reliable measure will produce similar results when administered under like circumstances" (Mills and Gobenschneider, p. 358).

"indicates that a particular approach is consistent across different researchers and different projects" (Creswell 2009, p. 232).

For example, suppose you created a survey instrument and administered it to a number of respondents. You can imagine that you would get a particular set of answers. The question of whether this survey is reliable is this: If you administered it again, how likely is it that it would yield the same answers?

One reason this might be unlikely is that the survey questions may be subject to different interpretations by different respondents. For example, suppose you are interested in characterizing and explaining recent trends in outdoor recreation. So you design a survey that asks the following multiple-choice question: "*How often do you go hiking in natural settings?*" And you provide the following possible answers for respondents to check off:

☐ All the time ☐ Often ☐ Sometimes ☐ Rarely ☐ Never

The problem is that there ambiguous terms in this question, including "hiking" and "natural settings." Would a nature walk be considered hiking? Would an urban park be considered a natural setting? Different respondents might have different things in mind when they are defining these concepts for themselves.

In addition, most of the response categories might mean different things to different respondents. For example, to one respondent, "rarely" might mean once every month or two, while another respondent might interpret it as once every couple of years or so. All of this might make it difficult to replicate your results in a follow-up study on a different set of respondents.

But the question of reliability goes beyond whether *you* would be able to replicate your findings, if you were so inclined. It is equally about making sure that *anyone* could replicate your findings, by using your tools and following your procedures. So in addition to mere replicability, there is an element of others being able to confirm your findings, as a check on how you did your study and, thus, the extent to which your conclusions are trustworthy.

In order to ensure reliability, the researcher Robert Yin suggests that when you conduct research, you should always imagine someone is looking over your shoulder, checking your work as you do it (Yin 2009, p. 45). This means documenting everything that you do, being explicit about your methodological assumptions, being consistent in the definition of your variables, and so forth.

Yin provides the following useful analogy. Think of yourself as an accountant whose calculations are subject to being audited at any time. So conducting research is a little like doing your taxes with the Internal Revenue Service looking over your shoulder!

In terms of specific things you can do to promote reliability in your research project, one important thing you can do is to exercise care in collecting, managing, and structuring your data. As we have seen, for certain types of data qualitative researchers sometimes create codes that help them to organize and categorize the data. In order for these coded categories to be useful, they must be consistently implemented, both within a given study and across studies.

If code definitions change as a study progresses—a process known as *code drift*—then there is a serious danger of inconsistency in how pieces of data are characterized. The same piece of data might be coded differently depending upon whether it was coded early or late in the data management phase. This would be bad enough, but one can imagine the havoc this practice would wreak if you then tried to compare codes devised by different researchers. Not only would it be unclear whether data were being coded correctly, it might not be clear what a particular code even meant.

There are several ways to combat code drift. Within a given study, codes should be written down, explicit, and clearly defined. If there are multiple coders, they should have common understandings of the conceptual categories, they should be in regular communication with each other and with the project leader, and their coding should be coordinated and documented. If codes are developed individually, then they should be cross-checked for consistency.

Maintaining code integrity both within and across studies is one of the key ways to increase study reliability. Some software packages contain reliability programs that permit coding to be compared with criteria for evaluating consistency across different codings.

Box 9.3 Checklist: Reliability

- ✔ Be careful in managing, organizing, and structuring the evidence.
- ✔ Codes should be written down, explicit, and clearly defined.
- ✔ Maintain consistency across different team members when defining codes.

To summarize our discussion, let us conclude with a comparison of the concepts of validity and reliability. As you can tell from the discussion of the last two sections, both concepts address the issue of credibility of the conclusions of a study. However, they are about different aspects of what makes these conclusions credible. Since students sometimes find these differences to be subtle, a simple visual, shown in Figure 9.1, may help make the differences clear.

As Figure 9.1 indicates, validity is about doing what you can to ensure that your study will, on average, yield the correct conclusion. You do this by carefully designing your study so that you can indeed interpret a relationship as a causal one. You employ variables that accurately measure the underlying theoretical constructs. And you exercise care in how you select people to participate in your study, to make sure they faithfully represent people in other settings that you would like to be able to say something about. If you do all these things, your conclusions will tend to home in on the "right answer" bullseye.

Reliability, on the other hand, is about being able to repeat the exercise and come up with roughly the same answer. You do this by carefully wording your survey questions; being careful about recording your steps; being transparent about your procedures; and not allowing the definitions of your variables to change in haphazard and untraceable ways. Notice that reliability does not necessarily

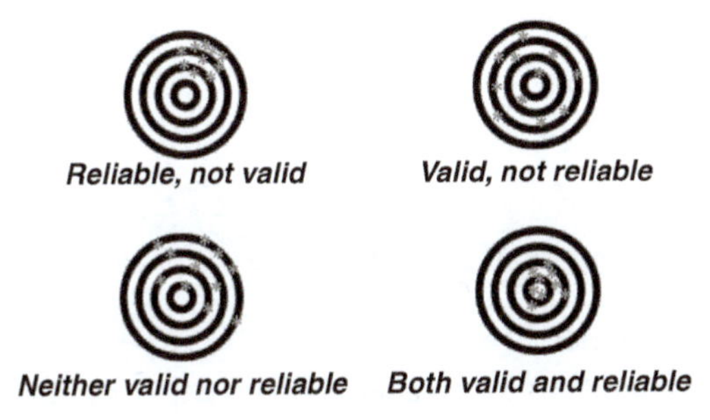

Figure 9.1 Validity vs. reliability.

mean that you home in on the "right answer." It simply means that whatever you have done can be checked to see if it can be done again.

The final thing that Figure 9.1 tells us is that both validity and reliability are important components of any research study. Validity without reliability doesn't do much good: we may think we have the answer, but how do we know for sure? And reliability without validity doesn't help much either: who wants to be able to replicate flawed studies? It is only when we have both validity and reliability that we have credible knowledge: trustworthy findings that can be checked and confirmed.

Summary: Choosing a qualitative approach

The discussion of this chapter should have impressed several things upon you. First is the importance of carefully considering your research question and thinking about whether it is best investigated using a qualitative or a quantitative approach. Each approach has its strengths, but as you know, the approaches are not equally applicable to answering all research questions. Some questions are simply better tackled using one approach or the other.

> **Advice:** Let your interests determine your question, and then select the approach best designed to help you answer it.

Second, even if you have decided to use a qualitative approach, there are many ways to proceed, again depending upon what you want to do. The next several chapters will describe various qualitative approaches, along with numerous examples to give you a sense for the types of questions that can be tackled using the different approaches. Chapter 15 will raise and describe an additional possibility: combining qualitative and quantitative methods into one study, or so-called *mixed methods*.

Finally, depending upon which qualitative approach you take, there may be a variety of kinds of data you can use and a variety of possible ways to subject it to analysis. It is probably useful to think broadly about what data you need to make your case, but I would take cues from existing studies to see what data they used. Not only will this give you ideas on types of data to use, it may point you towards particular sources of data for your own study.

Exercises/discussion questions

(1) Which of the following research questions seem amenable to a qualitative analysis, and why?

- Why do some popular referendums for local environmental protection pass while others fail?
- What factors determine whether businesses adopt green practices?
- Does increased incidence of drought conditions discourage visitations at national parks?

(2) Critique the following research designs for internal validity. If you found a relationship, would you feel comfortable with interpreting it as a causal one? Why or why not?

- A study of the role of political affiliation in determining support for climate change mitigation policy;
- A study of the role of religious beliefs in determining support for policies for increased protection of endangered species.

(3) Consider each of the following constructs and proposed variables with which to measure them. Would you be concerned about a possible lack of construct validity, and if so, why?

- Construct: *Personal happiness* Variable: *Job satisfaction*
- Construct: *Intelligence* Variable: *SAT score*

(4) Consider the construct *empathy*, which means the capacity to understand and share other people's feelings. Suppose you are trying to determine whether a particular person is generally empathetic. How reliable do you think the following ways to measure empathy would be? You observe the person:

- Giving $5 to a homeless person, while walking on the street with her boyfriend;
- Volunteering at the local hospital;
- Providing child care for his parents for free so they can go out to dinner;
- Crying at a sad scene in a movie.

(5) Consider the findings of the Bandura study, and critique its conclusions for external validity. Can we conclude that in general, observing violent behavior makes us act more violently?

(6) You are interested in conducting a study of student support for a policy of removing trays from all of the dining halls on your campus (in order to reduce food waste). For this study, you are considering surveying students who live on your residence hall floor. Comment on the likely external validity (that is, to the rest of the student body at your university) of the findings of this study.

(7) The administrators at your university are considering instituting a new energy conservation policy on campus that depends heavily on voluntary compliance by students. The policy includes measures like: turning off lights, unplugging computers, closing windows, and foregoing the use of space heaters. Before they announce it, you propose running a two-week pilot study in one residence hall over spring break, to see how well students comply with these voluntary measures. For this proposed study, you ask for student volunteers to participate. In your view, are there issues of either internal or external validity, and if so, what are they?

(8) Which of the following examples illustrate validity, and which ones illustrate reliability?

- Using your favorite chocolate chip cookie recipe to make banana bread.
- Using banana bread recipes from ten different cookbooks to make banana bread.
- Your alarm clock always going off at 6:00am when it is set for 7:00am.
- Weighing yourself on your own bathroom scale when you wake up, and then weighing yourself at the gym after a workout.

References

Creswell, John W. *Research Design: Qualitative, Quantitative, and Mixed Methods Approaches*. Los Angeles: Sage, 2009.

Heyink, J. W., and T. J. Tymstra. "The Function of Qualitative Research," *Social Indicators Research* 29(July 1993): 291–305.

Jones, Garett. *Hive Mind: How Your Nation's IQ Matters So Much More than Your Own*. Stanford: Stanford University Press, 2016.

Kaufman, Scott B. "Intelligent Testing: The Evolving Landscape of IQ Testing," *Psychology Today*, October 25, 2009, https://www.psychologytoday.com/blog/beautiful-minds/200910/intelligent-testing

Mahoney, James, and Gary Goertz. "A Tale of Two Cultures: Contrasting Quantitative and Qualitative Research," *Political Analysis* 14(Summer 2006): 227–49.

Seale, Clive. "Validity, Reliability and the Quality of Research," in Clive Seale (ed.), *Researching Society and Culture* (3rd ed.). Los Angeles: Sage, 2012: 528–43.

Seaman, David, and Harneet K. Gill. "Qualitative Approaches to Environment-behavior Research," in Robert Gifford (ed.), *Research Methods for Environmental Psychology*. West Sussex: Wiley, 2016: 115–36.

Svedsater, Henrik. "Economic Valuation of the Environment: How Citizens Make Sense of Contingent Valuation Questions," *Land Economics* 79(February 2003): 122–35.

Toppo, Greg. "Do video games inspire violent behavior?" *Scientific American*, July 1, 2015, https://www.scientificamerican.com/article/do-video-games-inspire-violent-behavior/

Yin, R. K. *Case Study Research: Design and Methods* (4th ed.). Los Angeles: Sage, 2009.

10 The case study method

Introduction

Let us begin a more detailed discussion of the qualitative approach by examining what is probably the most popular and well-known qualitative strategy: the *case study method*. Case studies have been used extensively to study various environmental issues, especially ones where theory is undeveloped and large numerical data sets are not available. Thus, understanding how to perform a case study will be an important tool in your research toolbox.

Consider, for example, the research questions of a number of environmental case studies listed in Box 10.1. This list should convey the wide applicability of the case study approach. In this chapter, the discussion of case study methodology will be liberally illustrated with material from most of these cases.

Box 10.1 Environmental case study examples

Study	*Research question*
Ando (2003)	How do interest group pressures influence the listing of endangered species under the US Endangered Species Act?
Berrens et al. (1998)	What have been the local economic impacts of the creation of habitat set-asides under the Endangered Species Act in the southwestern United States?
Clark and Slocombe (2011)	Can large-scale ecosystem management programs effectively protect large-scale carnivores such as grizzly bears?
Dhanda (2012)	How did a large health care company become an industry leader in sustainability practices?
Eick (2013)	How did an exemplary teacher use outdoor classroom and nature-study to connect to her science and language arts curriculum?
Guber (2001)	What explains the success or failure of local referendums for environmental protection?
Howe et al. (1990)	What have been the economic impacts of water transfers from farming to cities on the exporting areas in the western United States?
Menon et al. (2005)	What factors affect the success of local irrigation institutions in developing and managing water supplies?
Morris (2008)	Can environmental protection models based on local civic engagement be applied to large-scale environmental issues?

Source: Author.

What is a case study?

Case studies have the common feature that they all involve intensive study of one instance (or a very small number of instances) of some object of study, such as: an individual, event, activity, program, organization, or phenomenon. So, for example, the research questions listed in Box 10.1 focused on the listing decisions of one government agency (Ando), economic impacts in two watersheds in the southwestern United States (Berrens et al.), the implementation of one grizzly bear conservation program (Clark and Slocombe), and so forth.

The basic idea behind focusing on one or a small number of instances is to be able to really dig down deep, to understand the instance thoroughly in all of its real-life complexity (Gerring 2004, p. 352; Yin 2009, p. 18). The exercise is thus very different from the typical quantitative study, which strips away much of the complexity of a situation in order to estimate quantitative relationships or to perform simple hypothesis tests, as we have seen.

Digging deep means that case study researchers can consider a wide range of types of data, including documents of various kinds, interviews, and direct observation of a situation, as well as numerical data. All of these things might shed light on a real-world instance and, thus, all are considered admissible evidence for a case study (George and Bennett 2005, p. 6; Yin 2009, p. 11). And the fact that case studies may use numerical data indicates that they may have a quantitative component, though many do not.

Using different kinds of data presents both an opportunity and a challenge to case study researchers. On the one hand, having widely varying types of data at their disposal means that case study researchers may be able to investigate various dimensions of a wide range of phenomena. This may enable us to more fully understand the complexities of such phenomena than any quantitative analysis could.

On the other hand, researchers need to exercise care in combining and interpreting information from different sources. This is not always straightforward, particularly when different pieces of information taken from different sources seem to be saying different things. Generally speaking, the strategy for dealing with this issue is to consider the overall sense of the data, in a process referred to as *triangulation* (Kennedy and Luzar 1999, p. 584; Yin 2009, p. 18). Triangulation procedures will be discussed shortly.

Bottom line: Case studies involve intensive study of a small number of instances of individuals, events, entities, or processes that may use a wide variety of types and sources of information.

Why do a case study?

There are three general reasons why you might want to do a case study, which correspond to three basic kinds of case studies: *exploratory*, *descriptive*, and *explanatory* case studies (Yin 2009, pp. 7–8). Let us consider each of these in turn.

Exploratory case studies

If you have chosen a topic where not a whole lot is yet known, you might consider doing an exploratory case study. Exploratory case studies are often done in order to find out more about a largely unexplored area, with a potential eye to following up with a more detailed, structured study, if it seems warranted. So exploratory case studies can stand on their own, but they also often serve as preparation for a follow-up study, which might be undertaken either by the original researcher or future researchers.

For example, the researchers Douglas Clark and Scott Slocombe were interested in wildlife conservation programs in Alberta, Canada that were specifically targeted at grizzly bears (Clark and Slocombe 2011). They were specifically interested in why a new, large-scale collaborative effort between the federal government and provincial authorities turned out to be largely ineffective in maintaining grizzly bear populations. This type of collaborative approach had not been the subject of much previous study. So the authors undertook an exploratory case study in order to begin to understand the problems that might plague such an approach.

As another example, the researcher Mary Morris was interested in the effectiveness of an approach to environmental protection that emphasized local participation and civic engagement in environmental protection initiatives, or so-called *civic environmentalism* (Morris 2008). This is an approach that has been around for a while but which has only been applied to relatively local, small-scale environmental problems. She wondered whether it was a model that could also be used to combat large-scale problems, such as the issue of hypoxia in the Gulf of Mexico. Since little was known about how the approach might generalize to this new context, an exploratory case study seemed warranted.

In both of these examples, the researchers selected a research question that was on an understudied topic, as confirmed by an extensive examination of existing scholarly literature. They then went out and collected data appropriate to the respective topics.

Clark and Slocombe relied heavily on semi-structured interviews (see Chapter 17) of a variety of perspectives on the issue, including park managers, biologists, off-road vehicle users, and representatives of mining interests (Clark and Slocombe 2011, pp. 3–4).

Morris relied on a wide variety of sources of information on the issue of hypoxia in the Gulf of Mexico, including media reports, congressional hearings, case histories, and anecdotal information on fishing families based on fieldwork in the Gulf Coast area (Morris 2008, p. 1261).

These sources of data were tapped largely as a means of shedding light on the issues in a general way, where it was not at all clear what they would be ahead of time. In each case, a coherent picture emerged from that could serve as a basis for future, more in-depth studies.

Descriptive case studies

As the name suggests, descriptive case studies are largely concerned with describing what happens in a particular instance, such as an event, process, or natural phenomenon. You might, for example, be interested in what happened in a particular event, such as a flu epidemic (Neustadt and Fineberg 1983). Or you might be interested in how a business becomes an industry leader in adoption of sustainability practices (Dhanda 2013). Or you might be interested in the methods used by exemplary elementary school teachers in environmental education (Eick 2012).

In each of these examples, the researchers started with specific research questions and did intensive collection of information in order to answer those questions. So, for example, when Charles Eick examined elementary school environmental education, he posed the following two questions:

- "How does this teacher use the school's outdoor classroom and nature-study to connect to her science and language arts curriculum?" and
- "How does this teacher's nature-study approach to literacy learning impact children's state test results in reading and grammar for meeting Annual Yearly Progress (AYP)?"

(Eick 2012, p. 790)

And his case study sought to answer these questions through intensive observation of the teacher in action, audiotaped interviews, the keeping of detailed notes in a field journal, daily lesson plans, and assorted other documents.

It is sometimes presumed that descriptive case studies describe an instance, with no intent to explain what happened, or to generalize to other situations. However, this is not necessarily true. It is true that in some cases, the researcher just wants to understand what happened in a particular instance, such as the enactment of a major environmental treaty, or the experiences of a key government agency in regulating a particular pollutant. In these cases, instances are examined for their own sake, in which case the case study is referred to as *intrinsic* (Dhanda 2013, p. 668). However, many case studies that call themselves descriptive in fact contain elements of explanation and implications for other situations.

If you consider, for example, Eick's two research questions, interest in characterizing effective educational practices was very much in evidence. And he ended up drawing conclusions regarding how these practices might serve as a model for environmental education at other elementary schools (Eick 2012, p. 801).

As another example, the researcher Kathy Dhanda did a detailed descriptive case study of how a health care company expanded its sustainability practices over time (Dhanda 2013). This study involved not just describing what the company did, but also describing how it did it. And the practices undertaken by the company—including setting broad sustainability priorities and developing appropriate goals toward meeting these priorities—also had implications for other companies interested in increased sustainability (Dhanda 2013, pp. 676–7).

Explanatory case studies

Explanatory case studies are generally undertaken in relatively well-trodden areas where you have a pretty good idea of the issues and conceptual ways to think about them, based on a well-developed scholarly literature. In many cases, existing studies will provide much guidance in terms of a conceptual framework that informs how to think about the relationship among variables. Case study researchers are then able to investigate the extent to which particular case circumstances bear these out.

The researcher Deborah Guber recently undertook an explanatory case study in order to better understand the reasons for success or failure of local popular referendums on environmental issues (Guber 2001). Despite being the subject of a fair amount of previous research, it remained difficult to satisfactorily explain why some referendums passed while others failed. Specifically, the amount of campaign spending to sway public opinion on referendum seemed to have surprisingly little influence on the outcomes of many referendums.

To investigate this issue, Guber selected two referendums—one for California and one for Massachusetts—and examined survey data to gain insight into the voters themselves: their demographic characteristics and their perceptions of the issues as reflected by prior knowledge and how the issues were framed.

In the Massachusetts case, for example, Guber concluded that defeat occurred in part because opponents were successful in getting voters to think of a proposal to regulate product packaging as a packaging ban rather than a pro-recycling policy. Her approach enabled her to gain insights into the importance of issue framing in determining the outcomes of environmental referendums.

The takeaway message here is that when you do a case study, you have a choice of what kind of case study to do. As we have seen, which one you choose will depend upon your research interests. For one thing, you should ask yourself whether you are interested in description or explanation. Second, you should ask whether you are interested in understanding one instance really well on its own terms, or in generalizing to a broader class of instances.

Third, you should ask yourself what you think about the current state of understanding of a particular subject. If you have little to go on in terms of the findings of previous studies or ways to think about the subject, you might consider doing an exploratory study. This might be appropriate, for example, for studying a new situation or set of circumstances, with which we simply do not have much experience.

Bottom line: Case studies can be exploratory, descriptive, or explanatory. Which one you choose to do ultimately depends upon: (1) whether you are interested in description or explanation; (2) whether you want to understand a particular instance well, or if you wish to wish to understand a class of instances; and (3) the current depth of our understanding of particular issues, based upon how much they have already been studied.

Carrying out a case study

Now that we understand the various rationales for doing a case study, let us now consider the practical issues involved in actually carrying one out. As you might

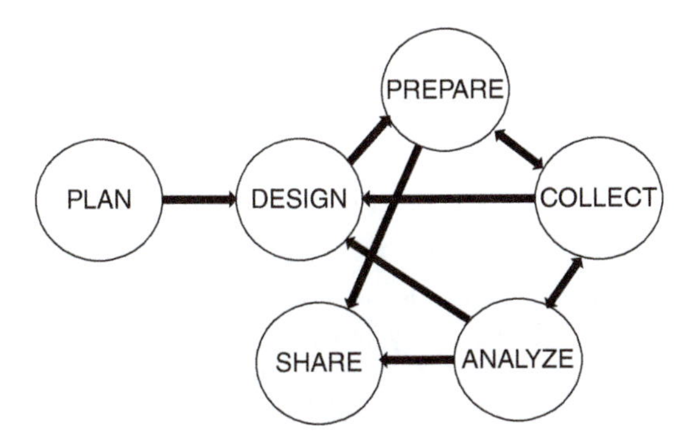

Figure 10.1 Performing a case study: a linear but iterative process.

Source: Yin, 2009.

guess, carrying out a case study can be a complex process. If we are trying to do justice to a complex picture and there are many sources of many different types of information, one can easily imagine not knowing where to start. The researcher Robert Yin, however, offers a very useful roadmap for doing a case study, as shown in Figure 10.1. Let us work our way through this roadmap.

Plan your case study

According to Yin, the process of doing a case study starts with preparation, at the "Plan" stage. Here, you consider your research question, decide whether it is best tackled using the case study method, and, if so, think about which case study approach would be best to use.

The key questions you should be asking yourself are:

- Am I interested in understanding one instance or a small number of instances really well?
- Am I interested in underlying processes, mechanisms, attitudes, or beliefs?
- Am I interested in understanding the instance(s) on its own terms, or am I interested in generalizing to a larger class of instances?
- How much do we currently know about the topic?
- What sort of data, both quantitative and qualitative, are likely to be available for my analysis?

Having read the previous section, I am presuming that you know how your answers will guide you in determining your next steps.

> **Bottom line:** Planning to do a case study entails making sure the case study method is appropriate to your research question and, if so, choosing which case study approach is appropriate. These depend upon your answers to these five questions.

Design your case study

Once you are satisfied that a case study is the way to go, and you know which case study approach to take, then it is safe to proceed to design your case study. In designing your case study, there are several factors to consider.

Define your unit of analysis

First, given your research question, you will need to define your unit of analysis. This is the object, individual, or entity that is the focus of your study (see Chapter 5).

This may sound pretty straightforward, but you actually have to be careful, because it may not always be clear exactly what the unit of analysis is. Recall, for example, the case study described earlier of a company that became an industry leader in sustainability practices.

It may seem obvious that the unit of observation is the company itself. However, depending on the research question, it is also possible for the unit of analysis to be divisions within the company, or particular executives within the company, or product lines. Without more information, we cannot know for sure. And which one it turns out to be may be crucial in determining the rest of the design of the case study, including what information to collect.

For example, if your focus was on the actions of top management, you might want to conduct interviews of the chief executive officer (CEO), chief operating officer (COO), and perhaps certain company officials who are specifically charged by the CEO with carrying out sustainability policy. However, if you were interested in the practical implementation of sustainability practices, you might want to examine key product lines or interview lower-level supervisors who carry out company policies on the factory floor. Or if you thought it was important to look at both of these factors, you might have to plan to collect data on all of these things.

The point here is simply that whatever you do in the way of collecting data will end up being governed by your choice of unit of analysis. As we shall see shortly, your unit of analysis could well change as you gather more information and discover the most important things to focus on. So it is probably best to consider your initial choice as being a tentative one and subject to change as your study progresses.

Develop theoretical propositions, if appropriate

The question remains of how you actually go about choosing your initial unit of analysis. Here, it may help to familiarize yourself with existing studies related to your topic. In many cases, existing studies may suggest theoretical propositions that help you choose your unit of analysis. Furthermore, they may help you structure your analysis and interpret the ultimate findings.

For example, consider again the study of the company adopting sustainability practices. A general research question might be: *Why did the company become an industry leader in sustainability?* The problem with this question is that it is extremely broad, and it provides us with little guidance on how to proceed.

Suppose, however, that existing studies suggest an important role played by top management in the adoption of new products and processes. This would suggest a more narrowly targeted proposition, such as: *Was it strong leadership at top management levels that enabled the company to develop appropriate goals toward meeting its sustainability priorities?* Notice how the theoretical proposition—*strong management is crucial*—culled from existing studies helps you narrow your focus and choose the appropriate unit of analysis.

On this point, it is important to keep in mind that clearly defined propositions based on existing studies may not always be available. This may especially be the case if you are focusing on a new situation or new circumstances, for which there is not a whole lot of information available to develop sensible propositions. This would probably be true, for example, of many exploratory case studies, where the research questions can often take the basic form of: *What the heck is going on?*

Bottom line: When available, specific theoretical propositions, derived from existing studies, can often provide useful focus to a case study.

Some important design features

Regardless of whether or not you have theoretical propositions, you will have to make certain decisions regarding the particular design features you will be using in your case study. By this, I mean that you will have to answer questions like: One case or multiple cases? And will you have single units of analysis or multiple units? Will your units of analysis coincide with the cases, or will they be defined at some sub-level?

Several possibilities for case study design types are illustrated in Figure 10.2, which is adapted from Yin (2009, p. 46). In Figure 10.2, each case is embedded within some larger context. A case design can involve a single case or multiple cases, and there can also be single units of analysis or multiple units of analysis.

For example, Eick's study of an elementary school teacher is an example of a single unit of analysis within a single case. Guber's study of environmental referendums is an example of a single unit of analysis within multiple cases. Studies of organizations such as the one by Dhanda may have multiple units of analysis, perhaps focusing on the entire company as well as divisions or individuals (for example, top-level management) within the company. Every case study can be placed into one of these four categories.

As always, which case design you choose depends upon the objectives of your research. Let us consider the advantages and disadvantages of the different options.

SINGLE CASE VS. MULTIPLE CASES

Under certain conditions, single case studies have distinct advantages. First, and perhaps most obviously, you may simply have an intrinsic interest in a specific

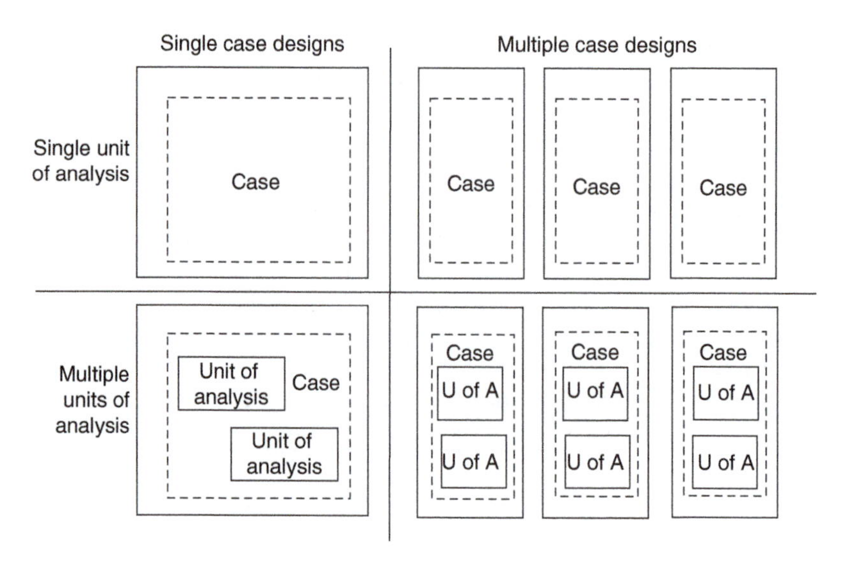

Figure 10.2 Design types for case studies.

Source: Author, adapted from Yin 2009, p. 46.

entity, event, or phenomenon, and you are not as concerned with generalizing to other similar ones. Furthermore, in some ways, by focusing on one instance rather than multiple instances, single case studies may be easier to do and less time-consuming (Yin 2009, p. 53). Importantly, you will not have to gather data on multiple instances.

On the other hand, examining multiple cases may allow you to be more confident in your conclusions. This is partly because you are simply bringing more evidence to bear to try to answer your research question. However, it is also because your conclusions will not depend upon the possible idiosyncrasies or special features of one individual instance. Examining multiple cases means that you are not putting all your eggs in one basket.

In addition, sometimes you are able to say more by doing a comparison of different cases. Deborah Guber, for example, focused on environmental referendums in two different states because they experienced different outcomes that she could compare and contrast. This permitted her to tie the outcomes to observed differences in how the issues were framed.

SINGLE UNITS OF ANALYSIS VS. MULTIPLE UNITS OF ANALYSIS

The issue of single vs. multiple units of analysis comes down to trying to say as much as you can with the evidence you have. Multiple units of analysis potentially mean more complementary evidence available to fill out a complex picture. For example, examining sustainability decisions made at the division level of a company, and by individual workers and supervisors, and by top-level management, may give you a more complete picture of how the entire company came to be "greener" over time.

In some cases, of course, there may simply not be information available to allow you to characterize multiple units of analysis. Furthermore, in focusing on multiple units of analysis, researchers warn of the potential danger of losing sight of the overall goals of a case study project (Yin 2009, p. 52). That is, if you focus a lot of attention on each of the separate units of analysis, it may be harder to keep in mind the larger picture that is the focus of your research question. The last thing you want to do is lose the forest for the trees, as they say.

Validity and reliability again

A final design issue concerns whether or not your case study will yield trustworthy conclusions. By this, we mean conclusions where the causation is clear, the variables chosen accurately capture the underlying theoretical concepts, and whether the conclusions are generalizable and replicable. Here, we are returning to the issues of *validity* and *reliability* that were discussed in Chapter 9.

Much of what we can say here will echo what was said in Chapter 9. You need to be careful about the possibility of confounding variables in order to correctly interpret any relationships you may find in the data (*internal validity*). You need to be careful about capturing your theoretical constructs accurately with the variables you use in your study (*construct validity*). You need to be concerned with *setting threats* and *selection threats* if you are interested in generalizing your conclusions to other settings (external validity).

And, finally, you need to be concerned about whether your findings could be replicated, by either you or another researcher (*reliability*). As we saw in Chapter 9, this means things like: asking unambiguously worded questions in survey instruments; being careful in collecting, managing, and structuring your data; and thoroughly documenting your procedures. Furthermore, you will want to try to avoid code drift if you are employing coding procedures to organize analysis of your data.

Data triangulation

Since you may well be using multiple sources of data, now may be a good time to return to the issue of *triangulation*, which we encountered earlier. The basic idea here is that when you are using multiple sources of data, you want all of the data to be saying the same thing. That is, you would like it all to lead you to one coherent conclusion.

To be clear, when we say data triangulation, we mean multiple sources of data that all speak to supporting one single fact that comprises part of your overall argument. This is as opposed to using different sources of evidence to document different parts of your argument. Data triangulation is about ensuring that the individual claims you are making have multiple sources of support. Figure 10.3, which is adapted from Yin, illustrates the argument (2009, p. 117).

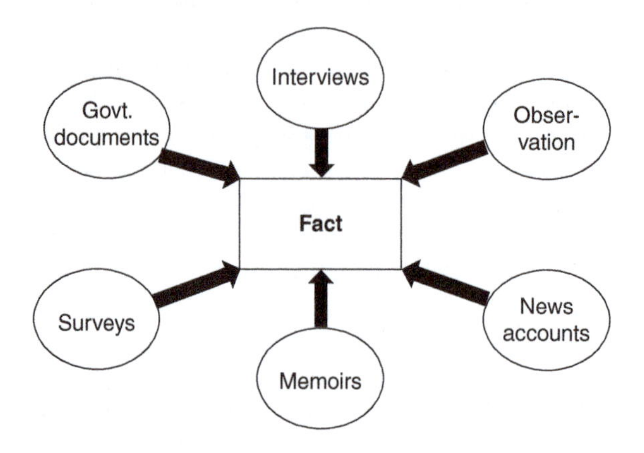

Figure 10.3 Data triangulation.

Source: Author, adapted from Yin 2009, p. 117.

As an example, suppose that you were doing a general assessment of the environmental curriculum design for a particular elementary school. As one part of the assessment, you were trying to document that a particular outdoor activity was effective in teaching environmental science. For evidence, you might use: classroom observations, student interviews, and in-class test scores. All of these varied sources of evidence speak to the effectiveness of the activity, and combining them might yield a more compelling conclusion than relying on only one source of data.

I will add that triangulating multiple sources of data is sometimes an effective way to promote construct validity. If you are drawing the same conclusions when you are measuring constructs in a variety of ways, this adds to the credibility of your conclusions. In the environmental curriculum example, investigating various measures of student learning may permit you to be more confident of the educational value of the activity.

Bottom line: Designing a case study entails: being clear on your unit of analysis; developing theoretical propositions to guide your study (if appropriate); selecting appropriate case design features; checking the validity and reliability of your design; and planning to triangulate your data, if you are using multiple data sources.

Prepare to collect data

Once you have planned and designed your case study, the next step is to prepare to collect data in order to support your argument. It turns out that collecting data for a case study may be a lot more challenging than you think. Hence the need for preparing yourself ahead of time.

In particular, when collecting data for a case study, it is generally not a simple matter of searching on-line, downloading data sets, or visiting libraries or archives (though doing these things may certainly be part of your overall data collection effort). You have to know what kind of information you are looking for. You may be interacting with people, trying to find out what they know. And because you never know in advance what you are going to find, you have to be prepared for surprises and unexpected turns, which may force a rethinking of aspects of your study. All of these things require a certain amount of preparedness, skill, and flexibility.

So in order to prepare for all of these contingencies (and more!), you are encouraged to consider the following points:

- Before starting to collect data, it will help *to be very clear about what kind of information you will need* in order to answer your research question. Keep in mind that there may be many different types of information at your disposal, as we have said. Being clear about what information you need will help you sift through what may at times seem like a mind-boggling mountain of information.
- To be clear about what information you need, it will help to *have a firm grasp of the issues* involved in your study. Being clear about the issues should help make it clear what specific information you need that will shed light on those issues.
- It will help to adopt the mindset of *bringing no biases or pre-conceived notions* to the task of collecting data. Leave your mind open to what you might discover when you visit a field site or interview a teacher or company official. Otherwise, there is a danger that your findings will reflect your preconceptions rather than a genuine and objective sense of the evidence.

The next few points are relevant if you are intending to conduct interviews as part of your case study. For more details, you should consult Chapter 17.

- First, if you are intending to conduct interviews, you will need to *develop an interview guide*. An interview guide is a detailed roadmap for the interview, including opening and closing scripts (containing specific issues you need to cover at the beginning and end of the interview) and the questions you intend to ask. The interview guide needs to be sufficiently detailed so that you can cover all of the topics you need to cover. At the same time, it has to leave room for flexibility in case the conversation veers in unexpected directions.
- As we shall see in Chapter 17, there is a real art to asking questions to elicit the specific information you seek. Part of preparing for the task of talking to people is thinking about how to *phrase questions in clear and unambiguous ways*. You should also keep in mind that talking to people is a social

interaction, which tends to go more smoothly—and tends to be more revealing—when it is relaxed, comfortable, and unforced.

- It is also *important to be a good listener*, to be able to listen carefully to what people are saying. This is both to encourage others to speak openly and to be able to hear and interpret what is being said. Here, it will again be useful to avoid bringing pre-conceived ideas to a conversation, so that you can hear what is actually being said, as opposed to what you think they are going to say.

Becoming good at asking and answering questions is not something that occurs overnight, and not everyone is equally good at them. But since everyone gets better with practice, you might consider practicing, perhaps with a friend or classmate, before you actually hit the field and do these things for real. Perhaps consider doing some of the exercises at the end of Chapter 17.

In your first case study or two, you may experience growing pains as you learn better ways to do these things. Just keep in mind what you have learned to help you do better the next time around.

- Finally, if your study involves working with human participants, you will need to *secure approval of your study* by the institutional review board (IRB) at your institution. The IRB will have a specific set of procedures (these vary somewhat across different institutions) that you will need to follow, so check with your IRB office to find out what these are. It is likely that you will have to provide a detailed description of your project, including its purpose, time frame, and intended outcomes. You will need to allow time for your application to make it through the IRB approval process, so budget time accordingly. For more information, see Chapter 18.

Collecting data

Let us begin our discussion of data collection by placing it within the larger context of how a case study is done.

Back to the linear, yet iterative, nature of case study procedures

Once you have done all of the necessary preparations to collect data, you should be forewarned that everything is about to become a lot more messy and nonlinear. Referring to Figure 10.4, which reproduces a modified Figure 10.1, the process so far has been a straight-line shot from planning the study to designing the study to preparing to collect data. In Figure 10.4, the boldfaced arrows from "PLAN" to "DESIGN" to "PREPARE" only go one way. So far, so good.

After "PREPARE," however, the picture becomes much more complicated in terms of next steps. It would seem that the logical next step after preparing to collect data would be to go out and collect it (arrow A). And in many cases, it is.

Notice, however, that Figure 10.4 indicates that you can also start thinking about steps that you will need to take to convey your findings to a wider audience (that is, moving down arrow D to "SHARE"). That is, you can already start

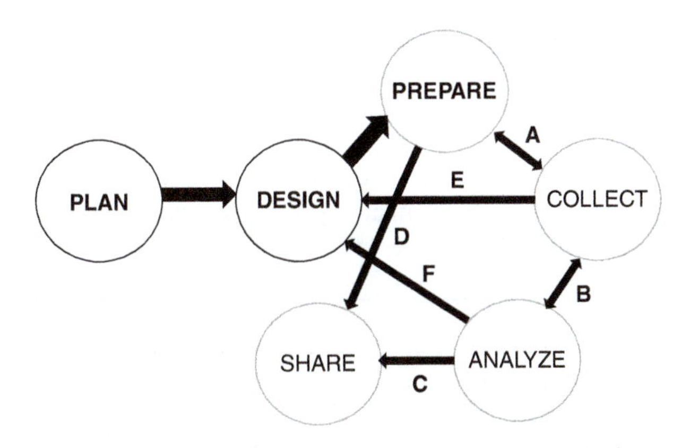

Figure 10.4 Now what?

Source: Author.

thinking about who your audience will be; what sort of data your audience might find compelling; and what sort of visual and textual materials you will need in order to make a compelling case. All this can, and perhaps should, be done before you start the formal process of collecting data.

However, if you do proceed to collecting data—following arrow A—notice that several things can happen after that. One would be the seemingly logical next step: perform your analysis of the data (arrow B), after which you share the results with your audience (arrow C). What we have just described—moving from A to B to C—is a linear process that strongly resembles what happens in most quantitative analyses (see Figure 10.5).

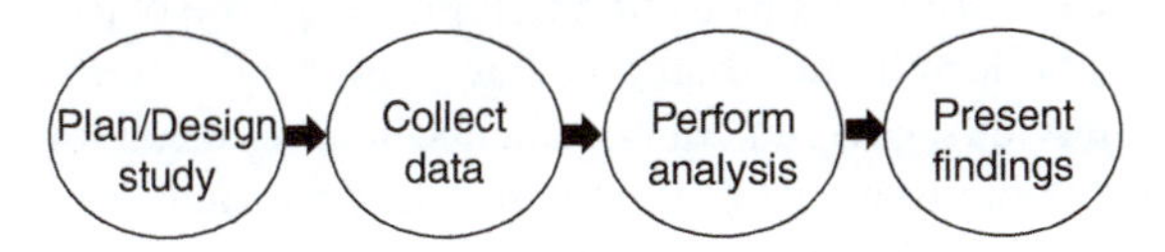

Figure 10.5 The linear quantitative approach.

Source: Author.

When doing a case study, however, there are many other things that can happen that make the entire process a lot less linear and more unpredictable. We have already seen one: reading existing studies may lead you to revise your unit of analysis. For another thing, the data may reveal new issues that you had not previously considered. This may require you to go back and do some additional preparation (arrow A) in terms of firming up your grasp of the issues and thinking more about your biases and preconceptions.

Sometimes, however, the new information contained in the data may require you to go back and do some broader rethinking of your study design (arrow E). If what you find surprises you, you may need to rethink some aspects of your study. This may entail going back and reading more studies to help you make sense of the new information. It is even possible that you may need to modify your research question. All of this is part of the iterative dimension of doing case study research.

Notice that the same thing can happen at the analysis stage. You may proceed from collecting data to analysis (arrow B), but performing the analysis reveals some surprising findings as well. This may also lead you to rethink some aspects of the design of the study (arrow F), which might require some extra different preparation to carry out, which may affect what data you collect, and so forth.

Bottom line: In case study research, collected evidence wears multiple hats. It serves as the evidentiary basis for analysis (arrow B), but it can also feed back into the design of a project, either directly (arrow E) or indirectly through the results of an analysis (arrow F). It can also affect how you prepare to undertake any new data collection (arrow A).

Some principles for data collection

With all this in mind, here are two important things to think about when you are collecting data for a case study. These principles are important to follow in order to produce a rich, robust study, to keep things organized as you are doing it, and to permit you and others to reproduce what you did.

TAKE ADVANTAGE OF MULTIPLE SOURCES OF DATA

At the risk of sounding like a broken record, case studies can rely on a wide range of types of data from a variety of sources. When available, different types of data culled from different sources can permit you to paint a rich picture of the object of your study. This picture might be far richer than one that relies merely on one single type of data, such as interviews, government documents, or news accounts.

You might, for example, be able to approach issues from different angles or gain multiple perspectives on a topic. Furthermore, different sources of data can complement each other, which might allow you to more convincingly support your arguments. For example, you could use data from EPA reports to identify firms who adopt green practices and then conduct field research at a selected group of those firms (Florida et al. 2001, p. 215). All of these things can serve to make your conclusions more compelling to your readers.

CREATE A CASE STUDY DATABASE

If you heed this advice and tap multiple types of data, it becomes crucial to systematically manage and document it. This is why you are encouraged to create a database that contains your various types of data and keeps them organized, allowing you to more easily consult the data as you are doing the study, and to be able to easily access it later if need be. This also makes it easier for others to see what you did, so they can confirm your methods and use of data. Thus, maintaining this database will enhance the reliability of your study.

Analyzing data

The final component we will discuss here is analysis of your data. Systematic analysis of data probably feels like a tall order, especially if you are using many different kinds of data. Here, the distinction between quantitative analysis and qualitative analysis seems sharpest. We can easily envision rows and columns of data in a spreadsheet and teasing out correlations. What is the analogy in qualitative research, for example, when you are doing a case study with data that can take every shape and form, possibly without any numbers at all?

This is actually a challenging question that many case study researchers have struggled with (Yin 2009, p. 127). However, here are a few things to keep in mind that you may find useful.

First, if you are feeling overwhelmed with a mass of data, you might try breaking it down into bite-sized chunks. One structured way to do this might be to pose questions that are smaller in scope than your overall research question, and bring data to bear to try to answer these narrower questions. The reason this strategy often works is that for every research project with a well-defined research question, there are countless sub-questions you have to answer, as components of your answer to the overall question.

For example, consider Guber's research question: *What explains the success or failure of local referendums for environmental protection?* In order to answer this question, she had to answer each of the following sub-questions along the way. How does the content of a campaign ad affect how people feel about a particular referendum? What sort of content? Given that there have been hundreds of environmental referendums, which ones do I focus on and why? Which referendums were more fiercely contested, and why? Answering each of these questions was a step along the way toward being able to provide a compelling answer to her overall research question. Each of these questions provided a focal point that helped her to organize her data.

To be concrete about this point, let us consider the first of these sub-questions: *How does the content of a campaign ad affect how people feel about a particular referendum?* Here, you might think it would help to collect data on the campaign ads and people's perception of the campaign ads for a particular set of referendums. So the relevant data might consist of: the content and wording of a set of referendums that you have chosen to study; information on the campaign ads run before the voting process occurs in each case; and perhaps some survey data on how people are responding to the campaign ads. Notice how the question itself provides suggestive guidance on what data you need to collect.

Second, many research questions are about relationships between or among variables. Here, it is often the case that the relationships are contained in theoretical propositions that may be based on some particular framing theory. A case study may then involve taking data that form an empirical pattern and seeing how it compares to the one suggested by a proposition. Doing this is sometimes referred to as *pattern-matching* (Yin 2009, pp. 136–41). If the patterns match, then this provides evidence for the proposition. If not, then this might lead us to conclude that there may be something else going on. The conclusion may be a new way of looking at things, perhaps in the form of a novel proposition.

So, for example, in Guber's case, there was a proposition out there in the existing literature that campaign spending is heavily determinative of the outcomes of public referendums. One of the reasons Guber chose to look more closely at a California referendum was that its outcome did not seem to conform to this proposition: the measure was resoundingly approved despite well-funded opposition. This outcome provided evidence that there might be other factors that were as, if not more, important than campaign spending in determining the success of a referendum.

If we think about Guber's example, it really came down to the following question: Does more campaign spending translate into more success at the polls? In order to be able to draw conclusions, she needed data that allowed her to establish the relationship between spending and electoral success. This meant that she needed variation in spending and she needed variation in electoral success. Without both of these, she could not hope to establish any sort of relationship between the two, positive or negative.

The question then becomes: When we do a case study, what strategies are available for us to obtain variation in the variables we are interested in? It turns out that there are several possible strategies. This is because even within one or a handful of instances, there are several ways in which the variables you are interested in may vary. First, the variables may vary over time. Second, they may vary cross-sectionally, perhaps across space. Finally, depending upon the topic and scope of inquiry, variables may exhibit variation both within and across cases. The fact that various dimensions for variation exist affords researchers numerous options to investigate the relationship among variables.

Temporal variation

First, a relationship among variables may reveal itself in how the variables move over time. For example, you might be interested in studying the effect of the regulation of endangered species in the United States. The enactment of the Endangered Species Act in 1973 provides variation in the extent of government regulation of endangered species, from basically none prior to 1973 to substantive regulation after that date. A before-and-after examination of population levels of certain species might provide some insights into the effectiveness of the Act.

More generally, the mere occurrence of specific events at particular points in time—the Kyoto Protocol, the Clean Air Act of 1970, the enactment of NAFTA, the construction of a hydropower dam, the institution of a zoning ordinance, the setting aside of a green space—the list goes on and on—may provide the variation necessary to characterize the covariation with another variable.

Cross-sectional/spatial variation

Second, the variable may vary cross-sectionally or spatially within the area that is the focus of the case study. For example, in the study by Berrens et al. that we shall encounter later in this chapter, the authors examine provisions for habitat conservation under the Endangered Species Act and investigate their impact on local economies within two watersheds in the southwestern United States (Berrens et al. 1998).

In each instance, the authors allowed for economic impacts that varied within sub-units of each watershed. In the multi-state Colorado River watershed, they allowed for varying impacts across states within the watershed, whereas in the small Virgin River watershed, the economic impacts varied across different counties. This permitted them to disaggregate the economic impacts based upon location.

Variation in studies involving multiple cases

Another important strategy for obtaining covariation is to consider multiple cases, where variation occurs across the cases. Indeed, in some instances using multiple cases may be the only feasible way of characterizing the relationship among the variables you are interested in.

Consider, for example, a 2005 study of local irrigation organizations in India that investigated the effect of different institutional arrangements on local efforts to develop and manage irrigation infrastructure. In this study, Vineetha Menon and his co-authors compared and contrasted several different local organizations, each managed and operated under a different institutional arrangement (Menon et al. 2005). These included two organizations managed by the government, one co-managed by the government and the local farmers, and three managed by the farmers themselves.

The idea behind their study was that the different nexuses of control might lead to different outcomes, in terms of how effectively irrigation facilities were operated and maintained. To put it plainly, whether an organization is managed by the government or by the farmers themselves might heavily influence a community's success in developing and managing its irrigation water supplies.

The decision to examine multiple organizations permitted the authors to examine the relationship between different institutions and different outcomes. This would not have been possible by examining just one organization. If they had examined only one organization, there would have been just one institutional arrangement and, hence, no way to see how different arrangements led to different outcomes.

Extended example: Berrens et al. on the Endangered Species Act

This discussion of how to carry out a case study may be clarified by a more detailed consideration of a particular case study. This case study examined implementation of the Endangered Species Act in two different watersheds in the southwestern United States (Berrens et al. 1998).

In this study, Berrens and his co-authors focused on the local economic impacts of implementing one particular feature of the Endangered Species Act: the so-called *safe minimum standard.* As its name implies, this policy establishes a minimum level below which an environmental resource (such as the flow of water in a river or an area of habitat) is not permitted to fall, unless the costs imposed on society are unacceptably high.

For example, the safe minimum standard is naturally applied to preservation of wildlife habitat, for guiding decisions to create habitat set-asides such as forests, game preserves, and stretches of river. The safe minimum standard is a criterion for evaluating the tradeoff between different uses of an environmental resource.

The following research question flowed naturally from this implication: *What is the local economic impact of implementation of the safe minimum standard for protection of endangered species?*

In posing this question, Berrens relied on a particular theoretical proposition that was based on a simple economic idea: Water resources are scarce within a given local watershed, which could impose economic costs as different activities compete for those water resources. This proposition generated a specific prediction: that set-asides for fish habitat could impose costs on farmers by depriving them of water.

In order to investigate whether this prediction held in the study area, Berrens et al. chose as units of analysis two individual watersheds—the Colorado River and Virgin River watersheds. They chose two watersheds instead of just one because this strategy provided them with cross-sectional and spatial variation that they could exploit.

So, for example, for the Colorado River watershed, which spans several states, they performed analysis on individual states within the watershed as well as the entire watershed itself. For the much smaller Virgin River watershed, they performed analysis on individual counties within the watershed. Thus, their strategy was to exploit spatial variation both within and across cases.

Their analysis proceeded with a detailed description of the study area, including information on the size of the local economies, a description of the local fish species that would benefit from critical habitat designation, and a brief history and description of local efforts to protect habitat.

A crucial issue was establishing interpretive criteria for evaluating the economic impacts of habitat set-asides. The method was essentially to establish a counterfactual baseline; that is, projections of economic activity under the assumption of no set-asides. In good part, this was accomplished by using an economic model to quantify the effects on jobs and total production activity.

These baseline projections were then compared to another set of projections under the alternative assumption that sufficient habitat consistent with maintaining a safe minimum standard had been set aside. The difference comprised the economic impacts of the set-asides themselves. Based upon these calculations, the study estimated the impact on both jobs and output.

One interesting feature of their findings was a somewhat counterintuitive result on the economic impact. Whereas they calculated a negative economic impact for the Virgin River watershed entailing the loss of dozens of jobs and over $100 million in output, the estimated impact on the Colorado River watershed actually turned out to be *positive*. Indeed, their estimated positive impact for the Colorado River watershed—nearly $1.3 billion in added output and over 1,800 new jobs—completely swamped the negative impact in the Virgin River watershed.

This result, which was seemingly at odds with the predictions of the theoretical proposition, encouraged them to look more closely to try to understand what was going on. The answer turned on a simple fact with important implications for future set-aside programs. The set-asides tended to be at higher elevations, where the alternative uses of water were of relative low value. Because this water was not diverted to maintain habitat in these areas, more of it was available for higher-value uses downstream.

This result underscores how case studies can sometimes provide unexpected insights when they encourage you to look more closely at anomalous results. It should be emphasized that obtaining this insight would not have been possible had they not considered spatial variation within their cases. Without such within-case variation, they would have had no way to distinguish between economic impacts at different locations within the Colorado River watershed, because upriver and downriver set-asides would have had identical impacts.

Conclusions

It is not surprising that case studies have been widely used in study of the environment, for several reasons. First, there are many contexts where sufficient quantitative data are not available, yet important questions need to be answered. Second, many environmental issues, such as ones involving the processes and mechanisms underlying an environmental relationship, do not in any case lend themselves to analysis using quantitative data. Third, sometimes there is considerable value to trying to understand the complex facets of an environmental issue. In general, there are a great many circumstances where the case study approach provides an attractive option for studying the environment.

Exercises/discussion questions

(1) Suppose you wanted to do a case study of the efforts of a small rural community to address the problem of growing depletion and contamination of local groundwater supplies. Would you conduct an exploratory, descriptive, or explanatory case study, and why? What information might be useful to gather to help you decide which one to do?

(2) Suppose you are interested in zoning ordinances enacted by local municipalities in the United States to reduce urban sprawl. Describe how you would go about selecting one or a handful of cases that would permit you to generalize to local municipalities in general.

(3) You are doing a case study of lead contamination in a neighborhood in a nearby large city. Design a case study with a single unit of analysis and specify what the unit of analysis is. Now design a case study that uses multiple units of analysis, again defining the units of analysis.
(4) Suppose you are doing a case study of the efforts of your local city government to promote energy conservation in all of its various departments. Design a study with a single unit of analysis. Design a study with multiple units of analysis. Can you see a way to design a case study using multiple cases?
(5) Consider the following research questions.

- Why did a novel wildlife conservation program fail?
- How did an exemplary elementary school teacher manage to be successful in using outdoor activities to teach environmental science?
- Why don't environmentally conscious citizens support policies to address climate change?

Come up with alternative wordings that use theoretical propositions to help refine and narrow the focus of your analysis.
(6) Consider a case study of elementary school environmental education based on observations in one teacher's classroom. Discuss the issues of validity that may arise in trying to generalize the conclusions to other elementary schools in other school districts.
(7) Read the case study by Guber. Consider the common components of case studies, as exemplified by Berrens et al.

- What is Guber's research question?
- What is her theoretical proposition?
- What is the implied cause-and-effect relationship?
- What are her units of analysis?
- What are her criteria for interpreting results?

References

Ando, Amy W. "Do Interest Groups Compete? An Application to Endangered Species," *Public Choice* 114(January 2003): 137–59.

Berrens, Robert P., David S. Brookshire, Michael McKee, and Christian Schmidt. "Implementing the Safe Minimum Standard Approach: Two Case Studies from the U.S. Endangered Species Act," *Land Economics* 74(May 1998): 147–61.

Clark, Douglas A., and D. Scott Slocombe. "Grizzly Bear Conservation in the Foothills Model Forest: Appraisal of a Collaborative Ecosystem Management Effort," *Policy Sciences* 44(March 2011): 1–11.

Dhanda, K. Kathy. "Case Study in the Evolution of Sustainability: Baxter International Inc.," *Journal of Business Ethics* 111(February 2013): 667–84.

Eick, Charles J. "Use of the Outdoor Classroom and Nature-study to Support Science and Literacy Learning: A Narrative Case Study of a Third-grade Classroom," *Journal of Science Teacher Education* 23(2012): 789–803.

Florida, Richard, Mark Atlas, and Matt Cline. "What Makes Companies Green? Organizational and Geographic Factors in the Adoption of Environmental Practices," *Economic Geography* 77(July 2001): 209–24.

George, A. L., and A. Bennett. *Case Studies and Theory Development*. Cambridge: Cambridge University Press, 2005.

Gerring, John. "What Is a Case Study and What Is It Good for?" *American Political Science Review* 98(May 2004): 341–54.

Guber, Deborah L. "Environmental Voting in the American States: A Tale of Two Initiatives," *State and Local Government Review* 33(Spring 2001): 120–32.

Howe, Charles W., Jeffrey K. Lazo, and Kenneth R. Weber. "The Economic Impacts of Agriculture-to-Urban Water Transfers on the Area of Origin: A Case Study of the Arkansas River Valley in Colorado," *American Journal of Agricultural Economics* 72(December 1990): 1200–04.

Kennedy, P. Lynn, and E. Jane Luzar. "Toward Methodological Inclusivism: The Case for Case Studies," *Review of Agricultural Economics* 21(Autumn/Winter 1999): 579–91.

Menon, Vineetha, Antonyto Paul, and K. N. Nair. "Dynamics of Irrigation Institutions: Case Study of a Village Panchayat in Kerala," *Economic and Political Weekly* 40(February 26–March 4, 2005): 893–904.

Morris, Mary Hallock. "When It Works and Where It Fails: Spatial, Temporal, and Budgetary Constraints to Civic Environmentalism," *Social Science Quarterly* 89(December 2008): 1252–76.

Neustadt, Richard E. and Harvey V. Fineberg. The Epidemic that Never Was: Policy-making and The Swine-Flu Scare. New York: Vintage, 1983.

Yin, R. K. *Case Study Research Design and Methods*. Thousand Oaks: Sage, 2009.

11 The ethnographic approach

Introduction

A second main qualitative approach that has been applied to study of the environment is the *ethnographic approach*. The ethnographic approach exemplifies many of the central features of qualitative research. It commonly focuses on one or a small number of instances, it generally relies heavily on non-numerical data, and it is centrally concerned with processes, mechanisms, attitudes, and belief systems. In addition, formal testable hypotheses are almost entirely absent. In many ways, ethnography is the quintessential qualitative approach.

Perhaps the most obvious way in which ethnography differs from typical case studies is in the types of evidence it generally relies upon. Whereas case study researchers use a wide variety of different types of data, ethnographers rely heavily on intensive observation of activities and behavior in their natural setting. In many cases, the ethnographer may actively participate in local activities along with the people being studied. This is why it is often said that ethnography is the *observer-participant* approach, which emphasizes the type of data being used and the way it is commonly collected.

What is ethnography?

The traditional definition of ethnography is stated well by two researchers, Hammersley and Atkinson:

> Ethnography is a particular method or set of methods which in its most characteristic form ... involves the ethnographer participating overtly or covertly in people's daily lives for an extended period of time, watching what happens, listening to what is said, asking questions—in fact, collecting whatever data are available to throw light on the issues that are the focus of the research.
>
> (Hammersley and Atkinson 1995, p. 1)

This definition reflects the disciplinary roots of the approach in the field of cultural anthropology, where researchers would go to a community, live there, and observe behavior on a day-to-day basis. Brian Hoey notes, however, that the definition has become broader over time:

> The term ethnography has come to be equated with virtually any qualitative research project where the intent is to provide a detailed in-depth description of everyday life and practice.
>
> (Hoey 2014, p. 1)

So the ethnographic approach involves focusing on lived experiences and behavior, which typically requires the researcher to spend an extended period of time in the context that is the subject of study.

Generally speaking, there are two distinctive features of the ethnographic approach. First, there is no clear dividing line between theorizing and empirical analysis. We have seen that the quantitative approach is *linear*: moving from research question to theory to generating testable hypotheses to data collection to hypothesis testing to findings and conclusions.

In sharp contrast, the ethnographic approach is a matter of constant and repeated interaction among theory, data collection, and data analysis (see Figure 11.1). This approach is thus reminiscent of the iterative case study approach. Data analysis guides theory development, which may result in collection of more data guided by this new theory, which leads to more data analysis, and so forth. In this way, theory is generated rather than tested, which is a feature of the qualitative approach in general, as we have seen.

Second, the ethnographic researcher is herself the research instrument, employing a variety of techniques in order to understand and document what is going on in a given setting. These techniques include: reading, recording, and analyzing written documents; establishing contact and rapport with so-called *gatekeepers* (individuals who can be instrumental in gaining access to a community); simple observation of events and interactions; direct dialog with people through conversations and interviews; careful and structured taking of field notes; and maintaining good interpersonal relations with persons within the observed community.

It may be apparent to you that the ethnographic researcher employs a very different set of skills than the typical quantitative researcher, who may spend much of her time downloading data from the internet and sitting at a computer doing

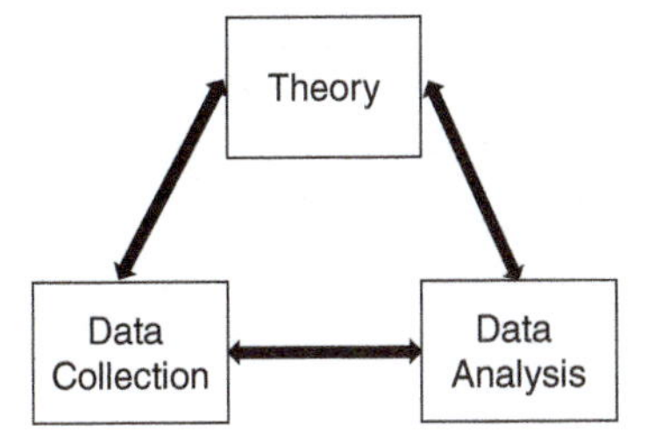

Figure 11.1 The non-linear approach of ethnography.

Source: Author.

data analysis. When deciding what kind of environmental study you would like to undertake, you are encouraged to think about your own skill set and comfort level with the different kinds of research tasks you will have to perform.

To help you think about how this approach could be applied to study of the environment, consider the following studies. Paul Lichterman (1995) did an ethnographic study of grassroots environmental groups along the west coast of the United States to understand the challenges of building political alliances across different multicultural groups in support of common environmental causes. Claudia Radel (2005) did an ethnographic study of women's agricultural community-based organizations in Mexico to understand factors that determined women's access to, and control over, land use. More recently, Kari Norgaard (2012) used an ethnographic approach in order to characterize the attitudes of rural Norwegians toward climate change.

More generally, the ethnographic approach has been applied to gain insights into a variety of environmental issues (see Box 11.1). In this chapter, we develop the goals and objectives of the ethnographic approach, see how the approach has been applied to study of the environment, and describe a number of practical issues involved in doing an ethnographic study.

The goals and objectives of ethnography

Ethnographic study has a long and rich history, and it is most heavily associated with the field of cultural anthropology, especially the famed anthropologists Bronislaw Malinowski, Franz Boas, and, later, Clifford Geertz. These anthropologists were interested in understanding culture through the lived experiences of members of the studied culture.

In the early twentieth century, Malinowski traveled to the South Pacific, where he conducted field research in Papua New Guinea and the Trobriand Islands. His most famous work, *Argonauts of the Western Pacific*, was an intensive ethnographic study of the Trobriand Islanders (Malinowski 1922).

Franz Boas was a German-American anthropologist who did intensive ethnographic fieldwork among the Inuit people on Baffin Island in northern Canada (Boas 1888).

Clifford Geertz conducted ethnographic research in Southeast Asia, and may be most famous for his description and cultural interpretation of cock-fighting in Bali (Geertz 1973).

Box 11.1 Some ethnographic studies of the environment

Study	*Topic*
Lichterman (1995)	Collaboration among grassroots environmental groups
Mathews (2005)	Firefighting on forest lands in Mexico
Norgaard (2012)	Attitudes toward climate change in rural Norway
Perry (2012)	Hydraulic fracturing in rural Pennsylvania
Radel (2005)	Women's access to land use in Mexico

Several things distinguish the ethnographic approaches of Malinowski, Boas, Geertz, and the legion of anthropologists who followed in their footsteps. First and perhaps foremost is the notion that true insight into cultures cannot be achieved by external observation, with the researcher keeping the members of the culture at arm's length. Rather, under the ethnographic approach, researchers immerse themselves in the culture, both observing and participating in day-to-day life for a significant period of time.

Malinowski coined the term "observer-participant" to denote the dual role played by the anthropologist doing ethnography. Mere observation is not sufficient, as it does not allow the observer to gain a real sense of the culture from the perspective of those being studied. It is only through actual participation that the researcher achieves a true sense of what it must be like to be a member of the culture.

This historical orientation toward "putting themselves in the shoes" of the members of the studied culture has some important implications for how ethnographic researchers interpret evidence. By seeing a culture through the eyes of its members, the data collected by researchers is almost by definition socially constructed, in the sense encountered earlier in Chapters 2 and 3.

In this important sense, ethnographic data are very different from the "objective" data favored by scientists and quantitative researchers in general. This means that the goals and objectives of ethnographic research have to be very different as well. Instead of searching for neutral and objective scientific truths, ethnographers search for *meaning*: what their lived experience means to members of the studied culture.

There is a broader implication of taking this *emic*, or insider's, perspective, which has to do with making normative judgments regarding the studied culture or its members. Cultural anthropologists have tried to be extremely careful to avoid judging cultures or societies relative to each other as "inferior" or "superior" in any sense. Making such judgments would not only impede their attempts to really understand a cultural experience; it also carries the danger of the entire ethnographic enterprise becoming one of enlightening the benighted masses to the wonders of the researcher's own cultural attitudes, values, and institutions. Cultures are what they are and should be understood on their own terms.

In doing an ethnography, there is a fine line to be drawn between description and interpretation. Is it the job of the ethnographic researcher merely to faithfully describe what she observes? Or should she go further and provide an interpretation of what she thinks it means? Many might argue the latter, but if so, how then does one avoid imposing one's own cultural values on the interpretation?

Among others, Clifford Geertz has attempted to resolve this quandary by arguing that ethnographers should interpret, but that any particular interpretation should be regarded as only one among many possible interpretations. The exercise is then similar to that of attempting to understand the meaning of a literary text, where there can be many interpretations (Walsh 2012, pp. 247–8). The takeaway message is that it is probably impossible to avoid making your own culturally based interpretation, but make it with a liberal dose of humility and be aware that others may interpret things differently.

The ethnographic approach in environmental studies

From its origins in cultural anthropology, the practice of ethnography has spread to contexts outside what were traditional community settings in non-western cultures. Recent examples include ethnographies of towns in rural Pennsylvania affected by hydraulic fracturing (Perry 2012); African-American families in inner-city neighborhoods in the northeastern United States (Burton 1997); the inner workings of the national environmental agency of Mexico (Mathews 2005); and the internet (Stoddart and MacDonald 2011). As you can see, the term ethnography has become considerably broader than its traditional meaning. But in all cases, it still refers to in-depth study of everyday life.

The application of the ethnographic approach to study of the environment has occurred as researchers have come to recognize its potential to provide insight into certain types of environmental issues. Many of these issues occur in the context of developing countries, such as rural land use, forest development, water management, and resource depletion. Anthropologists have taken the lead here, becoming increasingly interested in: (1) environmental issues with the growth of local environmental movements at field sites, (2) general burgeoning interest in environmental scholarship, and (3) various issues relating to recent trends toward greater globalization (Brosius 1999, p. 279).

However, the ethnographic approach has spread outside the discipline of cultural anthropology into sociology, and in the process, we are now seeing more environmental ethnographies in non-traditional settings. Let's examine a couple of recent examples.

Attitudes of rural Norwegians toward climate change

The sociologist Kari Norgaard was interested in better understanding public attitudes toward climate change (Norgaard 2012). It is well known that ongoing climate change has important distributional consequences, especially between developing and developed countries, which feeds into Norgaard's interest in environmental justice. She found it puzzling that many westerners exhibit seeming indifference to the issue, and she wanted to find out why.

Norgaard pursued an ethnography strategy, in which she lived in a rural community in western Norway for eight months and did dozens of interviews of local residents, made ethnographic observations, and combined this information with an analysis of popular media content. Her analysis centered mainly upon information gleaned from her interviews.

On the basis of these interviews, she concluded first of all that climate change was clearly a salient issue for many of her respondents. This enabled her to rule out the possibility that they were simply not aware of the issue. She was also able to conclude that it wasn't that they were simply not concerned about climate change and its impacts. On the contrary, they appeared to be very concerned. This left her wondering about the reasons for their apparent unwillingness to favor strong action to combat climate change.

The answer, she decided, lay in a set of psychological coping strategies commonly adopted by individuals when confronted with unpleasant information. When confronted by the troubling prospect of climate change causing significant changes in their local environment, and the fact that heavily oil-producing Norway is one of the leading contributors to climate change, local residents responded in two basic ways.

One was to devise various ways of promoting a feeling of security and stability in the face of changing times, what she called "tools of order." These included holding on to cherished traditions and creating narratives of Norwegian national identity that are tied up in their relationship to nature.

The other was to downplay their own contribution to climate change, which also took several forms. They talked about how they had suffered hard times in their history, and they emphasized their relatively small contribution to climate change compared to other countries and their generally positive relationship to the environment in other ways. These are examples of what she called "tools of innocence." Invoking tools of order and tools of innocence essentially allowed them to justify non-action on policy related to climate change.

It should be noted that, true to the qualitative approach, Norgaard did not begin with a theory and testable hypotheses. Rather, in pursuing her ethnographic work, she first observed the patterns in the data, and then tried to make sense out of them. She ended up developing a theoretical framework based upon the notions of tools of order and tools of innocence, which built upon previous studies that conceived of construction of social life and culture as a series of tools (Hollander and Gordon 2006). Notice how she combined two key features of much qualitative research: the interest in processes and mechanisms (as opposed to outcomes), and social construction.

Environmental community organizing in the western United States

The sociologist Paul Lichterman was interested in the experiences of grassroots environmental groups in developing alliances with other groups toward common causes (Lichterman 1995).

His interest in this issue stemmed from the apparent inability of many environmental groups to form effective alliances, especially across multicultural lines. The result has been an environmental movement that was largely white, middle-class, and relatively well-educated. He wanted to understand the factors that impeded the formation of multicultural alliances.

His study adopted the ethnographic approach, in which he spent two years as an observer-participant among environmental groups on the West Coast, examining internal structure, operations, and decision-making procedures as well as interactions among different groups.

There were two different types of groups: local Green organizations and anti-toxics organizations. The Green groups consisted largely of college-educated, middle-class whites. The study focused primarily on the relationship between

Green groups and an anti-toxics group—Hillviewers Against Toxics (HAT)—which consisted largely of low- to moderate-income African Americans. Preliminary contacts toward a possible alliance were made between Green groups and HAT, but apparently nothing came of these efforts.

In his field research, Lichterman found, first of all, that Green groups and HAT shared similar objectives and commitments to addressing local environmental issues, as well as what appeared to be a sincere willingness to work together. They communicated with each other and attended each other's meetings, workshops, and events. As an organization, the Greens were officially committed to promoting cultural diversity, opposing racism, and joining with communities of color to combat environmental degradation in their communities. None of this good will and good intentions was enough, however, to sustain a continuing effective alliance between the Green groups and HAT.

The problem, Lichterman concluded, had to do with different cultures of decision-making between the two groups. The Green groups emphasized individual empowerment, with members being encouraged to take personal initiative and to express personal opinions in meetings. Decisions were arrived at deliberatively and through consensus as issues were hashed out in extended discussions with broad participation.

HAT, on the other hand, downplayed individual empowerment, with the expectation that individuals serve as dutiful members of the group. Members were judged on the basis of how they contributed to the group, which was expected to speak with one voice on all issues. Lichterman provided the useful metaphor of likening the two types of groups to a choir. Whereas under the Greens model, the different voices sing in collective harmony, the HAT model is more like a "hearty chant in unison."

The cultural differences that gave rise to these different perspectives turned out to be fatal to the ability of these groups to form effective alliances with each other. In outreach efforts to HAT, the Green groups emphasized individual initiative in bridging gaps to multicultural communities. HAT, for its part, expected Green representatives at HAT meetings to speak with one voice in representing the Green groups, which resulted in miscommunication and some misunderstanding. Furthermore, Greens who attended HAT meetings, used to the participatory culture at Green meetings, were not always comfortable with what they perceived as a lack of democratic process.

Like Norgaard, Lichterman uses theory for framing his discussion and findings, rather than to generate testable hypotheses. Existing studies of alliance-building emphasize factors that differ across organizations, such as organizational structure, group ideologies, and ways in which members construct the collective identity of their groups.

One of Lichterman's main points is that though important, organizational and decision-making structures do not completely explain failures in alliance-building. Cultural differences can also matter a great deal. And this can have ongoing consequences for alliance-building, especially attempts to bridge gaps between different socioeconomic classes.

Ethnographic research procedures

Now that we have a sense for the ethnographic approach and how it can be applied to environmental issues, let us now turn to some practical nuts-and-bolts issues of performing an ethnographic study.

The questions are: What is sound ethnographic method, and what are the sorts of things we need to avoid? Let's divide up the ethnographic approach into several key issues: pre-fieldwork preparation, your role as ethnographic researcher, gaining access, collection of data, interviewing, and keeping field notes.

Preparation

Ethnography, of course, does not merely entail going and living somewhere and talking to people. There is much that goes into doing a careful ethnographic study, including important groundwork you need to lay before you even hit the field.

It is important to keep in mind that ethnographers need to walk a fine line between under-preparation and over-preparation. This is because ethnography is by definition open-ended, and you never know in advance what you are going to find. And what you find once you hit the field may very well lead you to rethink your study in important ways.

And yet, you need to go out there with some idea of what you are looking for. This means, first of all, that ethnographers need to familiarize themselves with a body of relevant literature, as with all good research. However, the process of doing a literature review for an ethnography is more fluid than it would be for a quantitative research project, which has a linear structure of: Theory—Testable Hypotheses—Data Collection—Data Analysis/Hypothesis Testing, as we have seen. Because ethnography is open-ended, data collection and analysis may open up new paths of inquiry, which may require familiarization with additional studies on further topics.

For example, given the nature of their research projects, both Norgaard and Lichterman had to familiarize themselves with how existing studies conceptualized culture, and Lichterman had to know what existing studies said about the factors determining the success of building alliances. But both had to hold out the possibility of unforeseen factors playing an important role and, if so, to know what existing studies said about them if they did. And they would only know this once they started collecting and analyzing their data.

Practically speaking, what all of this means is that you should emerge from your review of the literature with some problem statement or set of issues you would like to gain additional insight into. These are sometimes referred to as *foreshadowed problems* (Malinowski 1922; Smith 1974, p. 24). These are not as formal as testable hypotheses, but it is fine to think of them as working hypotheses that will be developed, refined, or modified in the process of observation and collection of data.

At this point, however, the focus of your study should still be quite broad, as you don't want to rule out possibly important factors before you even see what issues

Figure 11.2 The funnel shape of an ethnographic study.

Source: Author.

and patterns of evidence are emerging in the field. The subsequent process of data collection and analysis will naturally lead you to narrow your focus, to home in on the things that seem to really matter. In this way, the research process in an ethnography resembles a funnel: starting wide at the beginning and narrowing down to the essentials as your study progresses (see Figure 11.2) (Walsh 2012, p. 250).

> **Bottom line:** In doing ethnographies, we start with a broad focus and a tentative set of issues (foreshadowed problems) for investigation, based upon the findings of existing studies. This focus is gradually narrowed as the study proceeds and you collect data and gain insights into the key issues in your specific context.

Your role as researcher

Once you are in the field, you begin to face a number of practical concerns relating to acquisition of reliable data. The first issue you face is precisely what role to play within the setting of your research. As we have seen, Malinowski coined the term "observer-participant," by which he meant that the ethnographer's role is a dual one: both observing and participating in the life of the studied setting. However, there are several possibilities for doing this, which basically come down to how much of your role is that of (outside) observer, and how much is that of participant.

One possibility is to be a *complete participant*. This means to go into a setting and not let anyone know what you are doing. In this role, you are essentially going undercover, in hopes of obtaining the unvarnished "truth" about the situation, uncontaminated by people's awareness of your role and the possibility that they will treat you, and reveal information to you, differently as a result. This has been done, for example, in ethnographic studies of organized crime and religious cults. There is the danger of your cover being blown, with major consequences for your study (and potentially for you!). Furthermore, ethical objections can be raised to the practice, which after all involves deception (see Chapter 18). For these reasons, it is rare to find ethnographies where the researcher assumes this role, and it is probably one you should not consider.

At the other extreme is the possibility of being a *complete observer*. In this role, the researcher avoids all interaction with the studied culture and assumes a perspective of completely external observer. The advantage of this strategy is that you do not have to worry about the possibility that people are reacting to being observed. However, it is hard to see how, in many settings, one could logistically pull this off outside of the possibility of observing through a one-way mirror. Furthermore, trying to assume this role may limit the amount and types of information you can actually acquire, without the possibility of actual interactions, interviews, and conversation with members of the studied culture.

The other two possibilities—*participant as observer* and *observer as participant*—both involve participation and observation, but in differing degrees. The role of participant as observer stresses participation, while the role of observer as participant stresses observation. In both cases, the people being studied are aware of your role as researcher. However, your relationship to them is slightly different, the difference between actively participating in their lives and largely standing back and observing.

There are advantages to each strategy, but the basic tradeoff between the two comes down to objectivity versus full and complete information. The greater your level of active participation, the more difficult it may be to maintain a researcher's dispassionate detachment. However, the more you stand back and observe, the greater the danger that you may miss things. These include simply not seeing actions and events, and having an incomplete appreciation for what participation actually means to the people being studied.

Bottom line: If you do an ethnographic study, you will most likely want to assume a role that combines both participation and observation, one that combines both detachment and sufficient familiarity that you are really able to put yourself in the shoes of the people you are studying.

Gaining access to your setting

Once you have decided what role as researcher you want to play, the next step is to gain access to the setting you wish to study. This may seem as easy as relocating to the setting that is the subject of your study and settling in. However, once you get there, there may be all sorts of issues of access to the information you need to do your study. It may be difficult to know who you should be talking to. You may need to receive permission to attend meetings not open to the public. More generally, whenever there are private settings involved, one of your key tasks will be to gain admittance, not only physically but to specific sources of useful information. For this, it may help to identify *gatekeepers*; that is, strategically placed individuals who can facilitate access.

Who are these gatekeepers? They are not always easy to identify. They could be community leaders, key personnel in an organization, individuals who just happen to be well-connected within a community even if they have no formal position, certain long-time residents, and so forth. Their importance cannot be overstated. Sometimes, they can spell the difference between being able to get the information you need and not.

When you move to a setting, it may be well worth your while to invest some time in trying to identify who the gatekeepers are. Sometimes, this can be achieved by talking to people and explaining your purpose. Then, if nine out of ten people say: "You really have to talk to X," that may indicate that X is a gatekeeper.

Though gatekeepers are extremely valuable in general, one has to exercise a bit of caution when using them, as their objectives may not be completely consonant with yours as researcher. They may be concerned with the image of their community and how it will be depicted by you. They may want to keep certain sensitive or unpleasant things hidden. They may direct you to resources (e.g., people to talk to) that tend to serve their purposes rather than yours. None of this negates the potential value of gatekeepers, and sometimes tact, discreetness, diplomacy, and promises of confidentiality can address or mitigate some of these issues.

Bottom line: It can often be quite useful to spend some time identifying and getting to know the gatekeepers in a cultural setting. As long as you are careful, gatekeepers can greatly facilitate effective access to members of the setting.

Data collection

Once you have gained admittance, you can start collecting data. For this, it is important to establish good relations with those being studied including developing a degree of trust, since they may be suspicious of your intentions and motives to begin with. It is, of course, important to be respectful of local customs, to be sociable, and to be willing to engage people in normal social intercourse. Seemingly little things can make a big difference, such as the way you dress and comport yourself in general.

All of this is aimed at establishing rapport and earning trust, so that people are willing to share information with you. At the same time, there is a need to maintain a level of professional detachment, to not become so engrossed in one's role in the setting that one loses sight of the aims of the research project.

Assuming you have managed all of this successfully, the data that you collect on-site can come from a wide variety of sources, including simple observation, casual conversations, semi-formal interviews, and documents of various kinds. Given this potential wealth of information, the first thing you should ask yourself is: What do I need to know?

Regardless of your specific topic, there is a particular set of questions that often need to be answered in order to be able to fully characterize a setting and the action that takes place within that setting. These correspond roughly to the questions commonly asked by journalists when they are covering a news story: Who, What, When, Where, How, and Why? (Hoey 2014).

Who: Who are the key relevant actors in your setting? In Norgaard's study, it was the various residents of the locality she was studying. In Lichterman's study, it was the Green groups and the anti-toxics group (HAT), as well as certain key personnel within each organization.

What: What do these actors do? What else happens that is important in understanding the events and processes that occur and the meaning ascribed to them by the people involved? Here, many different things can be relevant, including actions, events, utterances, and social interactions. How much you rely on each of these things will depend upon the subject of your study.

For example, since Norgaard was interested in understanding individual attitudes, much of her data came from interviews and what people said in those interviews. Lichterman, on the other hand, was interested in inter-organizational dynamics, and so he focused much more on meetings and what happened in those meetings.

When: When do things happen? What you are looking for here are temporal patterns that shed light on what is happening in a particular situation. For example, do actions, utterances, or social interactions occur at specific times or follow any particular sequencing?

A good example of this is found at one point in Lichterman's study, where he ascribes significance to miscommunication between HAT and one of the Green groups that ended with a poorly attended rally, after which the Green group stopped contacting HAT (Lichterman 1995, p. 526).

Where: Where is the setting? What does it look like? Does it have significance in terms of how we interpret the data? Norgaard, for example, studied climate change attitudes among residents of rural Norway. This choice of setting permitted her to invoke several factors critical to her argument: a privileged western society, a significant contributor to global warming, and a natural setting where residents valued the environment.

How: How do things work? How do people behave? How do they view their interactions with others? The interpretive question here is regarding processes and mechanisms, and the factors that govern how these play out. This question was absolutely central to the Lichterman study, which compared the clash of two cultural norms: individualism vs. group-oriented behavior.

Why: Why did a thing happen? This is an interpretive question, where we are trying to understand the significance of an event, an interaction, or what someone said. There are tons of examples of this in both the Norgaard and Lichterman studies. The ultimate objective here is to take your interpretations of these individual happenings and weave them together into a coherent overall account.

Bottom line: It will be useful to keep in mind the six questions of journalism when thinking about how to characterize a cultural setting and what happens there.

Interviewing

In any case, much of your data are likely to derive from verbal interactions with people, in everything from informal conversations to formal interviews. In Chapter 17, we will see a much more complete discussion of proper interviewing methods, and you are encouraged to consult that chapter for more specific details. For now, you may want to keep several things in mind.

First, since ethnography emphasizes seeing things as they really are in the studied setting, the conversations you have with people should feel as unforced and natural as possible. Ideally, conversations would be spontaneous, unsolicited, and without specific agendas. This is one of the advantages to an extended stay in the studied setting, which makes these sorts of conversations easier and more likely to occur. If you can do this, great. However, since this is often not possible, you may well have to solicit and schedule interviews.

Second, when choosing whom to interview, you may well have to make a choice between trying to get a representative sample and a non-representative one that perhaps contains more useful information. Some potential interviewees may, for example, be especially thoughtful or reflective, or especially well-positioned to shed insights on the internal workings of organizations or communities.

Choice of interviewee should be made based on your careful assessment of who is likely to provide information most useful to your project goals. This also means that you are going to have to be careful in assessing the content of the information you collect. For example, if a gatekeeper points you to a particular person to talk to, you may want to think about the motivations of the gatekeeper when assessing that information.

Third, ethnographic interviews tend to be relatively unstructured and open-ended. Interviewees are generally not limited to specific choices defined by you, and the interviewer generally makes a conscious effort to try not to be directive in guiding the conversation down pre-determined paths.

At the same time, you as the researcher have specific information needs, so the conversation cannot be totally dictated by the interviewee. Thus, you will find yourself walking a fine line between giving the interviewee free rein and providing too much direction.

A good example of walking this fine line is found in the Norgaard study. In talking to local residents, she often found that global warming was not brought up spontaneously in their conversations. So, to gently nudge the conversation in that direction, she would ask people what they thought about the recent weather (Norgaard 2012, p. 86). This often served to turn the conversation to the topic she was really interested in, at which point she could ask some follow-up questions.

Bottom line: When conducting interviews in ethnographic research, it is best if the interviews feel as natural and unforced as possible. However, you should be prepared to have to guide the interviews in certain directions in order to obtain the information you require. You should also think carefully about whom to interview, in terms of best serving your needs for information.

Keeping field notes

A key component of ethnographic research is the taking and keeping of field notes. Here, you are keeping a written record of everything (relevant) that happens in the field, as you interview people, attend meetings, engage in casual conversations, and observe happenings and events. It is impossible to overstate the importance of keeping good field notes in doing an ethnographic study. As Brian Hoey puts it:

> [E]thnographers depend on their field notes to discover, to work through preliminary understandings, to develop interpretations, and eventually to reach their conclusions. Ethnography, in large part, may be said to take place in and through the field notes.
>
> (Hoey 2014, p. 6)

In order to make effective field notes, here are a few suggestions. First, it will help to keep in mind the funnel shape of the ethnographic research project you are undertaking. You are starting out with a broad focus and some general, perhaps vague, working hypotheses when you hit the field and start collecting data.

Since you may not know exactly what you are looking for, it will help to be thorough and comprehensive in what you write down: you never know what you may need later. It is a lot harder to try to reconstruct from memory events and utterances on matters that turn out to be important, rather than to discard what turns out to be unimportant! Your focus will start to narrow as you begin to see the patterns emerging in your notes.

It is, of course, impossible to write down literally everything that happens. So as a first pass, keep in mind the six journalistic questions discussed earlier for guidance as what to focus on. Keep a notebook with you at all times to jot down events and utterances, along with your own thoughts and ideas as they occur to you. Record speech verbatim if you can, but also pay attention to non-verbal behavior. Pay attention to context as well, including when and where things occurred, and who was present. You may find it difficult to write down everything that you need to when it happens, but do your best.

Afterwards, go back over your jottings and transcribe them into a more complete set of notes, filling in blanks and adding commentary and interpretation. It is important to do this as soon as you can before memory begins to fade.

Bottom line: Keeping good field notes is a crucial component of doing effective ethnography. Field notes should be comprehensive and should include not only the content of events and conversations, but also your own thoughts as these things occur. Furthermore, you will want to transcribe your notes as soon as you can afterwards, in order to obtain as accurate an account as possible.

It is also important to be in constant consultation with your notes. As your project progresses, new ideas will naturally occur to you, which may shed new light on notes you had taken earlier. This may create new gaps, new paths of inquiry. It will help to think about your old notes in the light of new evidence. Practically speaking, here are several things to keep in mind as you are going through this iterative process of note-taking.

First and perhaps foremost, it is important to view your notes with a critical eye with regard to what they are telling you about your object of study. When you read over your notes, ask yourself if they seem incomplete, and if so, in what way. Are there additional things you need to know, and if so, what things? How should you go about acquiring this additional information? Would it help to talk to additional people, and if so, who should you talk to and what might you need to ask them to get the information you need? Answering these questions may be particularly useful as you progress through the project and your understanding evolves over time.

One strategy you might find useful is to focus on things you find surprising. No matter how much you try to walk into a situation without preconceived notions, you will always have a few. It is impossible to be an entirely blank slate. Furthermore, ethnographic work is by its very nature serendipitous: you never know in advance what you are going to find.

All of this almost inevitably means that some things you experience in the field will surprise you: what happens, what people say. You should ask yourself what surprised you and why it surprised you. For example, are there important differences between what you believe to be true about people in the studied setting and what they believe about themselves? Where do these differences come from, and how do you explain them?

Your notes may also provide insight into how you are conducting your study. Are you taking the appropriate steps to obtain the information you need? Are you talking to the right people? How do people perceive you as researcher? Are the things they say and do in part a reaction to your very presence? Are you treating the people you are studying ethically and with respect?

One potentially useful strategy here is to share your findings with the people you are studying, as a way of validating your research. There are limitations to this strategy in that people may not be conscious of what they do, may want to rationalize their behavior, or may simply not be interested in an ethnographic account of their culture. However, their responses may stimulate new ideas and the possibility of new paths of analysis. Keep in mind that your ultimate objective is genuine insight into the studied culture, and all your efforts should be in service of this objective.

Bottom line: In taking field notes, it may help to take special note of things that challenge your preconceptions. It is often useful to note these things when they happen and then to evaluate your response critically.

Conclusions

You may have discerned from the discussion in this chapter that doing an ethnographic study entails a major investment in time and resources. This is certainly true and, thus, the challenges of doing an ethnographic study are not to be taken lightly. However, if you are interested in understanding better the things that ethnographies are particularly good at shedding light on—the meanings that people ascribe to events and actions, their interpretation of the world, and the consequences of these meanings and interpretations—then the ethnographic approach may well be for you.

Exercises/discussion questions

(1) Consider the four possibilities for the role that you as ethnographic research could play in the studied setting: complete participant, complete observer, participant as observer, and observer as participant. In which of the following settings would it make sense to play which role, and why?

(a) An Adele concert on campus, (b) life on the varsity women's basketball team, (c) life as a member of student government.

(2) Take your favorite television show that involves a portrayal of a real-life situation (this could, for example, be a sitcom, police crime show, or reality show). Watch one episode with a friend, each of you taking detailed ethnographic field notes on your own, keeping in mind the six journalistic questions. Obviously, you are assuming the role of complete observer.

Take two specific things that happen in the show and compare your respective interpretations of their significance toward contributing to the plot of the show. In addition, discuss the strengths and limitations of the complete observer approach, in terms of enabling you to understand what is going on in the observed culture, and to truly discern the meaning of events to its actual participants.

(3) Consider the living situation in a residence hall on your campus (not necessarily yours). You are interested in doing an ethnographic study to discover how social attitudes regarding new energy conservation measures on campus

are influenced by the social and cultural setting. How would you go about determining who would serve as a useful gatekeeper, and why?

(4) Attend a social event on campus, trying to keep detailed field notes on what events occur and your reactions at the time they occur. Note any difficulties that arise as you try to keep notes while not influencing people in the events as they happen. Afterwards, transcribe your notes and assess them for accuracy in fully capturing what you just experienced and your reactions to the overall experience.

References

Boas, Franz. "The Central Eskimo," *Smithsonian Institution via Gutenberg*, Sixth Annual Report of the Bureau of Ethnology to the Secretary of the Smithsonian Institution, 1884–1885. Washington: Government Printing Office, 1888: 399–670.

Brosius, J. Peter. "Analyses and Interventions: Anthropological Engagements with Environmentalism," *Current Anthropology* 40(June 1999): 277–309.

Burton, Linda M. "Ethnography and the Meaning of Adolescence in High-risk Neighborhoods," *Ethos* 25(June 1997): 208–17.

Geertz, Clifford. *Interpretation of Cultures*. New York: Basic Books, 1973.

Hammersley, Martyn, and Paul Atkinson. *Ethnography: Principles in Practice* (2nd ed.). London: Routledge, 1995.

Hoey, Brian A. "A Simple Introduction to the Practice of Ethnography and Guide to Ethnographic Fieldnotes," *Marshall University Digital Scholar* (June 2014), http://works.bepress.com/brian_hoey/12

Hollander, Jocelyn A. and Hava R. Gordon. "The processes of social construction in talk," *Symbolic Interaction* 29(2006): 183–212.

Lichterman, Paul. "Piecing Together Multicultural Community: Cultural Differences in Community Building Among Grass-roots Environmentalists," *Social Problems* 42(November 1995): 513–34.

Malinowski, Bronislaw. *Argonauts of the Western Pacific*. London: Routledge, 1922.

Mathews. Andrew S. "Power/Knowledge, Power/Ignorance: Forest Fires and the State in Mexico," *Human Ecology* 33(December 2005): 795–820.

Norgaard, Kari M. "Climate Denial and the Construction of Innocence: Reproducing Transnational Environmental Privilege in the Face of Climate Change," *Race, Gender & Class* 19(2012): 80–103.

Perry, Simona L. "Development, Land Use, and Collective Trauma: The Marcellus Shale Gas Boom in Rural Pennsylvania," *Culture, Agriculture, Food and Environment* 34(2012): 81–92.

Radel, Claudia. "Women's Community-based Organization, Conservation Projects, and Effective Land Control in Southern Mexico," *Journal of Latin American Geography* 4(2005): 7–34.

Smith, Louis M. "Reflections on Trying to Theorize from Ethnographic Data," *Council on Anthropology and Education Quarterly* 5(February 1974): 18–24.

Stoddart, Mark C. J., and Laura MacDonald. "'Keep It Wild, Keep It Local': Comparing News Media and the Internet as Sites for Environmental Movement Activism for Jumbo Pass, British Columbia," *Canadian Journal of Sociology* 36(October 2011): 313–35.

Walsh, David. "Doing Ethnography," in Clive Seale (ed.), *Researching Society and Culture* (3rd ed.). Los Angeles: Sage, 2012: 245–62.

12 Actor-network theory

Introduction

Actor-network theory is another qualitative approach that has been increasingly applied in recent years to study the environment. Originally developed as a way to think about science and technology, actor-network theory has come to be applied to a number of different environmental topics, including agriculture in developing countries, climate change, hydropower development, water governance, whaling, and wildlife conservation. In this chapter, we define what is meant by actor-network theory, discuss its goals and objectives, and examine two recent environmental studies that use actor-network theory. To provide a sense for the applicability of actor-network theory in environmental studies, Box 12.1 lists a number of recent environmental actor-network theory studies and the general topic of each study.

Box 12.1 Some actor-network studies of the environment

Study	*Topic*
Barnes (2012)	Desert reclamation in Egypt
Campbell (2004)	Rain-fed agriculture in Ghana
Campregher (2008)	Hydropower development in Costa Rica
Fleury et al. (2008)	Sustainable agriculture and rural development in the European Alps
Kishigami (2010)	Climate change and whaling among indigenous people in northwest Alaska
Soderbaum (1993)	Environmental policy
Suiyanata (2002)	Agriculture and land use in Hawaii

Source: Author.

An example: Rain-fed agriculture in Ghana

To understand what actor-network theory is all about, it might help to consider a concrete example. In a recent study, Michael Campbell was interested in the sustainability of rain-fed agriculture in Ghana (Campbell 2004). The coastal savannas in the studied area are susceptible to droughts, over-cultivation, and overgrazing, resulting in soil depletion and degradation. At the time of his study, technological solutions such as irrigation had not solved the problem because of chronic underfunding.

Campbell was interested in understanding a complex picture of social (gender roles, social networks, various demographics) and environmental (rainfall, soil quality) factors, and how all of these factors interacted to affect farming success. All of the traditional elements of a qualitative study were present. There was no real theory generating testable hypotheses, which would have been impossible anyway because of the absence of sufficient consistent, numerical data. And the author had a strong interest in characterizing underlying mechanisms and processes underlying local sustainable agriculture. This, as we have seen, is not the strong suit of the quantitative approach.

What Campbell quickly discovered were a large number of different factors, both environmental and social, that seemed to be important in determining sustainable farming practices. Moreover, there seemed to be major reciprocal influences among many of these different factors.

For example, the variability of rainfall affected farm sizes and the demand for mechanized practices, including tractors. It also increased the need for financing to tide farmers over during slow times. The need for financing in turn influenced gender relationships, since many of the farmers were male and many of the moneylenders were female. Social networks were used extensively to cope with rainfall variability, and the operation of these networks was influenced by the relative social status of different participants: male vs. female, young vs. old. The young were also more receptive to new emerging activities, such as long-distance trading and transport activities, which in turn affected the feasibility of sustainable farming.

We will return to this example shortly, but in the meantime, you might think about what research strategy you might use to tackle this complex, seemingly unwieldy project.

What is actor-network theory?

The idea behind actor-network theory is to treat systems as networks of connections, and to treat objects within networks as actors interacting through these connections. In Figure 12.1, for example, the nodes A are actors, and the lines C between the nodes are the connections. Environmental outcomes are understood as resulting from a complex interaction of actors across connections with various other actors.

To understand the approach taken by Campbell in our example study, it is important to note that the actors in a network need not be human actors but can be, for example, rainfall. The notion that inanimate objects like rainfall can be "actors" may seem strange to many people, so some actor-network theorists propose that they be given the more action-neutral term *actants* (Latour 1996, p. 369; Risan 2005, p. 787). We shall see other examples of actants in the example

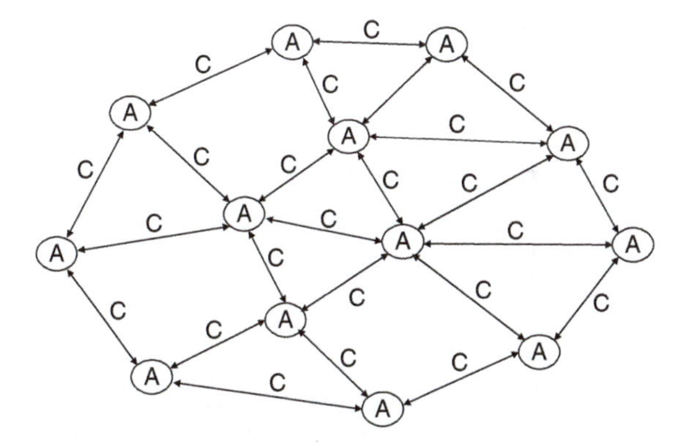

Figure 12.1 An actor-network.

Source: Author.

studies, including computers, ecosystems, wildlife, farm animals, water, microbes, and even ice.

Keeping in mind this broad definition of actors, let us consider more closely the notion of a network. Actor-network theorists emphasize that networks should be considered broadly as well. They emphasize this point because when we hear the word "network," many of us tend to think of it in a narrow technical sense, such as a network of power lines, or computers, or telephones.

Bruno Latour, one of the founders of actor-network theory, stresses that we should not think of networks in this way (Latour 1996, p. 369). Whereas power lines are constructed in fixed arrangements between producers, intermediaries, and final consumers, the networks Latour has in mind are fluid, with constantly varying configurations and intensity of connection, more like a social network like Facebook or Twitter.

Even with these broad definitions of actors and networks, it may be intuitive for us to grasp the notion of a bunch of networked actants, connected with and influenced by each other through the network. But where do these networks come from?

Unlike many real-world networks, the networks in actor-network theory are not consciously constructed by any of the actants, and no one comes in and constructs the network for them, like a power company might do to provide you and your neighbors with electricity. Rather, the networks form and evolve organically in connection with the actants that inhabit them. In the terminology of actor-network theory, actants and networks are *co-constructionist*: that is, they come into being together (Murdoch 2001, p. 111).

Furthermore, parts of networks can flicker out and disappear, connections can become weaker or stronger, and new connections can form, both with existing actants and with new, previously unconnected actants. The entire network is volatile, fluid, and emergent.

What determines what the network is going to look like? This ultimately depends upon the actants and the way that they interact with each other through the connections in the network. At any point in time, actants influence, and are influenced by, other actants. Each actant has its own perspective and interacts with other actants through *chains of translation* of their perspectives into language that can be understood by other actants (Callon and Law 1982). These interactions occur in so-called *spaces of negotiation*. At the same time, the connections in the network mediate and constrain the interactions among actants, in *spaces of prescription*.

Though conceptually different, these spaces of negotiation and spaces of prescription may well be the same spaces, which signifies that the same connections provide both opportunity for interactions and constraints on those interactions. At the same time, actions can reinforce or dilute connections, leading to changes in the network. Through these mutual interactions, networks and actants co-evolve in an organic process. Where they end up is unpredictable and depends very much upon the particulars of the situation.

With all this in mind, let us return to the Campbell study of Ghana. Given the complexity of the situation in terms of the many social and environmental factors and their interactions, Campbell decided that it could be fruitful to employ actor-network theory. This provided him with a framework to model the actants and their network connections. The actants included the largely male farmers and fishers, female money-lenders, tractor owners, a government-run irrigation project, rainfall, crops, soil fertility, fish stocks, and wildlife. These were all bound together into a network with varying connectivity across actants.

To characterize the actants and the connections, Campbell engaged in an intensive data collection effort involving surveys, semi-structured interviews (see Chapter 17), government records and reports, and scientific and agronomic observations. Using these data, Campbell was able to characterize relationships among actants that enabled him to establish the nature of the connections within the network.

These data confirmed, for example, the central importance of rainfall variability as a factor influencing rain-fed farming, which influenced crop production, farm sizes, demand for mechanized equipment such as tractors, and increased demand for business loans from money-lenders. All of these factors influenced the creation of what Campbell calls *socio-environmental networks*, the methods used by farmers to increase access to social and environmental resources. The study was thus able to document the true nature of the environmental problem—not low rainfall per se, but rather rainfall fluctuations—and the various adjustments made by local farmers to deal with the problem.

Goals and objectives of actor-network theory

It may still be unclear to you what actor-network theory buys us, in terms of explanatory power, compared to an ethnography or a detailed case study. To appreciate a bit more what it brings to the table, it may help to know some of its intellectual history. For this, let us consider again the quantitative approach, as exemplified by the scientific method.

Origins of actor-network theory in the sociology of science and technology

The scientific method, you will recall, involves a process of steady accumulation of improved understanding through repeated testing of hypotheses. Theory is formulated to generate falsifiable hypotheses, and then data are collected and considered in order to test these hypotheses. Theories are confirmed or discarded based upon the results of these hypothesis tests and, over time, we slowly inch toward a better understanding of the world. As Isaac Asimov reminds us, we are never entirely right, we only become relatively less wrong.

At some point along the way, some sociologists started asking themselves: "What's wrong with this picture?" These sociologists included Bruno Latour, Michel Callon, and John Law. The problem, they argued, was that it seems to be grossly incomplete and unrealistic by depicting a world in which social, political, and cultural factors play no part in the process of producing and disseminating scientific findings.

Certainly, on one level scientists were, and continue to be, correct in rejecting the intrusion of these factors into the practice of science. A signal cautionary lesson was provided by the experiences of the Soviet Union starting in the 1930s, when a man named Trofim Lysenko began to serve as director of the Academy of Agricultural Sciences. Under Lysenko's regime, the Academy rejected the notion of natural selection and advanced a number of pseudo-scientific claims that are now known to be demonstrably false. However, Lysenko's notions were supported by Joseph Stalin, who fired, imprisoned, or executed thousands of mainstream biologists (Roll-Hansen 2008; Babcock 2014). This entire sad episode spawned the term *Lysenkoism*, which today means any distortion or manipulation of the scientific process in order to advance political or social goals.

Nevertheless, Latour, Callon, Law, and others were troubled by the absence of social factors in the model of science. They believed there was a disconnect between this representation of scientific procedure and the way that science is actually done in the real world. As opposed to this tidy picture of science at work, they had a strong suspicion that the entire process of science—from what happens in laboratories all the way to dissemination of scientific findings to the broader public—was a good deal more messy and complex. This gave rise to a number of studies that looked inside the "black box" of science, aiming to shed light on how science is actually done and how laboratory findings actually become accepted as scientific knowledge.

A classic example is Latour's 1988 study *The Pasteurization of France*. This was an intensive examination of the French biologist Louis Pasteur, who is today most famous for his scientific discoveries regarding microbial transmission of disease that led to the process of pasteurization of milk.

In Pasteur's case, it was not simply a matter of doing the science and everyone else seeing the light. Rather, a variety of factors—scientific, social, and political—all played an important role in leading to the ultimate triumph of his ideas. Latour modeled this scientific process using actor-network theory, which treated a number of factors as actants within a complex network. These actants included farmers, newspapers, livestock, army doctors, government bureaucrats, and microbes (Latour 1988, pp. 59–145; Murdoch 2001, pp. 118–19; Luckhurst 2006, p. 6). By exploring the interactions among, and mutual influences of, these different actants, Latour helped us to decipher the complex picture that led to acceptance and application of his findings and ultimately led to widespread adoption of milk pasteurization.

Latour's application of actor-network theory to the practice of science has important practical implications for doing successful science. Science is not neat and tidy, but messy and complex. In the modern world, pure science does not exist, but rather is dependent upon funding from industry and government, the very existence of which can influence the scientific process. And to be effective, scientists cannot operate in isolation from the real world, but rather must be cognizant of the many social, economic, and political connections that influence how quickly and widely scientific findings will be disseminated to, and accepted by, society. According to this view, this awareness of the broader context could spell the difference between a scientist making a major difference or toiling for years in obscurity.

Application of actor-network theory to study of the environment

From its beginnings in the sociology of science and technology, actor-network theory subsequently spread to a number of other disciplines, including geography, anthropology, economics, education, and philosophy. Its application to environmental studies seems natural because of the complex nature of many environmental issues. Just think, for example, of the complex interplay of scientific, social, economic, and political factors surrounding the issue of climate change. Actor-network theory provides a framework for modeling complex systems, where many factors are interrelated in evolving, dynamic ways.

But the contribution of actor-network theory goes much farther than simply viewing environmental issues such as climate change as networks of connections among actants. By universalizing the notion of an actant to be virtually anything, actor-network theory deemphasizes the importance of humans, who find themselves as just one more node in a network, next to cows, ice, and microbes.

In actor-network theory, the influence of human actants stems not just from any intrinsic qualities but from the strength and power of their connections with other actants in the system. If the spaces in which they operate are largely spaces of prescription rather than spaces of negotiation, they may have little room to maneuver in terms of affecting environmental outcomes. To farmers wishing to irrigate their farms, for example, a severe scarcity of water can provide a powerful constraint on what they can accomplish and how they affect the environment.

This is not to argue that humans are not an extremely important part of the environmental picture in studies that use actor-network theory. Indeed, many such studies place humans in a prominent position in their analysis, just like Campbell did in the earlier example. But the fact that actor-network theory does not *automatically* privilege humans as special actors appeals to some researchers who subscribe to an ecological view of the environment, as opposed to an environmental landscape dominated by human actors (Murdoch 2001, p. 114; Campregher 2010, p. 785).

Furthermore, actor-network theory, by placing attention squarely on the connections between actants, and the nature of the spaces they represent, elevates the role played by social (and other) influences on human behavior. This includes the way that actions, ideas, and technologies are socially constructed. This was clearly seen in Latour's study of Pasteur, but we can also see social construction at play with many modern environmental issues.

Climate change science, for example, is not the tidy science of Karl Popper, but rather a messy affair that has come to be heavily politicized. The influence of politics can be seen in public reactions to scientific findings, with clear differences across different political persuasions and regions of the world. Some have also argued that political considerations can enter in at other stages of the research process, including when research agendas are being set and when laboratory findings are interpreted prior to public dissemination. And as we saw in Chapter 11, translating evidence on climate change into effective policy can depend in part on how citizens such as those in rural Norway socially construct climate change in their own personal lives.

You may notice some parallels between this description of actor-network theory and Chapter 11's discussion of the ethnographic approach. Cultural anthropology, the cradle of the ethnographic approach, focuses much of its attention on social and cultural influences on human behavior. It is almost as if humans are hard-wired into a social and cultural setting, which plays a very important role in influencing attitudes and behavior. This is very different from the rationalist approach emphasized by economists, for example, which emphasizes purposive, goal-oriented, individual behavior. Like ethnography, actor-network theory also stresses external influences on human behavior, which play out through the connections in the networks they occupy.

Another feature of the ethnographic approach is the deliberate and conscious attempt to see the world through the eyes and experiences of the peoples in the studied culture. Cultural immersion and thick description are key components of the researcher's attempt to put herself in their shoes, and to achieve a genuine understanding of their perspective.

Yet for some researchers, the traditional ethnographic approach does not go far enough. For them, the ethnographic researcher can still bring western baggage and a perspective of "otherness" that imposes a wall of separation between observer and observed, obstructing true understanding of the studied culture. Actor-network theory can be thought of as a conscious attempt to overcome this barrier (Campregher 2010, p. 786). Every participant in an environmental situation, even nature itself, is placed on equal footing with all other participants.

Bottom line: In actor-network theory, environmental problems are treated as complex, evolving networks among actants, both human and non-human. The approach also treats human and non-human actants symmetrically, in terms of position and influence within any given network.

Some environmental applications of actor-network theory

This discussion of actor-network theory has left open a number of practical questions of implementation. Perhaps the biggest question is how one moves past the basic actor-network set-up in order to draw meaningful conclusions regarding relationships among related variables. You may have also been wondering how actor-network theory practitioners model non-human actants, which many find to be one of the hardest features of actor-network theory for them to wrap their minds around. To address these and other issues, it may help to consider a couple of actual studies that have used actor-network theory to study specific environmental issues. These studies are chosen to illustrate different features of the actor-network theory approach.

Indigenous whaling in north Alaska

In a recent study, the anthropologist Nobuhiro Kishigami considers how Inupiat communities, whose way of life has traditionally been closely tied to subsistence hunting of bowhead whales, have been affected by recent climate change (Kishigami 2010). The Inupiat have been hunting bowhead whales for centuries, and in addition to providing sustenance, whaling forms an important basis for their culture, social lives, and ethnic identity. Whaling success has been aided by solid ice conditions, which both limits the geographical dispersion of whale migrations and provides shoreline locations for butchering whales. Beginning in the 1980s, climate change has warmed the local climate and reduced sea ice cover, with corresponding effects on whale migration patterns as well as less ice along the shoreline. All of this has made whaling more difficult.

There are major reserves of recoverable oil and natural gas on Alaska's continental shelf, which have been largely underdeveloped because of year-round sea ice. Reduced sea ice associated with ongoing climate change is encouraging both tourism and freight transport through Arctic waters. Reduced sea ice has encouraged oil and gas exploration by oil companies such as Royal Dutch Shell and Conoco Phillips. At the same time, the federal government has been more liberally granting leases to oil companies in order to promote energy security, especially in the wake of Hurricane Katrina. Increased drilling activity has been altering whale migration routes, forcing Inupiat whalers to have to travel farther to hunt.

All of this has led Inupiat whalers and environmental non-government organizations (NGOs) to bring legal action against both the federal government and oil companies. Environmental NGOs, including animal rights groups, have also been engaging in anti-whaling lobbying activities and publicity campaigns. Though primarily targeted at commercial whaling, these activities also adversely impact whaling by the Inupiat.

While all this has been happening, there have also been some internal changes within Inupiat society. These primarily relate to growing ethnic diversification due to an influx of non-indigenous job-seekers and growing income inequality.

Much of the network implied by this description is summarized in Figure 12.2, which is adapted from Kishigami (2010, p. 101). Figure 12.2 depicts changes in sea ice as a key actant, with direct linkages to climate change, marine transport, tourism, oil and gas development, oil companies, and the bowhead whales themselves. Another important actant is oil and gas development, which has connections to sea ice changes, oil companies, the leasing policies of the federal government, and also directly to the whales themselves and the prosecution of whaling.

Whaling itself is at the center of this particular network, with direct linkages to the whales and oil and gas development, but also to public opinion, environmental and animal rights NGOs, Inupiat societal changes, and an entire set of factors comprising the complex relationship of the Inupiat to the whales.

Kishigami concludes that there are a complex set of natural, social, cultural, economic, and political factors that are affecting Inupiat whaling: changes in sea ice, increased oil and natural gas exploration, oil company activities, increases in tourism and maritime shipping, US energy policy, the anti-whaling movement, and internal changes in Inupiat society.

Notice the ways that these actants, and connections among actants, have co-evolved over time, as actor-network theory suggests. Prior to recent climate change, Arctic sea ice largely stymied off-shore oil and gas development, making the connection between oil and gas development and whaling unimportant, if not non-existent.

Now that climate change has dramatically reduced Arctic sea ice cover, the connection between the two has become much stronger. For similar reasons, marine transport and Arctic tourism used to be non-factors but are no longer so. Finally, activist animal rights NGOs have become significant actants only in fairly recent days. All of this implies that the network used to be a simpler one, as depicted in Figure 12.3.

It should be pointed out that the nature of the research exercise here is clearly qualitative. There is no theory generating testable hypotheses, nor data analysis per se as you would see in a quantitative study. Kishigami does not attempt to quantify the relationships among actants through the network connections. Rather, the exercise is to delve into the complexities of the situation in order to identify important actors and influences and shed light on underlying processes and mechanisms.

Hydropower development in Costa Rica

The anthropologist Christoph Campregher recently applied actor-network theory to understand hydropower development in Costa Rica (Campregher 2010).

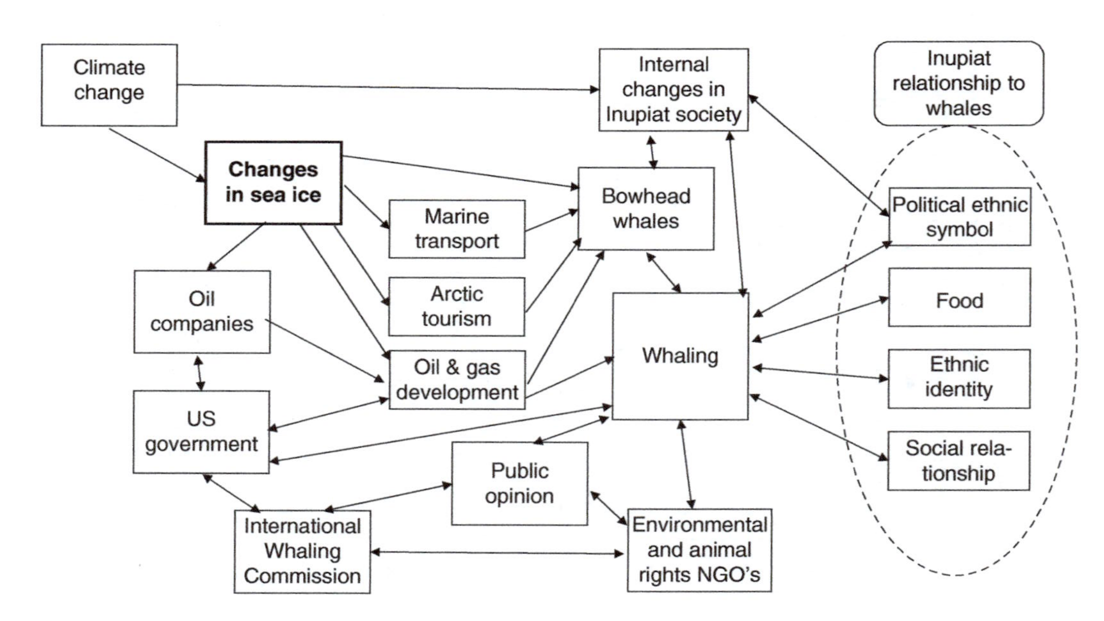

Figure 12.2 Actor-network, Kishigami.

Source: Author, adapted from Kishigami 2010, p. 101.

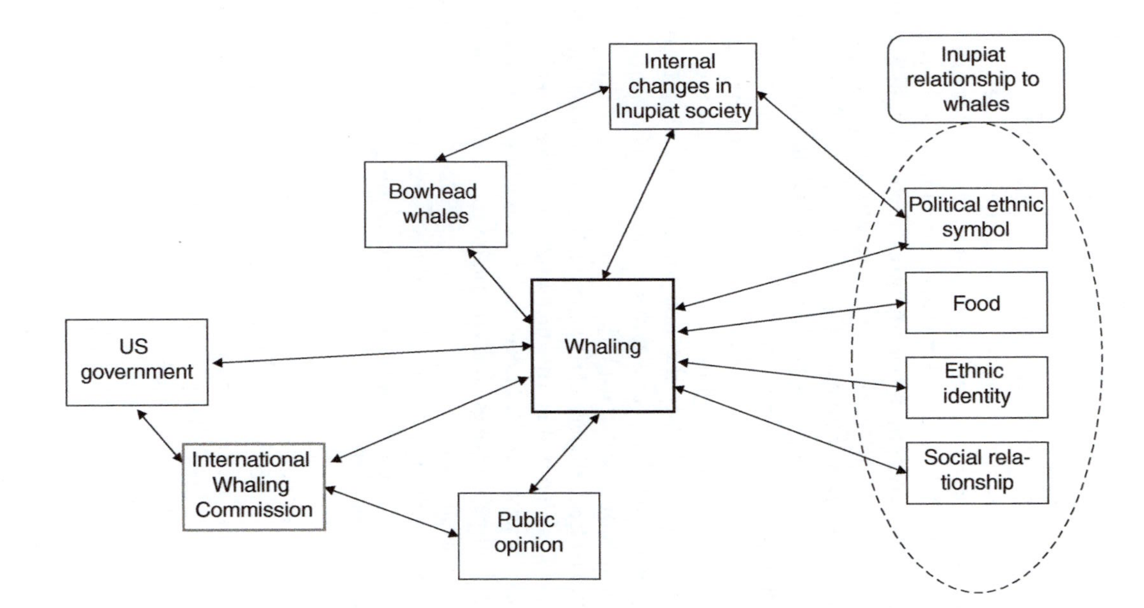

Figure 12.3 Historical actor-network, Kishigami.

Source: Author.

A key issue was the impact on local indigenous populations of building a hydropower dam. There were multiple actants: the hydropower developers, the indigenous peoples, and sociologists and anthropologists hired by the developers to work with the affected indigenous communities.

Complicating the picture was the fact that there were competing factions among the indigenous communities with varying attitudes towards hydropower development. The study focuses mostly on the political negotiations that took place among the interested parties.

Campregher's study is not, however, about explaining an outcome—whether a dam gets built. Nor is it about dissecting the political process whereby this occurs. Instead, he is interested in the question of how best to gather information on the positions of the different actants, in order to understand what is really going on. For this, he invokes the notion from actor-network theory that all actants in a network are to be treated symmetrically: that none are to occupy any special position by virtue of any quality, be it human-ness or anything else. As we have seen, this can serve to place humans in no special (especially dominant) relationship to nature, which appeals to many researchers.

Campregher uses this actor-network theory notion of symmetry to take the project sociologists and anthropologists on the one hand, and the indigenous communities on the other, and place them on equal footing. And then he goes one step further, placing *himself as the researcher* as just another actant in the network, with no special perspective or expertise.

All of this serves to treat all perspectives, including his own, as equally valid representations of a situation and its true meaning. Since every perspective has its blind spots, the only way to really understand what is going on is to give them all equal time. And all perspectives thus contribute to a complete and unified understanding of the dam project.

The study proceeds by alternately describing the perspectives of the main actants: first the developers, then the indigenous communities, and then finally, Campregher himself.

- *Developers*: The developers stress the economic benefits of the project, in terms of generating hydropower and providing local benefits such as jobs and opportunities for tourism, and to assuage concerns about environmental damages. They view their challenge as being to convince the locals that the project will benefit them, by providing information, answering questions, and addressing concerns. Their task is made more difficult by disputes over local land titles and the presence of different factions among the indigenous groups, some of who are strongly opposed to development.
- *Indigenous communities*: The perspective of the indigenous communities is quite different, as you might expect. There is strong resistance to the development project because of concerns over environmental impacts and bringing in migrant workers to build the dam. The indigenous communities value having control over development decisions that allow them to incorporate cultural, environmental, and economic factors. This would include not

necessarily building a dam but considering alternative development strategies, including eco-tourism and sustainable agriculture.
- *External researcher*: The perspective of the external researcher (Campregher) is to try to understand and describe the issues as objectively as possible, and to explain the positions of the different actors based upon sociological theories. He goes on to give his interpretation of the reasons for, and sources of, dispute between the two sides. He observes that in addition to an official entity that represents the region and ostensibly the interests of the indigenous peoples, there are roughly ten other groups that represent indigenous interests. These groups have generally worked to oppose the dam project, but their effectiveness has been diminished by various rivalries and tensions among the groups. The negotiations over the dam were shaped by a variety of factors, including local necessities, conflicts among these groups, and the presence of perceived alternatives to the dam project.

Having described the perspectives of the actants, Campregher goes on to explore how they are connected, in order to provide an interpretation that combines and reconciles the different perspectives. He connects the perspectives by interpreting each one as comprising a chain of translation of information derived from other actants.

The researcher translates information from his observations, and from a series of interviews and conversations with indigenous actors and the social scientists working for the developers. This information is interpreted through the lens of previous studies, which provide him with tools and language to make general statements.

The indigenous activist groups translate the on-the-ground reality among the indigenous communities into a representational picture for the social scientists working for the developers and other external organizations.

The social scientists translate the project plans and statistics into language understandable by the indigenous communities. They also provide backward translation of the reality of the communities into information that can be used and incorporated into the project development plans.

Campregher's approach is useful in couple of ways. First, by treating his own perspective as researcher as just another perspective on equal footing with all the rest, he can explore how his own cultural attitudes fit in with and relate to the subjects of his study. In doing so, he also places scientific knowledge and the self-knowledge within the communities on equal footing, as merely alternative representations of knowledge, each with its own truth.

Second, his focus on chains of translation permits him to highlight the ways in which different actants' positions are transformed and reconciled through their mutual interaction. This is the practice of social science that makes every attempt to be even-handed, objective, and culturally neutral.

The studies by Kishigami and Campregher provide a number of takeaway messages regarding the way actor-network theory studies can be done, as summarized here:

- Conceptualize your topic as a network of actants, potentially including non-human ones.

- Incorporate perspectives of the various actants, possibly including yourself.
- Model interactions as chains of translation between actants.
- Pay attention to how the network may evolve over time, through interactions among actants or outside forces.
- Draw conclusions on relationships among actants both through the connections and changes in the network over time.

Conclusions

To summarize, it is not only the inherent complexity of many environmental issues that has encouraged many researchers to apply actor-network theory to study of the environment. Many believe that the processes of interaction and communication among actants, the focus of actor-network theory, are crucial in understanding environmental outcomes. In addition, actor-network theory is a determinedly holistic approach that tries to account for a wide range of factors, entities, and types of connections. Finally, actor-network theory does not necessarily privilege human actors within a social-environmental network, which appeals to many researchers.

Exercises/discussion questions

(1) Consider the Campbell study of rain-fed agriculture in Ghana. Why not do this study as an ethnography? A case study? What is it about this study that makes it particularly suitable for the actor-network approach?

(2) The discussion in this chapter draws an analogy between a generic actor-network and a Facebook social network. What specific social factors determine the size and scope of one individual's Facebook network? What factors determine the strength of the connections in a Facebook network?

(3) One of the debates among scholars of actor-network theory is whether or not to draw distinctions between animate and inanimate objects as actants in a network. Woolgar (1991, p. 90–91) argues that it is "specist" (that is, to discriminate on the basis of species) to speak of users configuring computers to serve their needs. It is just as valid to think of computers as configuring users to *their* needs. For example, observing an interaction between computers and humans, he writes:

> Looking at the tape again, I am struck by the dignity of the machine in the face of the stumbling and mutterings of the human actants. For example, the machine sits there throughout the whole "wrong socket" episode, uncomplainingly. It must have known that the socket was not going to fit.

In response to the objection that humans are sentient and computers are not, he argues: "What entitles us to attribute intentionality to non-machines in the first place?"

What is your view of Woolgar's position that treating non-animate objects like computers amounts to discrimination on the basis of species?

(4) As illustrated in Campregher's study, in actor-network theory the researcher herself can be considered as just another actant in an actor-network, with no special role to play. Yet you as researcher do bring a particular set of useful skills to a research project, which seems to imply a unique role for you as researcher. How do you reconcile these two ideas?

References

Babcock, Christopher. "The Lasting Lesson of Lysenko," *Psychology Today*, January 11, 2014.

Barnes, Jessica. "Pumping Possibility: Agricultural Expansion Through Desert Reclamation in Egypt," *Social Studies of Science* 42(August 2012): 517–38.

Callon, Michel, and John Law. "On Interests and Their Transformation: Enrolment and Counter-enrolment," *Social Studies of Science* 12(1982): 615–25.

Campbell, Michael O'Neal. "The Role of Socio-environmental Networking in the Sustainability of Rain-fed Agriculture in the Coastal Savanna of Ghana," *GeoJournal* 61(2004): 79–88.

Campregher, Christoph. "Shifting Perspectives on Development: An Actor-network Study of a Dam in Costa Rica," *Anthropological Quarterly* 83(Fall 2010): 783–804.

Fleury, Philippe. "Implementing Sustainable Agriculture and Rural Development in the European Alps: Assets and Limitations of Local Projects Based on Multi-stakeholder Participation," *Mountain Research and Development* 28(August/November 2008): 226–32.

Kishigami, Nobuhiro. "Climate Change, Oil and Gas Development, and Inupiat Whaling in Northwest Alaska," *Etudes/Inuit/Studies* 34(2010): 91–107.

Latour, Bruno. *The Pasteurization of France*. Cambridge: Harvard University Press, 1988.

Latour, Bruno. "On Actor-network Theory: A Few Clarifications," *Soziale Welt* 47(1996): 369–81.

Luckhurst, Roger. "Bruno Latour's Scientifiction: Networks, Assemblages, and Tangled Objects," *Science Fiction Studies* 33(March 2006): 4–17.

Murdoch, Jonathan. "Ecologising Sociology: Actor-network Theory, Co-construction and the Problem of Exemptionalism," *Sociology* 35(February 2001): 111–33.

Risan, Lars Christian. "The Boundary of Animality," *Environment and Planning D: Society and Space* 23(2005): 787–93.

Roll-Hansen, Nils. "Wishful Science: The Persistence of T. D. Lysenko's Agrobiology in the Politics of Science," *Osiris* (2nd series) 23(2008): 166–88.

Soderbaum, Peter. "Values, Markets, and Environmental Policy: An Actor-network Approach," *Journal of Economic Issues* 27(June 1993): 387–408.

Suiyanata, Krisnawati. "Diversified Agriculture, Land Use, and Agrofood Networks in Hawaii," *Economic Geography* 78(January 2002): 71–86.

Woolgar, S. "Configuring the User: The Case of Usability Trials," in *A Sociology of Monsters: Essays on Power, Technology and Domination*. London: Routledge, 1991: 58–99.

13 Environmental discourse analysis

Introduction

Another qualitative strategy of growing popularity in recent years is *environmental discourse analysis*. The basic idea here is that we can tell a lot about environmental issues by examining the public conversations that surround them. By paying careful attention to what people say about environmental issues and how they say it, it is possible to discern a great deal about public attitudes toward various issues. Often, we can also explain a great deal about the policy outcomes that occur.

In this chapter, we define what is meant by environmental discourse analysis; provide two extended illustrations of environmental discourse analyses; discuss the rationale for doing this kind of analysis; and describe various things to consider when undertaking such an analysis.

What is environmental discourse analysis?

To define environmental discourse analysis, it will help to first define what is meant by a *discourse*, as environmental discourse analysis is simply the analysis of discourses in study of the environment. Box 13.1 lists several definitions that may be found in the literature.

Box 13.1 Definitions of discourse

- "A specific ensemble of ideas, concepts, and categorizations … through which meaning is given to physical and social realities" (Hajer 1995, p. 44).
- "A shared way of apprehending the world" (Dryzek 1997, p. 8).
- "A collection of interrelated texts that cohere in some way to produce both meanings and effects in the real world" (Maguire and Hardy 2009, p. 150).
- "A group of statements which provide a language for talking about—i.e., a way of interpreting—a particular kind of knowledge about a topic" (Tonkiss 2012, p. 406).

Source: Author.

The commonality in these definitions is the focus on language and texts and ways of talking about the world. The questions then become: How do we understand these discourses? What purposes do they serve? What do people accomplish by speaking in certain ways?

In order to answer these questions, it will help to first distinguish discourse from two other related concepts: *ideas* and *rhetoric*. All of these concepts—ideas, discourse, and rhetoric—are about ways of viewing, thinking about, and communicating what goes on in the world. However, they mean slightly different things.

Generally speaking, ideas are almost any set of beliefs, views, or conceptions of the world. Discourse takes some set of ideas and weaves them into a narrative that provides a particular interpretation of events. Finally, rhetoric refers to the specific linguistic ways in which ideas and discourses are expressed. You may think about it in this way: ideas provide the raw material for a discourse, which may be expressed in various ways through an assortment of rhetorical devices.

The field of discourse analysis has arisen as a systematic way of studying discourse and the role that it plays in society. Importantly, the focus of discourse analysis is not so much the ideas themselves, but rather how people fit these ideas together and how they communicate them to others. Discourse analysis aims to understand how and why specific discourses arise, why they take the form they do, and what purposes they serve.

There are different strains of discourse analysis, but the one most commonly applied to study of the environment is associated with the French philosopher and social theorist Michel Foucault. Foucault championed the view that ideas are powerful not only because of their content but also because of the way they are presented to others (Ludwig 2012, p. 146–7). Foucault thus stresses not so much the generation of ideas, but rather how they are communicated. In this approach, one can see parallels to the approach of Latour in his study of Louis Pasteur in Chapter 12.

This view thus focuses on the communication of ideas and how things spoken of are endowed with particular meanings. The idea here is that different people can take the same set of ideas and construct drastically different narratives that will mean very different things to different listeners.

A good example of this is provided by recent public discourse on climate change, which has become an extremely politically contentious issue, at least in the United States. The science of human-generated climate change is pretty settled, though there is enough uncertainty to accommodate two competing narratives within public discourse. To see this, consider Boxes 13.2 and 13.3, which contain excerpts from two recent news accounts regarding climate change. One of these is from the conservative network *Fox News* and the other is from the liberal newspaper *The Guardian*.

Box 13.2 News item: "A new low in science: Criminalizing climate change skeptics," *FoxNews.com*, 9/28/2015

The demand by Senator Whitehouse and the 20 climate scientists for legal persecution of people whose research on science and policy they disagree with represents a new low in the politicization of science.

The consequence of this persecution, intended or not, is to make pariahs of scientists who are doing exactly what we expect of researchers: to critically evaluate evidence and publish that work in the scientific literature.

Minority perspectives have an important and respected role to play in advancing science, as a mean for testing ideas and pushing the knowledge frontier forward.

Box 13.3 News item: "Fox News found to be a major driving force behind global warming denial," *The Guardian*, 8/8/2013

The study ... concluded that the conservative media creates distrust in scientists through five main methods:

1 Presenting contrarian scientists as "objective" experts while presenting mainstream scientists as self-interested or biased.
2 Denigrating scientific institutions and peer-reviewed journals.
3 Equating peer-reviewed research with a politically liberal opinion.
4 Accusing climate scientists of manipulating data to fund research projects.
5 Characterizing climate science as a religion.

The headlines tell us much. The *Guardian* headline speaks of climate "denial," while the *Fox News* headline refers to climate "skepticism." These keywords support two competing narratives on climate change. In referring to "climate skeptics," the *Fox News* article is supporting a narrative of healthy disagreements over scientific findings being stifled by self-serving zealots pushing their own agendas. In referring to "climate deniers," the *Guardian* article is supporting an alternative narrative of incompetent or disingenuous hacks whose only possible motive in challenging established facts must be that they are shilling for fossil fuel companies.

All of this illustrates an important principle of discourse theory: the way we speak about things can literally affect what others think they mean. Thus, when people engage in discourse, they are creating narratives for how the world is to be interpreted. One of the goals of discourse analysis is to decipher the messages that are being conveyed and how they are heard by listeners.

Discourse analysis goes further, however. As we have just seen, discourse may be actively being used strategically to further certain objectives of those engaging in the discourse. Foucault emphasized power relationships and the role of discourse in both preserving and challenging those relationships (Foucault 1979,

p. 27; Lipscomb and O'Connor 2002, p. 397). Under Foucault's approach, groups in power use discourse to influence the way the world is socially constructed by others in order to maintain their power. Groups out of power similarly use discourse in order to challenge those in power.

But the notion of discourse being used strategically is considerably broader than applying it only to power relationships. More broadly, discourse analysis seeks to understand a wide range of narratives, all of which relate to how the world is socially constructed. As generally practiced, discourse analysts assume there is no one true view of the world, only various interpretations of it. Discourse analysis examines the way that discourse-driven narratives are created and used strategically in a variety of public and social realms.

As the name implies, environmental discourse analysis takes the concepts and tools of discourse analysis and applies them to study of the environment. Here, the focus is on specific ways that people speak about environmental issues.

We have already seen that ways of speaking matter when talking about the environment, an idea applied to wilderness and climate change in earlier chapters. However, we have yet to see this idea explored in any systematic way. In this chapter, we will formalize the discussion, illustrated with specific environmental examples such as ozone depletion, acid rain, pesticides, and state regulations on flame retardant chemicals. Box 13.4 lists a few recent environmental discourse analyses, and the particular environmental issue examined.

Box 13.4 Some environmental discourse analysis studies

Study	*Environmental issue*
Litfin (1994)	Ozone depletion
Hajer (1995)	Acid rain
Lipscomb et al. (2002)	Nuclear waste disposal
Raymond and Olive (2009)	Flame-retardant chemicals
Maguire and Hardy (2009)	DDT
Ludwig et al. (2012)	Wildlife management

Two illustrations: DDT and regulation of flame-retardant chemicals

To convey a concrete sense for what an environmental discourse analysis looks like, let us consider a couple of recent studies.

DDT (Maguire and Hardy 2009)

You may be aware that the pesticide DDT was once widely used for pest control. Farmers used to spray it on crops and applied it to their livestock. Homeowners used it at home to control flies, roaches, and bedbugs. And suburban communities used it to control mosquitoes and other insects. In the 1950s and early 1960s, it was the single most widely used insecticide in the United States.

After that time, however, it went into a rapid decline as people became aware of a number of environmental damages associated with its use. This included its well-known impact on the thickness of the egg-shells of nesting raptors. In 1972, the US Environmental Protection Agency (EPA) banned its use nationwide. From a peak of nearly eighty million tons in 1959, its use fell to essentially zero by 1973, the effective year of the EPA ban (Maguire and Hardy 2009, p. 152). The decline in the use of DDT is a well-known episode exemplifying the rise of environmental protection in the United States over the last half century.

A common explanation for the decline of DDT was the publication of *Silent Spring*, by Rachel Carson, in 1962. This book, which chronicled the environmental hazards of chemical pesticides, was widely read and highly influential. It triggered a strong negative public reaction to the use of DDT. However, DDT was a highly effective and economically valuable pesticide, and the message of *Silent Spring* was vigorously resisted at the time by many scientists, farmers, and the chemical industry (Griswold 2012). Two researchers, Steve Maguire and Cynthia Hardy, wanted to answer the question: How was public consensus against DDT achieved in the face of strong support for its continued use by entrenched interests?

True to the qualitative approach, Maguire and Hardy used theory, not to generate hypotheses, but rather to provide an organizing framework to understand the episode. They viewed the phasing out of DDT as an example of what they call *deinstitutionalization*. By this, they simply mean that at any point in time, there will be a set of established practices, or institutions, which enjoy legitimacy and support from influential groups with an interest in their perpetuation. The process of deinstitutionalization is one in which these established, and often entrenched, institutions lose legitimacy and experience a decline in status. This leads ultimately to their demise and replacement with a new set of institutions. The downfall of DDT seems to fit well into this framework.

As Maguire and Hardy document, the downfall of DDT occurred through the actions of those who found themselves outside of a circle of those groups interested in perpetuating the practice of DDT spraying. The interested groups, or insiders, mainly included agribusinesses and chemical companies. The outsiders included certain scientists, non-governmental organizations, and members of the budding environmental movement. The outsiders triumphed by successfully creating a narrative of dangerous DDT that gradually resonated with more and more people over time.

In order to document the growing influence of the outsiders, Maguire and Hardy take a multi-pronged approach, based on multiple sources of textual evidence. They begin with an account of the timeline of the important events in the abandonment of DDT use. Based on this timeline, they then developed an account of the public discourse surrounding these events in government reports, scientific publications, and other public documents.

In order to correctly interpret this public discourse, they then turned to a detailed analysis in which they dissected the argument in *Silent Spring*, to identify the ways in which the book changed public discourse surrounding DDT. The assumption here was that *Silent Spring* was potentially the catalyst for the subsequent changes in public opinion on DDT. We have seen this basic strategy before in Chapter 10 on case studies: identifying an event and then observing the relationship between the event and some other variable of interest. In this case, the other variable is the public opinion on DDT.

The next step in the analysis was to examine precisely how discourse on DDT changed in the years after *Silent Spring*. The texts they examined were wide-ranging and included federal legislation, newspaper editorials, letters to the editor, science textbooks, scientific articles, and doctoral dissertations. They paid close attention to the ways in which both scientific discussions regarding, and public attitudes toward, DDT changed. In this way, they were able to pinpoint when changes in discourse occurred, and the form those changes took.

For example, Figure 13.1 reproduces a figure from the study, which summarizes a content analysis of articles appearing in the leading scientific journal *Science*. The figure reports the number of articles in each year from 1944 to 1972 that were about DDT, and the topic of each article.

Prior to 1960 or so, the vast majority of articles were about either chemistry/biochemistry or insects. This signifies that most of the discourse in *Science* prior to *Silent Spring* had a relatively narrow focus, likely relating to the chemistry of DDT and its effect on insects.

After *Silent Spring* came out in 1962, however, the focus of these articles changed, with many more articles about its environmental impact, birds and fish (likely how they were affected by DDT), and DDT regulation. A separate figure counting the number of doctoral dissertations on DDT tells a similar story.

Their findings related to three arenas potentially influenced by *Silent Spring*: scientific studies, public opinion, and government regulation. In each of these arenas, they documented a sea change in public discourse on DDT. Over time, scientific texts came to reflect a new narrative on its negative effect on human health and safety, food chains, birds, and ecosystems. Public opinion, as reflected in editorials and letters to the editor, increasingly challenged the continued use of DDT. Various governmental texts, including regulatory bills and government advisory reports, spoke increasingly negatively on the environmental impacts of DDT.

At the same time, by paying close attention to the discourse, the authors were able to observe ways in which the discursive treatment of DDT was not significantly altered. For example, though the government advisory reports indicated broad acceptance of the negative environmental impacts of chemical treatments like DDT, they were unwilling to sanction a complete switch to biological controls. Their careful reading of the public texts available at the time permitted the authors to document how public discourse on DDT did and did not change after *Silent Spring*.

Flame retardant chemicals (Raymond and Olive 2009)

Some of the distinctive features of environmental discourse analysis are also illustrated in a recent study undertaken by two political scientists, Leigh Raymond and Andrea Olive, who applied the approach to better understand recent attempts by various US states to regulate flame-retardant chemicals.

Flame retardant chemicals have been used for years in things like building materials, carpets, and mattresses in order to reduce the risk of fire. However,

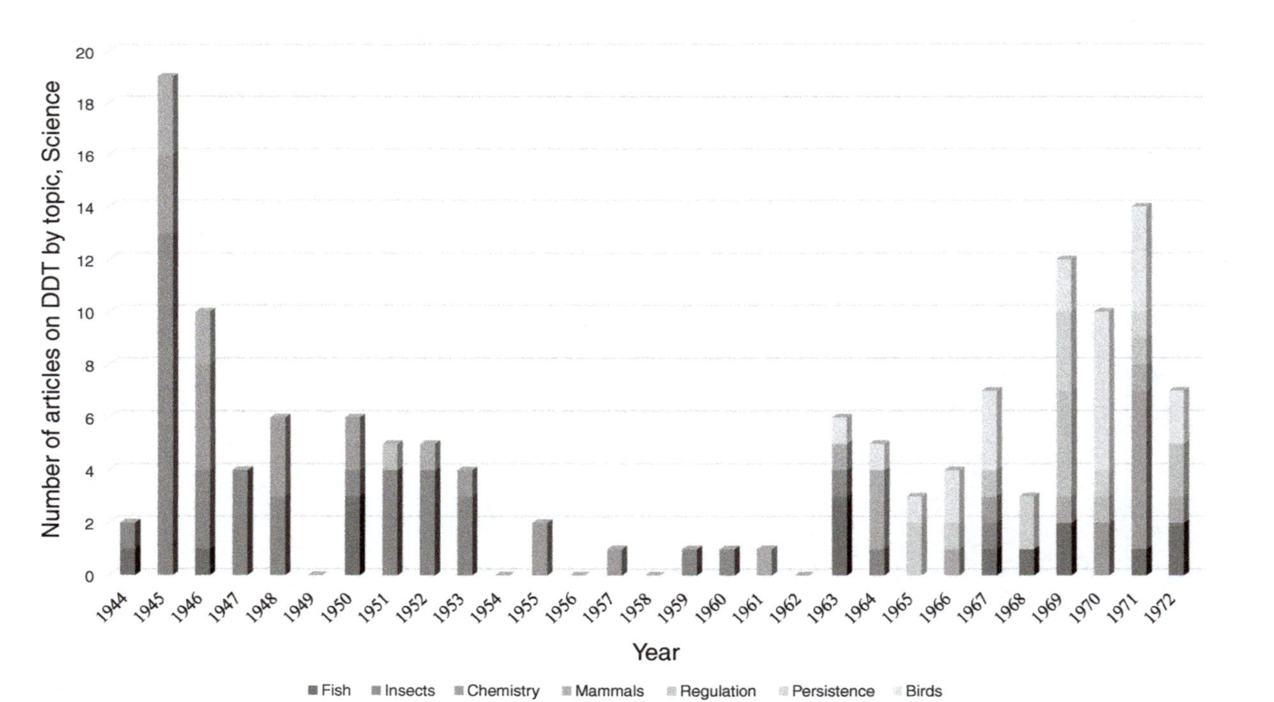

Figure 13.1 Number of Science articles on DDT by topic, 1944–1972.

Source: Maguire and Hardy 2009, p. 157.

in the 1990s people became increasingly aware of potential health risks associated with their use, and several states considered banning their manufacture and use. The study by Raymond and Olive focuses on three states in particular—California, Washington, and Minnesota—which experienced varying degrees of success in their attempts to regulate these chemicals within their respective states.

Raymond and Olive sought to shed light on the different regulatory experiences by examining the public discourse surrounding the political debates over regulation. Notice the notion of establishing the relationship among variables at work again: in this case, the relationship between public discourse and regulatory success.

Notice that, simply focusing on ideas leaves a lot of questions unexplained. There was a general idea out there that there were indeed health risks associated with the use of flame-retardant chemicals. Legislators and regulators in all three states would have had access to roughly the same idea, yet they ended up doing different things. Raymond and Olive asked whether it was possible that the way the idea was framed in differing narratives led to the different regulatory outcomes.

It turned out that the public discourse over the regulation issue varied across the states in systematic ways. A key issue lending support to bans on the chemicals was the accumulation of the chemicals in the environment: local ecosystems and, especially, breast milk. Its accumulation in breast milk turned out to be a very powerful idea that evoked a highly visceral negative response to continued use of the chemicals. However, scientific studies documenting its occurrence locally were apparently only available for California and Washington. As a result, the discourse in those states was largely framed in terms of the dangers to breast milk, whereas in Minnesota, the discourse focused more on the harder-to-document issue of general toxicity.

Another interesting aspect of the discourse was the way risk was portrayed. The effects of chemical accumulation only make themselves known gradually over time, and the science is not completely conclusive on the severity of its impacts. Under these circumstances, many scholars have suggested applying the *precautionary principle* to guide policy. The precautionary principle is thought to apply when a proposed action or policy may cause harm to the public or to the environment. It states that in the absence of scientific consensus that a particular action is not harmful, the burden of proof should fall on those taking the action to show that it is not harmful.

Despite its seeming applicability in the case, Raymond and Olive found it striking that the records of the public discourse contained numerous references to risk in various guises, but that mention of the precautionary principle itself by supporters of a ban was almost completely absent.

To understand why, they conducted a number of interviews with people involved in the legislative process in each state. These interviews strongly suggested that the term carried unwelcome connotations that supporters of a ban were anxious to avoid. One interviewee, for example, stated that the precautionary principle had become “a dirty word” associated with burdensome and unscientific regulation (Raymond and Olive 2009, p. 205). Thus, in order to bolster their case, they used other, less "loaded" language, which they believed would find more receptive ears.

On the basis of this analysis, Raymond and Olive drew two conclusions: one specific to the situation and one more general. One was that in the case at hand, discourse mattered. Neither ideas nor political economy considerations could fully explain the observed outcomes. Both sides tried to create compelling narratives favorable to their respective cases. And the final regulatory outcomes matched a story in which discourse played an important role.

Furthermore, the story provided insight into the policy importance of the precautionary principle. It was striking that ban supporters refused to use the language of the precautionary principle, feeling that doing so would hurt their cause. So even though the notion has many supporters among academics and policymakers, they concluded that its associated negative connotations may diminish its practical policy effectiveness.

Why do environmental discourse analysis?

The two preceding studies are suggestive of the ways that texts can be used to gain insights into environmental issues. At this point, however, it may be useful to be more explicit about the advantages of doing an environmental discourse analysis. The questions are: What exactly are the benefits of focusing on texts in order to shed light on environmental issues? What do examining and dissecting narratives give us that other approaches do not?

If you are considering doing an environmental discourse analysis, you probably find the qualitative approach appealing in general. This means that you may have an interest in the things the qualitative approach does well. Things like: shedding light on underlying processes in moving from A to B; recreating the subjective meaning of events to participants in those events; understanding the lived experiences of people in their society or culture; and gaining insights into how people socially construct various elements of their world.

Practitioners of environmental discourse analysis share many of these interests. They tend to see many environmental issues as messy, complex, and heavily contested. And they believe there are potentially important insights to be gained by characterizing the perspectives of various actors with a stake in how environmental issues are addressed. They do this, of course, by paying close attention to what people say about these issues. Written and verbal texts comprise the vehicles for their analysis.

Perhaps the defining characteristic of environmental discourse analysis is the assumption that language is not merely a passive medium that objectively describes environmental issues. Rather, it can actively affect one's subjective view of those issues. If so, the way that things are put may matter greatly. It matters, for example, whether you use the phrase "health risk" instead of "the precautionary principle," as we saw earlier. Similarly, the well-known environmental terms *sustainability*, *green revolution*, *spaceship earth*, and *population explosion* are not merely passive terms to describe things neutrally, but rather may actively affect how we think about those things.

If language matters and environmental issues are messy, complex, and heavily contested, this raises the possibility that competing sides on an environmental issue may engage in strategic use of language. Specifically, each side may try to create a self-serving narrative that resonates with others. And which narrative wins out can importantly affect what environmental laws are enacted and which environmental policies are implemented. Thus, understanding how narratives are constructed and what purposes they serve can provide important insights into environmental policy.

An important challenge for environmental discourse analysts is to understand which narratives will tend to win out, and why. Just because someone frames an issue in a certain way to create a particular narrative does not mean that narrative will be compelling to others. You could try to push a narrative that the moon is made out of green cheese, but it is unlikely you would get very far.

More generally, ideas matter in constructing a compelling narrative. But it also matters who is constructing the narrative, how much credibility they have, who the audiences are, and the context in which narratives are heard. At some point in the past, the notion that the moon is made out of green cheese was compelling for many people. And somebody pushing this idea would not have immediately lost all credibility with others. A key challenge for discourse analysis is to understand the interplay between narratives and the context in which they are created. The question is: What makes narratives compelling and under what conditions?

This turns out to be an important contribution of the environmental discourse approach, which attempts to shed light on why certain narratives catch on and others do not. And given the potential importance of competing narratives in influencing environmental policy, environmental discourse analysis can provide useful insights into why we get certain policies and the specific form those policies take.

The components of environmental discourse analysis

If there is one thing that characterizes the environmental discourse analysis approach, it is that it is difficult to identify any sort of standard approach. Different researchers use a variety of different frameworks, and much of the process is driven by what data are available, which determines the kind of analysis that can be done. Some have compared discourse analysis to riding a bike: "a process that one picks up by doing, perfects by practicing, and which is difficult to describe in a formal way" (Tonkiss 2012, p. 412).

However, a few general things can be said. As a form of qualitative analysis, environmental discourse analysis bears some strong methodological similarities to the qualitative approaches described in previous chapters. First, it tends to eschew formal hypothesis testing driven by theory. Rather, the researcher starts out with a general research problem informed, as always, by a survey of the literature. She then engages in an intensive collection of evidence that is subjected to analysis. This process of examining and considering the evidence feeds back into honing and refining the research question. The researcher gradually converges on the final research question, as well as conclusions based upon the evidence.

Let us consider the steps of the process in turn.

Defining the research problem

In some ways, defining the research problem is the most challenging step in the process, because it may not be clear exactly where you are going. Here, you may want to start out with a general idea, which gradually gets refined and focused through examination of evidence. In this way, the approach of an environmental discourse analysis resembles the funnel shape of the ethnography (see Chapter 11).

As an example, consider again the study by Raymond and Olive. As political scientists interested in environmental issues, they may have begun their project with only a general interest in the regulation of flame-retardant chemicals. But sifting through the evidence may have led them to realize the need to focus on regulation at the state level, which was where the regulatory efforts were taking place. Then when they examined more closely the regulatory experiences of different states, they may have noticed interesting differences in those experiences. This may have led them to question why those experiences were different.

In this way, from its initial nebulous form the research question gets gradually refined down to something more concrete and specific and, hence, more manageable; namely: What factors caused the regulatory experiences of different states to vary?

Bottom line: In defining the research problem in an environmental discourse analysis, you begin by reading relevant studies to give you a general research focus. Your focus gets gradually refined and narrowed as you gather more evidence, similarly to an ethnography.

Another factor to keep in mind when defining a research problem concerns your specific research objectives as a qualitative researcher. When doing an environmental discourse analysis, your objective is typically not to seek concrete solutions to specific problems. Rather, your main focus is typically on how both the problems and their solutions are talked about, with language and texts providing the evidence.

For example, an environmental discourse analysis on climate change would generally not pose a research question like: Should we focus on mitigation or adaptation strategies to combat climate change? Rather, we might pose the question: How is climate change understood, and how are the available strategies viewed, within the current political discourse? The research question is not so much about the problem itself, but rather on how it and its potential solutions are constructed by the opposing sides.

Bottom line: Discourse analyses do not generally focus on trying to explain environmental outcomes or to prescribe environmental policies. Rather, they focus on the narratives surrounding these outcomes or policies, in order to interpret the motivations and objectives of those who create the narratives.

Collection of evidence

Compared to the other qualitative approaches, the most distinctive feature of an environmental discourse analysis is the type of evidence it emphasizes. Rather than relying heavily on participant-observation or response analysis of surveys and interviews, environmental discourse analysis focuses primarily on texts, both oral and written. These could include news accounts, editorials, congressional or parliamentary debates, political speeches, government documents, books, scholarly articles, pamphlets, blogs, and so forth.

The point here is only partly that there are a great many kinds of evidence you can consider when you do an environmental discourse analysis. The focus on texts as one's primary source of evidence is particularly suited to getting at the issue of how environmental issues are socially constructed. This is because texts often speak directly to what events mean to the people participating in or affected by those events.

Consider again the Raymond and Olive study, whose texts consisted primarily of various documents from the legislative record, including hearings, testimony, and debates. These texts provided evidence of two competing narratives, one that emphasized the health risks involved in continued use of the flame-retardant chemicals, and another that emphasized the economic costs of banning a proven, effective method for reducing fire risk. Then, by carefully studying the statements made, a consistent, coherent picture emerged that both accumulation of chemicals in breast milk was a crucial factor leading to regulation, and the precautionary principle carried unwelcome rhetorical baggage.

Because there are so many different kinds of textual evidence, at some point along the way you will have to decide exactly which texts to use for your study. This is a challenging issue to say general things about, simply because there are so many different types of studies you could pursue and, therefore, so many different kinds of potentially appropriate texts. Here, let us simply consider a couple of examples, to give you an idea of the thought process of environmental discourse analysts.

International cooperation on ozone depletion

In *Ozone Discourses* (1994), Karen Litfin was interested in the discourse surrounding international negotiations over ozone depletion in the late 1980s, which culminated in the enactment of the Montreal Protocol in 1987. In this book, she documents how international cooperation to ban chlorofluorocarbons (CFCs) came to pass despite a great deal of scientific uncertainty regarding the connection between CFC production and ozone depletion.

Making her case required documenting how various interested parties—including government officials, environmental groups, and activist groups—framed the scientific evidence in such a way as to encourage preventive action. The texts she used to construct narratives for these respective groups included government agency reports, reports from environmental activist groups, and a wide variety of news accounts.

Acid rain

In *Politics of Environmental Discourse* (1995), Maarten Hajer examined the public discourse surrounding acid rain regulation in Europe during the 1970s and 1980s. In this research, he focused on two countries, the United Kingdom and the Netherlands, and constructed the relevant discourses that emerged in the public debates over regulation.

For example, in the United Kingdom, it came down to two competing narratives. One he called the *traditional pragmatist* narrative, advanced by regulation opponents such as industry trade groups and representatives of forest and energy interests. The other he called the *eco-modernist* narrative, advanced by supporters of regulation such as environmental groups, a government administrative agency on environmental pollution, and an environmental committee of the House of Commons. To construct these narratives, Hajer relied heavily on committee reports of the House of Commons and reports of the Forest Commission, Department of Energy, and Department of the Environment, all agencies of the government of the United Kingdom.

Elements of analysis

Once you have the data in hand, a number of methodological issues arise. The first is a general principle that one should approach the data with as few preconceptions as possible regarding what you think you are going to find. Let the evidence speak for itself.

This is often quite a challenge, since you will probably be sifting through a lot of evidence, and one simply cannot keep everything, or emphasize everything equally. At the same time, it is important not to discard evidence that is relevant in describing the actual discourse that is occurring. Above all, the objective is to make sure your characterization of discourses reflects the evidence as much as possible. If your interpretation is not consistent with the evidence you present, your analysis will not be compelling. With all this in mind, there are several strategies you could pursue.

Identifying key themes, issues and arguments

First, it will help to spend a fair amount of time identifying what appear to be the key themes, issues, and arguments to be found in the texts. This generally requires a careful reading of relevant texts that you have chosen, in which you look for regularities and patterns in the argumentation. Often it helps to keep an eye out for *keywords*, which may have been chosen for their power to convey and bolster a narrative. For example, in the earlier climate change example, "climate skeptics" and "climate change deniers" were important keywords in supporting the competing narratives.

As a more extended example, consider the famous study by Maarten Hajer on the politics of acid rain in Europe in the 1970s and 1980s. Hajer was interested in characterizing the evolution of the politics that led to major shifts in national policies regarding acid rain regulation.

By a close examination of various texts, Hajer was able to discern a shift from an old regime that emphasized a largely narrow, piecemeal, and non-science based approach to environmental regulation to a new regime that took a more broad-based approach based upon science, economics, and broader public participation in regulatory solutions. The old regime emphasized phrases like "end-of-pipe technologies" and "react-and-cure," whereas the new regime used very different terminologies like "anticipate-and-prevent," "pollution prevention pays," and "multi-value auditing" (Hajer 1995, pp. 25–8). These keywords added up to two distinct narratives that enabled Hajer to characterize and explain the evolution of European acid rain policy.

Patterns of association

In order to identify narratives, it can also help to notice how words and phrases are used in conjunction with each other to describe environmental issues or actors. In the earlier climate change example, the same *Guardian* article that referred to climate deniers also spoke about their "obstruction of climate solutions." This wording supported a narrative of there being solutions to the problem of climate change, which the deniers were simply obstructing for no good reason. Similarly, the *Fox News* article speaks of scientists "working hard to clarify uncertainties in the science." This phrasing paints a picture of diligent and conscientious scientists making a good-faith effort to get to the bottom of things. Such *patterns of association* can be quite useful in helping to see what narratives are being created.

Characterizations of affected individuals or groups: personalization and agency

Similarly, we can sometimes gain insight into narratives by paying close attention to how the accounts in texts characterize individuals or groups affected by environmental problems. There are several ways in which characterization can be used to support particular narratives. One way is through the use of *personalizing*—or *depersonalizing*—language.

You may have heard, for example, of islands in the Pacific Ocean vanishing under rising sea levels. There are two competing narratives that may be found here in news accounts. One depicts the vanishing islands as caused by climate change being directly responsible for rising sea levels. The other argues that climate change is only partly responsible, along with other factors, including the action of waves. These different narratives are sometimes supported by personalizing and depersonalizing language. One example of depersonalizing language is seen in the account found in Box 13.5.

Box 13.5 *News item*: "Scientist to liberal media: No climate change is not drowning Pacific islands," *Breitbart* 5/12/2016

The report … tracked the shapeshifting of 33 reef islands in the Solomon Islands between 1947 and 2014. It found that five had been washed away completely and six more had been severely eroded. The study blamed the loss on a combination of sea-level rise and high wave energy.

Contrast that to the account in Box 13.6, which is a climate change story about life in the Marshall Islands that personalizes the inhabitants. The two accounts evoke very different emotional responses from the reader, which serve to support each of the competing narratives of the impact of climate change.

Box 13.6 *News item*: "You're making this island disappear," *CNN.com*, August 16, 2016

Angie Hepisus heard her nephew, Mark, banging on the door and screaming in Marshallese.

"It's flooding! It's flooding! Get out!"

Her thoughts went immediately to her family on this fragile coastline in the middle of the Pacific, a place under increasing threat from climate change.

One of her cousins woke up that morning last spring to find herself floating, her plywood home filling up like an aquarium. Another, who lives in a house where the roof is held down by evenly spaced rocks, was so bewildered by the rush of water that had invaded her house at 4 a.m. that she actually licked her arm to be sure that, yes, this was saltwater, and, no, she wasn't having a nightmare.

A related device that is often used for characterizing affected individuals or groups concerns whether they are active participants in events or whether they are portrayed as victims of events beyond their control. For example, Box 13.7 contains more of the story of the experiences of people living in the Marshall Islands. This passage is a clear depiction of these people as victims of rising sea levels, which supports the narrative of climate change and its tragic consequences. In the terminology of discourse analysis, the Marshall Islands people lack *agency*: they are largely innocent, powerless victims caught up in circumstances beyond their control.

Box 13.7 News item: "You're making this island disappear," *CNN.com*, August 16, 2016

In the nine days I spent in Majuro, the crescent-shaped capital of the Marshall Islands, I learned there is nowhere on these islands to escape the floods. People, I was told, seek shelter on the second stories of buildings, or by climbing up the trunks of coconut trees. The only "hill" to speak of in Majuro is a bridge that's built over an inlet.

Bottom line: In performing environmental discourse analysis, it is useful to identify key themes in the texts, and to look for patterns of association between words and phrases and aspects of environmental issues. Also, pay attention to the use of personalizing and depersonalizing language.

Conclusions

Environmental discourse analysis is another qualitative approach that can be used to analyze and understand a wide range of environmental issues. It relies heavily on written and oral texts for evidence regarding narratives that are constructed to capture, represent, and understand environmental issues. The very nature of the evidence is not generally conducive to statistical analyses favored by quantitative researchers. But, as with all other qualitative approaches, it enables the researcher to dig deeper to understand attitudes, beliefs, and mechanisms for change. And proponents of environmental discourse analysis argue that it provides a more realistic and complete picture of how scientific and economic ideas get incorporated into environmental policy.

Exercises/discussion questions

(1) Find a couple of news items on hydraulic fracturing (fracking) that you think embody competing narratives, and briefly describe the different narratives they are telling. What are the different interpretations of fracking that the competing narratives are telling?

(2) Name another real-world example of deinstitutionalization in the area of environmental studies, and explain why it characterizes a situation of deinstitutionalization.

(3) One of the takeaway messages of the DDT episode described by Maguire and Hardy is that there are limits on the influence of changing discourse on policy. For DDT, what specific factors (political, economic, social, cultural) do you think limited the influence of discourse in affecting policy?

(4) As we saw, the Raymond and Olive study found that the phrase *precautionary principle* carried certain negative connotations for many interviewees. Suppose you are talking about climate change policy to someone who does not believe in anthropogenic climate change. Can you think of environmental phrases that such a person might consider "loaded"? What other, less loaded, phrases might you use instead? Do the same, assuming now that you are talking to someone who *does* believe in anthropogenic climate change.

(5) Give a real-life example of an environmental issue that involves an uneven power relationship among different groups. Characterize the narratives that the different groups are using to sway public opinion.

(6) Suppose you are a state senator interested in passing a state law to set aside logging areas for establishment of a nature preserve, in order to protect an endangered species of rare bird. Construct a narrative that supports establishment of the preserve that would be most compelling to employees of the logging industry.

(7) Find two news stories about a real-life environmental issue, where one story uses personalizing, and the other uses depersonalizing, language to support their respective narratives.

References

Curry, Judith. "A New Low in Science: Criminalizing Climate Change Skeptics," *FoxNews.com*, September 28, 2015, http://www.foxnews.com/opinion/2015/09/28/new-low-in-science-criminalizing-climate-change-skeptics.html

Delingpole, James. "Scientist to Liberal Media: No Climate Change Is Not Drowning Pacific Islands," *Breitbart.com*, May 12, 2016, http://www.breitbart.com/london/2016/05/12/scientist-to-liberal-media-no-climate-change-is-not-drowning-pacific-islands/

Dryzek, J. *The Politics of the Earth: Environmental Discourses*. Oxford: Oxford University Press, 1997.

Foucault, Michel. *Discipline and Punish: The Birth of the Prison*. New York: Vintage Books, 1979.

Griswold, Eliza. "How 'Silent Spring' Ignited the Environmental Movement," *New York Times Magazine*, September 21, 2012.

Hajer, Maarten A. *The Politics of Environmental Discourse: Ecological Modernization and the Policy Process*. Oxford: Clarendon Press, 1995.

Killingsworth, M. Jimmie, and Jacqueline S. Palmer. *Ecospeak: Rhetoric and Environmental Politics in America*. Carbondale, IL: Southern Illinois University Press, 1992.

Lipscomb, Michael E., and Robert E. O'Connor. "Democracy and Communicative Rifts: Foucault, Fish, and Yucca Mountain," *Administrative Theory and Praxis* 24(2002): 393–414.

Litfin, Karen T. *Ozone Discourses: Science and Politics In Global Environmental Cooperation*. New York: Columbia University Press, 1994.

Ludwig, Melanie, Friederike Gruninger, Eberhard Rothfuss, and Marco Heurich. "Discourse Analysis as an Instrument to Reveal the Pivotal Role of the Media In Local Acceptance or Rejection of a Wildlife Management Project: A Case Study from the Bavarian Forest National Park," *Erdkunde* (April–June 2012): 143–56.

Maguire, Steve, and Cynthia Hardy. "Discourse and Deinstitutionalization: The Decline of DDT," *Academy of Management Journal* 52(February 2009): 148–78.

Nucitelli, Dana. "Fox News Found to be a Major Driving Force Behind Global Warming Denial," *The Guardian*, August 8, 2013, https://www.theguardian.com/environment/climate-consensus-97-per-cent/2013/aug/08/global-warming-denial-fox-news

Raymond, Leigh and Andrea Olive. "Ideas, Discourse, and Rhetoric in Political Choice," *Polity* 41(April 2009): 189–210.

Sutter, John D. "You're Making This Island Disappear," *CNN.com*, August 16, 2016, http://www.cnn.com/interactive/2015/06/opinions/sutter-two-degrees-marshall-islands/

Tonkiss, Fran. "Discourse Analysis," in Clive Seale (ed.), *Researching Society and Culture* (3rd ed.). Los Angeles: Sage, 2012: 405–23.

14 Action research

Introduction

When you conduct research, you are always hopeful that your efforts will make a difference. Not only in contributing to a conversation among academic researchers, but also in helping to address real-world problems. These are not always the same thing. Or at least, the real-world impact of academic research is not always immediately apparent. All of the methods we have been discussing so far—both qualitative and quantitative—seem to be targeted at academic conversations with policy implications about things like environmental privilege, grassroots coalition-building, hydropower generation, ozone depletion policy, and the like.

There is, of course, nothing wrong with this: these types of studies, done correctly, can provide important and useful insights into environmental issues. Now, however, we are going to switch gears a bit and talk about a different type of research you could do: on-the-ground research that provides direct impetus for immediate action to address environmental problems. *Action research* has been a growing area of inquiry in recent years.

What is action research?

As with many of the other qualitative approaches that we have seen, action research has been defined in a number of different ways. Box 14.1 lists some representative definitions. Reading these definitions, you can why it is called action research. These definitions refer to pressing problems of practical concern to people: problems that you might want to take action on to try to address. In order to take effective action, naturally there is the need for research to determine what action to take, and why.

Generally speaking, all action research contains three basic components: *research*, *participation*, and *action* (Couch 2004, p. 147). Action research generates new knowledge to address a problem of practical concern. It makes a conscious effort to directly involve the people faced with the pressing problems in the performance of the research itself. This includes all aspects, including the focus of the research, its conceptualization, collection of data, and interpretation of the results. Then the results of the research put the people in an informed position to

Box 14.1 Some definitions of action research

- Research that brings together action and reflection, theory and practice in participation with others, in pursuit of practical solutions to issues of pressing concern to people (Druskat 2005, p. 953).
- Research [that] aims to contribute both to the practical concerns of people in an immediate problematic situation and to the goals of social science by joint collaboration within a mutually acceptable ethical framework (Rapaport 1970, cited in Small 1995, p. 942).
- A form of self-reflective enquiry undertaken by participants in social situations in order to improve the rationality, justice, coherence and satisfactoriness of (a) their own social practices, (b) their understanding of these practices, and (c) the institutions, programmes and ultimately the society in which these practices are carried out (McTaggart 1994, p. 317).
- A form of research that generates knowledge claims for the express purpose of taking action to promote social change and social analysis (Couch 2004, p. 146).
- A problem solving strategy that encourages academic researchers and community members to work together to: (a) identify and analyze community problems, (b) find solutions to those problems through the best methods of research, and (c) test those solutions in the community (Rajaram 2007, p. 139).

take action to address the problem. The researchers Susman and Evered refer to this as helping to develop "the self-help competencies of people facing problems" (Susman and Evered 1978, p. 588.)

To give you a sense for the action research approach as applied to the environment, here are a few recent examples.

Raju and Shah (2000)

In this study, the authors worked with local non-governmental organizations in rural India to improve local systems for the provision of irrigation water. In this heavily agricultural region, local farmers rely heavily on irrigation for crop production. The focus of the research was on water tanks, an integral component of the irrigation system that provide many benefits, including water storage, groundwater recharge, soil fertilization, and soil erosion control. In recent years, however, the tanks had fallen into disrepair. The authors saw the need for research not merely to support rehabilitating the tanks but also to provide a system for sustainable management of the tanks in the long-term. The research resulted in an action plan for ongoing sustainable tank management.

Stephen Couch (2004)

In this study, the author had students investigate whether potentially toxic emissions from local industrial facilities were having adverse health effects on residents of a local community. Representatives of the community had been concerned about various health effects, including both childhood and adult medical disorders and childhood learning disabilities. The students collected information on local health statistics and local levels of various toxins. They also combed the medical literature for studies on the connection between toxin levels and various health effects. In the end, they were able to document a higher incidence of brain cancer and childhood learning disabilities. They then provided a report of their findings to community leaders, who could use it to formulate an action plan.

Shireen Rajaram (2007)

In this study, students worked with a community grassroots organization in Omaha, Nebraska to investigate public awareness of the local dangers of lead poisoning. Lead is a known toxic substance, and there were various known sources of lead in certain neighborhoods, including: lead-based paint in homes, soil contaminated with lead from industrial emissions, and leaded gasoline. The researchers worked with a local community-based NGO on an outreach campaign to raise public awareness of the dangers of lead poisoning. In the end, the students produced a final report of their findings for public officials and community leaders, who could then formulate an action plan.

Tammy Lewis (2004)

In this study, students worked with local residents in a neighborhood in Newark, New Jersey to address various community issues. The starting point for the project was a report on community issues that had been generated by previous action research projects in the area. The research involved assessing community needs that had not already been previously addressed. In the end, the students produced two action guides: one to create a local community garden and the other to deal with problems associated with abandoned buildings.

Notice a common feature of all of these examples. They all involve working with residents in a community or local neighborhood to address an environmental problem faced by those residents. Action research is generally done at the local level to address a local problem. Seen in this way, action research bears a strong resemblance to *service learning*, a recent trend in higher education in which an important objective of student learning is to perform service to others.

Why do action research?

As we have seen, the central motivation for doing action research is to address a real-world problem, with the aim of trying to do something about it. You may find it puzzling that action research would try to distinguish itself from other research in this way, as you might think this should be the aim of *all* research. But the notion of action research originated in a belief by some that (too) much research is overly theoretical and does not address real-world concerns.

Furthermore, even when research does address real-world concerns, these researchers believe that some research does not necessarily translate into effective solutions. In the words of the management scholar Vanessa Druskat, action research is about "scholarship that works" (Druskat 2005, p. 952).

However, the reasons for doing action research go deeper than this. Think about what it would take to do "scholarship that works" within the typical context of action research: the neighborhood or community level. The standard model of research might involve going in, collecting information, performing an analysis, and reporting the findings.

For example, if you wanted to investigate the adverse local effects of toxic releases as Stephen Couch did, you might collect physical information on toxic releases, survey local residents for exposure and health issues, perform a statistical or spatial analysis, and present findings and policy prescriptions.

Action researchers believe this model might fail to achieve effective action to address the issue, because it does not sufficiently involve the local residents in the research. In neglecting to do this, it fails to take advantage of valuable information and expertise possessed by the residents themselves that could be useful toward addressing the problem. Furthermore, it may not take into consideration the beliefs and attitudes of the residents toward the problem and, thus, may not address their actual concerns. Finally, it runs the risk of not obtaining sufficient "buy-in" from residents into the proposed solutions, without which effective action may simply not occur.

In order to address these issues, the action research model involves the local residents in the research process every step of the way. They—or more commonly, people designated to represent them—would work with you to identify and characterize the problem; communicate to you their areas of concern; and partner with you in collecting information, performing analysis, interpreting results, and taking action based upon your findings.

In using this model, action researchers are explicitly taking issue with the way that research is done under the positivist/post-positivist model that we first encountered in Chapter 2 (Bryden-Miller et al. 2003, p. 11). As you recall, under that model research uses objective evidence toward the goal of eventually learning some objective truth. In order to achieve this goal, researchers maintain a dispassionate stance toward the subject of the research. They then go about their business in a value-neutral way; that is, trying not to promote any particular set of social or cultural values. Finally, under that model researchers have specialized expertise that is useful in carrying out the research.

In sharp contrast to the positivist model, most action researchers believe that there is no such thing as objective, impartial, value-free social science. Rather, they would argue that there are many sources of knowledge and that there are many equally valid ways of seeing and understanding the world (Bryden-Miller et al. 2003, p. 13; Billies et al. 2010, p. 278).

This means that your specific expertise as researcher is no more or less valuable than the knowledge brought to the research process by the local residents the research project is being designed to benefit. In this view, the action research project is a genuine collaboration among equals.

It should be added that there is very much a self-help element to action research. For many action researchers, the reason to collaborate is not merely to involve local residents in the research process. It also serves the important function of empowering them so that they are in a better position to work on and solve their own problems in the future. The idea, says one action researcher, is to

> provide people with the support and resources to do things in ways that will fit their own cultural context and their own lifestyles. The people ..., not the experts, should be the ones to determine the nature and operation of the things that affect ... their lives.
>
> (Stringer, as cited in Bryden-Miller et al. 2003, p. 14)

There are also benefits of doing action research for you, the researcher. Action research provides the opportunity to see environmental issues first-hand in the real world. It provides the opportunity to apply theoretical concepts and frameworks to real world issues. It allows you to see the world in all of its multidisciplinary complexity, often with scientific, economic, social, ethical, and policy issues being relevant to solving real-world problems. And it provides you with practice in problem-solving and critical thinking skills.

Bottom line: Action research is very much an action-oriented way to do research that involves collaboration with people as equals to address real problems in their lives. The purpose of collaboration is to ensure that any proposed actions are informed by their knowledge and perception of needs and, thus, are appropriate to their personal circumstances.

Carrying out an action research project

In order to carry out an action research project, there are a number of factors to consider. Perhaps the first is to consider the ultimate goals of your project and how it fits in to the larger context of practical, action-based solutions for the problem you have identified.

The spiral nature of action research

As we have seen, the objective of action research is to provide an informed basis for action to solve a problem or improve a situation. Within the broader context, however, the process does not end with a particular set of actions. Those actions will themselves have to be evaluated in order to ensure they are actually addressing the problem. Sometimes they do not, and then we may have to revise our thinking about what needs to be done.

For example, consider the study referred to earlier that created a guide to plan a community garden. The student researchers created what the faculty member assessed to be a very effective planning guide. However, the guide was not used by residents in the community for whom the guide was created.

The problem turned out to be that the residents didn't want a guide: they had thought that the students were going to work side-by-side with them to create a garden. So even though the action research had seemingly been successful, the actions fell short because of miscommunication between the student researchers and the local residents. All of this was revealed later in the post-mortem evaluation.

Though this was apparently not done in the community garden study, ideally there would be follow-up if an evaluation indicates the actions were ineffective. At this point, there might be more planning, perhaps rethinking of the project. Once this is done, then the project might be relaunched, hopefully with the issues addressed that caused the actions to fail the first time. In the community garden study, for example, there might be attention paid to addressing the miscommunication issues. In this way, there is gradual progression over time toward increasingly effective actions.

The social psychologist Kurt Lewin is commonly given credit as the father of action research (Lewin 1946; Susman and Evered 1978, pp. 586–7; Small 1995, p. 942). To characterize the above-described iterative process, Lewin has suggested the metaphor of action research as proceeding in a series of steps, spiral-fashion, toward increasingly improved action outcomes (see Figure 14.1).

In this process, one starts with a *plan* (and the means to carry it out), which leads to an *action*. The action is then *observed* to see the result and the researcher *reflects* on the outcome to determine whether the problem has been satisfactorily addressed. If the problem has not been addressed, then more planning is done, which leads to more action, and so forth.

The takeaway message here is that when you are thinking about the overall design of your project, you may want to keep in mind Lewin's observation and

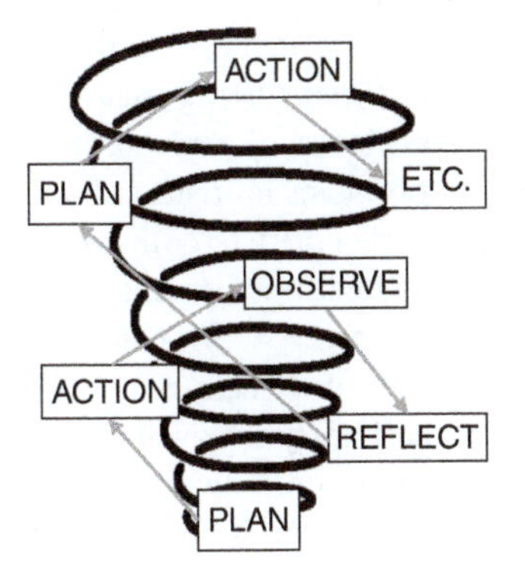

Figure 14.1 The spiral nature of action research.

Source: Author.

evaluation stages. Action research does not end with action: the actions should be evaluated before you can conclude that your research project is successful. This process of evaluation may well lead to further planning and action, either within the confines of your project or in future projects.

> **Bottom line:** An action research project is incomplete if it does not include evaluation of the proposed action for effectiveness in addressing the problem. The results of the evaluation become the basis for further research and actions, if warranted.

Collaboration with local residents

The community garden study also illustrates a key principle of action research: the need for an on-going relationship of mutual understanding and trust between the researchers and the residents in the community. As researcher, it is important to be extremely clear about your goals and objectives and to communicate these effectively to the community.

At the same time, it is important to be able to correctly assess the needs of the community. You should also assess the resources they can bring to the table to support the research process and to carry out any actions that might result. Mutual trust and understanding are essential toward promoting the effective communication needed to make all this happen.

Thus, perhaps the best way to begin an action research project is to identify and approach a set of residents or an entity that effectively represents the community, and to begin to cultivate a relationship with them.

For example, in the lead poisoning prevention study mentioned earlier, the author approached an entity called the Lead Safe Omaha Coalition (LSOC), a community-based non-governmental organization (NGO) whose objective was to eliminate local childhood lead poisoning through a variety of education, assistance, and advocacy programs. LSOC proved to be an extremely helpful collaborative partner. It facilitated entry into the community, supporting the study team's outreach and information-gathering efforts. And it was a key source of information on the local lead situation and the health problems it created.

Having a specific research topic may help you identify an entity to collaborate with. For example, knowing that they were interested in health issues related to lead exposure helped the previous researchers identify the LSOC as a suitable entity to work with. However, keep in mind that it may not be necessary to even have a specific topic before you approach an entity. Sometimes you may just have a general idea that you would like to make a difference, without knowing exactly how. In this case, it may work to approach an entity like a local NGO or development agency and simply ask them if they have any research that needs to be done.

For example, in the study cited earlier on the health impacts of toxic releases, the researcher simply approached a local grassroots environmental group and asked if they would like student researchers to work on a problem for them. Inquiring about the needs of the local residents helped ensure that the research would actually benefit them. And it probably went a long way toward persuading the residents that the objective of the research was to benefit them. This probably helped inspire feelings of trust in the project and toward the researchers.

Even so, it will help to be prepared for possible misunderstandings as you begin to develop a collaborative relationship with the local residents. The beginning of any relationship can be tricky to navigate, and action research collaborations are no exception. Students who have done action research projects in the past have not always been immediately welcomed with open arms.

Box 14.2, for example, reports some comments by students on their initial experiences in doing an action research project in Newark. Initially, the residents were suspicious and not entirely convinced of the value of working with the research team. You may want to be prepared for an initial breaking-in period during which you may have to convince local residents of your desire to genuinely partner with them toward achieving a mutual goal. In the above example, the residents soon warmed to the student researchers and they were able to comfortably work together.

Box 14.2 Some student comments, Lewis (2004) study

"Ignorantly, I expected the residents to want to talk about the project, but as I approached a table of residents in order to introduce myself, I received the cold shoulder by all of the residents except one."

"We felt as though we were invaders who were not welcomed."

One issue that may arise is possible miscommunication between local residents and an agency that supposedly represents them. If you approach a local agency, do not always assume that they are speaking faithfully for the interests of the local residents.

In one action research project, for example, the researcher discovered that a community officer had not fully consulted with community residents before inviting the research team into the community. The result was a sparsely attended kick-off meeting that generated feelings among the students that the local residents were passive and apathetic (Lewis 2004, pp. 100–01).

This example illustrates that there may be a great deal of value in spending time to make sure, early on in the process, that you know the true needs and wishes of the local residents. At this early stage, consulting widely and talking to a lot of people may save much time and wasted effort later on.

Finally, in establishing your relationship with local residents, it will help to communicate your genuine desire to work with them in a true collaborative partnership. This means listening carefully to what they are saying, understanding where they are coming from, and respecting their wishes and the value of the information they provide.

To reiterate, in an action research project, you are bringing in the local residents as full partners in the research. Your project is a two-way street. You need to be convinced that the research will benefit from their contribution. And *they* need to be convinced that your knowledge and expertise is just as valuable. Perhaps the best way to walk this fine line is to stress the importance of both of your respective contributions to the success of the project, and then to follow up by making them feel like bona fide partners in the enterprise.

You may find this to be a challenge sometimes if you are accustomed to doing other types of research projects in which you have sole responsibility for the research design. With action research, you may sometimes find yourself making compromises in order to accommodate the on-the-ground reality of working with local communities.

For example, in the lead poisoning study, the researcher wanted to administer a lengthy questionnaire to community residents. However, the community felt this would be an imposition on the residents, so the researcher settled for a shorter, less demanding survey. The researcher thus sacrificed the ability to answer certain questions for the sake of maintaining good relations with the community residents.

As another example, a different issue arose in the lead poisoning study having to do with the fact that the study involved research with human participants. This meant that participants in the survey needed to sign an informed consent form, a typical requirement of university ethics boards (see the discussion of institutional review boards in Chapter 18). This issue is a general one that arises with many action research projects.

The problem was that the community believed it to be inappropriate for respondents to have to sign consent forms, because the survey was supposed to be anonymous. Fortunately for the project, the ethics board approved the publishing of the results even though its guidelines had not, strictly speaking, been followed.

Issues of research methodology

Like the other forms of qualitative analysis that we have seen, the methods you use in action research will need to be tailor-made to your specific research needs. Like many research projects, your methods will depend both on the research question and on the nature of the evidence you will be dealing with. In general, however, the nature of action research dictates that qualitative methods are heavily emphasized.

There are several reasons for this. First is the fact that action research is generally done within the setting in which the problem is encountered, with the focus being on the particular needs of a community or neighborhood. This means that there is generally no issue of inference to a larger population: in most action research, the community IS the population. As we have seen, one of the key strengths of the quantitative approach is its application of statistical methods to make inferences from a sample to a population. This makes the external validity of your methods important. This issue is largely absent in action research.

Second, action researchers generally argue that many different kinds of evidence are legitimate sources of information on the needs of a community. This especially includes qualitative evidence of various kinds, many of which we have already encountered in previous chapters, including participant observation, interviews, documents, and texts. Some researchers argue for even broader notions of evidence, including things we have not encountered before, such as performances, artistic expressions, and emotions (Billies et al. 2010, p. 278).

The essential reason for the admissibility of so many different kinds of qualitative evidence has to do with the philosophy and objectives of action research. When one thinks about a local, perhaps environmental, problem, an important reason it is a problem is that people think it is. Thus, subjective attitudes, beliefs, and ascribed meanings play a big role in defining what a problem is.

To put it slightly differently, in action research there is an often an important element of social construction in defining problems and solutions (Brydon-Miller et al. 2003, p. 11). The use of so many types of qualitative evidence is in essence about respecting the views of local residents on the nature of the problem and what should be done about it.

All of this means that many of the research principles and methods that we have encountered in previous qualitative chapters may also be useful here. Keen observational skills, keeping detailed field notes, document analysis, surveying and interviewing skills, paying attention to discourses, and so forth will all potentially have important roles to play.

Conducting the research

Once you have established a collaborative relationship with a community and chosen a suitable research topic, you will need to prepare yourself for the research task. This may involve background reading on relevant issues, information-gathering, and orientation meetings with representatives of the local residents.

For example, for the study of lead poisoning awareness, students read research articles on lead poisoning prevention and attended a panel discussion organized by local neighborhood groups that provided information on the local lead situation and steps taken locally to address the problem.

At this point, the research proceeds, informed by the initial stage of information-gathering, including your literature review, if warranted by the study. Here, depending upon your topic, there are many ways the research could go, and you should be prepared for a variety of contingencies. In some cases, it may quickly become apparent what you need to do and how to do it.

For example, it became quickly apparent to the Newark research team that a guide to creating a community garden would be useful. In this case, the researchers benefited from an existing assessment report created by previous action research teams, which contained the idea.

In other cases, however, the project may proceed in fits and starts, with a winding path containing false starts, curves, and dead ends. If this happens, don't fret. This is partly the nature of an open-ended research process, where you never know ahead of time what you are going to find.

For example, in the study of toxic emissions in rural Pennsylvania, when the students began to search for data on local disease rates, they quickly discovered that a lot of data they were seeking was simply not available. This prompted an adjustment of their research strategy, to look more for data on various environmental indicators. They were still able to complete the project: it just turned out to have a slightly different orientation than they had originally intended.

More generally, it is important to keep in mind that information-gathering continues throughout the process, as dictated by your potentially evolving research problem.

> **Bottom line:** Conducting action research involves prior preparation in terms of reading appropriate studies and collecting other sources of information. It also may require flexibility on your part as new information is collected, which may necessitate rethinking of parts of the project.

Keep a research log

As you are proceeding through the research process, it will help to keep a detailed research log. This could, for example, be a notebook or Word document, in which you record activities, short-term objectives, and personal reflections. You should use it to keep track of what you have done, thoughts that occur to you along the way, data you have failed to find, what you need to still do to achieve your research goals, and how your research goals may be evolving. This research log will help you stay organized and efficient in your research.

Applying the findings towards action

Generally speaking, the end-result of an action research project is some sort of final report on your findings with specific information and/or recommendations for action. Keeping in mind that your research is intended to benefit the residents of a neighborhood or community, the report should be targeted specifically at them. This means it should be timely given their specific needs, it should be written so it is easily understood, and it should be clear in describing the particular action steps it is proposing.

Finally, it should ideally contain a way of observing and evaluating the results. Here, a couple of things can go wrong. One is that the proposed actions may not be taken by the local residents. For example, as we saw earlier, residents in the local neighborhood in Newark did not pursue the researchers' recommendation of planting a community garden. The other possibility is that the proposed actions may be taken, but they may be ineffective in addressing the issues. In either of these cases, a reassessment should take place to try to answer the questions: Why were the recommended actions not taken? Or if they were, why were they ineffective in addressing the issue?

Potential pitfalls

We have already seen a few of the things that can go wrong when you do an action research study. One additional general issue concerns the significant amount of time it often takes to coordinate the various participants in the study: students, faculty, community residents, and local community-based organizations. This includes the time and energy that must be invested in establishing and maintaining a good working relationship with the local residents and community organizations. The potentially sizable educational benefits from doing an action research study will have to be weighed against these costs.

A second issue relates to the fact that action research does not always fit easily into the busy personal and academic schedules of student researchers. A project may call for students to spend a considerable amount of time in the community, and it is not always easy to arrange specific, regular hours when the community field work gets done. This is not an insuperable obstacle, though, and it may be effectively addressed with careful advance planning and flexibility in other aspects of the course. For example, if your faculty member is willing, it may be possible to decrease other course assignments and commitments in order to accommodate more time spent on the project.

Bottom line: When conducting action research, budget plenty of time to coordinate with local residents and their representatives. This includes time and energy to maintain good working relations with them.

Conclusions

Action research has much to speak for it, especially for certain types of research projects that can be undertaken locally, for which effective collaborative arrangements can be made with relatively little time and effort. Done right, it is research that can make a difference, in terms of providing real solutions to environmental problems faced by local communities. And students can gain real insights into concrete real-world environmental problems and how to think about trying to solve them. In many ways, there is nothing like first-hand experience with the environmental problems faced by local communities to impress upon one the importance of these problems and the effect they have on people's lives.

Exercises/discussion questions

(1) If you initiate an action research project by contacting a local agency to determine a research need, how do you ensure that the agency officials are speaking on behalf of the local community?

(2) Can you think of some specific practical things you could do to get off on the right foot with residents of a local community with whom you are interested in collaborating? As the project proceeds, how can you make them feel like valued collaborators?
(3) What would you do if respondents in a community felt uncomfortable signing consent forms, but the ethics board at your university required them in order for your project to go forward?
(4) Suppose that you are planning to undertake an action research project with a local community in order to address a hazardous drinking water issue. Draw up a timetable, complete with specific tasks, that allows you to complete the project within a semester. In doing this, keep in mind the need to budget time for follow-up assessment of the actions taken.

References

Billies, Michelle, Valerie Francisco, Patricia Krueger, and Darla Linville. "Participatory Action Research: Our Methodological Roots," *International Review of Qualitative Research* 3(Fall 2010): 277–86.

Brydon-Miller, Mary, Davydd Greenwood, and Patricia Maguire. "Why Action Research?" *Action Research* 1(2003): 9–28.

Couch, Stephen C. "A Tale of Three Discourses: Doing Action Research in a Research Methods Class," *Social Problems* 51(February 2004): 146–53.

Druskat, Vanessa Urch. "Scholarship That Works," *The Academy of Management Journal* 48(December 2005): 952–5.

Lewin, Kurt. "Action Research and Minority Problems," *Journal of Social Issues* 2(1946): 34–6.

Lewis, Tammy L. "Service Learning for Social Change? Lessons from a Liberal Arts College," *Teaching Sociology* 32(January 2004): 94–108.

McTaggart, Robin. "Participatory Action Research: Issues in Theory and Practice," *Educational Action Research* 2(1994): 313–37.

Rajaram, Shireen S. "An Action-research Project: Community Lead Poisoning Prevention," *Teaching Sociology* 35(April 2007): 138–50.

Raju, K. V., and Tushaar Shah. "Revitalisation of Irrigation Tanks in Rajasthan," *Economic and Political Weekly* 35(June 3–9, 2000): 1930–6.

Small, Stephen A. "Action-oriented Research: Models and Methods," *Journal of Marriage and Family* 57(November 1995): 941–55.

Susman, Gerald I., and Roger D. Evered. "An Assessment of the Scientific Merits of Action Research," *Administrative Science Quarterly* 23(December 1978): 582–603.

15 Mixed methods

Introduction

Now that we have examined a number of qualitative approaches to environmental research, let us step back for a moment and consider where we are. We have now seen the two basic approaches: quantitative research and qualitative research. Though they go about their business differently, they both have the same objective: to answer questions we may have about environmental issues.

We have seen that the nature of our questions dictates which approach to take. Some questions involve theory generating testable hypotheses or understanding the quantitative relationship among variables. These questions lend themselves to the quantitative approach. Other questions are about environmental beliefs, attitudes, and the meanings that people ascribe to various phenomena. These questions lend themselves more to the qualitative approach. So far, the research universe seems to be divided up neatly into two separate and distinct camps.

Sometimes, however, we encounter questions where the distinction is not so clear-cut. If we think about issues like climate change, for example, we can think of a number of research questions, some of which seem more quantitative and others which seem more qualitative. And sometimes the quantitative and qualitative questions seem related.

Consider, for example, the qualitative study we encountered in Chapter 11 on the attitudes of rural Norwegians toward taking action on climate change. There, the author was interested in exploring why rural Norwegians seem apathetic, in order to gain insights into the causes and consequences of environmental privilege. Implicit in that study was an assumption that they really are apathetic. If this assumption were not true, that would take away a lot of the reason to even do the study. A complementary analysis might somehow test the hypothesis that they are, or at least provide systematic evidence to this effect. A quantitative analysis could do this.

This example illustrates why some researchers have proposed combining the quantitative and qualitative approaches in their research. This hybrid approach, called *mixed methods*, is the subject of this chapter.

What is mixed methods research?

As with the other qualitative approaches, mixed methods research has been defined in a number of slightly different ways. Box 15.1 provides a few of the definitions that can be found in the literature.

Box 15.1 Definitions of mixed methods research

"Mixed methods research is an approach to inquiry that combines or associates both qualitative and quantitative forms. It involves philosophical assumptions, the use of qualitative and quantitative approaches, and the mixing of both approaches in a study." (Creswell 2009, p. 4)

"Mixed methods research is … the class of research where the researcher mixes or combines quantitative and qualitative research techniques, methods, approaches, concepts or language into a single study." (Johnson and Onwuegbuzie 2004, p. 17)

"Mixed methods research combines elements from both qualitative and quantitative paradigms to produce converging findings in the context of complex research questions." (Lingard et al. 2008, p. 460)

"[Mixed method designs] include at least one quantitative method (designed to collect numbers) and one qualitative method (designed to collect words), where neither type of method is inherently linked to any particular inquiry paradigm." (Greene et al. 1989, p. 256)

Source: Author.

These definitions make clear some of the central features of mixed methods research. First and foremost, it involves bringing together the qualitative and quantitative approaches into a single study. Second, the approaches must complement each other to produce "converging" findings, which you may interpret as producing an overall picture that is coherent and consistent.

Implicit in these definitions is a third feature of mixed methods research; namely, that if it brings together the quantitative and qualitative approaches, it can exploit the features of both. Consider, for example, Box 15.2, which contrasts the mixed methods approach with the two approaches we have been considering so far.

For example, mixed methods researchers are not confined to using numerical data taken from census reports or other sources, as quantitative researchers are. Nor are they confined to using qualitative evidence provided by interviews, observation, textual documents of various kinds, and so forth, as qualitative researchers commonly are. Rather, they can use all kinds of evidence, both qualitative and quantitative.

Box 15.2 Mixed methods as a hybrid of quantitative and qualitative methods

Quantitative methods	*Mixed methods*	*Qualitative methods*
• Census/performance/ observational data	• Multiple forms of data	• Interviews, observation, documents
• Statistical analysis	• Statistical and text interpretation	• Textual interpretation
• Statistical interpretation	• Interpretation across databases	• Themes, patterns, interpretation
• Close-ended questions	• Closed- and open-ended questions	• Open-ended questions

Source: Author.

Similarly, mixed methods researchers are not limited to doing only statistical analysis or text interpretation. They can do both, and they may combine and synthesize their analyses across the different sources of evidence. And finally, when their research is based upon survey data, they can ask both close-ended and open-ended questions (for more on this distinction, see Chapter 16).

All of this opens up a world of possibilities for analysis. Let us now turn to two recent studies that use mixed methods, in order to illustrate the basic approach.

Two illustrative examples

Deforestation in the Brazilian Amazon

You have probably heard that there has been a dramatic reduction in the size of the Brazilian rain forest in recent years. This is just one example of *deforestation*, an environmental issue that afflicts many developing countries.

In the Brazilian rain forest, as in many other places where deforestation is occurring, many people blame population and economic growth for causing deforestation. Indeed, the statistical correlation between population growth and deforestation is quite high. If you took this finding at face value, you might be tempted to advocate for policies that limit local population increases, such as limitations on migration.

However, just because there is a strong correlation does not necessarily mean such policies are warranted. There is much about the connection between population growth and deforestation that we do not know. You will notice that this is the black box model of quantitative research argument that we have seen before (see Figure 15.1).

The researcher John Sydenstricker-Neto was interested in peering inside the black box to better understand the connection in the context of the Brazilian rain forest (Sydenstricker-Neto 2012). He suspected that there might be a number of economic, social, and cultural factors that could influence *how* population growth leads to deforestation. He wanted to determine what they were.

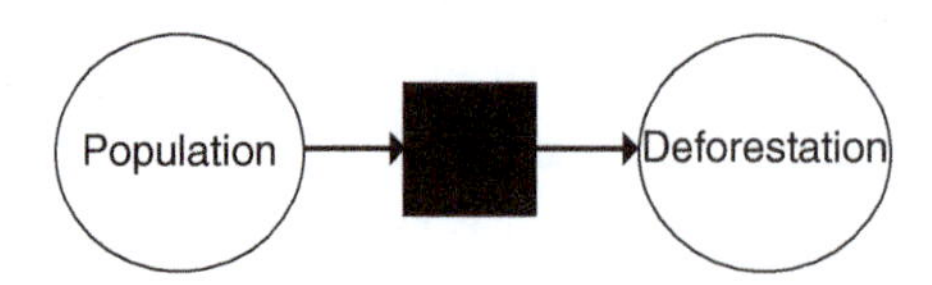

Figure 15.1 The black box model of quantitative research again.

Source: Author.

You might want to put yourself in his shoes for a second. *How would you go about trying to determine what factors influenced this relationship?*

Sydenstricker-Neto's answer was to pursue a mixed methods strategy. He saw the need for a quantitative component, for two reasons. One was to document that there was indeed a connection between population growth and deforestation, within the context of the Brazilian rain forest. The other was to investigate various population factors that influenced this connection, such as household age structure and factors related to labor supply.

To accomplish these objectives, he went out and collected data on land cover from GIS maps and correlated land cover variables with population variables, types of farming activity, and various demographic variables. His quantitative analysis showed that there indeed seemed to be a connection between population and deforestation. It also provided insights into various factors that seemed to matter, such as household income and farming background. Furthermore, it pointed to factors that did not seem to matter, like educational attainment level.

He then added a qualitative component, in order to be able to dig deeper into various factors that he wanted to understand better. For this part of the analysis, he conducted in-depth interviews of various farmers, which yielded some interesting additional insights.

For example, it turned out that differences in previous farming experiences influenced how farmers worked their lands, which affected how much they applied clear-cutting methods. Some farmers who had previously been involved in cattle ranching in southern Brazil were used to open-field production and were much more likely to clear-cut their lands. Others who had previously farmed in more traditional ways tended to leave the forests relatively undisturbed. Seeing the importance of previous life experiences would have never been possible without this second qualitative component of the study.

Similarly, through the interviews he was able to understand better why education did not seem to matter. He had hypothesized that more educated farmers would be less likely to clear-cut their lands, which made the quantitative finding of no correlation a bit of a puzzle. It turned out that farmers with little formal education tended to possess more traditional local knowledge about things like the uses of native plants, which made them less likely to clear-cut. The qualitative analysis thus shed light on some puzzles in the quantitative analysis.

Nature tourism in southern Africa

Our second example is taken from a recent study by two researchers, Julie Silva and Lila Khatiwada, on tourism and development in two African countries, Namibia and Mozambique (Silva and Khatiwada 2014). These countries have been trying to use tourism as a means for economic development, using an approach known as *community-based natural resource management* (CBNRM).

This approach has two components. First, land is set aside to provide protected areas for wildlife herds. Second, local communities are involved in management of these protected areas. In some of these programs, local residents receive compensation from tourism-related activities, which can include direct payments or investment in community assets. Thus, these wildlife management programs have two broad objectives: (1) to protect and manage wildlife and (2) to benefit local residents.

The concept of community-based natural resource management has been around for a long time. However, despite numerous studies that have examined their performance, it remains unclear how successful these programs have been in achieving their objectives. In particular, it remains unclear whether local communities have actually benefited from these programs.

In the authors' view, there are two key questions. Do communities involved in wildlife management programs reap more tourism-related economic benefits than communities that are not involved? Do extra benefits enjoyed by a community really translate into actual satisfaction with the management programs?

The first question is a largely factual one: Are communities benefiting from involvement in the programs? This question seems to lend itself to the following type of analysis. Select different communities, some involved and some not; choose indices of community benefit that can be compared across communities; investigate whether involvement confers greater benefits. As such, it seems eminently amenable to the quantitative approach.

The second question, however, is about perception: Do communities believe they are actually benefiting from these programs? This one seems harder to answer using the quantitative approach. To answer it, you would need evidence that speaks to their perceptions and beliefs about how well the programs are working for them, perhaps by administering questionnaires or interviews. This question seems to require the qualitative approach.

The authors view both of these questions as critical to their study. This leads them to pursue a mixed methods strategy in which they apply quantitative methods to answer the first question and qualitative methods to answer the second question.

To carry out their study, the authors selected eight communities, four involved in a management program and four not involved. These communities were divided equally between the two countries and were chosen to be comparable in other ways. They then conducted surveys on households selected through a largely random sampling process within each community. These surveys were designed to yield information on both questions.

To answer the first question, the surveys asked for information on household assets, consumption expenditures, and demographic characteristics. These responses then formed the basis for a statistical analysis of the relative benefits enjoyed by involved communities.

Though the results differed slightly between the two countries, households in involved communities seemed to benefit from involvement in the programs, on the whole. They enjoyed somewhat greater consumption levels and higher employment rates in tourism-related jobs than their counterparts in non-involved communities.

To answer the second question, the survey asked about experiences with tourism, plus a number of questions designed to assess perceptions of quality of life. The survey also permitted respondents to elaborate on their answers. The survey responses were then supplemented with interview data. In these interviews, respondents could describe their experiences with tourism and their perceptions of the benefits and costs of tourism.

Here, the responses conveyed that many residents did not consider themselves better off as a result of community involvement in conservation. This was a striking result that seemed contrary to the results of the quantitative analysis. The responses revealed various reasons for this.

First, some believed that in handing out jobs, park managers were not giving preferential treatment to local residents despite regulations requiring them to do so. Second, a number of respondents experienced crop- and livestock-related damages from wildlife, especially elephants. Third, some respondents chafed under restrictions on hunting and expansion of farming.

Finally, the authors speculated that part of the problem was the manner in which tourism revenues were re-invested in the communities. The programs called for tourism revenues to be used for community-wide projects rather than for providing direct payments into the pockets of community residents. This might have made it harder for residents to perceive that they were actually benefiting from tourism.

Bottom line: Qualitative and quantitative methods can sometimes nicely complement each other in the same research study, providing insights not obtainable using either approach alone.

Why do mixed methods research?

As these studies may make clear, mixed methods research is designed to provide a broader and deeper understanding of environmental problems than either approach can provide individually. The idea is that the quantitative and qualitative approaches each have their respective strengths and weaknesses.

The quantitative approach is really good at testing hypotheses and quantifying relationships among variables. It is less good at peering inside the black box to shed light on processes and mechanisms, or in divining the beliefs and attitudes of environmental actors. The qualitative approach is designed to shed light on these latter things, while it does not provide methods and techniques for formally testing hypotheses or quantifying relationships among variables.

The basic idea behind much mixed methods research is that many research questions are like the questions in the deforestation and nature tourism examples. They may benefit from analysis to test hypotheses or quantify relationships among variables. At the same time, they also benefit from digging deeper to explore mechanisms, processes, and attitudes. They don't want to merely understand *what*: they want to understand *how* and *why*. The parsimonious theories underlying much quantitative analysis—the ones that speak merely to what—just don't tell us enough (Klassen et al. 2012, p. 378).

Mixed methods research involves capitalizing on the strengths of each approach while minimizing its weaknesses. It is much more than merely collecting multiple forms of evidence, both qualitative and quantitative. Done correctly, it builds on the methodological strengths of the two approaches in a complementary way. And when it works, it makes several things possible.

We can investigate issues we could not otherwise

In the deforestation study, for example, the author was interested in more than simply quantifying the connection between population growth and deforestation, without looking inside the black box. He wanted to delve deeper into the social, cultural, and economic factors that, in his words, "mediated" the connection between population growth and deforestation.

To make his case, he needed to establish that in the local context, there was in fact such a connection. At this point he could then turn to evidence from his interviews to see what the mediating factors were. Combining the quantitative analysis (to establish the connection) with the qualitative analysis (to characterize the mediating factors) made an analysis of those factors both possible and meaningful.

We may be able to produce knowledge that neither individual approach can

In the nature tourism study, for example, important insights were produced by combining the findings of the quantitative research with the findings of the qualitative research. The quantitative analysis told us that community residents were better off by being involved in the management programs. Taken by itself, this finding would lead us to conclude that we should rely more heavily on these community-based programs in order to manage wildlife.

The qualitative analysis, however, told us that involvement in the programs was not making residents any more satisfied. The fact that they were better off by certain objective standards should make us think twice before concluding that the programs are a failure. Because the survey and interview results also indicated that residents in the communities did not want to end the programs, we could conclude that the programs needed to continue but be improved. And the responses gave us guidance regarding exactly how that should be done.

We can be more confident in our findings

This happens when the quantitative and qualitative findings seem to support and corroborate each other, adding up to a coherent picture that makes sense. In the deforestation study, for example, the quantitative analysis investigated a variety of factors that might affect farmers' propensity to clear-cut. Some of these factors seemed to matter, others did not. The qualitative analysis provided insight into why certain factors mattered and others did not, providing a more compelling overall interpretation.

We can interpret findings that would remain a mystery under a single approach strategy

Both studies provide good examples of this. In the nature tourism study, the quantitative component revealed that in objective terms, communities were indeed benefiting from involvement in the wildlife management programs. The qualitative component, however, documented that households in these communities were on the whole feeling no better off as a result of their involvement. The study was able to explain why local communities may be lukewarm in their support for CBNRM despite objective evidence that they do benefit.

In the deforestation study, the quantitative analysis indicated that there was no significant relationship between educational attainment and the propensity for farmers to clear-cut, which puzzled the author. Evidence from interviews, however, showed that farmers lacking formal education often possessed other, more traditional forms of knowledge that valued forest diversity. The author took this to mean that both formal and informal forms of education may matter in influencing whether farmers will clear-cut.

Choosing a mixed methods strategy

When you do a mixed methods study, many of the principles of the quantitative and qualitative approaches that we have already seen in previous chapters may be applied. Your study may call for statistical analysis of data to test hypotheses, visualization and organization of spatial data using GIS methods, divining meaning ascribed to events culled from interview data, ethnographic observer participation, discourse analysis, and so forth.

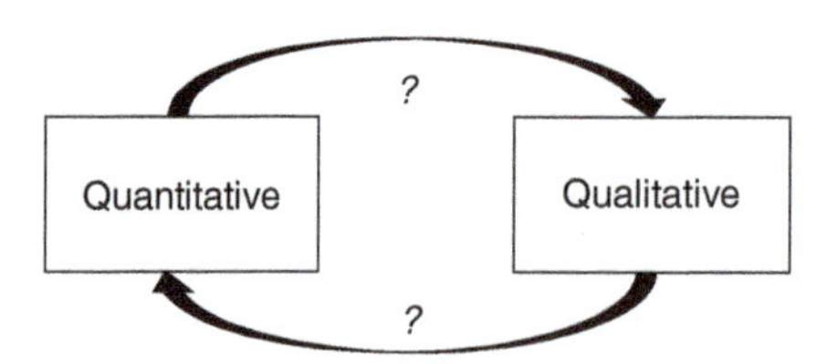

Figure 15.2 Mixed methods generally: how to fit the pieces together?

Source: Author.

All of these should be considered tools in your research toolbox. Which tools you use and how you use them will depend on your research question and the data you collect to try to answer it. The question is: How do you capitalize on such an embarrassment of riches to take full advantage of the mixed methods approach?

To understand how to proceed, it may help to begin by thinking about the structure of your research project. When we think about a project that contains both quantitative and qualitative components, we might ask ourselves: How do the quantitative and qualitative pieces fit together? (see Figure 15.2). Here there are two key issues: *emphasis* and *sequencing*, and two general approaches to doing a mixed methods study: *sequential* or *concurrent* strategies.

Sequential strategies

In all mixed methods research, you must decide how much weight to give to the quantitative vs. the qualitative components, and then sequencing follows naturally from that initial decision. In general, there are three possibilities:

- A mostly quantitative analysis with a supplemental qualitative component.
- A mostly qualitative analysis with a supplemental quantitative component.
- An analysis where both are weighted roughly equally.

Here, your research objectives matter a great deal. Your primary interest may be to do a quantitative analysis, perhaps to test a hypothesis. In this case, most of your argument will be devoted to carefully developing your quantitative analysis, with a supplemental qualitative analysis to aid in interpretation, or to provide additional insights. For this type of study, you generally do the quantitative analysis first, and then develop the qualitative component. When you do this type of study you are pursuing what is commonly known as a *sequential explanatory strategy*.

Figure 15.3 illustrates the sequential explanatory strategy. The research starts with the quantitative analysis, which consists of data collection and analysis. Then, after the quantitative analysis is done, the researcher moves to the qualitative analysis for further investigation. The boldfacing on the left-hand side signifies the relative emphasis placed on the quantitative component.

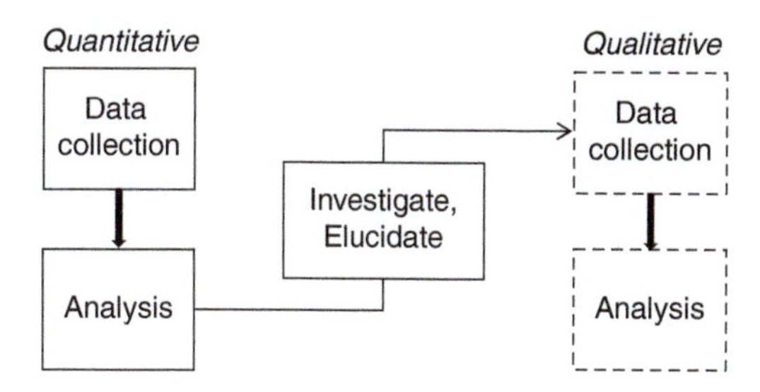

Figure 15.3 Sequential explanatory strategy.

Source: Author.

Rather than testing a hypothesis, you might be more interested in exploring the attitudes and beliefs of some group of people affected by an environmental problem. In this case, you may want to do a largely qualitative study, perhaps with some supplemental data analysis that expands upon your qualitative interpretations. In this type of study, you generally begin with the qualitative analysis, and then proceed to the quantitative component. This type of strategy is commonly known as a *sequential exploratory strategy* (Figure 15.4). Here, the sequential roles of the quantitative and qualitative analyses are reversed, with greater emphasis being placed on the initial qualitative component.

Let us now expand a bit on the whole issue of data collection. Both of these strategies require the collection of both quantitative and qualitative data. But when does the data collection occur? Generally, in both of these strategies, the data collection occurs sequentially, with the results of the first stage informing data collection at the second stage. This is in part because you never know what the first-stage analysis is going to reveal. So you wait to find out, and then once you see what is going on, only then are you in a position to know what additional data you will need to do the second-stage analysis.

If you think about this data collection process, you may have some concerns about the amount of time involved. These two sequential strategies both involve completing the first-stage analysis before turning to the second-stage data collection effort. Each data collection effort will take time. The question is: Given the time horizon of your project, will you have sufficient time to get all of this done?

Concurrent strategies

An alternative to either of these sequential strategies is to pursue a *concurrent* strategy. In concurrent strategies, data for both analyses are collected at the same time, and then the two analyses proceed simultaneously. These strategies have the obvious advantage of saving time, as you do not have to wait to complete one analysis before starting to collect data for the other. There are two main types of concurrent strategies: *concurrent triangulation strategies* and *concurrent embedded strategies*.

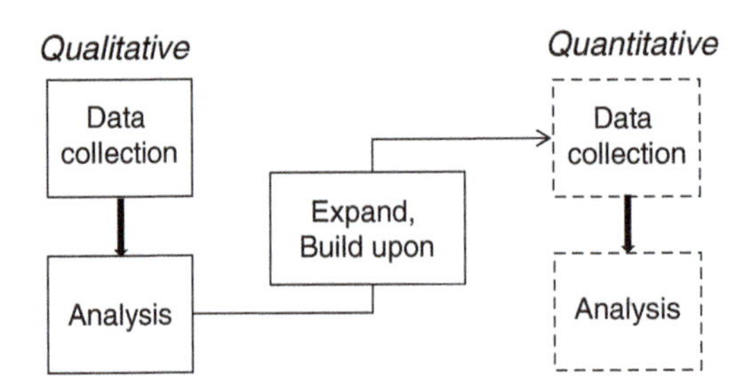

Figure 15.4 Sequential exploratory strategy.

Source: Author.

Concurrent triangulation strategies

Concurrent triangulation strategies emphasize the quantitative and qualitative components of your research design equally. This strategy is particularly suitable when you have a particular research question that you are trying to attack from multiple angles. The quantitative and qualitative data are both collected for whatever complementary insights they can provide on the research question.

Figure 15.5 illustrates the concurrent triangulation strategy. Here, the quantitative and qualitative components proceed in parallel. You collect data for both analyses during the initial stage, do your analyses, and then compare the results. The results of both analyses are weighted equally in reaching your final conclusions.

You may recall the notion of data triangulation that came up in the discussion of the case study method in Chapter 10. What we are discussing here seems similar: the need to be able to tell a coherent, consistent story when working with multiple sources and types of data.

Most of that earlier discussion applies here. We are still interested in using different types of data to support individual components of the argument. For example, you might perform both analyses separately and then support your interpretation of the quantitative results with extensive quotes from interviews or the answers to open-ended survey questions.

If you are so inclined, another possibility is to actually try to merge the data, perhaps by transforming one type of data into the other so they can be more easily compared. This is probably most commonly done by transforming qualitative evidence into quantitative data rather than going the other way. For example, you might be able to use computer software to analyze keyword counts in texts, as we saw in Chapter 9.

You should be aware of one challenge that may arise when the quantitative and qualitative data are collected concurrently. As we have seen, collecting all of your data at once may allow you to save time. On the other hand, collecting it all at once may limit your ability to pursue research avenues that arise unexpectedly during the course of your analysis. For example, if your quantitative

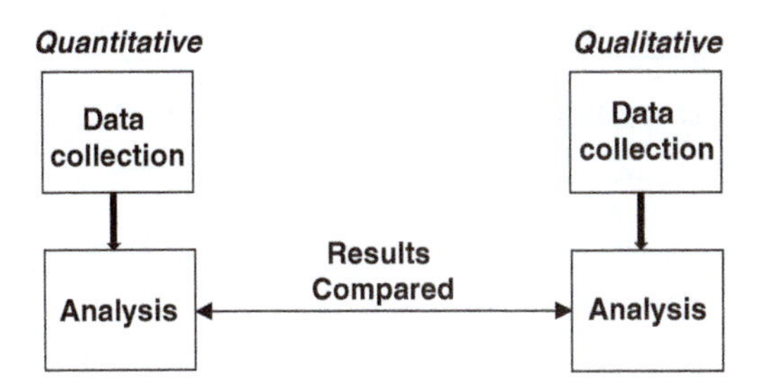

Figure 15.5 Concurrent triangulation strategy.

Source: Adapted from Creswell, 2009, p. 210.

analysis reveals an unexpected result, you may not be able to pursue it because the qualitative data you have already collected may not permit you to.

On the other hand, the melding of quantitative and qualitative analyses can provide strong validation of your research results. This occurs especially when the results of the two analyses tell the same story, and when the two approaches complement each other by compensating for each other's weaknesses. Done carefully, the concurrent triangulation strategy can be a powerful analytical method.

Concurrent embedded strategies

In contrast to concurrent triangulation strategies, concurrent embedded strategies place primary weight on either the quantitative or qualitative analysis, while casting the other analysis in more of a supporting role. Either the qualitative analysis is embedded in the quantitative analysis or vice versa.

In Figure 15.6, for example, the quantitative and qualitative analyses are being done concurrently, but one is being emphasized much more heavily. The other analysis is not developed as much: perhaps it is done mostly to fill in the blanks left by the other method. Or perhaps it addresses a slightly different, secondary question.

For example, in the earlier wildlife management study, it was important for the purposes of the study for the communities involved in the local wildlife management efforts to be similar to non-involved communities in other ways. So the authors used quantitative data on land area, rainfall, and income levels to show that they were indeed similar in these respects.

So how do we choose?

So: given all of these different strategies for doing mixed methods research, which one should you use? Here are a few things to consider.

What are your research objectives and what is the best approach to achieve them?

First, think carefully about your research objectives and the general approach you would like to take. By now, you are well aware of the many considerations that

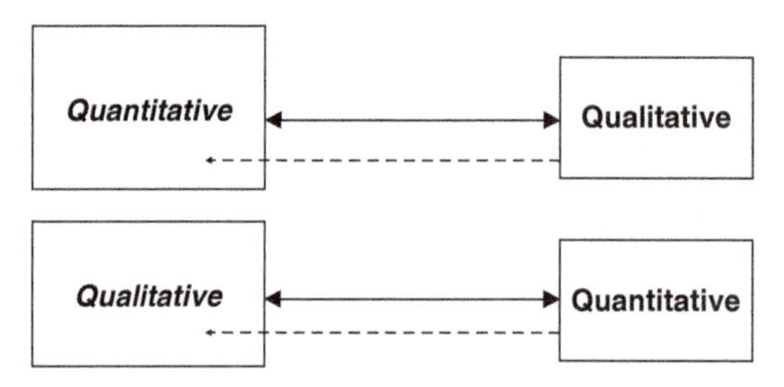

Figure 15.6 Concurrent embedded strategy.

Source: Author.

go into choosing a quantitative approach or a qualitative approach: hypothesis-generating theory vs. framing theory; interest in outcomes vs. processes; type of evidence available (i.e., numerical vs. textual).

If the nature of your research question is primarily quantitative, you might want to use a strategy that emphasizes the quantitative approach, such as the sequential explanatory strategy or a concurrent embedded strategy that emphasizes the quantitative analysis. But if it is primarily qualitative, you may want to use the sequential exploratory strategy, or the concurrent embedded strategy that emphasizes the qualitative analysis.

Finally, if your research question encompasses both quantitative and qualitative elements, perhaps because investigating outcomes and processes both provide important insights into your question, then you might consider using the concurrent triangulation strategy.

How much time do you have to complete your project?

As we have seen, sequential strategies take longer because the data collection efforts are not done simultaneously, but rather sequentially. So if your time is limited, you might consider adopting a concurrent strategy. You might also keep in mind that among the concurrent strategies, embedded strategies are generally smaller in scope than triangulation strategies. This is because you will focus most of your attention on doing either a quantitative analysis or a qualitative analysis. Embedded strategies are thus more manageable when you are pressed for time.

How do existing studies choose their approach, and why?

Sometimes you can get good ideas regarding the best strategy to pursue from studies that have already been done by other researchers. You can note similarities to your ideas in the sorts of issues they are addressing. You can also note the ways they structure and carry out their analysis and think about whether their methods and approach seem applicable to your research project. Here, of course, the literature review that you did for your project will be useful. Just keep in mind that your literature review will want to cover not only topics and ideas, but also methodologies.

Bottom line: Choosing a mixed methods approach depends upon your research objectives, which may lend themselves better to either quantitative methods or qualitative methods, or equally to both. When choosing an approach, keep in mind the amount of time you have to complete the study. Sometimes, it will help to consult existing mixed methods studies to see which approach they took, and why.

Data collection and analysis

As with all of the approaches we have seen so far, it will be important to engage in data collection and data analysis in order to carry out a mixed methods study. In this section, we will highlight a number of issues unique to the mixed methods approach.

Data collection

As with planning your study and choosing your approach, data collection is also influenced by what sort of study you want to do. Generally speaking, data collection for the quantitative and qualitative components of a mixed methods study is informed by the best practices of those respective methodologies.

For example, for the quantitative portion of your study you will have to think about issues of random sampling in order to be confident in generalizing your results to a larger population (see Chapter 5). For the qualitative portion of your study, however, you may be able to rely on non-random methods such as purposive or convenience sampling (see Chapter 16). You should review the discussions of each of those chapters to remind yourself of the issues and principles for good sampling.

Most of the additional data collection issues in doing mixed methods research involve the connection between the quantitative and qualitative components of your research. As with designing your study, the issues differ depending upon whether you choose a sequential or concurrent strategy.

Sequential strategies

As we have seen, one advantage of pursuing a sequential strategy is that the results of the first-stage analysis can inform the data collection effort at the second stage. Importantly, the findings from a first-stage quantitative analysis might aid in the design of a survey instrument that is administered in a second-stage qualitative analysis. This is because the first-stage findings might clarify what the important issues are, or identify potentially fruitful avenues of further inquiry.

In addition, a first-stage quantitative data analysis may reveal outliers that could be explored in a second-stage qualitative analysis. If the outliers emerge from answers to survey data, a second-stage analysis might involve interviews with those respondents whose answers do not fit the general pattern.

Concurrent strategies

As we have seen, if you pursue a concurrent strategy, the data for both the quantitative and qualitative analyses are collected at the same time, prior to doing any analysis. Because of this, data collection for concurrent studies may require more careful planning before you go out and collect the data. You will need to think about both of the individual pieces, and how you think the pieces fit together, because the data collection needs to service the overall goals of the project.

An important practical implication for data collection is to look for ways to structure the data collection to serve both components of the analysis. One common way to do this is to design a survey instrument that contains both close-ended and open-ended questions. The answers to the close-ended questions could then be subjected to quantitative analysis, while the answers to the open-ended questions could be subjected to qualitative analysis.

Bottom line: Data collection for a mixed methods study is informed by the best practices of each methodology. If you are considering a sequential strategy, keep in mind the extra time that may be needed to collect data, and weigh this against the added flexibility of having data collection in one stage that is informed by the results of the other stage.

Data analysis

As with data collection, most of the additional issues in data analysis are about the connection between the quantitative and qualitative components. The fact that the data used in the two approaches are so different presents challenges to the researcher in how to integrate the analyses of the different data sets.

The issue of integration is less acute in embedded strategies where one of the methodologies is playing a largely supporting role. In these cases, the contribution of the supporting methodology could be as simple as providing descriptive statistics or passages from interviews. The burden of telling the main story is chiefly being borne by its partner.

Where both methodologies are playing major roles as more-or-less full partners in the project, however, the issue of integration needs to be tackled head-on. Here, a common strategy is to transform either the quantitative or the qualitative data to make them comparable. This is literally a strategy of attempting to turn an apples-to-oranges comparison into apples-to-apples. Patterns and themes in the two types of data can then be meaningfully compared.

One strategy is to qualify the quantitative data. For this, one possibility might be to perform a *factor analysis*. Factor analysis is a statistical technique used to reduce the variability in multiple variables to a smaller number of underlying themes. You could apply factor analysis to a broad set of quantified variables to identify a smaller number of themes (factors) that could then be compared to patterns you observe in the qualitative data.[1] Most statistical packages such as SPSS, STATA, or R have the capability to do this.

The other data transformation strategy is to quantify the qualitative data. For example, you could take a text, identify themes, code them, and count the number of occurrences. For this, a software package such as MAXQDA or NVivo could be useful. The numerical occurrences of various themes could then be analyzed for patterns or relationships with other themes. Finally, you would compare the pattern of occurrences of the various themes to patterns or correlations in the quantitative data.

Some concerns about the mixed methods approach

You should know that researchers have debated the merits of the mixed methods approach, with some researchers expressing serious reservations. These reservations come down to three main issues: data transformation, data analysis, and practical issues of needed expertise.

Data transformation issues

This reservation comes down mainly to a concern about the merits of quantifying qualitative data. Some researchers urge caution in taking qualitative data and reducing it to numerical measures. In doing so, they argue that much of the rich, complex meaning of the qualitative data may be lost. Researchers who share this concern sometimes view with alarm the recent increasing emphasis on qualitative software packages that aid in identifying, coding, and counting themes found in texts and other qualitative sources of data.

Data analysis

In mixed methods research, data analysis is made a bit tricky by the fact that collection of quantitative and qualitative data often proceeds under different premises. As always, the question is how much you can say about what your findings mean. Do they generalize safely to other contexts, or do they apply only to the case at hand?

As we have seen, quantitative studies are designed to permit inference of findings in a sample to a larger population. In order for inference to be valid, however, our sample needs to be representative of the target population in relevant ways. In this case, however, how do we use the findings of a qualitative analysis based on convenience or purposive sampling in order to corroborate the quantitative findings? The problem is that there is no guarantee that a convenience sample will be representative of that target population for which the quantitative analysis is trying to draw inferences.

There are at least two solutions to this dilemma. The first is not to claim that your overall findings generalize to a larger population or, at least, to be highly circumspect in any claims you make. We have seen, for example, that all action research, and many case studies and ethnographies, make no claim to broader generalization. The differential sampling methods should not be an issue in these cases.

The second is to keep in mind the typically very different objectives of quantitative and qualitative research. The key distinction here is between research that quantifies relationships and research that explores underlying beliefs, attitudes, and ascribed meanings. There does not seem to be an inherent contradiction between the two kinds of research. Indeed, they may be viewed as augmenting each other in a logical way. If the quantitative component of your mixed methods study focuses on one and the qualitative component focuses on the other, the two elements of your study can be viewed as complementary parts. In the end, such a study may produce a final understanding that is greater than the sum of its parts.

Expertise

A final challenge presented by mixed methods research is the fact that it requires training and expertise in both quantitative and qualitative methods. Academic education has been traditionally discipline-based, with students being trained in either quantitative methods or qualitative methods but not both.

A mixed methods researcher who has been trained mostly in quantitative methods may find it difficult to meaningfully incorporate qualitative methods into the research project. And similarly for one who has been trained mostly in qualitative methods.

One solution to this problem may well be for researchers to work in teams, where different team members bring the different types of expertise to the research project. As we saw earlier, team research presents its own challenges, but it may provide the best way to address this issue.

Conclusions

Mixed methods research has become increasingly popular in recent years, as the methodology has become increasing refined and computer-based tools have emerged to address some of the practical issues of implementation. Its growing popularity stems in part from the appeal of the idea that we can use multiple methods to say more about environmental issues than either traditional methodology can by itself. It continues to present challenges to researchers because it requires training in both quantitative and qualitative methods, which many researchers do not have and which it is difficult to get in traditional discipline-based academic programs. However, as its methods continue to be refined and if disciplinary barriers gradually erode over time, the mixed methods approach may become increasingly popular and prevalent in environmental research.

Exercises/discussion questions

(1) Find a purely quantitative study and identify its research question and answer. Then describe a qualitative component you could add to it that would provide deeper insights into the issue. Restate the research question to take both components into account, splitting it into multiple questions if warranted. Keep in mind the *what* vs. the *how* and *why* distinction.

(2) Find a purely qualitative study and identify its research question and answer. Then describe a quantitative component you could add to it that would provide deeper insights into the issue. Restate the research question to take both

components into account, splitting it into multiple questions if warranted. Keep in mind the *what* vs. the *how* and *why* distinction.

(3) Suppose you have a semester to complete a mixed methods research project. State a research question (keeping in mind the earlier exhortation that it be an interesting one to you!) that is sufficiently narrow in scope that it would be feasible to pursue one of the two sequential mixed methods strategies described in the text. Create a detailed timetable, complete with specific tasks, that permits you to carry this out, saying as much as you can about the likely content of the second-stage analysis.

(4) Re-answer (3), where you instead consider using a concurrent triangulation strategy. Are you able to state a research question that is broader in scope? If so, how do you trade this increased breadth off against being able to provide fewer details about the second-stage analysis?

Note

1 For an intermediate-level, relatively non-mathematical treatment of factor analysis, see Foster et al. 2006, Chapter 6.

References

Creswell, John W. *Research Design: Qualitative, Quantitative, and Mixed Methods Approaches*. Los Angeles: Sage, 2009.

Foster, Jeremy, Emma Barkus, and Christian Yavorsky. *Understanding and Using Advanced Statistics*. London: Sage, 2006.

Greene, Jennifer C., Valerie J. Caracelli, and Wendy F. Graham. "Toward a Conceptual Framework for Mixed Method Evaluation Designs," *Educational Evaluation and Policy Analysis* 11(Autumn, 1989): 255–74.

Johnson, R. Burke, and Anthony J. Onwuegbuzie. "Mixed Methods Research: A Research Paradigm whose Time Has Come," *Educational Researcher* 33(October 2004): 14–26.

Klassen, Ann C., John Creswell, Vicki L. Plano Clark, Katherine Clegg Smith, and Helen I. Meissner. "Commentary: Best Practices in Mixed Methods for Quality of Life Research," *Quality of Life Research* 21(April 2012): 377–80.

Lingard, Lorelei, Mathieu Albert, and Wendy Levinson. "Qualitative Research: Grounded Theory, Mixed Methods, and Action Research," *British Medical Journal* 337(August 23, 2008): 459–61.

Silva, Julie A., and Lila K. Khatiwada. "Transforming Conservation into Cash? Nature Tourism in Southern Africa," *Africa Today* 61(Fall 2014): 17–45.

Sydenstricker-Neto, John. "Population and Deforestation in the Brazilian Amazon: A Mediating Perspective and a Mixed-method Analysis," *Population and Environment* 34(September 2012): 86–112.

16 Data collection I

Principles of surveying

Introduction

A great many qualitative research projects involve the collection of survey data, and some quantitative projects also use survey data. As we have seen, for example, the *North Shore Climate Change* project involved designing a survey instrument and administering it to tourists on the North Shore. In designing that survey instrument, we had to be extremely careful to follow a number of principles of correct survey design. It turns out that when you design a survey, there are many places you can go wrong. And if you do, there is a very real danger that your instrument will not serve its function: providing accurate information on which to base an analysis.

This chapter examines a number of issues of methodology regarding written surveys, in which respondents provide their responses on some written medium, including paper or electronic surveys. It is hoped that by the end of the discussion, you will have an appreciation for a variety of important considerations that go into good survey design. And that you will have learned a number of practical lessons for designing your own survey. Chapter 17 examines a similar set of issues involved in conducting oral interviews.

General principles of survey methodology

General survey methodology can be thought of as aimed at answering three fundamental questions: who to survey, what questions to ask, and how to ask them. These are the *Who*, *What*, and *How* questions of surveying methodology.

Figure 16.1 shows that these questions stem directly from your research question. Once you have formulated your research question, you need to start thinking about who you are going to survey to get the information you need. This takes us into an entire thicket of questions related to sampling (*who* to ask). The other two questions relate to your survey instrument: what it contains in terms of content (*what* questions to ask), wording, and format (*how* to ask these questions).

Sampling

As we have seen, in many cases of both quantitative and qualitative research the objective is to infer something about a population we are interested in

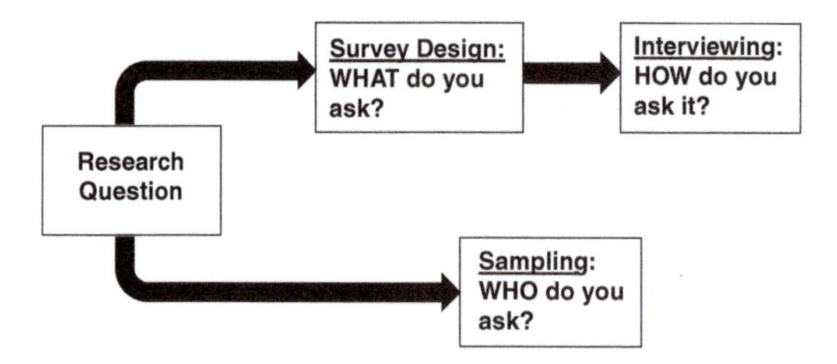

Figure 16.1 The Who, What, and How of surveying.

Source: Author.

understanding better. This is commonly known as the *target population*, the object of our interest (Figure 16.2). From the target population, we identify a *sampling frame*, which is a clearly defined representative subset of the target population, from which we draw our *sample*. In qualitative research, it is common to draw a distinction between the sample and the *respondents*, since not everyone who is sampled actually responds, in terms of information that can be used in the analysis.

Finally, it is commonly the case that there are *post-survey adjustments* to be made: filling in missing data and more generally, other sorts of adjustments we make for non-responses, data cleaning, and so forth. At the end of this process, we have a clean set of survey responses, ready for examination and analysis.

For example, consider the North Shore survey briefly described earlier. In that case, the target population was the set of tourists visiting the North Shore during the summer months, both for day trips and overnight visits. The sampling frame consisted of visitors to various destinations, including state parks, roadside rest areas, and outfitters. From this sampling frame, we selected a sample of 1,399 respondents speaking on behalf of roughly 4,200 individuals. Various post-survey adjustments were made to the sample responses, including culling responses that were clearly mistakes or typographical errors.

Survey design, interviewing

Figure 16.2 also shows the typical sequence of general steps involved in designing a survey and soliciting responses. Here, you begin with the *construct*: a variable, concept, or issue that your research project is concerned with. Because the construct is not always observable, you pose questions designed to provide your best *measurement* of the value of the construct (recall our discussion of construct validity in Chapter 9). Survey respondents provide *responses*, for which there might be follow-up questions to ensure that the response is in fact speaking to the question. Based on the information elicited by the follow-up questions, there may be an *edited response* tabulated as the actual final response.

For example, the construct of the North Shore study was the effect of climate change on recreational activity in general. To get at this issue, tourists

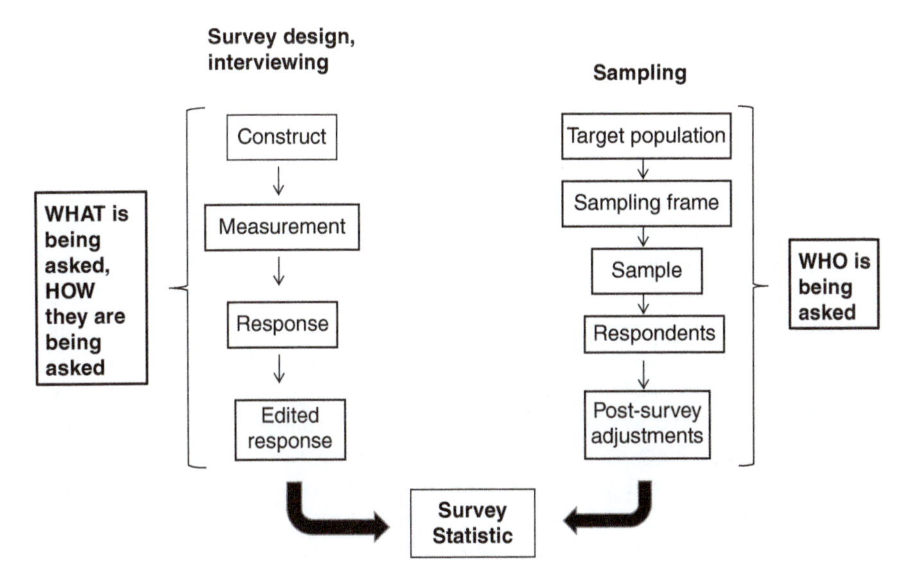

Figure 16.2 Components of the who, what, and how of surveying.

Source: Author.

were presented with climate change scenarios and queried about their trip-taking behavior. This was the way the researchers measured the construct. Tourists then reflected on the climate information and their personal preferences and gave their response. Finally, because of the electronic medium of the survey (surveys were administered on iPads), there were no follow-up questions and, therefore, no edited responses.

As a general matter, effective surveying is a matter of minimizing various kinds of errors that can arise when you design and administer a survey, and when you choose a sample of potential respondents. There are four basic kinds of error that you need to watch out for. In the process of sampling, you will need to worry about *coverage error*, *sampling error*, and *non-response error*. In the process of designing and administering your survey, you will need to worry about *measurement error*. Each of these concepts is explained in depth later on.

Adding all of these up gives you what surveying specialists refer to as *total survey error* (Weisbert 2005; Dillman et al. 2009, pp. 16–19; "Polling fundamentals"). Exemplary research projects that use survey data are ones that make every effort to minimize total survey error. The entire remaining discussion in this chapter can be viewed as a guide to how to accomplish exactly that.

Sampling

When we do a survey, we are commonly interested in inferring something about a larger population (the target population). In the earlier discussion of quantitative analysis, there were two extremely important issues: randomness in sampling and sample size. As we have seen, random sampling requires that every member of the population has an equal likelihood of being sampled, which is why it is sometimes referred to as probability sampling. Recall the metaphor of picking ping-pong balls out of a large rotating barrel with your eyes closed. If you sample randomly, then the pattern that emerges in the sample should closely mirror the underlying pattern in the population.

The reliability of your estimates, however, also depends upon the size of your sample. This is because when you sample randomly, literally any outcome within the population can happen in any given trial, and weird things can happen.

For example, suppose that half of the ping-pong balls in your rotating barrel are blue and the other half are red. This means that if you blindly grab a large number of ping-pong balls out of the barrel, roughly half of them should be blue. And this is likely to happen if you grab a thousand, or even a hundred, ping-pong balls. But if you grab only a handful of balls, there is actually a pretty good chance of getting either a large fraction of blues or a large fraction of reds. In this case, your sample will not give you a good sense for the actual proportions of blue and red balls in the barrel.

When you conduct a survey, both of these issues—random sampling and sample size—come into play. Generally speaking, there are a number of challenges both to sampling randomly and to constructing a large sample. Referring back to Figure 16.2, these occur at various stages in the overall sampling process and are manifested in various types of error.

Coverage error

The first potential issue occurs when moving from the target population to the sampling frame. Ideally, your sampling frame matches your target population exactly. This essentially means that every relevant subgroup in the population is also contained in the sampling frame, in the same proportions, and all irrelevant ones are excluded. So, for example, suppose you are interested in the opinions of US adults on a particular climate change policy. The best sampling frame would be one that covers all US adults and no one else.

Now suppose for reasons of feasibility you choose for your sampling frame a database of all cell phone numbers in the United States. There are at least two ways in which this sampling frame may differ from your target population. One is that some of those cell phone numbers may belong to teenagers. The other is that there may be some adults who do not have cell phones. So your sampling frame both excludes some relevant individuals and includes some irrelevant ones.

This is not necessarily fatal to your study, in terms of being able to obtain reliable results. But it can present problems, if either the included teenagers or the excluded adults exhibit different attitudes from those of the adults that comprise the target population of your study. For example, by not sampling the excluded adults, you may not be getting an overall accurate assessment of adults, if those excluded adults differ in some systematic way from the ones who are included.

When this occurs, we say that we have *coverage error*. See Box 16.1 for a famous example of coverage error from American history.

Box 16.1 Coverage error and the 1936 US presidential election

The 1936 presidential election pitted the incumbent Franklin Roosevelt, a Democrat, against a Republican challenger, Alf Landon. Prior to the election, the weekly magazine *Literary Digest* conducted a poll of readers asking who they were going to vote for in the election.

Literary Digest was highly experienced in polling and had a good track record, having successfully predicted the election outcome in the previous five presidential elections. And it polled a huge number of people by any standard: roughly ten million, of which over 2.3 million responded. By all indications, the results of its poll should have been extremely accurate. It predicted that Landon would win in a landslide, 57% to 43%, and that he would win over two-thirds of all the electoral votes.

As it turned out, *Literary Digest* was way off. Rather than winning only 43% of the popular vote, Roosevelt won 61%, and he captured 523 out of the 531 possible electoral votes. The debacle ended up striking an enormous blow to the credibility of the magazine, which folded two years later.

What went wrong? One issue was that *Literary Digest* chose a sampling frame that was horribly non-representative of the target population. The ten million voters polled were taken primarily from a database of automobile registration lists and telephone books (Squire 1988, pp. 126–7). Voters who happened to own cars and telephones were relatively wealthy compared to the general voting population. On the whole, these voters were much more likely to vote for the Republican challenger than the populist president.

Source: Dillman et al. 2009, pp. 3–4.

Sampling error

Another issue occurs in moving from the sampling frame to the sample. In an ideal but generally completely unattainable world, we would want to obtain information from everyone in the entire population. However, even with an extremely carefully done random sampling procedure, your characterization of the population is likely to be off. More accurately, any estimates you make of particular characteristics of the population, such as the nature of a relationship among variables, can only be said to be true not with certainty, but with some lesser degree of confidence. When your estimate does not perfectly match the true characteristic of the population because you are not sampling the entire population, we say that we have *sampling error* (Dillman et al. 2009, p. 17).

As it turns out, as a general rule, the smaller your sample, the greater is the likelihood of sampling error. Recalling the earlier ping-pong ball example, suppose you want to know what fraction of ping-pong balls in the barrel are blue, and your test is based upon the percentage of blue ping-pong balls you pull out of the barrel. If you pick just two balls, there is a really good chance that they will be either both blue or both red. Based on this tiny sample, your estimate of the proportion of blue balls would be way off: either zero or one. Even though you are sampling completely randomly, you get major sampling error because your sample is so small.

In order to minimize sampling error, the practical implications for your surveying effort would seem to be clear: try to randomly survey a lot of people. Sounds easy, right? However, there are a number of challenges to doing this successfully.

The first thing to keep in mind is that when you conduct a survey, not everyone is going to respond. Indeed, many may not. If you conduct a survey using regular mail, many of your envelopes may simply get thrown away into the trash, unopened. If you set up an electronic survey using a service like SurveyMonkey and then solicit participants from a target sample, many may not respond. Unlike picking ping-pong balls out of a barrel, there may a sizable difference between the size of your sample and the number of respondents.

This is a fact of life when it comes to surveying. However, later on in this chapter I will give you some suggestions regarding things you can do to increase your response rate. For now, just keep in mind that the number of surveys you solicit will in general need to be considerably larger than the number you can expect to be able to use in the end.

This brings up another important issue; namely, that surveying takes time and resources, and the budget for your research project is not limitless. This means that there may be practical limits to how large a sample you can consider trying to collect. Fortunately, it turns out that there are limits to how much additional accuracy you can achieve as you expand your sample size. This fact provides us with specific guidance on how large a sample you need to collect. This will depend upon various factors, including the size of your population, the likely division of your responses among different response categories, and how precise you want your estimates to be.

Consider, for example, Table 16.1, which is adapted from Dillman et al. (2009). Column one gives the population size. And given those population sizes, the rest of the columns list the sample sizes required to achieve a given level of confidence for different divisions of your responses into two categories.

So suppose I am a pollster trying to predict the outcome of the upcoming presidential election in my own town. Suppose the size of the target population is 10,000 (roughly the size of the voting population in my home town of Northfield, MN). Suppose also that I predict the division of my responses will be roughly 50–50 (say, the division of the vote in a hotly contested political race). Finally, suppose that I want a margin of error of three percentage points at a 95% confidence level (that is, I want to be within three points of the actual outcome 95% of the time). Table 16.1 tells us that I would need 965 completed survey responses.

Table 16.1 Sample size needed for 95% confidence level

	± 10%		± 5%		± 3%	
Population size	*50/50 Split*	*80/20 Split*	*50/50 Split*	*80/20 Split*	*50/50 Split*	*80/20 Split*
100	49	38	80	71	92	87
200	65	47	132	111	169	155
400	78	53	196	153	291	253
1,000	88	58	278	198	517	406
2,000	92	60	322	219	696	509
10,000	95	61	370	240	965	640
40,000	96	61	381	244	1,040	672
100,000	96	61	383	245	1,056	679
1,000,000	96	61	384	246	1,067	683

Source: Dillman et al. 2009, p. 57.

Table 16.1 tells us a couple of very interesting facts about sample sizes. First, for small populations, the size of your sample needs to be large relative to your population size. For example, if your population consists of only 100 individuals, you need to sample nearly everyone to achieve precise results (92 out of 100, for a 3% margin of error at a 95% confidence level in a hotly contested race).

However, for extremely large populations, you can make do with a sample size that is relatively small, comparatively speaking. If instead of 100, your population consisted of one *million* individuals, you would only need a sample size of 1,067—a fraction of 1% of the population—to achieve the same degree of precision under the same conditions. Great news for those of us interested in characterizing large populations, if we have the resources to do it.

Second, Table 16.1 indicates that you can make do with considerably smaller sample sizes if you are expecting relatively lop-sided responses. The required sample size when faced with an 80–20 split is considerably smaller than when faced with a 50–50 split, especially at larger population sizes.

Bottom line: Sampling error is centrally dependent upon sample size. Generally speaking, the larger the sample size the better, if you want to minimize sampling error. However, there are limits to the extra benefit you get from expanding your sample size, which depend upon various factors that vary across research projects. These include: the size of your population, the likely division of your responses into different categories, and the level of desired precision in your results. You should keep these in mind when you are negotiating the tradeoff between the objectives of your research project and the size of your research budget.

Non-response error

A related issue can arise in moving from the sample to the respondents. Ideally, we would like the group of actual respondents to mirror the sample in the ways important to the research question. Specifically, considering the fact that not all of those surveyed will actually respond, we would like the ones who do respond to faithfully reflect the ones who do not. When this does not happen, this is referred to as *non-response error*. In quantitative studies, the presence of non-response error is essentially the issue of *sample selection bias*, which we encountered in Chapter 7.

This issue apparently also came up in the *Literary Digest* poll fiasco, where we saw earlier that the choice of sampling frame significantly biased the predictions. However, even among the voters who had been sampled, there appears to have been significant non-response among Roosevelt supporters. This factor also made Landon's chances seem better than they really were. On the whole, both coverage error and non-response error contributed to the dismal performance of the *Literary Digest* poll (Squire 1988).

Methods of sampling

Let us now turn our focus to the practical matter of how we go about collecting our sample. In this discussion, our focus will be not so much on sample size, but rather on the issue of random sampling. We have already seen some general pitfalls when it comes to obtaining a random sample, especially coverage error and non-response error. In general, however, there are a number of issues in practical sampling that make the process look nothing like picking ping-pong balls at random from a barrel. There are two main types of non-random sampling: *purposive sampling* and *convenience sampling*.

Purposive sampling

One thing to keep in mind is that your sampling strategy will often depend upon the objectives of your research project. Non-random sampling may well be called for if, for example, you are interested in getting expert opinions on a particular topic, or if you want a wide range of opinions. In each of these cases, you would deliberately target a set of respondents, in the first instance a set of individuals possessing certain expertise that would be useful for your study. In the latter case, you might target a diverse set of individuals, according to some criterion you have in mind. Both of these strategies would be what we call *purposive sampling*, which is just what it sounds like: sampling with a particular purpose in mind (Nonprobability Sampling).

Another reason to engage in purposive sampling is if you simply want to ensure you have a sufficient number of respondents in each of a set of categories of respondents you are interested in. This type of sampling is called *quota sampling*:

you sample until you have filled your quota in all of the relevant categories (Seale 2012, pp. 144–5).

For example, if you are interested in climate change effects on recreational tourism, you may want to make sure you have enough of both day visitors and overnight visitors. So you could keep track of the number of respondents in each category as you go, and then stop when you have filled your quotas.

The advantage of quota sampling is that you can ensure that all groups you are interested in are adequately represented in your sample. At the same time, it may present challenges in terms of deciding which specific characteristics are important to your study.

Convenience sampling

The other type of non-random sampling is *convenience sampling*, which is also what it sounds like: basing your sampling procedure on what is convenient for you to get. Examples of this would be standing on a street corner soliciting passersby, or doing a survey of residents in your college residence hall.

The advantage of this strategy should be apparent: it makes the collection of responses relatively painless. The big disadvantage should also be apparent: collecting responses in this way in no way guarantees that your sample will end up being representative of the population you are interested in understanding better.

A sampling procedure that has elements of both convenience sampling and purposive sampling is called *snowball sampling*. Snowball sampling involves relying on referrals from respondents for other potential respondents. So, for example, you might ask the first people you survey whether they have any ideas for others you should talk to. And then you ask these folks the same thing. In this way, your sample snowballs, like a snowball rolling down a hill.

This method is unlikely to lead to a representative sample, but it has the advantage of allowing you to identify new potential respondents, which may be a difficult task in certain situations. And there are certain ways in which the issue of non-representativeness may be mitigated, such as starting out the sampling process with several individuals who are varied in key respects, so you can get coverage of different issues or characteristics. Your sample snowballs, if you will, in different directions (Seale 2012, p. 145).

Principles of effective surveying: Maximizing responses

By now, it is probably completely intuitive that you want to encourage as many people to respond to your survey as you can. Maximizing the response rate is of course an important means of ensuring a reasonable sample size. But it may also mean that you do not require as large a sample in order to get the same number of usable responses.

For example, a 30% response rate on a sample of 500 surveys yields the same number of responses as a 15% response rate on a sample of 1,000 surveys. Thus, anything you can do to increase your response rate may save you a great deal in terms of time, materials, postage, and so forth.

When thinking about measures to increase response rate, it may help to put yourself in the shoes of your potential respondents. After all, they may have jobs, they may be going to school, they may have families, and in general, there may be many things going on in their busy lives. When you solicit their participation in your survey, you are adding one more thing to the pile of things they have to do. They may want to help you out, but there may be many other things that take precedence. The question is: What can you do to try to keep your survey from falling to the bottom of their to-do list or, even worse, disappearing from their radar screen altogether?

Generally speaking, the answer is that you want to give them incentive to participate. There are at least three ways that you can do this: rewarding them for participation, making it relatively painless for them to participate, and inspiring confidence in them that your survey is a worthwhile endeavor to be involved in (Dillman et al. 2009, pp. 23–33).

Rewards for participation

Financial rewards work. Paying people to participate in your survey can be an effective way to get them to participate. Unfortunately, if you hope to get a decent-sized sample, substantial monetary payments to all respondents is beyond the budget of most research projects. However, there are ways to provide tangible rewards for participation that do not break the bank (see Box 16.2).

Many people, for example, respond to even token gifts, such as pens, gift cards, or coupons redeemable toward items such as movies, pizza, or printer cartridges. Another strategy that can keep your project costs down is to enter all participants into a drawing for some prize, like an iPad. If you do this, of course, you need to ensure that people understand that their reward for participation is not an iPad, but only a *chance* at winning an iPad. So be careful in how you communicate this to them.

As it turns out, however, there are a number of things you can do to effectively encourage participation besides invoking personal gain. This is because human beings are not only interested in money.

For one thing, they like to believe they are making a difference toward promoting social goals that they value. So one thing you should do is to provide them information about the survey: why it is being conducted and how the results will be used to benefit them and others. You may also want to stress the importance of their participation in the survey. If they see the value of the enterprise and how they can make a difference, they are more likely to want to be a part of it.

Second, human beings like it when they are shown respect, and they like feeling wanted and appreciated. So when you approach them about participating in your survey, ask for their help. Don't tell them they are one of the lucky ones to have been chosen to take the survey: they will never buy it and they will think that you think they are some kind of idiot. Acknowledge what is really going on: that you need them and you are relying on their generosity. In addition, there are all sorts of ways to ask questions, some of which come across as much more respectful of the respondents. We will go over a few of these ways in the next section. And lastly, don't forget to thank them in the end for their participation.

Box 16.2 Checklist: Rewards for participation

- ✔ Give tangible rewards.
- ✔ Provide information about the project.
- ✔ Ask for help.
- ✔ Show your appreciation.

Minimizing the pain

It is important to recognize that respondents incur costs when they participate in your survey: costs in terms of inconvenience, lost time, and, especially, the other things they could be doing with their time. So one thing you can do is to try to make participation as convenient for them as possible (see Box 16.3).

For example, if you are conducting a mail survey, make sure to include a self-addressed, stamped envelope. Or if you are conducting an on-line survey, when you send them an e-mail soliciting their participation, provide a clickable link that will open their browser and take them directly to the survey.

Second, you should make an effort to make the survey easy to complete. One thing this means is to keep it short and sweet. Here you may find yourself in a bit of a bind. There may be a lot of information you feel you need to ask for, but you don't want to overly tax the respondents by asking them to answer pages and pages of questions. If you do, they may not respond at all.

The bottom line is that you will have to balance the informational needs of your project against the onerousness of the task you are giving your respondents. One thing that will help is some careful planning: to think very carefully ahead of time about exactly what information you require, and to think about the most efficient way to get it, in terms of the questions you ask.

Another thing that will help is to try to make the survey as respondent-friendly as you can. This means, among other things, organized and clearly worded questions along with formats that make it easy to answer the questions. In the next section, we will discuss a number of wording and formatting issues that arise and suggest ways to encourage responsiveness.

Box 16.3 Checklist: Minimizing the pain

- ✔ Make it convenient to respond.
- ✔ Try to keep the survey as concise as you can, given your information needs.
- ✔ Make the survey clear and easy to read.

Inspiring confidence

The measures we have been talking about so far are mostly practical nuts-and-bolts ways of making it more appealing to respondents to participate in your survey. But in order for these measures to work, there is a larger question of credibility. You are asking them to participate in your survey, in return for which you will produce a piece of research. The question is whether they believe that if they help you out, their efforts will meaningfully contribute to something worthwhile. They have to have confidence in the enterprise and in you as the researcher.

There are several things you can do to try to earn their confidence (see Box 16.4). One general set of suggestions relate to the appearance of your survey instrument. It is important to make sure your survey instrument looks professional. Looks matter! Imagine your reaction if you received in the mail a handwritten, poorly worded survey. You would probably be tempted to throw it in the trash, figuring (correctly) that the author of the survey couldn't be bothered to put in the required amount of effort, so why should you.

Survey instruments should be carefully designed, neatly formatted, and attractive to look at. Including informational brochures about the project can convey professionalism, and as well as personalized cover letters printed on stationery with letterhead from your department, college, or university, if available.

Indeed, anything you can do to convey that you are associated with an authority that has general public legitimacy will tend to make people want to participate. These include, for example, logos of associated institutions such as government agencies, colleges, or universities, or well-known non-governmental organizations. These could be placed either on a hard-copy cover letter or on the first page of an on-line survey instrument.

Another thing that can inspire trust and encourage people to participate in your survey is a promise of confidentiality, as it is a common fear nowadays that sensitive information could be made public, with consequences for the respondent. The measures you take should include not just a statement promising that the information they provide will be kept confidential. You may also want to briefly explain the efforts that you will take to ensure the confidentiality of their responses.

Box 16.4 Checklist: Inspiring confidence

- ✔ Make the survey look professional.
- ✔ Obtain sponsorship of authority with recognized legitimacy.
- ✔ Provide assurances of confidentiality.

Principles of effective surveying: formatting and wording issues

Once you have taken steps to encourage maximum response, you need to take steps to try to ensure that the information you collect from your respondents is both accurate and serves the purposes of your research project. Here, we turn to the questions of what to ask, and how to ask it.

The things you ask about will of course be dictated largely by your research question and the information you require in order to answer it. So the discussion here will be of a general nature: issues that apply broadly across a wide range of different research questions. At this point, we are returning to the notion of *measurement error* and how to minimize it, which was briefly discussed earlier. By measurement error, we mean error that occurs when the answers of respondents are inaccurate or imprecise (Dillman et al. 2009, p. 18). Much of the discussion in this section will be about minimizing measurement error.

Quantitative or qualitative study?

To begin with, one key issue is whether you are undertaking a quantitative or qualitative study. Quantitative studies rely heavily on closed-ended questions, in which respondents are asked a question and given a menu of specific choices, from which they are asked to select an answer. The answer options are typically either numerical responses or responses to which numbers can later be assigned. All of this is because the quantitative approach requires responses that are consistent across different respondents in order to give validity to statistical analyses.

On the other hand, qualitative studies can rely on both closed-ended and open-ended questions. Instead of requiring respondents to pick only from a designated set of options, open-ended questions simply require respondents to write down a response. What they write down is (almost) completely up to them. So the difference between open-ended and closed-ended questions is akin to the difference between essay questions and multiple choice (Dillman et al. 2009, pp. 108–18).

One important implication, especially for qualitative research, is that answering open-ended questions requires more effort on the part of the respondent, just like it is harder for you to write an essay question than to answer a multiple-choice or true/false question. If your professor gave you a choice, you might be sorely tempted to simply not answer his essay questions. Similarly, the survey respondent is more likely to leave the open-ended question blank, which raises potential issues of non-response error if those folks differ in important ways from the ones who do respond.

There are a couple of ways to deal with this potential problem. One is to think carefully about how to ask your open-ended questions to make it as easy as possible for the respondent to answer. There are typically multiple ways to pose questions and still get the information you need. If you are playing with different wordings, you might consider getting feedback from other students in the class. The issues here are both content and clarity: not only do you want respondents to provide you answers, you also want to make sure they understand the questions.

The issue also speaks to the potential value of face-to-face or phone interviews, as opposed to some written instrument. It is a lot easier to ignore questions on a written survey than ones posed to you in real time by another human being. The tradeoff here is that interviews require a considerably larger investment of your time and energy. More details on interviewing principles are provided in the next chapter.

General issues

Regardless of whether you are doing a quantitative or qualitative study, there are certain general principles to consider when designing survey questions. Of course, you want respondents to answer truthfully and accurately. In part, this means to be aware of questions that respondents might be reluctant to answer. These would include, for example, questions about how much money they make, or questions on sensitive topics, such as run-ins with the police. Sometimes, judicious choice of wording can make people more comfortable about answering. For example, people generally feel more comfortable with answering questions about their income by choosing an income category rather than providing a specific number.

Also keep in mind that some questions are simply easier to answer than others. It is a lot easier, for example, for people to tell you how old they are than to tell you how they feel about specific policies regarding climate change. They may not *want* to tell you how old they are, but for most people, the information is right there at their fingertips. Opinions on climate change policy, on the other hand, require them to think about various issues: what the policy alternatives are, how serious they believe the problem of climate change is, who it affects, and so forth.

This means, of course, that the information you collect on their attitudes toward climate change policies may be subject to greater uncertainty than the information on their age and other demographic characteristics. They may be less likely to respond at all, increasing the chances of non-response error. Finally, it means that exactly *how* you ask your questions on climate change attitudes may greatly affect the response, making issues of wording even more important.

Another factor to consider is that answering certain questions may require respondents to recall things that happened in the past, about which their memories might be a little fuzzy. The point is more than the obvious one that memories tend to fade over time. There are certain types of things that it is simply harder for people to remember.

One is that it is hard to remember the precise details of specific instances of things you do on a regular basis, like going to class, cooking dinner, or driving your car. Another is that we often do not remember exactly when we did something, even which month or year. So if you ask someone which days he cooked spaghetti for dinner this past semester, he may well be unable to tell you. But he may well be able to tell you how many times this month, and perhaps exactly when, he cooked a romantic spaghetti dinner for his girlfriend. If there are ways to phrase questions so that they are about more recent or more memorable events, you are likely to obtain more accurate information.

Wording issues

By now, you can probably see that the way that questions are worded is extremely important. Let's now turn to some common issues, and suggestions for how to deal with them.

To begin with, it is important to keep in mind that there are MANY ways to word a question. In deciding how you want to word a question, there are three main issues: (1) making sure you are asking questions in ways that they CAN be answered; (2) making sure the respondent knows exactly what you are asking; and (3) making sure you are not inadvertently biasing the responses in how you pose the questions. There is a real art to wording questions, but you can avoid many sources of error by following a few simple principles.

How to make sure you are asking questions in ways that they can be answered

The first thing to keep in mind is that you want to make sure that the question is worded in such a way that the respondent can actually answer it. To see what I mean, let us consider two important rules.

RULE: MAKE SURE THE QUESTION APPLIES TO THE RESPONDENT

Consider the question: Who is your cell phone provider? This may seem like a straightforward question to ask on a survey. The problem, however, is that some respondents may not have cell phones. So how are they likely to respond? If you give them a space in which to write an answer, they may write "None," which may tell you what you want to know. But they may also just skip the question, leaving you wondering whether they in fact have no cell phone provider or just chose not to answer. Regardless of which one it is, you will be forced to discard the answer.

One way you may be tempted to deal with this issue is to make the question conditional. You could, for example, ask: If you have a cell phone, who is your cell phone provider? This may not, however, solve the problem, because they may decide the question does not apply to them and just skip it. The general rule here is to make sure that each question requires an answer from every respondent. So in this example, the best thing to do would be to provide a filter question first, like: "Do you have a cell phone?" Then pose the question only if they answer yes. And if they answer no, instruct them to skip to the following question.

RULE: ASK ONE QUESTION AT A TIME

This may seem like silly advice, but here's what I mean. Sometimes questions are worded in such a way that two different questions are being asked at once. For example, consider the following question: Do you like to eat fruits and vegetables? This question is actually asking two questions, one about fruits and one about vegetables. The problem is that some people may like to eat cherries but hate broccoli, and vice versa. Such people will not know how to answer this question.

RULE: MAKE SURE YOU INCLUDE ALL POSSIBLE RESPONSES

Another problem can arise if you ask a question and provide a set of possible responses that don't include all possibilities. For example, consider the following question: From which of these sources did you find out about the terrorist bombing attacks in Paris? Suppose you provide the following four responses: radio, television, another student, my parents. The problem is, of course, that there are other sources from which the respondent may have heard about the attacks, like a newspaper or the internet. If you are going to provide a limited set of responses, you need to make sure you have covered all the possibilities. If you are unsure you have, then adding an "Other" category will at least ensure the question can be answered.

RULE: MAKE SURE YOUR ANSWER CATEGORIES DON'T OVERLAP

Here, the danger is that if categories overlap, then more than one category may be correct, and the respondent may choose both or not know which one to choose. Consider, for example, the following categories, in response to the question: What is your annual income?

- Less than $25,000
- $25,000 to $50,000
- $50,000 to $75,000
- $75,000 to $100,000
- More than $100,000

It is possible, even if unlikely, that a respondent may recall having made $50,000, in which case she will not know whether to mark the second category or the third. In this case, you might state the categories as follows instead:

- Less than $25,000
- $25,000 up to $50,000
- $50,000 up to $75,000
- $75,000 up to $100,000
- More than $100,000

Here, the respondent who recalls making $50,000 is much more likely to mark the third category.

How to make sure the respondent knows what you are asking

In general, the idea here is to put yourself in the shoes of your potential respondents and ask yourself what they could possibly find unclear about your questions. For most surveys, the general rule is to keep your questions concrete, specific, short, and simple.

RULE: USE CONCRETE AND SPECIFIC WORDS

The key reason to ask questions that are concrete and specific is to minimize the amount that respondents have to interpret what you mean. The more they have to interpret, the greater is the danger that they will misinterpret and answer a different question than the one you intended. Consider the following example. Suppose you are doing a sociological study of various factors that encourage family cohesiveness, including eating meals together. You want to find out how often a given respondent's family eats together, so you ask the following question (see Dillman et al. 2009, p. 84): How many times did you eat together as a family last week? Is this question likely to yield useful information for your study?

On the surface, the question seems pretty clear, concrete, and specific, but let's dissect it. Probably the biggest source of ambiguity is in the phrase: "eat together as a family." The questions are: How might the respondent interpret this question, and will different respondents interpret it differently? Some might interpret this phrase as: where everyone is present at sit-down meals at the kitchen table. Others may also count take-out pizza where everyone is camped in front of the television. Still others may count family picnics, snacking in the car on the way to grandma's house, or tailgating before the Saturday afternoon football game of the local university. And if different respondents interpret the question differently, the answers may simply reflect their differing interpretations as opposed to providing a consistent measure of family cohesiveness.

So what can be done about this question to make it less open to interpretation? It depends on what your measure of family cohesiveness is. But let's suppose it is sit-down meals, perhaps because you happen to believe that pizza in front of the TV does not promote the same amount of family bonding and communication. One possible rewording might be: How many meals did you sit down to eat at home as a family last week? This would (likely, but see exercise (5) at the end of the chapter) rule out meals camped in front of the television or eaten on the fly on the way to something else.

RULE: AVOID DOUBLE NEGATIVES

Another related interpretive issue arises when you use double-negatives. In 2006, for example, the Roper organization was interested in public opinion on a bill that would prevent foreign companies from owning cargo operations in US seaports ("The Perils of Double Negatives"). But it was also interested in whether the wording of the question would affect responses. So it presented the following questions to different groups of respondents, and asked whether the respondent agreed:

> *Would you favor or oppose a bill that would prevent any foreign-owned company from owning cargo operations at seaports in the United States?*
>
> *Would you favor or oppose a bill that would allow* only *US companies to own cargo operations at seaports in the United States?*

If you examine these two questions, they are saying the same thing but the first one is employing a double-negative (*oppose-prevent*). As it turned out, 38% of respondents said they would favor the bill when presented with the first statement, whereas nearly 68% favored the bill as described in the second statement.

The likely explanation is that respondents were confused by what the first question was actually saying. In addition, there is something in our psychological makeup that makes it more difficult to agree with a "not" statement (Dillman et al. 2009, p. 88). By employing the double negative, we probably get an understatement of actual public support for this bill.

RULE: USE SIMPLE AND FAMILIAR WORDS

One of the first principles of effective surveying is a simple one: you want respondents to understand the question. If you use longer, less-commonly used words, you increase the chances that they will not know what you mean. So instead of "highest priority," you might say "most important." Instead of "household occupants," you might say "people who live here" (Dillman et al. 2009, p. 83).

RULE: ASK SHORT QUESTIONS

It is also a good idea to keep your questions short and sweet. The longer they are, the more information respondents have to process, and the greater the chance they will misread or misinterpret what they are being asked. One piece of advice here is to write your question and then look for ways to eliminate unnecessary words. This is the same exhortation that you have received from faculty members in your writing classes: avoid being verbose. For example, there is probably no reason to write "due to the fact that" when you can simply say "because".

RULE: WRITE COMPLETE SENTENCES

Given the last two rules, it is tempting to use incomplete sentences in order to save space, but unfortunately, this can create confusion. For example, suppose your survey contains questions asking for demographic information. You might be tempted to simply specify: "Age" or "Ethnicity" or "Your city or town" or "Highest level of educational attainment," followed by a box in which to write in their answer. Dillman provides the following cautionary tale against doing that (Dillman et al. 2009, p. 87).

Consider the following set of incomplete-sentence questions:

> *Number of years lived in Idaho*
> *Your city or town*
> *Your county*

These questions were once asked consecutively in a survey. Seem difficult to misinterpret, right? It turns out that nearly one fifth of all respondents entered not the *name* of their city or town, but the *number of years* they had lived in their city or town, without saying what city or town it was. Apparently, the first question framed how they interpreted the next question. To make matters worse, in response to the "Your county" question, several respondents answered "United

the chances of getting more "agree" responses. Both make it less likely that you will be able to glean their true attitudes toward carbon taxes.

RULE: FOR BIPOLAR QUESTIONS, PROVIDE FIVE OR SEVEN RESPONSES, BUT NOT MORE

Obviously, to have a balanced scale around a neutral center, you need an odd number of response options. The above balanced scale example provides five, but you could consider seven, as in Box 16.9. More options increases the cognitive burden on the respondent, but it also provides potentially useful finer gradations of opinion. More than seven options, however, probably imposes too much of a burden on the respondent for too little gain.

Box 16.9 Balanced scale, seven response options

- ☐ Completely disagree
- ☐ Mostly disagree
- ☐ Slightly disagree
- ☐ Neither agree nor disagree
- ☐ Slightly agree
- ☐ Mostly agree
- ☐ Completely agree

RULE: FOR UNIPOLAR QUESTIONS, PROVIDE NO MORE THAN FOUR OR FIVE OPTIONS

For unipolar questions, it is not important to have an odd number of response options, though you certainly could. For example, consider the following question: How important is it to limit greenhouse gas emissions? In this case, you could easily provide four options, as in Box 16.10. For some unipolar questions, five response options might also work well, as shown in Box 16.11. However, more than five response options is probably too much for a unipolar scale.

Box 16.10 Four response options, unipolar questions

- ☐ Very important
- ☐ Somewhat important
- ☐ Slightly important
- ☐ Not at all important

Box 16.11 Five response options, unipolar questions

- ☐ Completely successful
- ☐ Very successful
- ☐ Somewhat successful
- ☐ Slightly successful
- ☐ Not at all successful

Box 16.12 Checklist: Rules for formatting survey questions

- ✔ Have respondents rank only a few items at a time.
- ✔ Randomize the ordering of your response options.
- ✔ Use forced-choice questions.
- ✔ Choose an appropriate scale for your responses.
- ✔ Limit the number of response options.
- ✔ For bipolar questions, provide a balanced scale of possible response options, from positive to negative.
- ✔ For bipolar questions, provide five or seven response options, but not more.
- ✔ For unipolar questions, provide no more than four or five options.

Piloting the survey

If you have followed all of these suggestions, there is a good chance that your survey will be effective in allowing you to collect accurate information. However, in the interest of leaving nothing to chance, a final recommendation here is to pilot your survey. That is, before you actually administer it to your chosen sample of respondents, you might try it out on a smaller number of respondents: do a dry run, if you will.

Piloting your survey might be really useful because it may reveal problems with your survey that you did not anticipate. Perhaps, despite your best efforts, the instructions are unclear. Perhaps the wording on some questions is ambiguous and difficult to interpret. Obviously, it would be best to know these things early and, especially, before you administer your survey for real.

If you do pilot your survey ahead of time, it might be useful to ask some questions of those respondents that would help you redo the survey if necessary. These would include questions regarding both format and content. Was the layout of the survey clear and easy to follow? Were the instructions clear? Were there any places where it was unclear what was being asked? You might also ask how long it took to complete the survey. If this turned out to be inordinately long, you might consider reducing its length, perhaps by cutting out some questions that are not as important for respondents to answer (Phellas et al. 2012, p. 197).

Conclusions

When constructing and administering a survey instrument, there are many ways you can go wrong. The idea behind good surveying practice is to try to minimize various sources of error that can result in unreliable responses. The main sources of error are coverage error, sampling error, non-response, and measurement error. These can be addressed with a combination of careful sampling, and careful wording and formatting of survey questions. In the end, following a few simple rules can steer you away from a number of problems that could result in the collection of unreliable survey information.

Exercises/discussion questions

(1) Consider the *Literary Digest* debacle in predicting the results of the 1936 election. Suppose you sampled randomly from a database of automobile registration lists *today*. How representative do you think this would be of the current voting population?

(2) You want to take a survey to gauge support for the 2020 U.S. presidential candidates. Keeping in mind the population you are interested in, describe what you think would be an appropriate sampling frame, and explain why you think it would give you accurate results.

(3) You wish to quantify the willingness-to-pay of North Shore tourists for policies to mitigate climate change. Suppose that you are interested in the population of all tourists on the North Shore during the summer months. Critique the following sampling frames:

- Daytime tourists at the visitor's center of Gooseberry Falls, the largest and southernmost state park.
- Random motorists stopping at a scenic overlook half-way up the North Shore.
- Customers at several randomly selected fast food places along the North Shore.
- Customers at a supermarket in Grand Marais, which is located toward the northern end of the North Shore.

(4) Suppose you want to reassure respondents to your survey that their responses will be kept confidential. What efforts could you tell them you are going to take that you think they would find reassuring?

(5) Consider the proposed resolution to the ambiguous wording question on page 301: How many meals did you sit down to eat at home as a family last week? In your opinion, does this completely solve the interpretive problem? How might you reword this question to address the remaining ambiguity?

(6) Critique the following survey questions for both clarity and possible bias:

- How concerned are you about climate change: very concerned, somewhat concerned, not so concerned, or not concerned at all?
- Do you think global warming is an environmental problem that is causing a serious impact now, or do you think the impact of global warming won't happen until sometime in the future, or do you think global warming won't have a serious impact at all?
- In order to help reduce global warming, would you be willing to pay more for electricity if it were generated by renewable sources like solar or wind energy?
- Do you think climate change is caused by human activity?
- Thinking about what is said in the news, in your view is the seriousness of global warming generally exaggerated, generally correct, or is it generally underestimated?

References

Dillman, Don A., Jolene D. Smyth, and Leah Melani Christian. *Internet, Mail, and Mixed-Mode Surveys: The Tailored Design Method*. Hoboken: Wiley, 2009.

"Nonprobability Sampling," *Research Methods Knowledge Base*, n.d., https://www.socialresearchmethods.net/kb/sampnon.php

"The Perils of Double Negatives," *Mystery Pollster*, March 21, 2006, http://www.mysterypollster.com/main/2006/03/the_perils_of_d.html

Phellas, Constantinos N., Alice Bloch, and Clive Seale. "Structured Methods: Interviews, Questionnaires and Observation," in Clive Seale (ed.), *Researching Society and Culture* (3rd ed.). Los Angeles: Sage, 2012: 181–205.

"Polling Fundamentals – Total Survey Error," *Roper Center for Public Opinion Research*, Cornell University, https://ropercenter.cornell.edu/support/polling-fundamentals-total-survey-error/

Seale, Clive. "Sampling," in Clive Seale (ed.), *Researching Society and Culture* (3rd ed.). Los Angeles: Sage, 2012: 134–52.

Squire, Peverill. "Why the 1936 Literary Digest Poll Failed," *Public Opinion Quarterly* 52(Spring 1988): 125–33.

Weisberg, Herbert F. *The Total Survey Error Approach*. Chicago: University of Chicago Press, 2005.

17 Data collection II

Interviewing

Introduction

Another common way to collect evidence for a qualitative study is to conduct interviews. Depending upon your project, interviews can be a rich source of detailed information that speaks to the ideas, attitudes, and beliefs of individuals in their interactions with the environment. Done correctly, research based on interview data may reveal many insights into human–environment interactions that cannot be obtained using any other data collection methods.

Why conduct interviews?

There are several reasons why you might want to conduct interviews rather than simply mailing out a questionnaire or administering a survey on-line. For one, it is possible to obtain much more detailed and complete information regarding peoples' attitudes and beliefs when they are being interviewed. You have much more to go on: not only what they say but also their body language and a whole set of other non-verbal cues. In addition, unlike the typical questionnaire, you have the opportunity to ask follow-up questions when answers are vague or unclear; you can probe for more elaboration of the answers; and you can pursue unexpected avenues when they arise.

The downside is that doing interviews is a good deal more time consuming than administering written surveys. And compared to surveys, doing an interview requires a lot more skill and specialized expertise. This is especially true when the interview is relatively unstructured, so that you as the interviewer have to maintain control over the interview while not being overly directive and intrusive. This takes a lot of skill, practice, and experience. However, if you have sufficient time and resources and the skills and expertise to pull it off, interviewing can be an extremely effective way to collect evidence for your study.

Overview of the interview-based study

There is a logical sequence of steps involved in doing an interview-based study (see Figure 17.1). These steps parallel those taken under most qualitative approaches. The study begins with *thematizing*: thinking about the reasons for

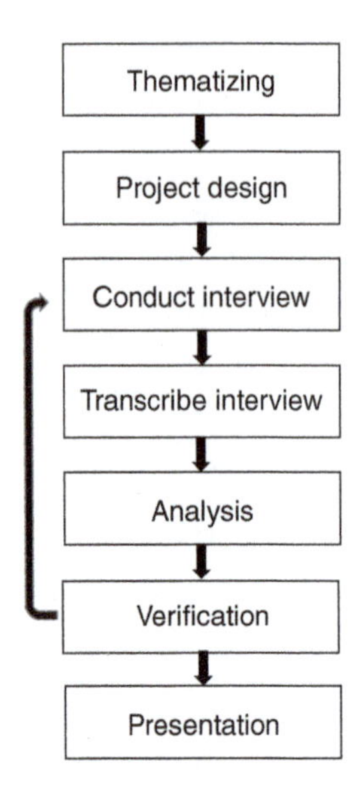

Figure 17.1 The stage of an interview-based study.

Source: Author.

undertaking your study, especially what you hope to accomplish and why. If you have gotten this far, you have already formulated a research question and decided that the information you need to answer it can be best obtained by interviewing a certain group of people.

The next step is the *project design* phase of your study. Among other things, this involves thinking carefully about your research question and precisely what information culled from interviews you need to answer it. It may be that there are a series of sub-questions that need to be answered, and your interviews should be designed to answer each of these in turn.

During the project design phase, you will be thinking about specifically who you need to interview, what questions you need to ask, and what interview format will best serve your purposes. For most interviews, an important goal of the design phase is the creation of an *interview guide*, which contains your interview questions in the format and sequence you intend to follow during the interview. The elements of the project design phase are described in the sections entitled: *Recruiting participants and Preparing for the interview.*

The next step is to use the interview guide to *conduct your interview.* Here, all of the practical nuts-and-bolts principles of interviewing theory and method come into play. These include issues in: (1) preparing to conduct the interview, (2) actually conducting the interview itself, and (3) various things you need to do to get the interview material ready for transcription after the interview is over. All of these elements of interviewing are described below in the section entitled: *Conducting the interview.*

The next phase is taking your interview material and *transcribing* it into a form suitable for analysis. This phase is much more than simply writing everything down.

During the interview you will have taken extremely detailed notes: not just what was said, but everything that happened in the interview. This includes your own thoughts and interpretations of things as they occurred, in real time. The transcription task is taking that jumble of material and starting to give it structure and meaning.

After transcribing the material you enter the *analysis* phase, where you try to figure out what this mass of material means for your research question. Here, you begin by coding the data into units of meaning and then organizing the codes into categories or themes. These form the basis for your analysis of what they all mean when considered together. In order to make sense out of all this material, you will typically develop a theoretical framework that most fully explains or describes your data.

Finally, there is a *verification* phase, in which you take various steps to ascertain the validity of your findings and interpretations. For example, verification may include going back to the interview transcripts and conducting a *negative case analysis*. Negative case analysis entails looking for cases that appear to contradict your interpretations and seeing if there is anything you need to rethink. Transcription, analysis, and verification are described below in the section entitled: *Analysis*.

Figure 17.1 also conveys an important feature of the interview-based methods approach, as represented in the arrow from the verification box back up to conducting the interview. Sometimes—not always but sometimes—your data analysis and verification steps may lead you to conclude that you need to collect more interview data.

It may be, for example, that an initial set of interviews raises some additional questions you had not thought of before, or perhaps it reveals some puzzling anomalies in your findings. And perhaps the only way to resolve these is to conduct more interviews, in which you probe new experiences identified by your initial analysis. Or perhaps the initial analysis identifies other people you need to interview.

Or finally, perhaps the initial analysis reveals that you are thinking about the issue in the wrong way, and you need to adjust your mindset or rethink your preconceptions. New interview data may be needed to help you explore this new thinking. Through this iterative process, you move gradually towards a more complete, coherent picture of what is going on. If you think about it, we have seen this iterative process before: it resembles the linear but iterative process of conducting a case study that we encountered in Chapter 10.

Recruiting participants

Once you have a clear idea of what you want to accomplish in your research, the next step in an interview-based study is to make arrangements for people to be interviewed. Here, there are two important issues: determining whom you wish to interview, and gaining access to those people.

Whom to interview: Issues of sampling

To put this discussion in a familiar context, let us think about the issue of whom to interview in terms of what we already know about the principles of good sampling.

As we know, there are two basic kinds of sampling: *random*, or probability, sampling and *non-random* sampling. Random sampling is preferred when we want to make inferences about a larger population, as in many quantitative studies. However, for many qualitative studies, we can rely upon non-random sampling methods such as purposive or convenience sampling because broader inference is not a central goal of the study. Since interviewing is done mostly for qualitative studies, interview-based studies commonly use non-random methods to select their respondents.

If you think about it this way, all the principles of non-random sampling discussed in Chapter 16 apply to your study. Purposive sampling may be used when your study calls for interviewing experts in a particular area, or if you want to solicit a wide range of opinions on a topic. If you need responses for different categories of respondents, you may want to do quota sampling to ensure you have enough responses in all the categories.

In interview-based studies, convenience sampling methods such as snowball sampling are commonly used. Snowball sampling involves referrals provided by respondents to other potential respondents. This is a relatively painless way to generate a good-sized sample. You might go back and review some of the discussion in Chapter 16 and think about how that discussion applies to conducting interviews.

Gaining access

When you are at the point of actually wanting to start interviewing, the practical issue arises of how to go about approaching potential respondents. This is not always a simple matter. Imagine someone contacted you out of the blue and told you she wanted to take up an hour or more of your time asking you a lot of questions. My guess is that you might not be terribly receptive.

This general issue of *gaining access* to respondents is an extremely important one for successful interviewing. Think about what is needed here: *we need a foot in the door*. And for this, it would help if we had someone who could vouch for us.

This brings us back to the issue of *gatekeepers* that we encountered in the chapter on ethnography. Recalling that discussion, gatekeepers are individuals who can facilitate access within a local setting because they are connected, influential, or highly informed about the local situation. Perhaps they are local officials, long-standing residents of a community, or officers in an organization. Identifying these folks is not always a simple matter, but because they have a lot of pull or know a lot of people, it could really help to have them on your side.

When dealing with gatekeepers, there are several things to keep in mind. Most importantly, they are doing you a favor by facilitating access to their community or organization. This means that it will be helpful to make it worth their while, or at the very least, provide all assurances that your study will not do damage to them or their community. This means things like getting all necessary permissions; making sure there is informed consent; offering to share all of your findings with the community; being sensitive to any concerns they may have about your study; and promising to preserve confidentiality.

Preparing for the interview

In preparing to conduct the interview, there are two basic questions. What kind of interview should you conduct? And what do you need to do to be prepared for that interview? Let us take these one at a time.

What kind of interview?

Once you know who you are going to interview, the next step is to begin to prepare for the interview itself. The first question concerns how much structure to impose on the interview. It turns out that a wide variety of interview structures are possible in practice. However, in principle you may think of there being three basic types: *unstructured*, *structured*, and *semi-structured*.

In all of these types of interviews, you walk into the interview with a clear idea of the focus, topic, and goals for the interview. Above all, this means being prepared with a game plan. The difference lies in how you go about conducting the interview.

Unstructured interviews

Unstructured interviews are ones that have little if any structure, in terms of what specific questions you ask and the order in which you ask them. It is more like a directed conversation. They generally do not require a structured interview guide. Questions tend to be open-ended, giving maximum flexibility for the respondent to express herself in her own way.

As the interviewer, you go in there with a plan regarding what you want to talk about and what you want to get out of the interview. Just be prepared for unexpected turns: unexpected responses or unanticipated insights. When these occur, the unstructured nature of the interview permits you to pursue them.

Unstructured interviews are called for when you have developed a reasonably well-defined research question and general understanding of a topic, but there are still a lot of things you do not know. Consequently, you are hesitant to place many constraints on how respondents respond, because the responses—especially the unexpected responses—can really do a lot to fill in the missing gaps in your understanding.

You should be forewarned that unstructured interviews are challenging to do, because they require a lot of skill on the part of the interviewer. This includes the ability: to establish a rapport with the respondent; to really see the meaning of what is being said; to recognize potentially fruitful new research avenues on the spot; and to deftly guide the conversation to ensure you are getting the information you need.

Structured interviews

As opposed to unstructured interviews, structured interviews impose a lot of structure on the interview. All questions are written down ahead of time in a detailed interview guide, and respondents are given only limited options for how to respond. This mainly means that the interview will consist mostly of close-ended questions, ones where the respondent can choose from a handful of pre-chosen responses. The interviewer simply asks the prepared questions, and there is no opportunity for follow-up if answers are surprising or unclear. All respondents are asked the same questions and the ordering and phrasing of the questions are kept consistent across interviews.

So why might you want to do a structured interview? Structured interviews are best suited to situations where you have a clear research focus and well-developed ideas about your topic. You may even be in a position in your research to pose and test hypotheses. If so, structured interviews have the nice feature that they provide consistent data across respondents. Every respondent is being asked the same things and the responses can be consistently tabulated, compared, and analyzed. They are thus amenable to quantification and statistical hypothesis testing.

Another advantage of structured interviews is that they don't require a lot of training to conduct successfully. The interviewing procedure is straightforward and mechanical: get in, ask your questions, and get out. This is much easier than having to manage a meandering conversation that could go anywhere. Furthermore, it places fewer demands on you in terms of your interpersonal skills. As the interviewer, you should be pleasant and courteous, but you do not have to establish any sort of real rapport with the respondent.

Semi-structured interviews

Semi-structured interviews provide a middle ground between structured and unstructured interviews and, in some ways, provide the best of both worlds. As the name suggests, semi-structured interviews have some of the features of both. They commonly use a detailed interview guide that includes clear instructions to the interviewer and a combination of close-ended and open-ended questions. While questions are written down ahead of time, the semi-structured format permits the interviewer some flexibility in pursuing unexpected themes that may arise in the open-ended questions.

Semi-structured interviews are useful in a study that is already well-developed in terms of your research question and understanding of the topic, but which you suspect might benefit from probing for further insights in certain areas. This means that your study could contain both qualitative and quantitative components. The responses to your close-ended questions can provide the basis for a statistical component to your study. On the other hand, the open-ended questions permit you to pursue unexpected avenues and, perhaps, engage in theory development. As we have seen, these correspond roughly to quantitative and qualitative analyses.

A final reason many researchers find semi-structured interviews to be appealing is that they consider the skill requirements to be able to pull it off, both in expertise and interpersonal skills, to be manageable. Conducting a semi-structured interview does require more skill than conducting a structured one, because unexpected turns can occur in the interview. However, it does not require nearly as much skill as navigating the unpredictable waters of an unstructured one. So given the added flexibility and greater ranges of information that can be collected, these researchers find them to be well worth the extra costs.

Preparing yourself for the interview

Perhaps the most important way to prepare for the interview is to develop an interview guide to be used during the interview. For most kinds of interviews, a detailed interview guide is an indispensable resource and well worth spending a fair amount of time and thought to create. Here are a few general principles to keep in mind for developing an effective interview guide that serves your purposes.

Generally speaking, an interview guide contains interview questions, generally in the order they will be asked during the interview, and instructions for the interviewer in conducting the interview. The questions are specifically targeted at the focus of your inquiry and reflect both what you already know about the topic and what you want to learn from the respondents.

When formulating your questions, you should keep in mind the specific information needs of your research project, but also the type of interview you are doing. As we have seen, structured interviews benefit from highly detailed and structured guides. Everything that is going to happen in the interview is written down, essentially leaving nothing to chance. Interview guides for unstructured and semi-structured interviews, on the other hand, are generally looser, with more free-form questions. In writing your questions for these types of interviews, one thing to keep in mind is that you may write down follow-up questions, in anticipation of receiving certain kinds of answers.

In addition to considering the type of interview you are doing, you may also want to consider the specific type of project you are doing. Information needs vary for quantitative vs. qualitative analyses and for different types of qualitative analyses. For example, if you intend to do a statistical analysis of how responses correlate to demographic characteristics of the respondents, make sure you collect information on all of the characteristics you are interested in. A case study may also benefit from collecting this kind of information. On the other hand, if you are doing unstructured interviews for an ethnographic study, you may not need to worry about collecting the same information.

When you first write down a specific question for the interview guide, consider it a work in progress. Writing interview questions that are clear, concise, and to the point is a challenging exercise, as it is sometimes difficult to predict the reaction of the respondent. Therefore, it may be a good idea to try out your questions on friends or classmates before going out into the field. This will give you an opportunity to modify and refine them appropriately if need be.

The order in which the questions are asked may be more important than you think. There is a general ebb and flow to unstructured and semi-structured interviews that reflects the social dynamic between interviewer and respondent. Rapport, general comfort level, and trust are all factors in conducting interviews, and they have implications for the order in which you ask the questions. In the next section, we will discuss this idea in more detail.

A final thing to keep in mind in preparing for an interview is that you may be bringing your own attitudes, biases, and preconceptions to the interview. This means that in conducting the interview, there is a fine line you will have to walk. On the one hand, you have to go into the interview with a specific agenda and certain goals, in terms of what you want to find out. On the other hand, it is important not to project your own ideas onto your respondents, to filter their responses through your own preconceptions. Rather, you want to keep an open mind, to truly listen to what people are telling you. As one researcher put it: "The main task in interviewing is to understand the meaning of what the interviewees say" (Kvale 1996).

Box 17.1 Checklist: Preparing for the interview

- ✔ Develop a detailed interview guide, anticipating the need for follow-up questions.
- ✔ Tailor your questions to the type of interview you are conducting.
- ✔ Seek feedback on your questions prior to the interview.
- ✔ Pay attention to the order in which you ask questions.
- ✔ Be aware of your own biases and preconceptions.

Conducting the interview

To begin with, you need to select a suitable location to hold the interview. It is important that this setting be a comfortable one free of distractions. This means, for example, that you probably don't want to hold the interview in a busy coffee shop or restaurant. Much better would be using a conference room where you can take steps to ensure you won't be disturbed, or going to someone's home while the kids are off at school. The idea here, of course, is to make it possible for the respondent to give her complete and undivided attention to the task of responding thoughtfully to your questions.

A word of warning: since quiet, undisturbed settings may well be ones where few people come by, you might want to give a little thought to issues of safety (yours). Use your common sense and try not to put yourself in situations that could be dangerous, such as far off, out-of-the-way places. If something feels wrong when you get there, feel free to decline to do the interview. At the very least, let friends or family know where you are going and when to expect you back.

Preliminaries

Before turning to posing the questions that are the heart of the interview, it is good practice to begin with a preamble that addresses various important issues (see Box 17.2).

Box 17.2 Checklist: Preamble

- ✔ Explain the purpose of interview, perhaps the goals of the research.
- ✔ Explain the interview format.
- ✔ Explain how you propose to proceed.
- ✔ Indicate how long interviews usually take.
- ✔ Provide assurances of confidentiality.
- ✔ Provide your contact information.
- ✔ Ask if they have any questions.

First and perhaps foremost, you should begin by explaining the purpose of the interview: what your project is all about and what you are trying to accomplish in doing the research. You should also let them know what to expect by explaining the format of the interview, how you propose to proceed, and how long you expect the interview to take. You should also make it clear up front that their answers will be kept in strictest confidence. Make sure you give them your contact information so they can get hold of you if they have any questions or concerns. And, finally, ask if they have any questions before you begin. It is probably a good idea to include all of this in your interview guide, to make sure you do not forget anything.

Conducting the interview: General considerations

In actually conducting the interview, there are several general things to keep in mind. The first is that, except perhaps for structured interviews, you are engaged in a social interaction with the person being interviewed. You are not grilling him for information: you are trying to gain his trust so that he feels comfortable sharing information with you. At the same time, you are trying to steer the interview in a certain direction to get the information you need. This all adds up to the need to take a firm, but gentle approach.

> The more comfortable you make someone feel, the better interview you're ultimately going to get.
>
> Katie Couric, journalist

The second general thing to keep in mind is that the interview is about them, not you. It is about them sharing with you what they know. This means, first of all, that you should do a lot more listening than talking. It also means that you should minimize talking about your own experiences, or offering your own opinions on things. Every minute you spend doing these things is one fewer minute to hear what they have to say.

The third thing to keep in mind is the need to faithfully preserve what the interviewee says so that you can accurately reproduce it later. Audio recorders can be very useful in this regard. However, you should keep in mind that not everyone will feel comfortable being recorded. And some may not agree to being recorded, which of course you have to respect. It is also important to not let the audio device substitute for carefully listening to what the respondent is saying during the interview. Audio-recording an interview should be viewed as a useful tool during an interview. It should not be used as a crutch (Yin 2009, p. 109).

Taking *field notes* should be done in any case, because you will want to record non-verbal things going on as well, such as eye contact, perceived discomfort or nervousness, body language, and so forth. Since taking notes during an interview can be distracting, however, you may want to delegate it to a second person to sit in on the interview as designated note-taker. That is, if the interviewee feels comfortable with this arrangement.

Box 17.3 Checklist: General considerations

- ✔ Be firm but gentle.
- ✔ Talk less, listen more.
- ✔ Minimize sharing your own experiences.
- ✔ Avoid giving your own opinions.
- ✔ Audio record the interview, if possible.

If recording is not possible, consider bringing along a second person to take notes.

Progression of the interview

After the preamble comes the interview itself, and here are a few things to consider about how the interview should unfold. Here, it helps to keep in mind that the best respondent is a comfortable respondent. Hence, it is probably best to start off with easy, straightforward questions that they can answer with confidence. This will feed into their comfort level with the process and enable you to more quickly establish a rapport. Then, once it feels like you have established a rapport, you can turn to topics that are more sensitive and/or controversial.

It will also probably help for them to see the progression of the topics and for them to know where they are in the process. For this, it will help if you provide *guideposts*: points of transition between the major topics of the interview. Just let the respondent know that you have no more questions about the topic you have just been talking about and you are ready to move on to the next topic.

Finally, the interview should end by providing respondents the opportunity to comment on the interview, or on topics covered in the interview. And, of course, express your appreciation to the respondent for her participation, and provide your contact information should she want to get hold of you later on.

Principles for asking questions

The questions you ask are the heart and soul of your interview, so it is important that certain principles be followed to ensure that you get reliable information; that is, information that accurately reflects the knowledge and beliefs of the respondents.

RULE: ASK ONE QUESTION AT A TIME

If this one sounds familiar, that is because it came up in the last chapter on surveying. With interviewing, the same basic issues arise. Sometimes, simply through careless sentence construction, we may inadvertently ask multiple questions when we think we are only asking one.

When you ask, for example, how many times a week someone eats his fruits and vegetables, you are actually asking two questions, one about fruits and another about vegetables. The problem is that the answers to the two questions may be different, and the respondent may not know which one to answer. Or the respondent may guess, and then end up answering a different question than the one you think you are asking. One small difference from surveying is that the respondent may ask you for clarification, but it would be better not to have to rely on this.

RULE: AVOID YES OR NO QUESTIONS

It is tempting to ask questions that can be answered with a simple "yes" or "no," but make every effort to resist. Such questions seem to invite clear and unambiguous responses. The problem with yes or no questions is that they do not provide the opportunity for the respondent to expound on the subject, which leaves you the interviewer with limited information and no rich description. This defeats the purpose of interviewing.

RULE: AVOID "WHY" QUESTIONS

This may sound like a surprising rule. After all, isn't the goal of the interview to find out what the respondent thinks about the topic? Why wouldn't you want to know why he feels the way he does? The problem with "why" questions is that they pressure respondents to explain themselves, to justify their answers. Interviews are probably better spent asking "what" and "how" questions. *What* questions invite respondents to share what they know and believe, and *how* questions invite them to provide context for their decisions.

RULE: MAINTAIN AS NEUTRAL A POSTURE AS YOU CAN

As the interviewer, you have a lot of influence over the respondent, perhaps more than you know. What you say and the way you say it can really affect the answers you get. All of this means that you have to be careful what you say. Importantly, try to be as neutral as you can, particularly about sensitive or controversial topics. This means to avoid the use of loaded or biased language when asking questions. If you don't, their responses may reflect your opinions and feelings as much as theirs.

This also means that when listening to the responses, you need to be aware of, and perhaps rein in, your own reactions to what you are hearing. If, for example, you express surprise at a response ("Wow, *really*?"), this may convey to the respondent that she didn't give the "correct" answer. Or if you jump to take notes and start scribbling feverishly ("Wow, that's *really* interesting. I've GOT to write that down."), this may signal that this is something she *should* be saying. The danger is that neither provides a true read on her experiences and beliefs.

RULE: AVOID LEADING QUESTIONS

Related to maintaining a neutral posture is trying to avoid asking leading questions. Leading questions are questions that are phrased in ways that seem intended to elicit a particular answer. As an example, consider the following question: "Climate deniers are a bunch of crazies, aren't they?" Asking questions in this way should be avoided because you are denying the respondent the opportunity to articulate her true views on the subject. By interjecting your own opinion into the question, you reduce the chances that you will find out how she truly feels.

RULE: CONSIDER REFRAMING A QUESTION IF YOU GET A NEGATIVE OR UNEXPECTED REACTION THE FIRST TIME

All experienced interviewers will tell you that despite our best intentions, interviews do not always go smoothly. Sometimes this can occur just because of the way we ask questions. Respondents may misunderstand what you are asking. Or they may simply feel uncomfortable answering certain questions that may be of a sensitive or controversial nature. Awkward moments can arise because it is hard to anticipate what the reaction to particular questions will be.

If this happens, feel free to momentarily backtrack and restate your question. If it seems as if the respondent does not understand the question, you might consider reframing it to make it clearer or more concrete. If possible, it might help to refer back to something covered earlier in the conversation. If you perceive discomfort with answering a question, ask yourself where you think the discomfort is coming from. It may be that the respondent is worried you will judge her based on what she says. Again, reframing the question may help to address this issue.

RULE: DON'T INTERRUPT

One cardinal rule of effective interviewing is not to interrupt the respondent when she is responding to a question. The reason is that interrupting may cause her to lose her train of thought. She may be in the middle of telling you something important and if you interrupt, that moment might be gone forever.

This rule may sound like a no-brainer, but it is sometimes a tough rule to follow. For one thing, there may be times you feel like the interview is going off the rails and you want to get it back on track. Whatever you do, do not abruptly cut in. Seek an opening and gently nudge the interview back toward where you want it to go.

For another thing, your respondent may be "on a roll" and saying a lot of things that you would like to pursue with follow-up questions. Be patient. Let her say her piece, and once she is done, come back to what she said and ask your follow-up questions then.

RULE: EXPLORE UNCLEAR OR UNEXPECTED RESPONSES

During the course of an interview, it is common to get responses you don't expect or responses where it is unclear exactly what is being said. When this happens, you can *probe* further, either asking clarifying questions or asking the respondent to elaborate on her answer. The objective in probing more deeply is to make sure you see and understand the entire picture.

There are several things to think about when you probe more deeply. First, the type of probing you do will depend upon what is keeping things from being clear or complete. Perhaps a particular piece of the narrative seems incomplete, in which case you might ask: "And then what happened?" Or perhaps a point merits elaboration, in which case you might ask: "Can you give me an example?" Or finally, perhaps the interview seems to be getting off track. In this case, you could try to bring things back by saying: "You mentioned that..."

Notice that these probes are short and simple: you don't want the respondent to lose her train of thought. The less you intrude, the more likely it is that you will get the complete, unvarnished picture.

Finally, try to probe sparingly, and vary your probes if possible. You want the interview to feel comfortable and natural. A series of rapid-fire "And then what happened?" will feel anything but.

RULE: PAY ATTENTION TO NON-VERBAL CUES

When you conduct an interview, there is a lot going on, including things not being said. Non-verbal cues include things like: body language, tone of voice, and how comfortable the respondent appears to be with the interview questions. These are all important sources of information for you as the interviewer. Paying attention to them may help you decide to slow down, to reframe questions, to probe more deeply, to change the subject, and so forth. All of these, appropriately chosen, will make your interview more productive.

RULE: TOLERATE SILENCE

For many inexperienced interviewers, one of the hardest things about interviewing is to feel comfortable when nothing is being said, what some people have called "the dreaded lull." It's like dead air time on the radio: you wonder what is going on. It feels awkward. And you are sorely tempted to fill the silence with words. Try to resist. Lulls can be extremely useful toward making an interview successful.

There are two particularly important places where lulls can occur: after you have asked a question, and after the respondent has answered. In both cases, lulls can serve a useful function. After you have asked a question, the respondent may be organizing her thoughts, thinking about how to respond. The last thing you want to do is to interrupt her train of thought. Give her time.

Perhaps the less obvious place to tolerate a lull is after the respondent has answered. She's finished: why would you possibly not want to step in now? The answer is that she may not be finished. Given a little extra time, she may expand on what she has already said, or she may take the conversation in a new direction. In either case, waiting briefly before stepping in may provide you with important new information.

> If you resist the temptation to respond too quickly to the answer, you'll discover something almost magical. The other person will either expand on what he's already said or he'll go in a different direction. Either way, he's expanding his response, and you get a clear view into his head and heart.
>
> Jim Lehrer, journalist

This is why some veteran interviewers recommend the *five second rule*: Ask your question, listen carefully to the answer, and then, when the respondent seems to have finished his answer, wait five seconds before you turn to the next question. You never know what will happen in those five seconds.

Box 17.4 Checklist: Principles for asking interview questions

- ✔ Ask one question at a time.
- ✔ Avoid yes or no questions.
- ✔ Avoid "why" questions.
- ✔ Maintain as neutral a posture as you can.
- ✔ Avoid leading questions.
- ✔ Consider reframing the question if you get an unexpected or negative reaction the first time.
- ✔ Don't interrupt.
- ✔ Explore unclear or unexpected responses.
- ✔ Pay attention to non-verbal cues.
- ✔ Tolerate silence.

Principles for keeping field notes

Even if you are video- or audio-recording the interview, it is crucial to keep detailed notes on what goes on in the interview. These *field notes* should contain everything of note that takes place during the interview. This includes their answers to your questions; interpretive thoughts that occur to you along the way; and any non-verbal cues you pick up on that seem significant. It is crucial to keep complete and detailed field notes so that later on, you can accurately reconstruct what happened in the interview.

For taking and keeping field notes, you will need a notebook. In order to keep the material organized, it is recommended that you keep their answers and your interpretations separate. To do this, take each page in your notebook and draw a line down the middle so that each page has two broad columns. Label the left column "Interview notes" and label the right column "Field notes." The left column will contain their answers and follow-up questions that occur to you as you go along. The right column will contain your interpretations of what is being said, as well as non-verbal cues you pick up on.

For example, consider the sample field notes shown in Figure 17.2. The interviewer is interviewing someone about a local community problem of water pollution in a nearby lake. The interview has progressed to the stage where some sensitive questions are being asked about how to address the problem. In the left-hand side column, the interviewer has written the content of the respondent's answers and follow-up questions as they occur. The right-hand side contains interpretive comments on things as they occur.

There are two important things to notice here. The first is that rather than merely recording what is going on, the interviewer is making analytical sense out of the responses. When, for example, the respondent expresses her belief that there is "no political will to do anything to clean up the water," the interviewer interprets this as relating to the level of social capacity within the community. When the respondent later on expresses her belief that "people look down on you if you express environmental views," this seems to confirm that social capacity is an important part of the story.

The second thing to notice is the use of verbal and non-verbal cues. Consider the entries at the top of the page, when the respondent expresses her opinion that "people don't care about the lake." Here, the interviewer has noted several things that suggest the respondent is nervous about expressing this opinion: "seems nervous," "keeps looking at recorder & notebook," and "wants confirmation of confidentiality." All of these verbal and non-verbal cues provide added useful information about how to interpret the content of the answer.

Immediate post-interview issues

You are not quite done when the interview is over and you have turned off the audio recorder. The first thing to do is to verify the recorder worked. In the off-chance it did not, you may need to reschedule the interview.

Then, as soon as you can find somewhere to do it, carefully go back over your notes. Here, you re-read them carefully, making sure they make sense to you and

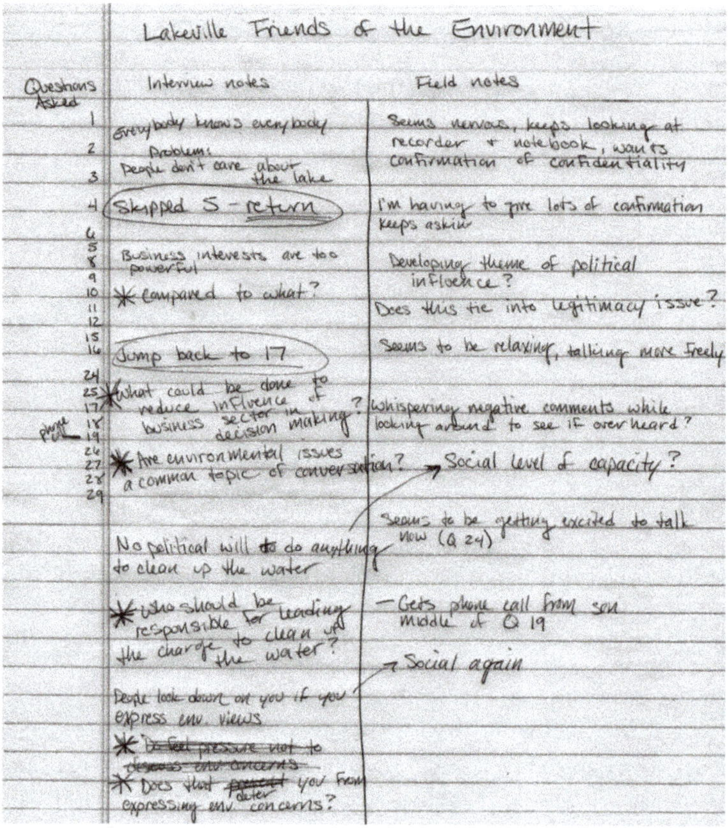

Figure 17.2 Sample field notes.

Source: Amanda Sames.

fully capture your best sense of what went on in the interview. In addition, now would be a good time to fill out your interpretations, which you may not have had time to be comprehensive about during the interview. It is important to do all of this as soon as possible after the interview, before memory starts to fade.

Analysis

Once you have your interview records in good shape, the next step is to subject the records to analysis. Here, there are three distinct stages: data familiarization, data reduction, and data interpretation and verification.

Data familiarization

During this important initial stage, you are getting ready to put all of the pieces together. Data familiarization is essentially about preparing to organize the data for analysis. This requires first that you step back and consider the larger picture, beginning with your study objectives. Remind yourself of exactly what you are trying to understand about your topic, and remind yourself of your rationale for going out and interviewing the particular respondents that you did. Specifically, what sorts of insights did you expect them to be able to provide?

The next step is to immerse yourself in the data from your interviews. First, transcribe your audio recordings and proofread them for accuracy and legibility. Similarly, you may need to write up and proofread your field notes if the notes you took in the interview are sloppy, disorganized, or hard to read.

Finally, re-read the interviews, noting recurring themes, general patterns, and any big ideas that seem to be emerging. Practically speaking, you will want to be making notes when you find something of interest. During this last step, you are beginning to engage the data analytically, thinking systematically about what it all means. In most cases, this thought process will be informed by theoretical propositions derived from your literature review.

Data reduction

In this next stage, you begin processing and organizing the data into meaningful themes and categories. This is done in a process called *coding*. Coding means going through the transcriptions line by line and creating *units of meaning* such as ideas, beliefs, types of actions or behaviors, processes, or outcomes. These units of meaning are then organized into a system of codes by grouping related ones together into themes or categories. This process formalizes and organizes the general themes and patterns found in the data.

Consider, for example, Figure 17.3, which contains a sample code system for a study of collaborative watershed management. This coding was done using the software program MAXQDA. In this coding document, the interview transcripts have been coded to document an analytical framework applied to understand both the outcomes expected from collaboration and the challenges to achieving successful collaboration (see left-hand side bottom box).

So, for example, based upon material from interviews, the researcher has identified three potential general barriers to successful collaboration, coded as "Limited range of effectiveness," "Managing competing agendas," and "Getting the necessary stakeholders to attend." These general barriers were constructed from units of meaning derived directly from the interview material.

To illustrate, consider one of these barriers, "Managing competing agendas." From the interviews the researcher had identified five related units of meaning: "Too large of a group makes collaboration challenging," "Can be difficult to reach agreement," "Some people just want to protect their turf," "Difficult to engage participants representing different groups," and "Politics can affect successful implementation of outcomes."

By considering all of these units of meaning, the researcher decided that they could all together be described as "Managing competing agendas." Thus, the general barrier was built from the ground up, from the units of meaning that emerged from dissecting the interviews.

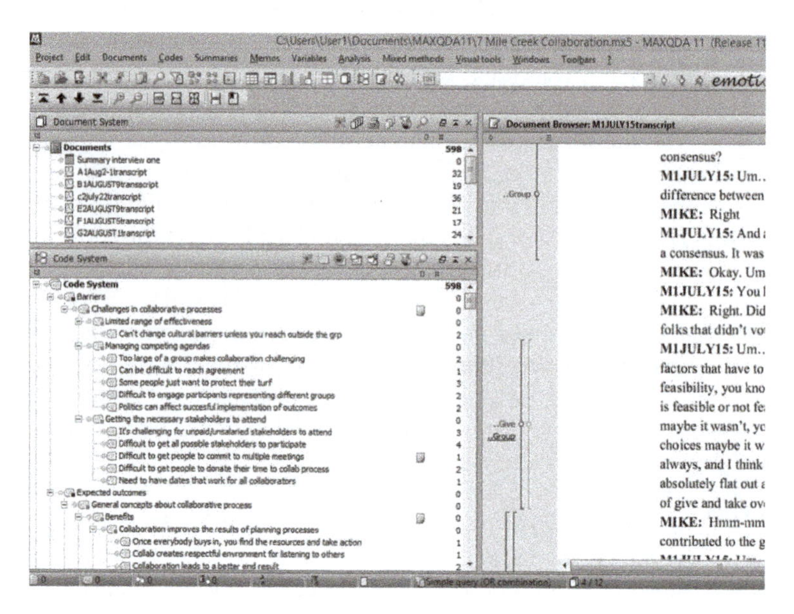

Figure 17.3 Some sample code, MAXQDA.

Source: Amanda Sames.

Data interpretation and verification

Once you have organized the data into general themes, the final stage is to subject the themes to analysis to determine their meaning. Here, you are trying to tell the most coherent and compelling story you can. This means a story where all the pieces fit together and make sense in a theoretically consistent way, with no loose ends. As with many qualitative approaches, you may be generating a theory as you do all of this, one which explains or describes your data as parsimoniously as you can.

In order to confirm your theory and the story you are telling, one strategy you can pursue is to perform a *negative case analysis*. This means going back and re-reading the transcripts of the interviews and looking for cases that contradict the interpretations you have come up with. If you do not find any negative cases, this makes your story that much more compelling. If you do find negative cases, this may force you to rethink some of your interpretations, and the resulting story will also be more compelling. Either way, you end up with a more convincing bottom line.

Conclusions

As you can probably tell from this discussion, conducting interviews can be a challenging proposition. It generally requires: good interpersonal skills, facility in managing a directed social interaction, and the ability to read between the lines and understand what people really mean. But it also offers the potential for tremendous rewards in terms of being able to obtain richly textured information you cannot get in any other way. For certain types of environmental projects, these rewards can make interviewing well worth it.

Exercises/discussion questions

(1) You are a reporter who arrives at the scene of a burglary, and you are interviewing a next-door neighbor so you can write a news story about the incident. Critique the following interview questions and suggest improvements.

- Were you home alone when the burglary occurred?
- When you went over to the house, was the door smashed open?
- Was the security alarm going off?
- Why do you think anyone would break into that house?
- So did you go home afterwards and go to bed?

(2) Pair up with another student and take turns performing interviews of each other. For these interviews, you may pick any topic that both partners are interested in (i.e., hobbies, childhood fears, employment experience, political beliefs, etc.). Each of you should write your own interview guide to use in the mock interview. When you do your interviews, each person being interviewed should answer the questions, while taking notes on what the interviewer did well, and what could be improved. Please pay attention to the following things:

- Whether you ever felt cut off.
- Whether the questions were easy to understand and respond to.
- Whether there were uncomfortable moments.
- What made you open up and talk more freely.

(3) Go to this link: http://www.youtube.com/watch?feature=player_embedded &v=z4Ezruu1oeQ

This link takes you to an interview of the actress Mila Kunis by a relatively inexperienced interviewer, Chris Stark. Watch the interview and answer the following questions:

- How effective was the interviewer at eliciting the information he was after?
- What did he do well, and what mistakes did he make?
- If you were in his shoes, what would you have done differently?

(4) Suppose you are the owner of a small software company, and you are interviewing someone who has applied for a job as an entry-level computer programmer. Compose a set of questions that will give you enough information regarding whether to hire him or not.

(5) As an exercise in taking field notes, pair up with another student and take turns describing to each other a recent experience you have had with a job, internship, or extracurricular activity. While one student speaks, the other should take detailed field notes on what is being said, gently interrupting for clarification if needed. The notes should include both interview notes (what is being said) and field notes (your interpretation of what is being said, along with any visual cues you pick up on). Afterwards, read your field notes carefully, making sure that they accurately capture what you think was said. Also, fill in any additional points of interpretation that you may not have managed to get down during the interview.

References

Kvale, Steinar. *Interviews: An Introduction to Qualitative Research Interviewing.* Thousand Oaks: Sage, 1996.

Marshall, Catherine, and Gretchen B. Rossman. *Designing Qualitative Research.* Los Angeles: Sage, 2011.

Phellas, Constantinos N., Alice Bloch, and Clive Seale. "Structured Methods: Interviews, Questionnaires and Observation," in Clive Seale (ed.), *Researching Society and Culture* (3rd ed.). Los Angeles: Sage, 2012: 181–205.

Seidman, Irving. *Interviewing as Qualitative Research* (4th ed.). New York: Teacher's College Press, 2012.

Yin, R. K. *Case Study Research: Design and Methods* (4th ed.). Los Angeles: Sage, 2009.

18 Ethical issues in environmental research

Introduction

When conducting environmental research, there may be times when you will question whether what you are doing feels like the right thing to do. After all, you have been raised to distinguish right from wrong in so many different ways. You treat people honestly, and you do not confuse or mislead them if you can help it. You give credit where credit is due and you do not try to take credit for something you did not do. You don't repeat things to others that have been told to you in confidence. You don't make things up that are not true. All of these things are common sense: they are ways that decent people treat each other.

It turns out that these and many other common sense intuitions apply when you are doing research. They apply, for example, in your interactions with those whom you are studying. These could be people being interviewed by you or participating in your survey, or those in a local community with whom you are collaborating in an action research project. They apply to your interactions with fellow research team members. And they apply to people outside of your research project but who might be influenced or impacted by your research. These could be policymakers, other researchers, and even the general public. In doing research, your actions have consequences for others.

This is why, when doing research, it is important to keep in mind a number of ethical issues. While it is important to advance the state of our understanding on various environmental issues, it is equally important to do so in a way that does not deceive or take advantage of others, or put them at risk. Studying research ethics can help ensure that these things do not happen. These ethical issues are the subject of the present chapter.

What are research ethics?

To answer this question, it will be useful to define ethics more generally. Probably the best way to understand what is meant by ethics is to think about rules that we choose to live by because they prescribe proper ways to treat people. We are all familiar, for example, with the so-called *Golden Rule: Treat others the way you would like to be treated.* As another example, doctors are guided by the *Hippocratic Oath*, which requires *First, do no harm*. These are informal rules, or *norms*, that provide guidance on how to live our lives. This is perhaps the most common definition of ethics: norms for how to conduct ourselves both personally and professionally that distinguish between acceptable and unacceptable behavior (Resnik 2015).

Thought of in this way, research ethics is all about acceptable versus unacceptable ways of doing research. To begin to understand the difference, let us consider a few concrete examples.

Some actual examples of potentially unethical research

The history of research is littered with examples of research projects where ethically questionable decisions were made. In some cases, they involved violating norms of basic decency regarding the proper way to treat other people. Examples of this include:

- Medical experiments performed by Nazi physicians on people held in World War II concentration camps. These included exposing people to extreme temperatures, mustard gas, and various poisons, which resulted in numerous deaths (Berger 1990).
- A forty-year study of the US Public Health Service that examined the progression of untreated syphilis in African-American men in Alabama. In this case, the researchers not only misled the men regarding the study objectives, they withheld penicillin that would have effectively treated the disease (Landau 2010).
- During the Cold War era, the US Atomic Energy Commission sponsored a study in which mentally disabled children were fed radioactive oatmeal, in order to see how the nutrients were digested (*New York Times*, January 1, 1998).

In these examples, it is clear that the conduct of the researchers was unethical, as every reasonable person would agree that the participants in the study were mistreated. One simply does not treat other people this way. However, there are a great many instances where the ethical issues are not as black-and-white. Let us consider a few notorious examples of research that have raised various ethical issues.

Milgram obedience experiment

In the 1960s, the Yale psychologist Stanley Milgram was interested in the issue of obedience to authority figures. Specifically, he wanted to know how far people would be willing to go to perform acts that went against their personal beliefs just because an authority figure ordered them to. The backdrop for this study was the war trial of the Nazi war criminal Adolph Eichmann, who was eventually found guilty of war atrocities for his role in carrying out the Holocaust. The burning question was whether Eichmann and others were just following orders, and could others be expected to do the same things under the same circumstances?

In the experiment devised by Milgram, participants were paired up and given the respective roles of "teacher" and "learner." They were taken to a room where the learner was strapped into a chair. The teacher was then taken into a different room where he (the subjects were all men) was told that he was supposed to teach the learner sets of word pairs. At every incorrect response, the teacher was told to administer an electric shock to the learner. With every incorrect response, the shocks were to get more severe.

In actuality, no shocks were administered, but the teacher was not told this: he believed that he was administering real shocks, of increasing intensity. As part of the experiment, a tape recorder played pre-recorded sounds of screams of pain whenever a shock was administered. But while many of the teachers expressed discomfort and misgivings about inflicting pain on the learners, when told to continue, many of them did so. In fact, an alarmingly large number of all of the teachers were willing to administer the maximum shock of 450 volts.

It should be stressed that no physical harm came to the learners, who were never actually shocked. However, the ethics of this experiment have been questioned, on the grounds that it inflicted severe emotional distress on those playing the role of teacher (Abbott 2016).

The Stanford prison experiment

In the early 1970s, Philip Zimbardo, a faculty member in the psychology department at Stanford University, was interested in prison psychology. At the time, abuse of inmates by prison guards was considered a potentially serious problem. Zimbardo was interested in why abusive behavior occurred and, in particular, whether guards were predisposed to such behavior or whether it was triggered by working in the prison environment. So he designed an experiment in which he simulated a real-life prison situation in the basement of the psychology building at Stanford and recruited students to participate in the experiment (MacLeod 2008).

Half of the participants were assigned the role of inmates and the other half were assigned the role of guards. Inmates were mock-arrested at their homes and mock-charged with armed robbery. They were then taken to the "prison," where they were given smocks and stocking caps to wear, and they were confined to tiny 6 by 9 foot cells. The other half were assigned the role of prison guards, for which they were given prison guard attire to wear and wooden batons to carry. They were also given sunglasses to wear so that they would not make eye contact with the inmates, and they were instructed not to call the inmates by name, but rather by an assigned number.

The experiment was designed with various safeguards. The participants all knew, of course, that it was not a real prison. The students chosen to participate were predominantly white, middle-class, healthy, psychologically well-adjusted males. Those who played prison guards were given an orientation session that laid out clear guidelines for how they were to treat the "prisoners." They were not, for example, allowed to physically mistreat the prisoners, or to withhold food and drink. All participants were told that they could terminate their participation at any time.

Thinking about the way this research project was set up, before reading further, you might ask yourself what you think the ethical issues were.

What happened next was remarkable. The participants fell quickly into their respective roles. The guards began to harass, insult, and intimidate prisoners. If prisoners disobeyed the rules, they were made to do pushups, stripped, sprayed with fire extinguishers, or had mattresses removed from their cells so that they had to sleep on the cold concrete floor.

For their part, the prisoners began to behave like real inmates: initially staging rebellions against the conditions, but soon exhibiting submissive behavior and showing signs of emotional distress. One prisoner had to be released after thirty-six hours after becoming emotionally distraught. The experiment was scheduled to run as long as two weeks, but it was terminated after six days after an outside observer complained strenuously about the abuse the student prisoners were being subjected to (Zimbardo 2007).

India driver's license study

In this 2007 study, several economists investigated bureaucratic corruption in India. They were interested in a common way that corruption occurs in developing countries: the offering of bribes to local officials responsible for administering public services. Their study involved recruiting volunteers and providing them with financial incentives to bribe local officials in order to receive their driver's licenses more quickly (Bertrand et al. 2007).

Before reading further, can you see the ethical issue?

One might argue that just bribing officials to circumvent the law is itself unethical. However, some might argue (and in fact have argued) that offering a bribe is not necessarily unethical because in some cultural contexts, it is just the cost of doing business. Here, however, the ethical problem is that if the volunteers were successful in getting their driver's licenses more quickly, this would have had the definitely undesirable effect of potentially putting unsafe drivers on the road. Thus, the experiment could have posed a hazard to public safety. Serious ethical concerns have been voiced about this study for that reason (Ravallion 2014).

Facebook mood contagion study

In 2012, some researchers were interested in the psychological effect of negative content that appears in social media. They investigated this issue using the social media service Facebook, asking the question whether negative content affects the moods of Facebook users. In order to perform a controlled experiment, the researchers secretly manipulated the news feeds of hundreds of thousands of Facebook users. Some of the users were shown content that contained mostly happy and positive words. Others were shown content with mostly unhappy and negative words. The researchers found that negative news feeds tended to result in more negative status messages.

Before reading further, ask yourself whether or not you think the researchers behaved unethically and why.

It should be mentioned, first of all, that the behavior of the researchers was almost certainly legal. There is an explicit statement in Facebook that users must permit Facebook to use their data for "data analysis, testing, and research." However, many felt that what the researchers did was unethical. When news of the experiment broke, it was condemned by many people, especially Facebook users, who believed that their rights had been violated. A Facebook spokesman was forced to issue a statement explaining what they had done, emphasizing the value of the research and the safeguards they had used to keep the data secure. Later, one of the researchers also issued a statement that grudgingly conceded that doing the study may not have been justified, given all the anxiety it provoked (Meyer 2014).

General ethical considerations

The Milgram obedience experiment, the Stanford prison experiment, the India driver's license study, and the Facebook mood manipulation study all illustrate some potential ethical pitfalls of conducting research. These studies were all carefully conceptualized and rigorously executed, following many principles of good research. They all had well-defined research questions, they chose logical approaches and methodologies given their research questions, and their research arguably had the potential to significantly benefit society. Yet all four studies could be fairly criticized for violating various ethical norms. Let us now turn to a discussion of a number of important ethical principles, in order to better understand how to avoid behaving unethically in your own research.

Ethics vs. laws

The first thing to keep in mind is the important distinction between ethics and laws. As we have seen, ethics are informal norms that distinguish between acceptable and unacceptable behavior. Laws, on the other hand, are the official formal rules that a society has set in place to govern people's behavior. Just because a particular behavior is legal, this does not mean it is ethical, as we saw in all four of our examples. On the other hand, ethical behavior can be illegal. For example, many would consider the acts of civil disobedience of Mahatma Gandhi and Martin Luther King to be highly ethical, even if they were illegal under the laws prevailing at the time.

What all of this means is that it is often harder to determine what behavior is unethical than to determine what is illegal. If you wonder about whether doing something is illegal, it is relatively easy (though not always trivial!) to find out by reading local ordinances or the state legal code, or by consulting a lawyer. However, to determine if something is unethical, there are no such official sources to examine. Much of it comes down to the fuzzier notions of right and wrong, about which reasonable people can sometimes disagree. And nowhere is this truer than in the case of research ethics.

Ethical behavior: Adding to our knowledge base

One thing that it will be important to keep in mind is your primary objective in doing research; namely, to add to what we know. This means that you should:

- Do research carefully, thoroughly, and evenhandedly.
- Maintain an open mind about the outcome of the research.
- Conduct your research in such a way that the findings honestly and objectively reflect the true sense of the evidence.
- Report your findings to others in a clear, honest, and transparent manner.

These are all principles of good research, of course: we all try to do the best we can on every one of these points. Ethical lines can be crossed, however, when you deliberately violate one of these rules.

To make all of this more concrete, consider the *North Shore Climate Change* study. One aspect of that study was to survey tourists to ask about their willingness-to-pay for hypothetical programs to mitigate climate change. We did our best to word the survey questions neutrally and even-handedly; to sample tourists at various locations along the North Shore in order to obtain a representative sample; to analyze the data carefully using appropriate methods; and to report our findings objectively. We would have been behaving unethically if we had done any of the following:

- Deliberately worded our questions in a leading way to get particular answers.
- Deliberately sampled tourists who we believed were likely to give us inflated responses.
- Deliberately shaded our analysis to get the answers we wanted.
- Deliberately misreported or misrepresented our findings.

The operant word here is "deliberately." In previous chapters, we have seen the many challenges of doing good, careful research. For example, it is not easy to word survey questions in a clear, even-handed way. In our case, however, we were behaving ethically because we made a good faith effort to avoid doing the things on this list. What is unethical is taking deliberate actions in conducting your research in order to mislead others.

It is an unfortunate fact that there are numerous recorded cases of serious unethical behavior by researchers. In May of 2015, the *New York Times* ran a story that listed a number of high-profile cases where scientists were found to have committed research fraud (Roston 2015). These cases included studies on attitudes toward gay marriage, vaccines and autism, stem cell production, herbicides and cancer, and learning among primates. The charges included falsified data, faked experiments, and questionable scientific methods. In many cases, published studies had to be retracted. In other cases, a researcher lost government funding or was stripped of his graduate degree. In one particular case, a researcher ended up committing suicide.

Why did they do it? The answer has to do with the high-pressure world of academic research. Often, researchers are under enormous pressure to publish their research. Raises, promotions, endowed chairs, government funding, or status within one's profession can all depend upon the ability to publish. With so much at stake, some researchers struggle to maintain and apply ethical standards in their research practices.

I hope it is clear what the ethical issues are. By engaging in fraudulent research, you are not serving the objective of adding to our knowledge base because in the end, you produce findings that are simply not true. And sometimes this can have serious consequences for society. In one of the cases listed in the *New York Times* article, a researcher published an article claiming that vaccinations for measles, mumps, and rubella could lead to increased autism in children. Even though the study was retracted, it provoked fears among parents in Britain and the United States, many of whom stopped vaccinating their children. One consequence may have been a spike in the number of cases of measles in the United States (Rowan 2015; CIDRAP 2016).

Furthermore, when cases like these come to light, it tends to reflect poorly on scientific research in general. Legitimate, ethical research can end up being painted with the same brush. The last thing we want to do is to have people lose faith in the integrity of the research process.

Taking credit only where credit is due

Another set of ethical issues in research has to do with taking credit for your work. Everybody wants acknowledgment for the good things that they do. If you were to discover a cure for cancer, you would want people to give you credit for this great accomplishment. And of course, there is nothing unethical about feeling this way. You can perhaps see, then, that it would be unethical to try to take credit for someone else's work: say, someone else had discovered a cure for cancer and you tried to claim that the discovery was yours. In a way, this is a version of the *Golden Rule*: Treat others the way you want to be treated.

Perhaps the most obvious and most common way researchers can try to take credit for the work of others is to take someone else's work and pass it off as their own. Once when I was in graduate school, I took a year off to work for a government agency in Washington, DC, and one of my tasks was to read and vet reports submitted by government contractors. As I was sitting there one day reading a report, I started experiencing *déjà vu*, a feeling that I had experienced something before. The passages I was reading were really familiar.

As it turned out, dozens of pages of the contractor report had been lifted wholesale from a book on natural resource economics. I noticed this only because I had just taken a course that had used this book. Since the contractor had likely been paid tens of thousands of dollars for writing this report, this behavior was clearly unethical.

This contractor's behavior was an example of *plagiarism*. Plagiarism is taking someone else's words or ideas and representing them as your own, without giving credit to the other person. To understand plagiarism, consider the following passage from Samuel Hays' classic environmental history book *Conservation and the Gospel of Efficiency*:

> "Until the spring of 1908 the Roosevelt administration's natural resource program moved forward without interruption. It had expanded from piecemeal irrigation, forest, range, and mineral measures to the most comprehensive water development program yet devised."
>
> (Hays 1959, p. 122)

Here, I have been extremely careful to give Hays full credit for his work. I have taken the original passage, not changed a word, enclosed it in quotation marks, and provided clear attribution to Hays and where to find the passage in his book. If you read the references at the back of this chapter, you will also see that I have provided a complete bibliographical citation of the book. All of this is for the benefit of the reader so that it is easy to go find the passage, if desired. But it is also for Hays' benefit, so that everyone knows that the work is his.

Verbatim, or direct, plagiarism

So what would constitute plagiarism in this case? In its most extreme form, the words or ideas are simply reproduced verbatim without attribution. For example, consider the following passage I have composed:

> Until the spring of 1908 the Roosevelt administration was extremely successful in advancing its conservation goals. Its *natural resource program moved forward without interruption. It had expanded from piecemeal irrigation, forest, range, and mineral measures to the most comprehensive water development program yet devised.* However, at this point, it began to encounter stiff resistance from Congress and from within the administration.

Here, I have used Hays' exact words, and I have not given him any credit for these ideas. By not giving credit where credit is due, I would clearly be behaving unethically if I tried to represent this passage as my own research. This is *Plagiarism rule #1: If you quote verbatim, you must use quotation marks and provide a citation.*

However, even if you do not quote verbatim, you could still be guilty of plagiarism if you do not give credit to an original source. Here, there are two additional cases: *paraphrase plagiarism* and *mosaic plagiarism*.

Paraphrase plagiarism

When you paraphrase someone else's words, you are using your own words to convey their meaning. This may be fine: it depends on how much are your own words and how much are those of other person. If your paraphrase is not much different from the original, however, then you must give credit. For example, consider the following paraphrase of Hays' passage:

> Until early 1908 the natural resource program of the Roosevelt administration advanced without interruption. From a set of piecemeal measures in irrigation, forest, range, and minerals, it had expanded to the most comprehensive water development program yet devised.

In composing this passage, I have clearly just taken the original passage and basically just moved words around, while retaining Hays' exact original meaning. If I do not now give Hays credit for these ideas by citing him, I am committing paraphrase plagiarism. The minor effort I have expended to put things into my own words does not allow me to pass off the ideas as mine.

Mosaic plagiarism

Mosaic plagiarism means rewriting the passage, perhaps with some original ideas of your own, but liberally taking bits of the original material and inserting them here and there into the passage. For example, consider the following passage:

> The progressive era was a time of important broad-based advances in natural resource conservation. As before, the programs of the Roosevelt administration *moved forward without interruption*. However, rather than being comprised of piecemeal management programs for *irrigation, forest, range, and mineral* resources, the administration was able to push through a highly *comprehensive water development program.*

In composing this passage, I have created a "mosaic" of bits of the original material (all of the italicized phrases). However, even though most of the wording is mine, the fact that I am using verbatim phrases from Hays still means that I have to give him credit for them.

One takeaway message here is that there is a bit of a gray area when it comes to determining exactly what constitutes plagiarism. As we have seen, all research is to some extent derivative of previous research. The question here is: How different does your writing have to be from previous writing in order to be considered different enough? Here, I think it pays to play it safe: when in doubt, give credit. In some cases, there will be no question, as when you quote a long passage verbatim. But in general, whenever you are using someone else's specific ideas or phrases, you will probably want to make sure you let people know.

> **Bottom line:** Plagiarism does not only mean using someone's else's words verbatim without attribution. You can also be committing plagiarism if you, without attribution: (1) move words about without changing the *meaning* (*paraphrase plagiarism*), or (2) use verbatim bits of someone else's work (*mosaic plagiarism*). The general rule is: When in doubt, provide attribution credit.

Working with human participants

Three examples given earlier—the Milgram obedience experiment, the Stanford prisoner experiment, and the Facebook mood manipulation study—all raised serious ethical issues because of how the people participating in the studies were treated. Whenever your research involves working with people, you have to keep in mind that those people have certain rights that must be respected. These include the rights to: well-being, safety, privacy, and justice, as well as the right to not be deceived by the researcher. Ethical issues can arise when any of these rights are violated.

When conducting research, we sometimes find ourselves having to walk a fine line between advancing knowledge and respecting the rights of individuals. By advancing knowledge, research can confer important benefits to society. Who could doubt that society would be better off if we were to discover a cure for cancer, or a costless way to burn fossil fuels without generating greenhouse gases?

However, sometimes research discoveries come at a cost when the rights of individuals are violated. At some point we have to say on ethical grounds that the benefits are not worth the costs. Whatever might have been the benefits of the Nazi cold temperature and mustard gas experiments, no reasonable person would say they justified the many deaths that occurred to the subjects of those experiments.

On the other hand, some valuable research projects might entail relatively minor violations of the rights of study participants. In such cases, we might conclude that the researchers were behaving ethically.

For example, once when I was in college, a psychology major friend of mine asked me to participate in a research project he was doing for his senior thesis. The project involved pairing up students to jointly perform a simple task that required cooperation. His hypothesis was that more stressful tasks would cause people to blink their eyes more. Of course, he did not tell me, or any other participant, that he would be counting how often I blinked while I was doing these different tasks. If he had told us, this would have completely contaminated the data. At the same time, not telling me did not harm me in any way. So in this case, I would argue that less-than-full disclosure was completely justified ethically, in order to further the objectives of the research.

Many research projects involving human participants fall somewhere in the middle between these two extreme cases. You might, for example, consider the Facebook mood manipulation study to fall more into the gray area (see Figure 18.1). For projects in the gray area, making the right ethical decision becomes a judgment call on your part, in which you have to decide whether the risks or potential harm to participants are justified. But you should consider the burden of proof to be on you to justify doing the study, if there are any appreciable risks to the participants.

However, your ethical task does not end when you have decided that the general concept of the study, including the likely costs imposed on participants,

No costs to participants		Large costs to participants
Eye-blink study	Facebook mood manipulation study?	Nazi medical experiments, US Public Health syphilis study
Ethical		Unethical

Figure 18.1 Ethical research: the costs to participants.

Source: Author.

is ethically acceptable. At this point, there are a number of additional ethical considerations.

Voluntary participation

A key ethical notion in research is that participation in a study must be completely voluntary. One of the things that made the various Nazi experiments so ethically heinous is that the subjects of the experiments were given no choice but to participate. It may seem to you that this issue does not apply to you and your research. After all, you may be saying to yourself, how in the world could I force someone to participate in my study if he or she did not want to?

It turns out that you could well encounter ethical issues in this area, because the distinction between voluntary and involuntary participation is not completely clear-cut. Consider, for example, our earlier discussion of ethnographic methods in Chapter 11. As we saw, when doing ethnography, one possible approach is *complete participation*: basically, to go undercover and not tell anyone what you are doing. If you adopt this approach, however, it is not clear that people are participating in your study voluntarily. They may not wish to be observed by you, and you are not giving them the opportunity to refuse. Similarly, because the Facebook mood manipulation study was done surreptitiously, it cannot be said to have obtained the voluntary participation of Facebook users.

Second, some potential participants in a study may simply not really be in a position to refuse to participate, even if they know fully what the research project is all about. People incarcerated in prisons, for example, may not feel that they can say no, if they believe that certain benefits (like early release time, library privileges, longer hours permitted outside) are conditional on their participation.

Third, some potential participants may not be competent to give consent to participate. For example, suppose your research project involved working with young children. One important aspect of voluntary participation is understanding what voluntary participation means. Young children may not really comprehend what participation actually entails and, therefore, they may not be in a position to assess its consequences for them. The same principle would apply to mentally incompetent adults.

Fourth, in some cases it may be extremely difficult logistically to obtain voluntary consent to participate in your study. Consider, for example, the ethnographic study of environmental community organizing we encountered in Chapter 11. As part of his study, the researcher attended several public meetings where many things were said in public that he wanted to use in his study. It would have been extremely difficult for him to obtain consent ahead of time from every individual who happened to speak at those meetings. A possible solution here might have been to distribute leaflets at the meeting, informing attenders of the research and asking them to let the researcher know if they do not wish to be included.

Finally, remember that people can change their minds. They may originally agree to participate but then decide at some point that they prefer not to. As we saw earlier, this was one of the safeguards built into the Stanford prison experiment. Giving consent at one point in time does not mean agreement for all time, and, as a researcher, you will have to respect this. If they change their minds and you force them to participate anyway, this is not voluntary participation.

Informed consent

Closely related to the notion of voluntary participation is the notion of informed consent. Participants have to know what they are getting into: if not, they will be unable to give informed consent. This means that they must understand clearly what the research project is all about, what their participation entails, and what the potential risks are to them. All of this is so that they can decide whether or not participation is in their own best interest.

One important way in which informed consent is not given is when the researcher engages in deception regarding the aims of the study or the participant's role in it. This was the case in the Tuskegee syphilis study, as the subjects were not told that the study was about the progression of syphilis. If they had known, they might well have decided that they did not want to participate.

There are a couple of things to consider when you are seeking to obtain informed consent from potential participants. First, you need to provide information about the study that is appropriate, meaningful, and understandable to them. You do not want to provide too little detail, but at the same time it is possible to provide too much, to the point that the participant is overwhelmed. Similarly, you don't want to provide information that is filled with technical details and jargon that the participant would not understand. The information you provide should be clear, jargon-free, and pitched at an appropriate level. Only if all of these things are true can a person make a truly informed decision about participation.

Second, information can be given either verbally or in written form, by providing an information sheet. If possible, you might consider making up a consent form to be signed by both you and the participant. However, this is not necessary in all circumstances. For example, if you solicit participation in an on-line survey, the mere fact that they respond would be sufficient to indicate consent.

Confidentiality

A final key ethical concern is confidentiality: the right of participants in a research study to have information about them kept private.

The issue of confidentiality often occurs when you are collecting information from people, either in an interview or survey. By participating in a survey or interview, they are potentially revealing much about themselves. This could include their attitudes on controversial issues or their experiences with sensitive topics. If you have collected demographic information, this might contain information on their income, religious affiliation, educational attainment level, and gender identification. There are many reasons why they would want to keep these things confidential.

When you assure respondents that their answers will be kept confidential, you are promising them that no one else will have access to their specific information. To ensure this is the case, there are several steps you will need to take once you have collected the data. Normally, you would want to make the answers anonymous, so that no one else could tie an answer to a particular respondent. You could do this by expunging all names in the database. However, it is important to know who provided which answers, so that you can establish patterns in the data. Therefore, you may want to create a coding system, so that each respondent is given a coded number. These coded numbers could be a separate column in a spreadsheet, and could be then used as identifiers for each of the set of responses.

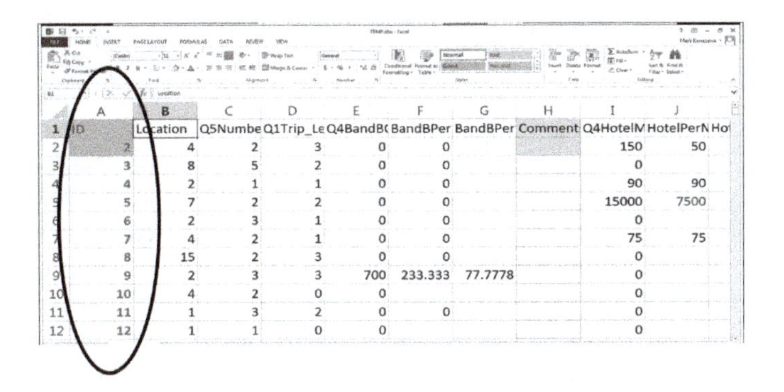

	A	B	C	D	E	F	G	H	I	J
1	ID	Location	Q5Numbe	Q1Trip_Le	Q4BandB(	BandBPer	BandBPer	Comment	Q4HotelM	HotelPerN
2	2	4	2	3	0	0			150	50
3	3	8	5	2	0	0			0	
4	4	2	1	1	0	0			90	90
5	5	7	2	2	0	0			15000	7500
6	6	2	3	1	0	0			0	
7	7	4	2	1	0	0			75	75
8	8	15	2	3	0	0			0	
9	9	2	3	3	700	233.333	77.7778		0	
10	10	4	2	0	0				0	
11	11	1	3	2	0	0			0	
12	12	1	1	0	0				0	

Figure 18.2 An anonymized database.

For example, consider the spreadsheet fragment shown in Figure 18.2. This fragment is taken from the spreadsheet used to organize and manage the survey responses in the *North Shore Climate Change* study. Every respondent has been given an identification number, shown in column A as ID. This makes it impossible for anyone to connect the answers to any particular respondent.

Another potential issue of confidentiality occurs when you are summarizing and reporting the data. If you have subdivided the responses into different categories, it may be that the number of responses in certain categories is so small that the responses of individual respondents can be identified.

For example, suppose that someone had surveyed all the faculty at Carleton College regarding their attitudes toward climate change. It would violate confidentiality if a research paper reported that Japanese-American senior faculty in the economics department favored mitigation procedures. Even though my name is never mentioned, it would be extremely easy to figure out this statement referred to me, as I am the only faculty member at Carleton who fits this description.

Bottom line: When working with human participants in your research project, every effort should be made to keep the information about them confidential. This should be done in such a way that no one, seeing the data, could connect the content of the information to the participant.

Institutional review board approval

It turns out that on all college and university campuses today, research involving human participants has to pass muster with an institutional review board (IRB). These IRBs are committees typically consisting of faculty and administrators whose function is to determine whether ethical guidelines are being followed. IRBs exist because federal law requires that all academic research be screened to ensure against human rights violations. The IRB process involves assessing research projects for the potential for harm to participants in a study.

As part of the vetting process, researchers need to submit a research proposal to the IRB committee. These proposals must contain sufficient information on your procedures and the human participants so that the IRB can determine whether they are being exposed to any sort of unacceptable risk. The IRB committee will be very interested, for example, to see any survey instruments or interview scripts that you have developed. In addition, you may be required to develop a consent form for participants to sign before the research begins. This form will contain a statement that the participants' rights will be protected. You should check the IRB procedures at your institution to make sure you know what information you need to include in your proposal.

It is important to keep in mind that the IRB review process can take time, especially if the IRB committee decides that changes need to be made in your research design. Therefore, you are strongly encouraged to submit your proposal early and, in particular, well before you plan to begin interacting with the participants. You may be required to pass your proposal before a faculty research advisor (at my institution, this is a requirement of the review process). Obtaining input ahead of time from a faculty advisor can be extremely useful toward ensuring that you are meeting IRB guidelines.

To give you a concrete sense of the thinking of your IRB and what it will be looking for, consider a study done in 2009 by the psychologist Jerry Burger. Burger wanted to replicate the Milgram obedience study, but he wanted to include safeguards to be sure he was treating the participants ethically. Among the safeguards he used:

- He carefully screened potential participants so that he could exclude some who he thought might react negatively to the experience.
- He told participants multiple times that they could withdraw from the experiment at any time and still receive their participation fee.
- He had the person ostensibly receiving the shocks enter the room almost immediately after the experiment was over to reassure the participant he was fine.
- The entire experiment was overseen by a clinical psychologist who was instructed to terminate the study if there were signs of excessive stress.

(Burger 2009, p. 2)

Notice that the potential risks to the participants were not completely eliminated. The initial screening process may not have been foolproof. During the experiment, the people administering the shocks may have experienced some psychological trauma. However, the IRB at Burger's institution approved this study, deeming the safeguards sufficient to avoid imposing excessive risk on the participants.

Box 18.1 Checklist: Obtaining IRB approval

✓ Research proposal should be sufficiently detailed to enable the IRB to assess risk to human participants.
✓ When feasible, create a written consent form.
✓ Leave plenty of time for the IRB process to be completed.
✓ Get input from your faculty research advisor.
✓ Check the IRB guidelines at your institution.

Conclusions

The bottom line point of this chapter is that the research process is not only about obtaining new knowledge. It is about obtaining it in socially acceptable ways. We do not misrepresent findings, steal ideas from others, or trample on others' human rights. We do our best to advance the frontiers of our understanding openly and honestly, we give credit where credit is due, we respect people's privacy, and we respect their rights to be physically safe and secure and emotionally well-adjusted. In some cases, we may well forego pursuing a particular research strategy, simply because the costs are too high.

To ensure that you do not cross ethical lines, it will help to be deeply conscious of how your research affects others. If you see serious potential for your research to benefit others in meaningful ways, consider that to be a strong argument in favor of pursuing that research. When you envision potential negative consequences for others, take them seriously and take what steps you can to avoid or minimize those consequences. Perhaps the best thing you can do is to bring a sense of personal integrity to your research, one that guides you at every step along the way. You have a good sense for how to treat others, be they family, friends, or even total strangers. Just bring this same sense to the research process.

Exercises/discussion questions

(1) Consider the Milgram obedience study and recall the notion of *external validity*; that is, whether the results of a study will generalize to other times and settings. If someone were to perform the same study today, do you think the findings would be the same? That is, do you think the Milgram study has external validity to the present time?

(2) Would you consider the following illegal acts unethical?

- Driving 70 mph in a 65 mph zone.
- Driving 100 mph in a 65 mph zone.
- Running a red light to get a critically injured friend to the hospital emergency room.
- Smoking within 100 feet of the entrance of a public building (New York).

(3) Suppose you are engaged in an ethnographic study and have established a cordial relationship with certain members of the community. A couple of them send you a request to friend them on Facebook. What do you do? Discuss the ethical issues.

(4) Suppose you are engaged in an ethnographic study and have established a cordial relationship with certain members of the community. One of them asks you if she can take a look at your research diary. What do you do? Discuss the ethical issues.

(5) A few years ago, the on-line dating website OKCupid was interested in seeing whether its compatibility ratings were effective in connecting date-seeking users to each other. So it altered the compatibility ratings of a set of randomly chosen users to see if this affected their inclination to connect with others. However, it did this without letting them know what was going on. OKCupid's user agreement states explicitly that personal data provided by users may be used for research and analysis. Was the behavior of OKCupid ethical or unethical? Discuss.

References

Abbott, Alison. "Modern Milgram Experiment Sheds Light on Power of Authority," *Nature* 530(February 18, 2016): 394–5.

Berger, Robert L. "Nazi Science: the Dachau Hypothermia Experiments," *New England Journal of Medicine* 29(May 1990): 1435–40.

Bertrand, Marianne, Simeon Djankov, Rema Hanna, and Sendhil Mullainathan. "Obtaining a Driver's License in India: An Experimental Approach to Studying Corruption," *Quarterly Journal of Economics* 122(November 2007): 1639–76.

Brownlee, Shannon, and Jeanne Lenzer. "Does the Vaccine Matter?" *The Atlantic*, November 2009, https://www.theatlantic.com/magazine/archive/2009/11/does-the-vaccine-matter/307723/

Burger, Jerry. "Replicating Milgram: Would People Still Obey Today?" *American Psychologist* 64(January 2009): 1–11.

Hays, Samuel P. *Conservation and the Gospel of Efficiency*. Cambridge: Harvard University Press, 1959.

Landau, Elizabeth. "Studies Show 'Dark Chapter' of Medical Research," *CNN*, October 1, 2010.

MacLeod, Saul. "Stanford Prison Experiment," *Simply Psychology* 2008, https://www.simplypsychology.org/zimbardo.html

Meyer, Robinson. "Everything We Know about Facebook's Secret Mood Manipulation Experiment," *The Atlantic*, June 28, 2014, http://www.theatlantic.com/technology/archive/2014/06/everything-we-know-about-facebooks-secret-mood-manipulation-experiment/373648/p

Ravallion, Martin. "Taking Ethical Validity Seriously," *Development Impact*, World Bank, March 17, 2014, http://blogs.worldbank.org/impactevaluations/taking-ethical-validity-seriously

Research Methods Knowledge Base. *Ethics in Research*, http://www.socialresearchmethods.net/kb/ethics.php.

Resnik, David B. "What is Ethics in Research and Why is It Important?" National Institute of Environmental Health Sciences, December 1, 2015, http://www.niehs.nih.gov/research/resources/bioethics/whatis/

Roston, Michael. "Retracted Scientific Studies: A Growing List," *New York Times*, May 28, 2015, http://www.nytimes.com/interactive/2015/05/28/science/retractions-scientific-studies.html?_r=0.

Rowan, Karen. "U.S. Spike in Measles Cases Due to People Skipping Vaccination," *Live Science, January 29*, 2015, http://www.livescience.com/49637-measles-cases-us-vaccination.html

"Settlement Reached in Suit over Radioactive Oatmeal Experiment," *New York Times*, January 1, 1998.
"Study Relates Vaccine Refusal to Rise in Measles, Pertussis," Center for Infectious Disease Research and Policy (CIDRAP), May 21, 2016, http://www.cidrap.umn.edu/news-perspective/2016/03/study-relates-vaccine-refusal-rise-measles-pertussis
Zimbardo, Philip. *The Lucifer Effect: Understanding How Good People Turn Evil*. New York: Random House, 2007.

19 Writing a research proposal

Introduction

As part of the process of doing a research project, you may be called upon to write a research proposal. This may, for example, be part of the requirements for a course, or for writing a senior thesis at your college or university. The research proposal is exactly what it sounds like: a proposal for doing a research project that will need to pass muster with someone, in your case probably a faculty advisor.

There will be certain things that the proposal reader will be looking for. These include things like a specific, well-defined research question, a good familiarity with existing relevant studies, and a clear, feasible plan of action for collecting evidence. Discussing these things and more will enable a reader to get a good sense for whether what you propose to do is feasible, original, useful, and interesting.

But you should also view writing a research proposal as an opportunity to really refine and clarify your thinking on exactly what it is you want to do. Sometimes, by working things out carefully in your own mind, you may notice weaknesses in your approach, or questions that need to be answered. These include questions such as:

- Is my research question clearly and specifically posed?
- Am I clear about exactly what the unanswered questions are given the studies that have already been done?
- Have I chosen the right methodological approach?
- Am I thinking about the right kind of evidence that would allow me to answer my research question?

These are all questions that it would be useful to answer ahead of time before you have progressed too far in your project.

Overview: The elements of a research proposal

In order for the research proposal to serve its purpose, there are a number of issues it will have to address, relating to the motivation for doing the study;

what the study hopes to accomplish; and how the research will be done. In general, research proposals should contain a number of specific elements that are designed to address these issues. These elements are listed in Box 19.1. The overall proposal should be written as a sequential narrative, in which each element of the proposal builds on the previous elements. By the end, the reader should have a good sense for both the value and feasibility of the research.

Box 19.1 Checklist: Research proposal

- ✔ Introduction
  - ✔ Statement of problem
  - ✔ Purpose statement
- ✔ Review of literature
- ✔ Questions/hypotheses
- ✔ Methods and procedures
- ✔ Plan of work
- ✔ Works cited
- ✔ Supporting material

The remainder of this chapter discusses each of the elements of this checklist in turn.

Introduction

The first element of a research proposal is the introduction. This is a crucial first step in which you provide the motivation for your project, while also providing the reader with a clear roadmap of your study. These are the important questions of *Why* and *What*: why the study needs to be done, and what you specifically propose to do. These questions are addressed in two important elements of your introduction: a statement of the research problem, and a statement of your research purpose.

Why: *Statement of research problem*

The most successful research proposals are ones that provide the strongest argument for why the proposed project is worth doing. This means, first and foremost, a clear statement of a problem that your reader would agree is important, relevant and timely. Good candidates for such problems are ones that address current environmental issues, particularly ones with major consequences for some identifiable group. We have seen a number of examples of such studies in this book. Some of these are listed in Box 19.2 along with a statement of their research problem.

Box 19.2 Illustrations of research problem statements

Study	*Research problem statement*
Berrens et al. (1998)	Not known how successful safe minimum standards are for preserving wildlife habitat.
Guber (2001)	Not known why some environmental referendums succeed and others fail.
Howe et al. (1990)	Magnitude of the impact of water diversions on irrigating farmers not known.
Lichterman (1995)	Not known why multicultural alliance-building on environmental issues often fail.
Norgaard (2012)	Not known why informed people in wealthy countries often do not show much concern about their role in contributing to climate change.

An important common feature of these research problem statements is that they all point to some gap in our understanding of an environmental issue. Without this gap, of course, there would be no need for another study. Implicit here is that the authors did their homework, meaning that they did an exhaustive search for existing studies that might have supplied the missing knowledge. It was only when they were satisfied that no such studies existed that they were able to conclude that this really was a research problem worth exploring further.

For example, Box 19.3 contains an excerpt from the study of Maguire and Hardy on DDT (see Chapter 13). The authors apparently became interested in "outsider-driven deinstitutionalization" when they recognized that the notion seemed to apply to the case of DDT. Then, when they read further and found little in existing studies that dealt with deinstitutionalization, they realized that they had a potential contribution to make.

Box 19.3 Statement of a gap: Maguire and Hardy (2009)

Despite its importance, outsider-driven deinstitutionalization [abandonment of existing institutional practices] has not been studied in detail. In fact, empirical studies of any form of deinstitutionalization are rare (Ahmadjian & Robinson, 2001; Scott, 2001). When it has been examined, it has often been studied indirectly, as a by-product of research on the adoption of new practices. As a result, little is known "about the work done by actors to disrupt institutions." (Lawrence & Suddaby, 2006: 238)

To summarize, this discussion points to a couple of important issues to consider when creating your research problem statement. First, you need to identify an environmental issue or problem into which it is useful and important to provide insight. Second, it is important to thoroughly read the studies of other researchers who have examined the problem. Only when you have done both of these things can you be satisfied that you have a research problem worth studying further. Again, your objective is to answer the question: "Given what previous studies have found, why is *this* study needed?"

What: The purpose statement

As opposed to the research problem statement, which states what the problem is and why it is important, the purpose statement is a statement of your research strategy for addressing the problem. Writing an effective purpose statement requires that you provide details and be very clear about what you propose to do. To help you to be as clear as possible, it is recommended that you write a sentence starting with: "The purpose of this study is …" and complete it with a clear declarative statement of your main objective in doing the study. Writing this sentence serves two purposes. First, it will clarify in your own mind exactly what it is that you propose to do. Second, when inserted into your proposal, it will provide a clear, concise statement to the reader of precisely what your proposed research project is all about.

There are a number of other things you will want to include in your purpose statement. Perhaps most importantly, you will need to convey the specific methodology you intend to use. At the most general level, you will need to convey whether you will be pursuing a qualitative, quantitative, or a mixed methods strategy. Then, depending upon which strategy you choose, you will want to tailor-make your purpose statement to the specific demands of that strategy.

Quantitative purpose statements

Of the three types of statements, quantitative purpose statements are the most uniform both in content and format. Generally speaking, these statements will focus on the relationship among variables.

For example, consider the purpose statement in Box 19.4, taken from a recent study of aquatic invasive species and their effect on local property values. Here, the authors have named the specific variables—*Eurasian watermilfoil* and *property values*—that are suspected to be related. Notice also that they have been very specific about two other factors that it will be important to know: the identity of the participants (property owners) and the research site (forests of northern Wisconsin). These four factors—(a) the variables we are interested in, (b) the relationship among them, (c) the participants in the study, and (d) the site where the research takes place—are all important to mention in your purpose statement.

Box 19.4 Sample quantitative purpose statement

The purpose of this study is to estimate a hedonic model of lakeshore property values to quantify the effects of a common aquatic invasive species—Eurasian watermilfoil ...—on property values across an extensive system of over 170 lakes in the northern forest region of Wisconsin. (Horsch and Lewis 2009, p. 391)

Qualitative purpose statements

As we have seen, there are a wide variety of qualitative approaches. Because of this, qualitative purpose statements can be quite varied in content and format, depending upon the research problem and the specific qualitative approach you have decided to take. Generally speaking, qualitative purpose statements do not speak to quantifying a relationship, as quantitative purpose statements commonly do. Rather, they are often stated as an *exploration* of a particular phenomenon or process, or the behavior or attitudes of a specific set of research participants (see Box 19.5).

Box 19.5 Sample qualitative purpose statement

This article explores the importance of issue-framing (i.e., how issues are symbolically presented) in initiative campaigns using survey data from two prominent and contrasting case studies—the first, a successful 1986 toxics initiative in California intended to protect drinking water supplies; the second, an unsuccessful 1992 recycling initiative in Massachusetts. (Guber 2001, pp. 120–1)

This emphasis on research as being exploratory in nature means that qualitative purpose statements are often broader and more open-ended than quantitative ones. This does not mean that they can be nebulous and lack specifics. But as we have seen, qualitative research is often about inductively starting with the evidence rather than deductively using a theoretical framework and well-defined testable hypotheses.

For many qualitative projects, one's ideas almost necessarily have to start broadly and acquire more specific focus as we see what the evidence says. We saw this, for example, earlier when we encountered the ethnographic approach, where we saw that ethnographic studies often exhibit a characteristic "funnel" shape, starting broad and narrowing down as the study progresses. One's purpose statement may well have to accommodate this initial broad focus.

One thing that can give focus to a qualitative purpose statement is a framing theory. This framing theory can provide a conceptual structure that you can use to organize your thoughts. In Box 19.6, for example, we see a purpose statement where the author is proposing to use a conceptual structure she calls "the construction of innocence" as a means for organizing and understanding the evidence she will be collecting on climate change attitudes in a small Norwegian town.

> *Box 19.6* Sample qualitative purpose statement
>
> In the present paper, I evaluate the material and symbolic significance of both climate change denial and a phenomenon I call 'the construction of innocence' in terms of their role in reproducing global material and ideological power relations along the lines of race, class and gender. (Norgaard 2012, p. 82)

Again, there are no testable hypotheses; rather, framing theory simply provides a coherent conceptual way to think about your evidence. And as we have seen, it can often derive from existing studies that have applied a theory to a different topic. Thus, it may provide a link to existing scholarship, which may well help you to identify unanswered research questions. In Norgaard's case, she bases her framing theory on earlier work by two other researchers who developed concepts for understanding psychological denial of negative outcomes and personal involvement (Norgaard 2012, p. 87).

Mixed methods purpose statements

Finally, if you are using a mixed methods approach, you will probably be using a combination of these approaches. In this case, your purpose statement should not only speak to both approaches but also describe how the approaches will complement each other. This means that you will want to clearly state the overall objective of the study, provide information on the quantitative and qualitative components, and discuss how the components complement each other.

Consider, for example, the mixed methods deforestation study by John Sydenstricker-Neto that we saw earlier in Chapter 15. That study contained two complementary components: (1) a quantitative component in which he documented a connection between local population growth and deforestation; and (2) a qualitative component in which he examined factors that influenced this connection.

Box 19.7 contains Sydenstricker-Neto's purpose statement. In it, he is making clear the main focus of his study: the relationship between population and deforestation. He is also making clear that the study is not just about quantifying this relationship. It is also about investigating various mediating factors that may influence this relationship. So it reads very much like a mixed methods purpose statement. And he reinforces this impression by discussing a wide variety of types of evidence—both qualitative and quantitative—that he intends to use.

Box 19.7 Sample mixed methods purpose statement

This paper examines the contribution of the "population factor" as a cause of deforestation in Machadinho D'Oeste, Rondônia, Brazilian Amazonia, an area with significant small-scale farming. Conceptually, the paper shows that socioeconomic status and mediating factors (i.e., education, managerial skills, previous rural experience, integration into the local, and regional contexts), and attitudes and behaviors toward the land parcel development mediate migrants' relationships with the local environment. The analysis combines multiple data sources (i.e., demographic census, household survey, land-cover maps, in-depth interviews) and analytical approaches (i.e., fuzzy sets statistics, remote-sensing/GIS analysis, interpretivist qualitative assessment) to examine the complex interrelationships between [land-use and land-cover change] and human population. (Sydenstricker-Neto 2012, p. 86)

Review of related literature

Once you have discussed in broad terms why you want to do your study and what you propose to do, it is then time to provide more specific details. The reader of your proposal will need to be convinced of two things. First, that there is a need for research on your proposed topic. Second, that you are knowledgeable about the topic, both in terms of what other researchers have done and what remains to be done at this point, in order to further advance our understanding. A good literature review will address both of these points (Abdulai and Owusa-Ansah 2014, p. 4).

At this point, it might be useful to distinguish between the studies you may have referenced in your problem statement and the literature review for a research proposal. In both cases, you are invoking previous studies in order to make the case for your proposed research. However, the way they use existing studies differs in certain subtle yet important ways.

Studies in your problem statement

Recall that the purpose of your problem statement is to briefly state why your study is needed. Here, the operant word is "brief": the problem statement is not an extended treatment of existing research. Rather, it is a hook to draw the reader in and convince her of the general merit of what you propose. Consequently, you are generally only going to want to invoke studies that justify your study in the broadest terms.

Recall, for example, the statement of a gap in Box 19.3. There, in order to justify their study, the authors needed to document that institutionalization was an understudied issue, especially when it is driven by outsiders. To make this case, all they did was to cite three studies: two that corroborated the claim that hardly any empirical studies of the issue exist, and one that corroborated that we know little about how external actors cause it to occur.

They then go on to argue, citing a couple more studies, that while studies of the influence of actors within institutions do exist, the influence of internal actors cannot be generalized to describe the influence of external actors. All of this is sufficient to justify looking at the influence of external actors on institutional practices, such as the widespread use of DDT.

Studies for a research proposal

The literature review for a research proposal goes further than just providing broad justification for your study. Rather, it may develop more fully the definitions of important concepts or variables; discuss relevant theories that either generate hypotheses or frame our understanding of an issue; and perhaps discuss methods that have been used by other researchers. Your objective here is to demonstrate command of the topic and that you are aware of important recent developments, both in terms of findings and research methodologies.

At the same time, the literature review should still be relatively brief, speaking primarily to the main themes and findings in existing studies. This means that you want to be somewhat selective in citing studies, choosing only the ones that are directly relevant to the points you are making. However, at the end of the literature review, you want to make sure you make it clear what your point of departure is: where you are going in your research that builds upon what we already know.

You should also keep in mind that this literature review may not be the final word in identifying relevant studies. Once you actually undertake your research project, you may well come across additional studies that will help further inform or refine your study. This will be true no matter what kind of study you do. However, it is especially true of many studies with a qualitative component, since the process of exploration and theory generation may well lead you in new and unexpected directions.

It may also be the case that as your study progresses, certain strands in the existing literature become less relevant, leading you to decide that certain studies you included in your proposal literature review are no longer important to cite. In any case, the literature review for your final study may well look different from the one you write for your research proposal.

A word of warning: when writing a literature review, it is generally not a good idea to make broad, general statements like: "Little is currently known about [a particular topic]." It is tempting to make statements like this, because you want to convey that there is a gap in our understanding of your topic. However, such statements can easily lead a discerning reader to conclude that you have simply not done your homework to really determine what studies have been done and what they have concluded.

Rather than arguing in general terms that little is known, focus more on specifically what it is about the topic that we do not know. This will force you to read and cite studies that speak directly to particular aspects of your argument.

More generally, there are a number of things that can go wrong when you write a literature review. Box 19.8 lists some common problems of literature reviews.

Box 19.8 Checklist: Common problems of literature reviews

- ✔ Fail to cite influential papers
- ✔ Fail to keep up with recent developments
- ✔ Fail to critically evaluate cited papers
- ✔ Cite irrelevant or trivial sources
- ✔ Lack organization and structure
- ✔ Are repetitive and verbose

(adapted from Wong n.d.)

Research questions/hypotheses

Once you have done all this, you are now in a position to state specifically what you propose to do. Your earlier purpose statement described the general thrust of your study, based upon a research problem you have identified. The literature review provided guidance based upon what previous researchers have found and the theories and methods they have used. It is now time to take your general idea and refine it into some specific questions you want answers to. Again, there will be some important differences depending upon whether you are doing a quantitative, qualitative, or mixed methods study.

Quantitative studies

As we have seen, quantitative studies commonly involve either quantifying a relationship among variables or testing a hypothesis. This means that you can either pose a research question or a testable hypothesis, depending upon your study goals. Either one can speak to one or both of these objectives (Creswell 2009, pp. 132–36). For example, Box 19.9 contains some examples of research questions from recent quantitative studies.

Two of these research questions are about quantifying a relationship among variables, while the third states a hypothesis. Before continuing, make sure you can tell which are which.

Box 19.9 Some sample quantitative research questions

Leones et al. (1997): What were the impacts of depleted summer streamflows on whitewater rafting in New Mexico in the early 1990s?

Scott et al. (2007): What is the impact of changes in climate variables associated with climate change on national park visitations in the Canadian Rocky Mountains in the late 1990s and early 2000s?

Loomis and Keske (2012): Did consumer expenditures and willingness to pay (WTP) for nature-based recreation fall during the Great Recession?

The first two, by Leones et al. and Scott et al., are, of course, the questions stated as aimed at quantifying a relationship among variables. Notice that they are stated specifically enough that you have a good idea of what data they probably used to answer the question. It appears that Leones et al. used data on streamflow levels and some measure of rafting activity. Scott et al. probably used data on climate variables and visitation activity at national parks. Notice also that each research question is highly specific about the time frame and location of the study, as well as the study participants. Your research question should be specific enough for your reader to be able to discern all of these things.

The research question by Loomis and Keske is the one stated as a hypothesis. The difference from the first two is in the way it is stated, so that it can be answered "yes" or "no." These answers would correspond to competing hypotheses about the impact of the Great Recession. Notice also that this research question contains essentially all of the same information as the first two regarding data needs, time frame, location, and study participants. Though the last two factors are not clearly stated, one can infer that the authors will use data on nature-based recreationists at some location, in order to test their hypothesis.

Qualitative studies

Like quantitative studies, qualitative studies pose research questions that derive directly from their purpose statements. However, unlike quantitative studies, qualitative studies typically pose research questions that are exploratory in nature. This is, of course, completely in line with the exploratory nature of many qualitative studies in general. As a result, qualitative research questions tend to be open-ended, in terms of the likely answers of the inquiry.

For example, consider the research questions from the DDT study that are contained in Box 19.10. Though filled with way too much jargon for my taste, they illustrate some common features of qualitative research questions.

Box 19.10 Sample qualitative study research questions

If outsiders are to bring about the abandonment of practices, what happens to their problematizations (that is, claims and arguments that corroborate the ineffective nature of existing practices) during this process of translation?

What role does the process of translation play in outsider-driven deinstitutionalization? (Maguire and Hardy 2009, pp. 151–2)

Notice that there is no sense of quantifying any relationships or testing hypotheses. Rather, they use words such as: "what happens to" and "what role." These words leave everything open-ended. The spirit of the research exercise is that they just want to see what happens to these problematizations, not that they have any clear idea ahead of time based, say, on some theory. Similarly, they pose no clear idea, and certainly no hypothesis, regarding precisely what the role of translation will be. True to the qualitative approach, they are engaging in the inductive method and this is coming across in their research questions.

Mixed methods studies

Finally, the research questions for a mixed methods study will address both the qualitative and quantitative components of the study. For example, consider the research questions contained in Box 19.11. These questions were taken from a study of nature tourism in southern Africa.

> *Box 19.11* Sample mixed methods research questions
>
> In this paper, we specifically address two research questions: Do households located in areas with ICDPs [integrated conservation and development programs] receive more tourism-related benefits than households that are not? And do economic benefits increase local residents' satisfaction with tourism-related development? The first question lets us examine whether nature tourism succeeds as a means of economic accumulation for local residents, and whether ICDPs better facilitate the delivery of these benefits. The second question investigates the relationship between monetary benefits and quality of life within areas pursuing a tourism-based development strategy, and whether this varies among people who live in areas involved in ICDPs and those that do not. Thus, our analytical framework considers both the monetary and nonmonetary dimensions of ICDPs currently being implemented in parts of southern Africa. (Silva and Khatiwada 2014, p. 19)

The mixed methods approach is illustrated with the double-barreled research questions. The first—Does location in a conservation area confer extra tourism benefits on local households?—appears suited to a quantitative analysis that correlates location with monetary benefits. The second—Do these extra benefits translate into increased satisfaction for those households?—seems suited to a qualitative analysis, since it would probably have to rely on qualitative measures of satisfaction, such as those gleaned from a survey. As always, these questions are clear about the research participants (local households that may or may not be served by the ICDPs) and the site location (rural southern Africa).

Methods and procedures

In this section, you describe your plan of action: the specific methods and procedures you will use to answer your research questions. This section should contain everything that your reader will need to know to determine whether your methodology is sound. When writing this section, a good rule of thumb is that you should provide enough specific details so that another competent researcher could actually do your study for you. The main elements of this section are listed in Box 19.12.

Box 19.12 Checklist: Elements of a Methods and Procedures section

- ✔ Context for empirical analysis
- ✔ Sampling issues
- ✔ Survey instrument/interview script
- ✔ Plans for data analysis
- ✔ Ethical considerations

Context for empirical analysis

Given what you have already written up to now, it should be clear whether you intend to do a qualitative, quantitative, or mixed methods study. Nevertheless, it will not hurt to reiterate the particular approach you propose to take, especially if you are doing a qualitative study. As we have seen, there are a variety of such approaches, and being specific about which one you are using will help your reader evaluate the overall merit of your proposal.

For example, Box 19.13 contains excerpts from the beginning of several methods sections of recent environmental studies. Though these excerpts are from the final completed studies, they could easily serve in the methods section of a proposal. In each case, the reader is given a good sense for the basic approach: in three instances, the authors are proposing to do a case study, and in a fourth instance, the author is proposing to do an ethnography.

Box 19.13 Opening context for your methods description

Howe et al. (1990): "This is a case study of a seven-county reach of the Arkansas River in southeastern Colorado, an area from which a large amount of agricultural water already has been transferred to urban uses and for which there is the prospect of even larger future transfers" (p. 1201).

Campregher (2010): "The context of our case study is a hydroelectrical project called Hydroelectrical Project El Diquis, …, which is planned to be constructed in southern Costa Rica, and the construction of which affects the indigenous community of Térraba" (p. 787).

Maguire and Hardy (2009): "We used a single, exploratory case study, following a common research method for building theory" (p. 153).

Norgaard (2012): "This paper uses data from a larger eight month ethnographic study on the role of cultural context in how people experience global climate change that combines 46 interviews and media analysis" (p. 86).

The examples also illustrate another common function of the opening context: providing specific information on the setting of the study, like the seven-county area in southern Colorado, or the community of Terraba in southern Costa Rica. The other two examples illustrate that this information need not be contained in the opening sentence. However, it is a good idea to identify the setting early in this section, to help the reader better evaluate the merits of your proposal.

In the Howe study, the authors had just gone through a lengthy discussion, on a conceptual level, of external damages to farmers resulting from transfers of water from rural areas to cities. The reader is then expecting that the methods section will be about investigating and perhaps quantifying these potential damages. Here, she is not disappointed.

I should point out that this sentence, though a bit long, does a nice job of reinforcing the rationale for doing the study. It says that the issue of transfers is already an important one at the site of the study, and that it is only going to become more important over time. This sentence thus serves the really useful function of impressing upon the reader why the proposed study is an important one to undertake.

Sampling

The reader of your proposal will be very concerned with your method for collecting evidence. The basic issue here is whether your study has *validity*, which has two components. First, does it have *internal* validity? That is, are the conclusions warranted on the basis of the arguments and evidence presented? Second, does it have *external* validity? Are the conclusions generalizable to larger contexts? The reader will be assessing how you propose to collect your evidence in order to see if it supports your study's validity, and here is where sampling comes into the picture.

As before, the issues with regard to sampling vary somewhat depending upon whether you are doing a quantitative or a qualitative study. A good part of the difference concerns the different kinds of evidence to be collected. Let us consider each of these approaches in turn.

Quantitative studies

For quantitative studies, there are two basic ways in which you will be collecting data. You may either be using existing data sets collected by third parties like government agencies or generating the data yourself, perhaps by conducting a survey.

If your data are coming from a third party, you will want to specify the particular variables you intend to use, as well as the specific source of these variables. Suppose, for example, that you are interested in doing a quantitative study of endangered species, perhaps to estimate an environmental Kuznets curve (see Chapter 4). Recalling the quantitative databases listed in the appendix to Chapter 5, you would want to specify that you will be using particular statistics on different species taken from the *Red List of Threatened Species*, IUCN. Naming specific variables, and the sources of those variables, will again convey both that you have done your homework and whether your approach is sound.

If you are proposing to generate the data yourself, you will want to be careful to specify how you propose to get a reasonably random sample, which is key to the external validity of quantitative studies.

For example, for the *North Shore Climate Change* study, we gave a lot of thought to the challenges of sampling to get a reasonably representative sample of visitors to the North Shore. We decided that the best way to obtain such a sample was to conduct the survey in person at a variety of venues along the North Shore, including state parks, roadside rest areas, outfitters, and resorts. The problem, of course, is that there is certainly an element of convenience sampling to this method. Therefore, in our proposal we had to make the case that this sampling method was warranted by the choice of multiple venues and the lack of suitable alternatives.

You will also want to be explicit about who the survey will be administered to. Here, you may want to describe your target group of participants, perhaps including information on demographic characteristics, if relevant to your study. Your reader will be interested in how you selected the target group and, in particular, what selection criteria you used. Keep in mind that the reader will have to be persuaded that the selection criteria are appropriate given the objectives of the study.

Qualitative studies

For many qualitative studies, your evidence is less likely to come from third-party sources. Rather, it will often be data you have generated yourself, from surveys or interviews. In general, the task of supporting validity is harder than for quantitative studies because you will often be working with a non-random sampling procedure, such as convenience or snowball sampling. If so, this means that you will need to clearly state your rationale for your sampling approach and the potential limitations in terms of the conclusions you can draw. Do not worry about undermining the case for doing your study. It is better to show that you recognize the possible issues that may arise than to raise doubts in the mind of the reader that you are unaware of them.

Here, you will again have to provide a description of the participants, keeping in mind the objectives of your proposed study. The choice of participants will have to make sense given what your study hopes to accomplish.

Consider, for example, the ethnographic study by Kari Norgaard of climate change attitudes among privileged groups in developed countries (Norgaard 2012). In this study, the author chose to interview residents of a small town in Norway, arguing in effect that the information garnered in these interviews would provide a good sense of the attitudes of environmentally privileged residents of developed nations in general. By many metrics, Norway is an environmentally privileged society. Furthermore, the residents of the town were by all accounts well-informed about climate change. Thus, the author could make a compelling case for interviewing these particular people.

Survey instrument/interview guide

As we have seen, in many cases you will be collecting data by administering a survey or conducting an interview. If so, it will be important to provide details about the particular instrument you will be using.

Surveying

If you are conducting a survey, the reader will be interested, of course, in the questions you propose to ask, and you will want to make sure to include the actual proposed survey in your supporting materials (see *Supporting materials* below). If you have been careful, you will have followed the principles for effective formatting of surveys and effective wording of survey questions discussed in Chapter 16, and your reader will be persuaded that your methodology is sound.

In addition to the survey itself, you are going to want to provide details regarding how you intend to administer the survey. For example, will it be done in person, on-line, by phone, or through the mail? How many responses will you be looking for? What is your time frame for obtaining your target number of responses? This time frame will need to be consistent with the timetable you will be proposing for completion of your study (see *Plan of work* below).

Interviewing

Similarly, if you are planning to conduct interviews, it will be important to provide your reader with specific details. In general, you want to convey that doing interviews makes sense given your research objectives; that the people you propose to interview are suitable for your purposes; that you have a feasible plan for gaining access to those potential interviewees; and that you are budgeting sufficient time to conduct all of the interviews that you will need.

Keep in mind that if you propose conducting either a structured or semi-structured interview (see Chapter 17), you will have to prepare a detailed interview guide. This interview guide will contain your interview questions and, if appropriate, instructions for whoever will be conducting the interview. This interview guide will need to be submitted as part of the supporting materials for your proposal.

It goes without saying that you should plan to follow the principles for preparing good interview guides. These include: tailoring your questions to the type of interview you are conducting; paying careful attention to the order in which you ask questions; seeking feedback on your questions prior to the interview; and anticipating the possible need for follow-up questions. You may want to review the material in Chapter 17 when you are preparing your research guide.

If you propose conducting an unstructured interview, you will probably have to spend time justifying why an unstructured interview is warranted given the goals of your study. This is because unstructured interviews are much more difficult to do than structured, or even semi-structured, interviews, as we have seen. They really require a lot of skill, and your reader is going to need to be reassured that: (1) an unstructured interview needs to be done, and (2) you have the skills and preparation to pull it off. You might want to discuss things with your faculty advisor before you decide to go down this path.

When considering conducting interviews, a key issue is gaining access to potential interviewees. Consenting to an interview is a major commitment for a potential interviewee, much more than the commitment required to fill out a survey. You are asking them to spend a significant amount of time responding to questions posed by a complete stranger. As a result, you should be prepared for some people to be reluctant to participate in an interview.

This means that even prior to preparing your proposal, you should be seeking out agreement in principle by people in your target group to be interviewed by you. Here, it may help to approach *gatekeepers*: people in a community, neighborhood, or organization who are in a position to facilitate connection-building. They may be able to vouch for your project, or point you in the direction of people who are willing to participate. It will significantly strengthen a proposal if you are able to say that you have people already lined up to participate in the interviews.

Methods of data analysis

In this section, you want to describe your general strategy for analyzing your data, providing as many specific details as possible. If you are doing a quantitative analysis, you will want to name the primary variables you are interested in. If your analysis involves quantifying a relationship, you may want to state the model explicitly, including the primary variables along with control variables, if appropriate. If your analysis involves testing hypotheses, it will help to provide explicit statements of the hypotheses.

You should also provide details regarding the specific statistical techniques you intend to use, such as factor analysis or regression analysis. Providing these details will show your reader that you have thought carefully about the appropriate statistical techniques to use. In addition, knowing the details will help the reader assess the soundness of your method.

In all likelihood, you will be using a data management spreadsheet such as Excel and/or a statistical software package such as R, SAS, SPSS, or STATA. If you are doing a spatial analysis, you may be using spatial software such as ArcGIS. In any case, you will also want to include in your proposal the name of the software you will be using. Providing this information will: (1) convey to the reader that you have thought through the details of your data analysis, and (2) allow the reader to assess whether what you propose is feasible and appropriate given the analytical needs of the project.

If you are doing a qualitative analysis, you will want to provide details on your general strategy for managing and analyzing the evidence. In some cases, you will be doing a lot of work manually. For example, if you propose conducting interviews, you will have to spend time transcribing data from your field notes and audio recordings of the interview. You may also spend time doing manual coding of themes that emerge from the interviews. It will be useful to mention in your proposal that you recognize you will have to spend some time transcribing and coding the data. You will also want to build time to accomplish all of these things into your plan of work and, especially, the timetable for when things get done.

Depending upon your project, you may also be doing some of this data management and analysis electronically. Some of the data you collect may then be subject to statistical analysis, in which case you may also be using packages like Excel, R, and/or SPSS. With qualitative data, you may also be planning to use computer packages like NVivo or MAXQDA. In any case, you should specify which packages you will be using and what you will be using them to accomplish.

Ethical considerations

Finally, there are number of ethical issues that you will want to address in your proposal. As we saw in Chapter 18, these issues include *informed consent*, *protection from harm*, and *confidentiality*. Your research proposal should briefly discuss how you will address these issues.

Informed consent

As we have seen, participation in a study should be voluntary, and participants need to understand what they are getting themselves into. Your proposal should describe how you will inform the participants what the research is about and how you will obtain their consent to participate. If you are planning to conduct a survey or interviews, make sure that the survey instrument or interview script also contains the preamble that informs the respondent about the project. This will convey to your reader that you are providing accurate, clear information about the project.

Some types of studies, such as ethnographies or action research, entail more extensive involvement and contact with people (say, in a local community or organization) than merely taking a survey. Here, obtaining informed consent can be trickier, as it becomes more of a challenge to ensure that everyone affected by the research both understands what the research is for and is willing to participate.

We saw that this was true, for example, of the ethnographic study of forging alliances among grassroots organizations described in Chapter 11, where the author attended large public meetings and every attender was, technically speaking, a participant in the study. You can see how this might also have been true of many of the action research projects described in Chapter 14.

In cases like these, your proposal should discuss any steps you intend to take to inform affected people about the project. This might include making contacts with local community leaders, gatekeepers, or organizational officials.

Furthermore, if the proposed research is likely to involve multiple groups of people, you may want to mention your intention to reach out to as many of these groups as is feasible. It might be important to do this if certain contact people may not be in a position to speak for all affected groups. For example, in one of the action research projects described in Chapter 14, we saw some miscommunication between a local public official and some of those within the local community, which created some challenges for the researchers.

Confidentiality

When doing surveys or interviews, a big issue is confidentiality; namely, keeping the information you collect secure and private. Any well-designed survey instrument or interview script will contain an explicit confidentiality statement. This statement constitutes a promise to the respondents that the collected information will remain confidential.

However, the issue of confidentiality goes beyond this disclaimer statement. In your proposal, you will also want to detail the steps you will take to ensure that this information will remain confidential. These may include anonymizing responses (so that no one can connect specific answers to specific individuals); measures to securely store the data during the term of the project; and measures to dispose of the data after the project's completion.

Protection from harm

For most of the types of studies you will probably be considering, protecting study participants from harm will likely not be an issue. The ethical stricture against inflicting harm on research participants is most compelling in medical and psychological studies, where there can be real and potentially serious consequences to the physical and psychological well-being of the participants (recall some of the examples from Chapter 18). However, harm can occur in less obvious ways, of which you should be aware. These include (1) harm to others not directly participating in the study and (2) harm to interpersonal relations among participants (such as in a workplace).

An example of harm to others is provided by the driver's license study that we read about in Chapter 18. In that study, the potential for harm—in terms of unsafe drivers and more dangerous roads—was built directly, if unintentionally, into the research design. If you see possible hazards such as this in your proposed research, you will want to speak to this possibility in your proposal. The reader may well decide that the potential dangers are sufficiently small to not warrant changing your research plans. However, if they are potentially serious enough, this may prompt a useful discussion between you and your faculty advisor to consider alternative, perhaps less problematic, methods that will still permit you to answer your research question.

An example of harm to interpersonal relations is provided by the following example cited by the researchers Suki Ali and Moira Kelly (Ali and Kelly 2012, p.

63). They use the example of a study of workplace inequalities, where the researchers propose to conduct focus groups involving both workers and supervisors. One can easily imagine how a frank exchange of views within this setting might well create hard feelings and erode trust between workers and supervisors. These effects could linger for a long time after the researcher has departed the scene.

It is incumbent upon you as a researcher to think carefully about your research design in order to avoid creating situations like this. It might help to put yourself in the shoes of the participants and view what you propose to do from their viewpoint. If you decide that there is a serious danger of inflicting harm, you might consider modifying your research design. If in doubt, at the very least you should mention the issue in your proposal and see if your reader has ethical concerns about what you propose. Better yet, you might discuss the issue directly with your faculty advisor to gain her insights on the seriousness of the issue and whether a modification of your research plans may be warranted.

Plan of work

As a final step in your proposal narrative, you should provide specific details for precisely what you plan to do, in what order, and over what time frame. Now that you have done the research for your proposal, you have done all of the leg-work to: identify a research problem; survey literature to identify a gap in our knowledge; pose a well-defined research question; and speak to the methods you will be using to answer it. At this point, the question is how you will actually carry out the research.

You might consider dividing the project up into different phases that correspond roughly to data collection, data analysis and interpretation, and writing. The research will progress in roughly this order. However, as we have seen, qualitative studies are more fluid and open-ended than quantitative studies, sometimes calling for additional literature review in response to evolving ideas or unexpected findings. Furthermore, you are encouraged to regularly spend time throughout the process organizing and writing up your ideas and findings as the project progresses.

When writing up your plan of work, it will be important to consider the time frame of the project and make sure you allocate sufficient time to each phase while still being able to meet the overall project deadline. In doing this, you should be realistic about how much time each phase will take. For example, if your reader thinks you are being overly optimistic about how long it will take you to collect your data, she may reject the proposal or ask you to revise the project parameters and scope.

But even so, you should build buffer time into your timetable, since it is difficult to anticipate in advance all of the issues that might arise along the way. A deadline for completion of a rough draft should occur at least two weeks in advance of the final deadline, to allow you to polish and refine your argument, perhaps with the input of a faculty advisor.

If you are doing a group project, it will also help to be specific both about the particular responsibilities of each member of the team and when they should be doing what. For example, all members of a team might be responsible for reviewing the literature on the general issue, but you might consider dividing up responsibilities on subtopics, such as data collection, statistical techniques, and familiarization with statistical software. In a group endeavor, it will help for there to be complete clarity on which team member is responsible for doing what.

Finally, you should include in your proposal a detailed timetable for your plan of work. For research projects lasting a semester or less, this timetable should include week-by-week details: that is, precisely what will be done (and for group projects, by whom) in each week.

Works cited

And, finally, you should provide a detailed bibliography, which contains every single primary and secondary source from your literature review. This bibliography should also include scholarly sources of information on specific analytical techniques you intend to use, as well as all sources of data. You should consult a standard source of writing style for the particular format of the citation entries, or consult your faculty advisor to see if she has particular format preferences.

Supporting materials

A number of different types of supporting materials are appropriate to be included in your proposal, as further evidence for the reader to make an informed assessment of your proposed research. These include:

- Verbatim instructions to participants.
- Survey instruments. If an instrument is copyrighted, permission in writing to reproduce the instrument from the copyright holder or proof of purchase of the instrument.
- Interview guides.
- Sample of informed consent forms.
- Cover letters sent to appropriate stakeholders.
- Official letters of permission to conduct research.

(adapted from Pajares 2007)

Conclusions

Research proposals are an extremely important part of the research process. How carefully you construct your proposal can spell the difference between approval and rejection of your research project. In writing your proposal, you should keep in mind its fundamental function: to let the reader know exactly what you have in mind for your research. The reader will have to be persuaded that you have done your homework to identify an original, interesting research question and that you have the skills and qualifications to carry out the project. But you are also encouraged to view it as an opportunity to organize your own thoughts on precisely what it is you want to accomplish, and how.

Exercises/discussion questions

(1) Consider the following passage from Lichterman (1995). Briefly write, in your own words, the problem statement.

> In 1990 large US environmental organizations such as the Sierra Club received letters from minority activists charging them with neglecting racial diversity in personnel and program agendas. However, some white, grass-roots environmentalists had already recognized a lack of diversity in their small, volunteer groups. Like feminists, new leftists, and other grass-roots activists before them, these activists hoped to build bridges across race lines. They attended a "multicultural alliance-building workshop" at which they told stories of racisms they had practiced in their own lives that they were now trying, sometimes tearfully, to exorcise. Despite such efforts, these environmentalists accomplished relatively little in their multicultural alliance-building quest, and appeared fated to remain a largely white, highly educated middle-class group, similar to radical feminist, anti-nuclear, and other recent movement groups.
>
> Impediments to multicultural alliance building have received little theoretical attention. Both movement scholars and activists have remarked on difficulties in relations between mostly middle-class whites and people of color from varied socioeconomic backgrounds in the civil rights movement (Carson 1981; McAdam 1988a); the new left and youth movements (Breines 1982; Mansbridge 1983; Kazin 1995); the women's movement (Albrecht and Brewer 1990; Anzaldua and Moraga 1982; Adams 1989); and, in anti-toxics activism (Bullard 1993). These works have not developed a cultural analysis of barriers to multicultural alliances. In the 1980s and 1990s, activists of color protesting toxic waste siting practices they deem unfair have entered grass-roots environmentalist arenas previously dominated by middle-class, well-educated whites (Bullard 1989, 1990, 1993; Capek 1993; Commission on Racial Justice 1987; Russell 1989). Grass-roots environmentalism thus offers an important opportunity for conceptualizing difficulties in multicultural alliance building
>
> (pp. 513–14).

(2) As an analogy to doing an exploratory case study, consider Christopher Columbus' voyage to the New World in 1492. When he went to Queen Isabella to ask for support for his voyage, he probably had to justify not only asking for support but also for the amount of support she would give him. For

example, he probably had to provide some reasons for asking for three ships (Why not one? Why not five?). He also probably had to provide some reasons for going westward (Why not south? Why not south and then east?). He also probably had some criteria for recognizing the Indies when he actually encountered it. In short, his exploration must have begun with some rationale and direction.

Put yourself in Columbus' shoes. How would you justify asking for support from Queen Isabella to do your exploratory study? How would you justify asking for three ships? Sailing west? What criteria would you propose? (Adapted from Yin 2009, pp. 28–9.)

(3) Suppose you have an entire semester to complete a research project. Compose a research question that reflects your own personal interests in the environment, and create a week-by-week timeline to accomplish all of the things that need to be done to complete the project.

References

Abdulai, Raymond Talinbe, and Anthony Owusa-Ansah. "Essential Ingredients of a Good Research Proposal for Undergraduate and Postgraduate Students in the Social Sciences," *SAGE Open* (July–September 2014): 1–15.

Ali, Suki, and Moira Kelly. "Ethics and social research," in Clive Seale (ed.), *Researching Society and Culture* (3rd ed.). Los Angeles: Sage, 2012: 58–76.

Berrens, Robert P., David S. Brookshire, Michael McKee, and Christian Schmidt. "Implementing the Safe Minimum Standard Approach: Two Case Studies from the U.S. Endangered Species Act," *Land Economics* 74(May 1998): 147–61.

Campregher, Christoph. "Shifting Perspectives on Development: An Actor-network Study of a Dam in Costa Rica," *Anthropological Quarterly* 83(Fall 2010): 783–804.

Creswell, John W. *Research Design: Qualitative, Quantitative, and Mixed Methods Approaches*. Los Angeles: Sage, 2009.

Guber, Deborah L. "Environmental Voting in the American States: A Tale of Two Initiatives," *State and Local Government Review* 33(Spring 2001): 120–32.

Horsch, Eric J., and David J. Lewis. "The Effects of Aquatic Invasive Species on Property Values: Evidence from a Quasi-experiment," *Land Economics* 85(August 2009): 391–409.

Howe, Charles W., Jeffrey K. Lazo, and Kenneth R. Weber. "The Economic Impacts of Agriculture-to-Urban Water Transfers on the Area of Origin: A Case Study of the Arkansas River Valley in Colorado," *American Journal of Agricultural Economics* 72(December 1990): 1200–04.

Kumar, Ranjit. *Research Methodology: A Step-by-Step Guide for Beginners* (3rd ed.). Sage: London, 2011.

Leones, Julie, Bonnie Colby, Dennis Cory, and Liz Ryan. "Measuring Regional Economic Impacts of Streamflow Depletions," *Water Resources Research* 33(April 1997): 831–38.

Lichterman, Paul. "Piecing Together Multicultural Community: Cultural Differences in Community Building among Grass-roots Environmentalists," *Social Problems* 42(November 1995): 513–34.

Loomis, John, and Catherine Keske. "Did the Great Recession Reduce Visitor Spending and Willingness to Pay for Nature-based Recreation? Evidence from 2006 and 2009," *Contemporary Economic Policy* 30(April 2012): 238–46.

Maguire, Steve, and Cynthia Hardy. "Discourse and Deinstitutionalization: The Decline of DDT," *Academy of Management Journal* 52(February 2009): 148–78.

Norgaard, Kari M. "Climate Denial and the Construction of Innocence: Reproducing Transnational Environmental Privilege in the Face of Climate Change," *Race, Gender & Class* 19(2012): 80–103.

Pajares, F. *Elements of a Proposal*, 2007, http://des.emory.edu/mfp/proposal.html

Scott, Daniel, Brenda Jones, and Jasmina Konopek. "Implications of Climate and Environmental Change for Nature-based Tourism in the Canadian Rocky Mountains: A Case Study of Waterton Lakes National Park," *Tourism Management* 28(2007): 570–79.

Silva, Julie A., and Lila K. Khatiwada. "Transforming Conservation into Cash? Nature Tourism in Southern Africa," *Africa Today* 61(Fall 2014): 17–45.

Sydenstricker-Neto, John. "Population and Deforestation in the Brazilian Amazon: A Mediating Perspective and a Mixed-method Analysis," *Population and Environment* 34(September 2012): 86–112.

Wong, Paul T. P. "How to Write a Research Proposal," *International Network on Personal Meaning*, http://www.meaning.ca/archives/archive/art_how_to_write_P_Wong.htm

Yin, R. K. *Case Study Research: Design and Methods* (4th ed.). Los Angeles: Sage, 2009.

Index